CONTENTS

IMC Unit 1 The Investment Environment Syllabus

By the end of this Unit, learners should be able to demonstrate:

- An understanding of the UK financial services industry and international financial markets

- An understanding of and ability to critically evaluate the outcomes that distinguish between ethical and compliance driven behaviour and apply the CFA Code of Ethics and Professional Standards to business behaviours of individuals

- An understanding of the Financial Conduct Authority's (FCA's) use of principles and outcomes based regulation to promote ethical and fair outcomes, and the ability to apply the regulatory advice framework in practice for the consumer

- An understanding of the FCA's responsibilities and approach to regulation, and the role of the Prudential Regulation Authority (PRA) for dual regulated firms, and an understanding of and ability to apply the FCA principles and rules as set out in the regulatory framework, and FCA Handbook

- An understanding of legal concepts relevant to financial advice

- An understanding of how the retail consumer is served by the financial services industry, the range of skills required when advising clients and an ability to apply the investment advice process

- An understanding of the UK tax system as relevant to the needs and circumstances of individuals and trusts

- An ability to analyse the taxation of investments as relevant to the needs and circumstances of individuals and trusts, and an ability to apply the knowledge of personal taxation to the provision of investment advice

- An ability to analyse the role and relevance of tax in the financial affairs of individuals and trusts

The detailed content of **Syllabus version 11**, which is tested from **1 December 2013**, is set out below.

The **Chapter-Section** reference in the right-hand column indicates where in this Study Text each learning outcome is covered. For example, learning outcome 1.1.3 is covered in Chapter 1 Section 3.

Learning outcome	Chapter–Section
1. Financial markets and institutions	**Chapter 1**
• Demonstrate an understanding of the UK financial services industry, in its European and global context	
• Demonstrate an understanding of UK and international financial markets	
1.1 Introduction to financial markets	
1.1.1 Explain the functions of the financial services industry in allocating capital within the global economy	1 – 1
1.1.2 Evaluate the role and impact of the main financial institutions	1 – 2
1.1.3 Explain the role of government including economic and industrial policy, regulation, taxation and social welfare	1 – 3
1.2 The role of securities markets in providing liquidity and price transparency	
1.2.1 Differentiate between a financial security and a real asset	1 – 4
1.2.2 Identify the key features of: a common equity share, a bond, a derivative contract, a unit in a pooled fund, and a foreign exchange transaction	1 – 4

STUDY TEXT

Unit 1 – The Investment Environment

Syllabus version 11

In this edition

- A **user-friendly format** for easy navigation
- **Exam tips** to put you on the right track
- A **Test your knowledge** quiz at the end of each chapter
- A full **index**

BPP LEARNING MEDIA

Published November 2013

ISBN 9781 4727 0404 7
e ISBN 9781 4727 0155 8

British Library Cataloguing-in-Publication Data
A catalogue record for this book
is available from the British Library

Published by
BPP Learning Media Ltd
BPP House, Aldine Place
142-144 Uxbridge Road
London W12 8AA

www.bpp.com/learningmedia

Printed in United Kingdom by Ricoh
Ricoh House, Ullswater Cresent
Coulsdon, CR5 2HR

Your learning materials, published by BPP Learning Media Ltd, are printed on paper sourced from sustainable, managed forests.

BPP
LEARNING MEDIA

Learning outcome		Chapter–Section
1.2.3	Identify the functions of securities market in providing price transparency and liquidity	1 – 4
1.2.4	Identify the reasons why liquidity and price transparency are thought to be important for the efficient allocation of capital costs when trading in securities markets	1 – 4
1.2.5	Calculate round trip transaction costs incorporating bid-ask spreads, dealing commission and transaction taxes, both in percentages and in absolute amounts	1 – 4
1.2.6	Identify the types of securities and the market conditions where price transparency, liquidity and depth are likely to be high / low	1 – 4
1.2.7	Define liquidity risk and identify why it is important	1 – 4
1.3 Types of financial markets		
1.3.1	Identify the main dealing systems and facilities offered in the UK equities market	1 – 5
1.3.2	Identify the nature of the securities that would be traded on each of the above systems and facilities	1 – 5
1.3.3	Explain the structure and operation of the primary and secondary UK markets for gilts and corporate bonds	1 – 5
1.3.4	Explain the motivations for and implications of dual listing of a company	1 – 5
1.3.5	Compare and contrast exchange trading and over-the-counter (OTC) markets	1 – 5
1.3.6	Distinguish between the following alternative trading venues: Multilateral Trading Facilities, Systematic Internalisers, Dark Pools	1 – 5
1.3.7	Distinguish between a quote-driven and order-driven market	1 – 5
1.3.8	Explain the roles of the various participants in the UK equity market	1 – 5
1.3.9	Explain high-frequency trading, its benefits and risks	1 – 5
1.4 Settlement procedures in the UK		
1.4.1	Explain the clearing and settlement procedures for UK exchange traded securities	1 – 6
1.5 The UK Listing Authority and prospectus requirements		
1.5.1	Explain the role of the Financial Conduct Authority (FCA) as the UK listing authority	1 – 7
1.5.2	Identify the source of the listing rules as Financial Services and Markets Act 2000, and relevant EU directives	1 – 7
1.5.3	Explain the main conditions for listing on the Official List, AIM and ISDX	1 – 7
1.5.4	Explain the purpose of the requirement for prospectus or listing particulars	1 – 7
1.5.5	Identify the main exemptions from listing particulars	1 – 7

Learning outcome	Chapter–Section
1.6 Information disclosure and corporate governance requirements for UK equity markets	
1.6.1 Explain the disclosures required under the disclosure and transparency rules relating to directors' interests and major shareholdings	1 – 8
1.6.2 Explain the purpose of corporate governance regulation and the role of the Financial Reporting Council (FRC) in promoting good corporate governance	1 – 8
1.6.3 Explain, in outline, the scope and content of corporate governance regulation in the UK	1 – 8
1.6.4 Explain the London Stock Exchange (LSE) requirements for listed companies to disclose corporate governance compliance	1 – 8
1.6.5 Explain the continuing obligations of LSE listed companies regarding information disclosure and dissemination	1 – 8
1.6.6 Explain, in outline, the UK company law requirements regarding the calling of general meetings	1 – 8
1.6.7 Distinguish annual general meetings and other types of company meetings	1 – 8
1.6.8 Distinguish between the types of resolution that can be considered at company general meetings	1 – 8
1.6.9 Distinguish between the voting methods used at company meetings	1 – 8
1.6.10 Explain the role and powers of a proxy	1 – 8
1.7 International markets	
1.7.1 Explain the structure, features, regulatory and trading environment of international markets, including developed markets and emerging markets	1 – 9
1.7.2 Explain the structure and operation of the primary and secondary markets for Eurobonds	1 – 9
1.7.3 Explain the settlement and clearing procedures overseas, including the role of international central securities depositories, and the different settlement cycles and challenges in managing global assets	1 – 9
1.8 The principal-agent problem: separation of ownership and control	
1.8.1 Explain how capital markets allow the beneficial ownership and the control of capital to be separated	1 – 10
1.8.2 Distinguish between beneficial owners (principals) and the various agents involved in the capital allocation process	1 – 10
1.8.3 Explain how conflict between the interests of agents and principals gives rise to the 'agency' or 'principal-agent' problem	1 – 10
1.8.4 Identify examples of agency costs such as: expropriation, perquisites, self-dealing, and higher cost of capital, which arise when the agency problem is known to exist	1 – 10
1.8.5 Identify the main reasons why it is argued that reducing the agency problem benefits the investment profession and society as a whole	1 – 10

Learning outcome	Chapter–Section
2. Ethics and investment professionalism	**Chapter 2**
• Demonstrate an ability to critically evaluate the outcomes that distinguish between ethical and compliance-driven behaviour	
• Demonstrate an ability to apply the CFA Code of Ethics and Professional Standards to the business behaviours of individuals	
2.1 Ethical and compliance driven behaviour	
2.1.1 Describe the need for ethics in the investment industry	2 – 1
2.1.2 Identify the ethical obligations to clients, prospective clients, employers and co-workers	2 – 1
2.1.3 Identify positive and negative behavioural indicators	2 – 1
2.1.4 Critically evaluate the outcomes which may result from behaving ethically – for the industry, individual advisers and consumers	2 – 1
2.1.5 Critically evaluate the outcomes which may result from limiting behaviour to compliance with the rules – for the industry, firm, individual advisers and consumers	2 – 1
2.2 CFA Code of Ethics and Professional Standards	
2.2.1 Identify the elements of the CFA Code of Ethics and Professional Standards	2 – 2
2.2.2 Explain the professional principles and values on which the Code of Ethics is based	2 – 2
2.2.3 Apply the Code to a range of ethical dilemmas	2 – 2
3. The regulation of financial markets and institutions	**Chapter 3**
• Demonstrate the ability to apply the regulatory advice framework in practice for the consumer	
• Demonstrate an understanding of the UK financial services industry, in its European and global context	
• Demonstrate an understanding of the Financial Conduct Authority's responsibilities and approach to regulation	
• Demonstrate an understanding of UK and international financial markets	
• Demonstrate an ability to apply the FCA's principles and rules as set out in the regulatory framework, and FCA Handbook	
• Demonstrate an understanding of where the PRA may also be involved for dual-regulated firms	
3.1 European Union Directives, Regulations and Guidance	
3.1.1 Explain the legal status of EU Directives and Regulations within the UK	3 – 1
3.1.2 Explain the role and powers of the European Securities and Markets Authority	3 – 1

Learning outcome		Chapter–Section
3.1.3	Explain the purpose and scope of the Markets in Financial Instruments Directive (MiFID) with respect to: passporting, roles of the home and host state, core and non-core investment services, financial instruments covered by the legislation	3 – 1
3.1.4	Explain the purpose and scope of the Undertakings for Collective Investment in Transferable Securities (UCITS) Directives	3 – 1
3.1.5	Explain the purpose and scope of the European Market Infrastructure Regulation (EMIR)	3 – 1
3.2 UK regulation		
3.2.1	Describe and distinguish between the roles of the Financial Conduct Authority (FCA), Prudential Regulation Authority (PRA), Bank of England, Financial Policy Committee (FPC) and HM Treasury	3 – 2
3.2.2	Explain the different roles of the FCA and PRA for dual-regulated investment firms	3 – 2
3.2.3	Explain the scope of the Financial Services and Markets Act 2000 (as amended by the Financial Services Act 2012)	3 – 2
3.2.4	Explain the scope of the Regulated Activities Order 2001 (as amended) in terms of: regulated activities, specified investments	3 – 2
3.2.5	Explain the purpose and scope of the FCA's rules regarding Senior Management Arrangements, Systems and Controls (SYSC)	3 – 2
3.2.6	Explain the function of the following bodies/persons: the Panel for Takeovers and Mergers, the Department for Business Innovation and Skills, the Office of Fair Trading, the Competition Commission, and the Information Commission	3 – 2
3.2.7	Explain the make-up of the Panel on Takeovers and Mergers (the takeover panel) and how it is financed	3 – 2
3.2.8	Explain the regulatory status of the City Code on Takeovers and Mergers	3 – 2
3.2.9	Explain the main provisions of the City Code including the bid timetable	3 – 2
3.2.10	Explain the purpose and scope of the Trustee Act 2000, the rights and duties of the parties involved, the nature of the trust deed, and the investment powers of trustees	3 – 2
3.2.11	Explain the significance of the Pensions Act 2004: scheme-specific funding requirement, the Pensions Regulator, the Pension Protection Fund	3 – 2
3.2.12	Explain the purpose of a Statement of Investment Principles	3 – 2
3.3 The Financial Conduct Authority objectives and high level standards		3 – 3
3.3.1	Explain the role and statutory objectives of the Financial Conduct Authority (FCA)	3 – 3
3.3.2	Identify and distinguish among the blocks of the FCA Handbook	3 – 3
3.3.4	Explain the application and purpose of the FCA's Principles for Businesses (PRIN 1.1.1 & 2)	3 – 3
3.3.5	Explain the consequences of breaching the FCA's Principles for Businesses (PRIN 1.1.7-9; DEPP 6.2.14 & 15)	3 – 3

Learning outcome		Chapter–Section
3.3.6	Explain, in outline, the procedure for authorisation of firms, including knowledge of the threshold conditions, and liaison with the PRA where relevant	3 – 3
3.3.7	Explain the application and purpose of the Statements of Principles and Code of Practice for approved persons (APER)	3 – 3
3.3.8	Define an Approved Person	3 – 3
3.3.9	Define a Controlled Function	3 – 3
3.3.10	Identify the types of controlled functions defined within the FCA Handbook (SUP 10A)	3 – 3
3.3.11	Identify the main assessment criteria in the FCA's Fit and Proper Test for Approved Persons (FIT)	3 – 3
3.3.12	Explain the application procedure for approved persons (SUP 10A) and how the PRA may also be involved	3 – 3
3.3.13	Explain the procedure for an approved person moving within a group and how the PRA may also be involved (SUP 10A)	3 – 3
3.3.14	Explain the requirements relating to training and competence (TC 1-3)	3 – 3
3.3.15	Explain the professionalism requirements that have to be met by retail advisers and investment managers	3 – 3
3.4 Regulation of investment exchanges		
3.4.1	Explain the role of an investment exchange	3 – 4
3.4.2	Explain the need for, and relevance of, investment exchanges needing to be recognised by the FCA	3 – 4
3.4.3	Explain how the Bank of England regulates clearing houses in the UK	3 – 4
3.4.4	Identify the recognised investment exchanges and clearing houses in the UK	3 – 4
3.4.5	Identify and distinguish the roles of LSE, NYSE Liffe, and LCH.Clearnet	3 – 4
3.4.6	Identify the features of trading systems for derivatives	3 – 4
3.4.7	Identify the main features of the regulation of derivatives	3 – 4
3.4.8	Identify the main features of clearing and settlement for trading on derivatives exchanges, and when trading over-the-counter (OTC)	3 – 4
3.4.9	Explain the arrangements for market transparency and transaction reporting in the main derivative markets	3 – 4
3.4.10	Explain the impact of MiFID and International Accounting Standards on the regulation of derivative markets	3 – 4
3.5 FCA Business Standards		
Accepting customers for business (client categorisation)		
3.5.1	Explain the purpose of client classification	3 – 5
3.5.2	Distinguish between a retail client, a professional client and an eligible counterparty (COBS 3.4, 3.5 & 3.6)	3 – 5

Learning outcome		Chapter–Section
3.5.3	Apply the rules relating to treating a client as an elective professional client (COBS 3.5.3)	3 – 5
3.5.4	Apply the rules relating to treating a client as an elective eligible counterparty (COBS 3.6.4)	3 – 5
3.5.5	Apply the rules relating to providing clients with a higher level of protection (COBS 3.7)	3 – 5
3.5.6	Apply the rules relating to client agreements (COBS 8.1)	3 – 5
Financial promotions and other communications with customers including information about the firm		
3.5.7	Explain the purpose and scope of the financial promotions rules and the exemptions from them (COBS 4.1)	3 – 5
3.5.8	Explain the fair, clear and not misleading rule (COBS 4.2)	3 – 5
3.5.9	Explain the rules relating to communications with retail clients (COBS 4.5)	3 – 5
3.5.10	Explain the rules relating to past, simulated past and future performance (COBS 4.6)	3 – 5
3.5.11	Explain the rules relating to direct offer promotions (COBS 4.7)	3 – 5
3.5.12	Explain the rules relating to cold calls and other promotions that are not in writing (COBS 4.8)	3 – 5
3.5.13	Explain the rules relating to systems and controls in relation to approving and communicating financial promotions (COBS 4.10)	3 – 5
3.5.14	Explain the record keeping requirements relating to financial promotions (COBS 4.11)	3 – 5
3.5.15	Explain the rules relating to distance marketing communications (COBS 5.1)	3 – 5
3.5.16	Explain the rules relating to providing information about the firm and compensation information (COBS 6.1)	3 – 5
3.5.17	Explain the rules on adviser charging and remuneration (COBS 6.3 & 6.4)	3 – 5
3.5.18	Explain the FCA's approach to temporary product intervention	3 – 5
Identifying client needs (suitability and appropriateness)		
3.5.19	Explain the rules relating to assessing suitability (COBS 9.2)	3 – 5
3.5.20	Explain the rules relating to assessing appropriateness (COBS 10.2)	3 – 5
3.5.21	Explain the rules relating to warning a client about the appropriateness of their instructions (COBS 10.3)	3 – 5
3.5.22	Identify circumstances when assessing appropriateness is not required (COBS 10.4, 10.5 & 10.6)	3 – 5
3.5.23	Identify circumstances where own authority or expertise is limited and there is the need to refer to specialists	3 – 5
3.5.24	Distinguish between independent advice and restricted advice (COBS 6.2A)	3 – 5

Learning outcome	Chapter–Section
Dealing and managing	
3.5.25 Explain the rules relating to best execution (COBS 11.2)	3 – 5
3.5.26 Explain the rules relating to client order handling (COBS 11.3)	3 – 5
3.5.27 Explain the rules relating to the use of dealing commission (COBS 11.6)	3 – 5
3.5.28 Explain the rules on personal account dealing (COBS 11.7)	3 – 5
3.5.29 Explain the purpose of the principles and rules on conflicts of interest, including: identifying, recording and disclosing conflicts of interest and managing them to ensure the fair treatment of clients (PRIN 2.1.1, Principle 8, SYSC 10.1.1-7, 10.1.8/9 & 10.2)	3 – 5
Investment research	
3.5.30 Explain the rules relating to investment research produced by a firm and disseminated to clients (COBS 12.2)	3 – 5
3.5.31 Explain the rules relating to the publication and dissemination of non-independent research (COBS 12.3)	3 – 5
3.5.32 Explain the disclosure requirements relating to the production and dissemination of research recommendations (COBS 12.4)	3 – 5
Product disclosure – packaged products	
3.5.33 Explain the obligations relating to preparing product information (COBS 13.1 & COLL 4.7)	3 – 5
3.5.34 Explain the rules relating to the form and content of a key features document and a key investor information document (COBS 13.2, 13.3, 14.2 & COLL 4.7)	3 – 5
3.5.35 Explain the rules relating to cancellation rights (COBS 15)	3 – 5
3.5.36 Distinguish between packaged products and retail investment products	3 – 5
Record keeping and reporting information	
3.5.37 Apply the rules relating to record keeping for client orders and transactions (COBS 11.5)	3 – 5
3.5.38 Apply the rules relating to occasional reporting to clients (COBS 16.2)	3 – 5
3.5.39 Apply the rules relating to periodic reporting to clients (COBS 16.3)	3 – 5
3.5.40 Explain the rules relating to reporting on the progress of an authorised fund to unitholders (COLL 4.5)	3 – 5
Client assets and client money rules	
3.5.41 Explain the concept of fiduciary duty	3 – 5
3.5.42 Explain the application and purpose of the rules relating to custody of client assets held in connection with MIFID business (CASS 6.1)	3 – 5
3.5.43 Explain the rules relating to the protection of clients' assets and having adequate organisation arrangements (CASS 6.2)	3 – 5
3.5.44 Explain the rules relating to depositing assets with third parties (CASS 6.3)	3 – 5
3.5.45 Explain the purpose of the rules relating to the use of clients' assets (CASS 6.4)	3 – 5

Learning outcome		Chapter–Section
3.5.46	Explain the rules relating to records, accounts and reconciliations of clients' assets (CASS 6.5)	3 – 5
3.5.47	Explain the application and general purpose of the client money rules (CASS 7.2)	3 – 5
3.5.48	Explain the rules relating to the segregation of client money (CASS 7.4)	3 – 5
3.5.49	Explain the rules relating to records, accounts and reconciliations of clients' assets (CASS 7.6)	3 – 5
3.5.50	Explain the rules relating to mandate accounts	3 – 5
3.6 FCA Supervision and redress		
3.6.1	Explain the FCA's risk based approach to supervision and the enforcement and disciplinary powers of the FCA	3 – 6
Complaints handling, the Financial Ombudsman Service and the Financial Services Compensation Scheme		
3.6.2	Explain the FCA rules relating to handling of complaints (DISP 1.3)	3 – 7
3.6.3	Explain the role of the Financial Ombudsman Service (DISP Introduction and DISP 2)	3 – 7
3.6.4	Apply the rules relating to determination by the Financial Ombudsman Service (DISP 3)	3 – 7
3.6.5	Distinguish compulsory from voluntary jurisdiction (DISP Introduction)	3 – 7
3.6.6	Explain the procedure and time limits for the resolution of complaints (DISP 1.4, 1.5 & 1.6)	3 – 7
3.6.7	Apply the rules relating to record keeping and reporting concerning complaints (DISP 1.9 & 1.10)	3 – 7
3.6.8	Explain the purpose of the Financial Services Compensation Scheme (FSCS) (COMP 1.1.7)	3 – 7
3.6.9	Identify the circumstances under which the FSCS will pay compensation (COMP 1.3.3, 3.2.1, 4.2.1 & 4.2.2)	3 – 7
3.6.10	Identify the limits on the compensation payable by the FSCS (COMP 10.2.1, 10.2.2 & 10.2.3)	3 – 7
3.7 Financial crime		
3.7.1	Explain the various sources of money laundering and counter terrorism regulation and legislation (FCA rules, Money Laundering Regulations, Proceeds of Crime Act 2002)	3 – 8
3.7.2	Explain the role of the Joint Money Laundering Steering Group (JMLSG)	3 – 8
3.7.3	Explain the main features of the guidance provided by the JMLSG	3 – 8
3.7.4	Explain the three stages involved in the money laundering process	3 – 8
3.7.5	Explain the four offence categories under UK money laundering legislation	3 – 8
3.7.6	Explain the meaning of 'inside information' covered by the Criminal Justice Act (CJA) 1993	3 – 8
3.7.7	Explain the offence of insider dealing covered by the CJA 1993	3 – 8

BPP
LEARNING MEDIA

Learning outcome	Chapter–Section
3.7.8 Identify the penalties for being found guilty of insider dealing	3 – 8
3.7.9 Explain the FCA's powers to prosecute insider dealing	3 – 8
3.7.10 Describe the behaviours defined as market abuse (MAR 1.3, 1.4, 1.5, 1.6, 1.7, 1.8 & 1.9)	3 – 8
3.7.11 Explain the enforcement powers of the FCA relating to market abuse (MAR 1.1.4, 1.1.5 & 1.1.6)	3 – 8
3.7.12 Explain the main features of the Bribery Act 2010	3 – 8
4. Legal concepts	**Chapter 4**
• Demonstrate an understanding of legal concepts relevant to financial advice	
4.1.1 Explain legal persons and power of attorney	4 – 1
4.1.2 Explain basic law of contract and agency	4 – 2
4.1.3 Explain the types of ownership of property	4 – 3
4.1.4 Explain insolvency and bankruptcy	4 – 4
4.1.5 Explain wills and intestacy	4 – 5
4.1.6 Identify the main types of trusts and their uses	4 – 6
5. The regulatory advice framework	**Chapter 5**
• Demonstrate an understanding of how the retail consumer is served by the financial services industry	
• Demonstrate an ability to apply the investment advice process	
• Demonstrate an understanding of the range of skills required when advising clients	
5.1 Types and characteristics of investors	
5.1.1 Describe and compare different types of investors	5 – 1
5.1.2 Explain how needs differ amongst different types of investors	5 – 1
5.1.3 Explain the main needs of retail clients and how they are prioritised	5 – 1, 5 – 2
5.2 The client's financial objectives	
5.2.1 Explain the importance of establishing and quantifying a client's objectives	5 – 2
5.2.2 Explain the need to prioritise objectives to accommodate a client's affordability	5 – 2
5.3 The client's current circumstances	
5.3.1 Explain the importance of the fact find process in establishing a client's current financial circumstances and requirements	5 – 2
5.3.2 Identify the factors shaping a clients' circumstances	5 – 2

Learning outcome		Chapter–Section
5.4 The client's attitude to risk		
5.4.1	Analyse the main types of investment risk as they affect investors	5 – 2
5.4.2	Explain the role of diversification in mitigating risk	5 – 2
5.4.3	Analyse the impact of timescale on a client's attitude to risk	5 – 2
5.4.4	Explain the key methods of determining a client's attitude to risk	5 – 2
5.5 Advice and recommendations		
5.5.1	Explain why asset allocation always comes before investment or product selection	5 – 2
5.5.2	Explain the key roles of charges and the financial stability of the provider as criteria within the fund selection process, and the use of past performance	5 – 2
5.5.3	Explain the importance of stability, independence and standing of trustees, fund custodians and auditors in the fund selection process	5 – 2
5.5.4	Identify benchmarks and other performance measures	5 – 2
5.5.5	Explain the importance of reviews within the financial planning process	5 – 2
5.6 Skills required when advising clients		
5.6.1	Describe the need for advisers to communicate clearly, assessing and adapting to the differing levels of knowledge and understanding of their clients	5 – 4
5.6.2	Identify and apply suitable investment solutions to suit different needs of retail clients	5 – 1, 5 – 2, 5 – 4
5.7 The objectives of pension funds, life assurance and general insurance companies and the factors that impact upon their investment decisions		
5.7.1	Explain the features and objectives of the following funds in the UK: pension funds (defined benefit (DB) and defined contribution (DC), life assurance and general insurance funds	5 – 3
5.7.2	Distinguish among the typical asset allocations for DB and DC pension funds, life assurance and general insurance funds	5 – 3
5.7.3	Explain the return objectives of the major fund types	5 – 3
5.7.4	Classify funds by their income/capital growth requirements	5 – 3
5.7.5	Explain the effect of each of the following on a fund's asset allocation: time horizons, liability structure, liquidity requirements	5 – 3
5.7.6	Explain the taxation of the various types of funds in the UK	5 – 3
5.7.7	Explain the effect that tax legislation may have on the stock selection and asset allocation of a fund	5 – 3
5.7.8	Identify other types of legal requirements that affect pension funds, insurance funds and private retail clients	5 – 3

Learning outcome	Chapter–Section
6. Taxation in the UK	**Chapter 6**
• Demonstrate an understanding of the UK tax system as relevant to the needs and circumstances of individuals and trusts	
• Demonstrate an ability to analyse the taxation of investments as relevant to the needs and circumstances of individuals and trusts	
• Demonstrate an ability to analyse the role and relevance of tax in the financial affairs of individuals and trusts	
• Demonstrate an ability to apply the knowledge of personal taxation to the provision of investment advice	
6.1 The UK tax system and the taxation of investments	
6.1.1 Describe the principles of income tax applicable to earnings, savings and investment income in the UK	6 – 1
6.1.2 Describe, in relation to income tax, the system of allowances, reliefs and priorities for taxing income	6 – 1
6.1.3 Explain the taxation of the income of trusts and beneficiaries	6 – 4
6.1.4 Describe the system of national insurance contributions (NICs)	6 – 2
6.1.5 Describe the principles of capital gains tax (CGT) in the UK	6 – 3
6.1.6 Describe the principles of inheritance tax (IHT)	6 – 4
6.1.7 Explain the limitations of lifetime gifts and transfers at death in mitigating IHT	6 – 10
6.1.8 Explain the implications of residence and domicile in relation to liability to income, capital gains and inheritance tax	6 – 1, 6 – 3, 6 – 4
6.1.9 Explain the system of UK tax compliance including self assessment, Pay As You Earn (PAYE), tax returns, tax payments, tax evasion and avoidance issues	6 – 5
6.1.10 Describe the principles of stamp duty land tax (SDLT) as applied to property transactions – buying, selling and leasing	6 – 6
6.1.11 Describe the principles of stamp duty reserve tax (SDRT)	6 – 6
6.1.12 Explain how companies are taxed in the UK	6 – 7
6.1.13 Describe in outline the principles of Value Added Tax (VAT)	6 – 8
6.1.14 Analyse the taxation of direct investments including cash and cash equivalents, fixed interest securities, equities and property	6 – 9
6.1.15 Analyse the key features and taxation of indirect investments including pension arrangements, Individual Savings Accounts (ISAs), onshore and offshore life assurance policies, Real Estate Investment Trusts (REITs), Venture Capital Trusts (VCTs) and Enterprise Investment Schemes (EISs)	6 – 9

Learning outcome	Chapter–Section
6.2 Investment advice and tax planning	
6.2.1 Evaluate the tax considerations shaping clients' needs and circumstances	6 – 10
6.2.2 Analyse the key principles of income tax planning	6 – 10
6.2.3 Analyse how the use of annual CGT exemptions, the realisation of losses, the timing of disposals, and sale and repurchase of similar assets, can mitigate CGT	6 – 10
6.2.4 Calculate the most common elements of income tax and NICs, CGT, and IHT, including the impact of lifetime transfers and transfers at death	6 – 1, 6 – 2, 6 – 4, 6 – 9, 6 – 10
6.2.5 Select elementary tax planning recommendations in the context of investments and pensions advice	6 – 3, 6 – 10

1

Financial markets and institutions

INTRODUCTION

In this first chapter of the Study Text, we look at the place of the financial services industry within the economic system, and at the main institutions and markets within the industry. We examine also the roles of the national Government, and the status of EU legislation in the UK.

The London Stock Exchange operates a market place for trading bonds and other securities in the UK and operates the trading platforms SETS and SETSqx.

The Financial Conduct Authority (FCA) operates as the UK Listing Authority (UKLA), to regulate company listings.

The creation of Multilateral Trading Facilities (MTFs) has been a challenge to the mainstream exchanges, with MTFs taking a significant market share of transactions.

CHAPTER CONTENTS

1 FUNCTIONS OF THE FINANCIAL SERVICES INDUSTRY

Learning objective	1.1.1 **Explain** the functions of the financial services industry in allocating capital within the global economy

1.1 The monetary economy

Money is the main **medium of exchange** in our society. In a **barter economy**, goods and services are exchanged one for another. If someone works to harvest corn, and is given corn in payment for their labour, this is a barter exchange. The use of money as a medium of exchange creates much flexibility in economic transactions. If the harvester is paid in money instead of corn, he may be able to use that money to buy cooking pots and meat. He cannot subsist only on corn.

Most measures of 'money' include balances (for example, at banks and building societies) as well as notes and coin. Money functions as a medium of exchange because:

- It is **divisible** into small units (pounds and pence, dollars and cents)
- There are **sufficient quantities of money** to use for transactions
- Money is **generally accepted** by all parties in transactions

The modern **monetary economy** involves a huge variety of types of transactions involving money. Because money is a recognised medium of exchange among people, it is accepted that debt relationships between people, and claims by one person or institution over another, can be expressed in monetary terms.

The **financial services industry** covers various activities within our monetary **economy**. At the national level, we have the economy of the United Kingdom, with its own currency, the pound sterling. The financial services industry also operates within an international framework, resulting from both the multinational nature of many financial services activities and from various international agreements and regulatory influences. As a member of the **European Union (EU)**, the United Kingdom is subject to EU legislation.

1.2 The flow of funds in the economy

The **flow of funds** in an economy describes the movement of funds or money between one group of people or institutions in the economic system and other groups.

If we begin by ignoring the country's imports and exports of goods and services and foreign investments, we can start to build up a picture of the flow of funds by identifying three sectors in the economy.

- The **personal sector** – mainly individuals or households
- The **business sector** (or industrial and commercial sector) – ie companies and other businesses
- The **government sector** – ie central government, local government and public corporations

Within each of these three sectors, there are continual **movements of funds**.

- Individuals will give money or lend money to other individuals.

- Companies will buy goods and services from other companies, and may occasionally lend money direct to other companies.

- Central government will provide funds for local government authorities and loss-making nationalised industries.

As well as movements of funds within each sector, there are flows of funds between different sectors of the economy.

These flows of funds can be shown in a diagram.

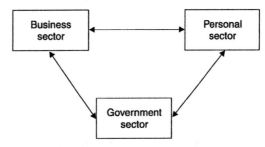

Flow of funds ignoring financial intermediation

But reality is not quite so simple, and our analysis of the flow of funds in the UK should also take account of two other main factors.

- The **overseas sector** comprises businesses, individuals and governments in other countries. The UK economy is influenced by trade with the foreign sector and flows of capital both from and to it.

- **Financial intermediaries** – explained in what follows.

1.3 Financial intermediation

An intermediary is a go-between, and a financial intermediary is an institution which **links lenders with borrowers**, by obtaining deposits from lenders and then re-lending them to borrowers. Such institutions can, for example, provide a link between savers and investors.

The role of **financial intermediaries** such as banks and building societies in an economy is to provide means by which funds can be transferred from **surplus units** (for example, someone with savings to invest in the economy) to **deficit units** (for example, someone who wants to borrow money to buy a house). Financial intermediaries develop the facilities and **financial instruments** which make lending and borrowing possible.

If no financial intermediation takes place, lending and borrowing will be direct.

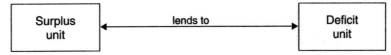

If financial intermediation does take place, the intermediary provides a service to both the surplus unit and the deficit unit.

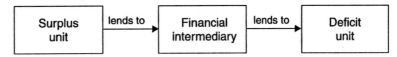

For example, a person might deposit savings with a bank, and the bank might use its collective deposits of savings to provide a loan to a company.

Financial intermediaries might also lend abroad or borrow from abroad, and a fuller version of a diagram depicting the flow of funds is thus as follows.

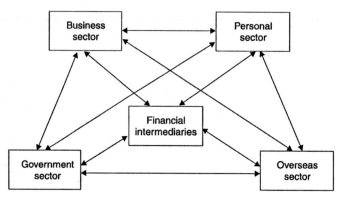

Flow of funds in an open economy, showing the role of financial intermediation

A **financial intermediary** is a party bringing together providers and users of finance, either as a broker facilitating a transaction between two other parties, or in their own right, as principal.

UK financial intermediaries include the following sectors of the financial services industry:

- Banks
- Building societies
- Insurance companies, pension funds, unit trust companies and investment trust companies
- The Government's National Savings & Investments (NS&I)

In spite of competition from building societies, insurance companies and other financial institutions, banks arguably remain the major financial intermediaries in the UK.

The clearing banks are the biggest operators in the retail banking market, although competition from the building societies has grown in the UK.

There is greater competition between different banks (overseas banks and the clearing banks especially) for business in the wholesale lending market.

Financial intermediaries can link lenders with borrowers, by obtaining deposits from lenders and then re-lending them to borrowers. But not all intermediation takes place between savers and investors. Some institutions act mainly as intermediaries between other institutions. Almost all place part of their funds with other institutions, and a number (including finance houses, leasing companies and factoring companies) obtain most of their funds by borrowing from other institutions.

1.4 Benefits of financial intermediation

Financial intermediaries perform the following functions.

- They provide obvious and **convenient** ways in which a **lender can save money** to spend in the future. Instead of having to find a suitable borrower for their money, lenders can deposit money. Financial intermediaries also provide a ready **source of funds for borrowers**.

- They can aggregate or 'package' the amounts lent by savers and lend on to borrowers in different amounts (a process called **aggregation**). By aggregating the deposits of hundreds of small savers, a bank or building society is able to package up the amounts and lend on to several borrowers in the form of larger mortgages.

- Financial intermediaries provide for **maturity transformation**, ie they bridge the gap between the wish of most lenders for liquidity and the desire of most borrowers for loans over longer periods. For example, while many depositors in a building society may want instant access to their funds, the building society can lend these funds to mortgage borrowers over much longer periods, by ensuring that it attracts sufficient funds from depositors over this longer term.

By pooling the funds of large numbers of people, some financial institutions are able to give small investors access to professionally managed **diversified portfolios** covering a varied range of different securities through collective investment products such as unit trusts and investment trusts.

Risk for individuals is reduced by **pooling**. Since financial intermediaries lend to a large number of individuals and organisations, losses suffered through default by borrowers or capital losses are pooled and borne as costs by the intermediary. Such losses are shared among lenders in general.

1.5 Management of risk

For most people, **risk** means the chance that something will go wrong. Taking a risk means doing something that could turn out to be damaging, or could result in a loss.

Individuals can face various risks, such as a risk of physical injury, ill health or death, a risk of damage to property or theft of property, a risk that an investment will lose money, a risk that their bank or other financial institution may fail, and so on.

Insurance, of various kinds, offers ways of reducing various risks, by transferring the risk to an insurer who bears risks for many others in exchange for premiums collected from each insured party.

Various financial instruments made available through the financial services industry allow individuals to expose themselves to **investment risks** that they may wish to run, in the hope of a positive return on their investment.

Businesses, likewise, face various risks. A business may lose customers or key staff, its products may fail, changes in the law may curtail its activities, and so on. A company is owned by its members – that is, its **shareholders**. When a company is exposed to risks, this will affect the value of the shareholders' stake in the company. However, there are other stakeholders in a company who may stand to lose from the risks that a company is exposed to: these other **stakeholder groups** that could be affected include providers of debt finance (often, banks), employees and directors. As with individuals, insurance offers a way in which businesses can manage various risks.

Financial products offer ways in which individuals and businesses can **manage** risk.

It is not the aim of **risk management** to eliminate risks entirely. The aims of risk management can be formulated as follows.

- Make an assessment of risk when taking decisions, and keep investment risk within acceptable limits

- Avoid unnecessary risks and prevent unnecessary losses

- Reduce the frequency of adverse outcomes when the risk probability is high, and reduce the impact of adverse outcomes where the severity of the risk is high

Risk cannot be totally eliminated, for either individuals or businesses. Indeed, regulators see it as both **impossible and undesirable to remove all risk** and failure from the financial system.

Exercise: Risk

Set out some reasons why it could be undesirable to remove all risk from the financial system.

Solution

If there were no risk in the financial system, companies would not be able to raise finance through the system for risky ventures such as developing new medicines or investing in innovative technologies.

People may wish to take risks with money that they can afford to lose, to give the possible prospect of high returns if an investment turns out well.

Many of the things that people would like to do, such as buy their own home, are subject to market forces that inevitably involve risks: house prices might fall, so that someone with a mortgage might find that the house comes to be worth less than the mortgage loan on the house.

Removing all risk from transactions could mean that excessive resources are spent on bureaucracy to regulate institutions and markets. Alternatively, a 'risk-free' financial system might involve the State effectively 'underwriting' all the risks that an individual might face: this suggests an economic system with a very high level of State control, which many would consider to be undesirable.

2 MARKETS AND INSTITUTIONS

Learning objective	1.1.2 **Explain** the role and impact of the main financial institutions

2.1 Capital markets and money markets

The capital markets and the money markets are types of market for dealing in capital.

- **Capital markets** are financial markets for raising and investing largely **long-term** capital.
- **Money markets** are financial markets for lending and borrowing largely **short-term** capital.

2.2 Long-term and short-term capital

What do we mean by **long-term** and **short-term** capital?

- By **short-term capital**, we mean capital that is lent or borrowed for a period which might range from as short as overnight up to about one year, and sometimes longer.

- By **long-term capital**, we mean capital invested or lent and borrowed for a period of about five years or more, but sometimes shorter.

- There is a **grey area** between long-term and short-term capital, which is lending and borrowing for a period from about one to two years up to about five years, which is not surprisingly referred to as **medium-term** capital.

2.3 Banks

Banks can be approached directly by individuals (**retail** business) and businesses for medium-term and long-term loans as well as short-term loans or overdrafts.

The major clearing banks, many investment banks and foreign banks operating in the UK are often willing to lend medium-term capital, especially to well established businesses.

2.4 The gilt-edged market

The **gilt-edged market** is a further major capital market in the UK. The government borrows over the medium and longer term by issuing government stocks (called 'gilt-edged stock' or 'gilts'). Trade in second-hand gilts will continue until the debt eventually matures and the government redeems the stock.

The **primary** gilts market is the market for the sale of new gilt issues. There is an active **secondary** market in second-hand gilts with existing holders selling their holdings of gilts to other investors in the gilts market.

2.5 Providers of capital

Providers of capital include **private individuals** in the retail sector. This includes those who buy stocks and shares on the Stock Exchange, and those who deposit money with banks, building societies and National Savings & Investments (NS&I). NS&I is a government institution set up to borrow on behalf of the government, mainly from the non-banking private sector of the economy.

There are also, of course, important groups of **institutional investors** which specialise in providing capital and act as financial intermediaries between suppliers and demanders of funds. Many financial services organisations now have diversified operations covering a range of the following activities.

- **Pension funds**. Pension funds invest the pension contributions of individuals who subscribe to a pension fund, and of organisations with a company pension fund.

- **Insurance**. Insurance companies invest premiums paid on insurance policies by policy holders. Life assurance policies, including life-assurance based savings policies, account for substantial assets, which are invested in equities, bonds, property and other assets.

- **Investment trusts**. The business of investment trust companies is investing in the stocks and shares of other companies and the government. In other words, they trade in investments.

- **Collective funds. Unit trusts and Open-ended Investment Companies (OEICs)** are similar to investment trusts, in the sense that they invest in stocks and shares of other companies.

- **Venture capital**. Venture capital providers are organisations that specialise in raising funds for new business ventures, such as 'management buy-outs' (ie purchases of firms by their management staff). These organisations are therefore providing capital for fairly risky ventures.

2.6 Overview of capital markets

The role of financial intermediaries in capital markets is illustrated in the following diagram.

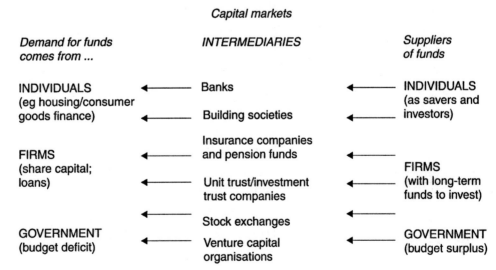

Capital markets

2.7 Changes in capital markets

Recent years have seen great changes in the capital markets of the world.

- **Globalisation of capital markets.** The capital markets of each country have become internationally integrated. Securities issued in one country can now be traded in capital markets around the world. For example, shares in many UK companies are traded in the USA. The shares are bought by US banks, which then issue ADRs (American Depositary Receipts) which are a form in which foreign shares can be traded in US markets without a local listing.

- **Securitisation of debt.** Securitisation of debt means creating tradable securities which are backed by less liquid assets such as mortgages and other long-term loans.

- **Risk management (and risk assessment).** Various techniques have been developed for companies to manage their financial risk such as swaps and options. These 'derivative' financial instruments may allow transactions to take place 'off-balance sheet' and therefore not easily evident from the company's financial statements. The existence of such transactions may make it more difficult for banks and other would-be lenders to assess the financial risk of a company that is asking to borrow money.

- **Increased competition.** There is much fiercer competition than there used to be between financial institutions for business. For example, building societies have become direct competitors to the retail banks, and foreign banks have also competed in the UK with the big clearing banks. Banks have made shifts towards more fee-based activities (such as selling advice and selling insurance products for commission) and away from the traditional transaction-based activities (holding deposits, making loans).

Securitisation of debt involves disintermediation. **Financial disintermediation** is a process whereby ultimate borrowers and lenders by-pass the normal methods of financial intermediation (such as depositing money with and borrowing money from banks) and find other ways of lending or borrowing funds; or lend and borrow directly with each other, avoiding financial intermediation altogether. Securitisation of debt provides firms with a method of borrowing from non-banks. Although banks might act as managers of the debt issue, finding lenders who will buy the securitised debt, banks are not doing the lending themselves.

2.8 The money markets

The UK **money markets** are operated by the banks and other financial institutions. Although the money markets largely involve **wholesale borrowing and lending** by banks, some large companies and the government are also involved in money market operations. The money markets are essentially shorter term debt markets, with loans being made for a specified period at a specified rate of interest.

The money markets operate both as a **primary market**, in which new financial claims are issued and as a **secondary market**, where previously issued financial claims are traded.

Amounts dealt in are relatively large, typically being at least £50,000 and often in millions of pounds. Loans are transacted on extremely 'fine' terms – ie with small margins between lending and borrowing rates – reflecting the **economies of scale** involved. The emphasis is on liquidity: the efficiency of the money markets can make the financial claims dealt in virtually the equivalent of cash.

2.9 The banks and the banking system

There are different types of **banks** which operate within a banking system, and you will probably have come across a number of terms which describe them. **Commercial banks** make commercial banking transactions with customers. They are distinct from the country's **central bank**.

- **Clearing banks** are those that operate the clearing system for settling payments (eg payments by cheque by bank customers).

- The term **retail banks** is used to describe the traditional High Street banks. The term **wholesale banks** refers to banks which specialise in lending in large amounts to major customers. The clearing banks are involved in both retail and wholesale banking but are commonly regarded as the main retail banks.

- **Investment banks** offer services, often of a specialised nature, to institutional investors and to corporate customers. These banks operate as brokers, as underwriters and as advisers in corporate actions such as mergers and takeovers.

These categories are not mutually exclusive: a single bank may be a retail clearing bank, with wholesale and investment banking operations.

2.10 Building societies

The **building societies** of the UK are **mutual** organisations whose main assets are mortgages of their members. Among their liabilities are the balances of the investor members who hold savings accounts with the society. The **Building Societies Act 1986** requires that at least **50%** of a building society's funds must be raised from share accounts held by individual members.

The distinction between building societies and banks has become increasingly blurred, as the societies have taken to providing a range of services formerly the province mainly of banks, and banks have themselves made inroads into the housing mortgage market. Some building societies now offer cheque book accounts, cash cards and many other facilities that compete directly with the banks.

The building society sector has shrunk in size over the last twenty years or so as a number of the major societies have either converted to public limited companies and therefore become banks or have been taken over by banks or other financial institutions.

2.11 The central bank

A **central bank** is a bank which acts on behalf of the government. The central bank for the UK is the **Bank of England ('the Bank')**.

The Bank is a nationalised corporation, and it has two **core purposes**: **monetary stability** and **financial stability**.

Functions of the Bank

- It acts as **banker to the central government** and holds the 'public deposits'. Public deposits include the National Loans Fund, the Consolidated Fund and the account of the Paymaster General, which in turn includes the Exchange Equalisation Account.

- It is the **central note-issuing authority** in the UK – it is responsible for issuing bank notes in England.

- It is the **manager of the National Debt** – ie it deals with long-term and short-term borrowing by the central government and the repayment of central government debt.

- It is the manager of the Exchange Equalisation Account (ie the UK's **foreign currency reserves**).

- It acts as adviser to the government on **monetary policy**.

- The Bank's **Monetary Policy Committee (MPC)** acts as agent for the Government in carrying out its monetary policies. Since May 1997, the MPC has had operational responsibility for **setting short-term interest rates** at the level it considers appropriate in order to meet the Government's inflation target.

- It acts as a **lender to the banking system**. When the banking system is short of money, the Bank of England will provide the money the banks need – at a suitable rate of interest.

- The Financial Services Act 2012 (FSA 2012) established an independent **Financial Policy Committee (FPC)**, and the **Prudential Regulation Authority (PRA)** – a subsidiary of the Bank – as a new prudential regulator, and created new responsibilities for the Bank as the **supervisor of financial market infrastructure providers**.

2.12 The central bank as lender of last resort

In the UK, the **short-term money market** provides a link between the banking system and the government (Bank of England) whereby the Bank of England lends money to the banking system, when banks which need cash cannot get it from anywhere else.

- The Bank will supply cash to the banking system on days when the banks have a cash shortage. It does this by buying eligible bills and other short-term financial investments from approved financial institutions in exchange for cash.

- The Bank will remove excess cash from the banking system on days when the banks have a cash surplus. It does this by selling bills to institutions, so that the short-term money markets obtain interest-bearing bills in place of the cash that they do not want.

The process whereby this is done currently is known as **open market operations** by the Bank. This simply describes the buying and selling of short-term assets between the Bank and the short-term money market.

The Bank acted as lender of last resort to the bank Northern Rock, when the bank became unable to raise enough funds on the wholesale money markets during 2007.

2.13 The UK's position in financial services

Learning objective	1 Demonstrate an understanding of the UK financial services industry, in its European and global context

2.13.1 Overview

The financial services industry is a key sector of the UK economy. The UK financial services industry employs over 1 million people and net overseas earnings from the industry amount to over 5% of national output or GDP.

With a long history going back to the time of merchant adventurers who sought finance for world-wide overseas trading, the 'Square Mile' of the **City of London** is the centre for the UK financial services industry. The City is the largest centre for many international financial markets, such as the currency markets. The UK has the world's largest share in the metals market (95%), Eurobond trade (70%), the foreign equity market (58%), derivatives markets (36%) and insurance (22%).

2.13.2 Banking

While there are over 300 **banking** groups and building societies operating in the UK, the ten largest UK-owned banking groups hold some 70% of UK households' deposits. Building societies hold over 20% of household deposits.

The UK has the greatest concentration of foreign banks, numbering around 500 compared with around 300 in the USA, in the world. London accounts for 19% of global cross-border bank lending, more than any other financial centre. The total assets of the UK banking system have been measured to exceed £3,000 billion, of which approximately 55% belongs to foreign banks. The assets of UK-owned banks, totalling around £1,300 billion, are dominated by around a dozen retail banks, with national branch networks serving domestic, personal and corporate customers.

The banks and building societies form a significant part of the market for financial services. A banking institution could maintain access to a full range of products and product providers by setting up an independent arm. However, few have maintained a wholly independent stance. Most have either formed tied links to life insurance companies ('life offices') or have acquired or set up their own insurance companies which mainly or wholly offer products to clients introduced through the bank or building society. The **universal bank** model involves providing financial services of various kinds, including advisory services, in addition to deposit and lending services.

2.13.3 Insurance

UK **life insurance companies** sell various products within the UK retail market, including collective investment schemes such as unit trusts, OEICs and investment trusts, pension products and individual life insurance. The development of life assurance provision by **banks** is known as **bancassurance** or **all finanz**. The Association of British Insurers (ABI) defines **bancassurers** as 'insurance companies that are subsidiaries of banks and building societies and whose primary market is the customer base of the bank or building society'.

The UK has a major **general insurance** and **reinsurance** market ranging from personal motor insurance to insurance for space satellites. Reinsurance is a process by which a company – for example, a life office writing new business – can sell or pass on the risks on its policies to a third party **reinsurer**.

The UK insurance business generates premium income in the UK insurance market of over £170 billion annually. This makes the third largest such market in the world, exceeded only by the US and Japan. The London market – centred on **Lloyds** of London – is the global market leader in aviation and marine insurance, with market shares of 31% and 19% respectively.

Lloyds acts as a major reinsurer for life assurance. Lloyds is a long-established market in which **underwriting syndicates** operate independently. Syndicates are made up of companies and individuals (Lloyds **'names'**) who provide capital and assume the risk of liabilities they insure or reinsure. Syndicates are run by **managing agents** who appoint **underwriters** to write (assess) risks on behalf of the syndicate.

2.13.4 Pensions

With a rapidly ageing population, there is a **pensions crisis** worldwide. Many countries are passing the burden for pensions provision from the state sector to the private sector.

Domestically, the UK pensions market is of great importance, and a higher proportion of pension payments are provided by the private sector in the UK than in nearly any other country.

2.13.5 Fund management

Collective funds such as unit trusts and investment trusts need to be managed. In the **fund management** sector, the value of assets under management exceeds £4 trillion. Around one quarter of these funds were managed on behalf of overseas clients. The UK fund management sector offers liquid markets, with the opportunity to trade in large blocks of shares, and a relatively liberalised operating environment combined with protection against abuse. More funds are invested in the London than the ten top European centres combined. Edinburgh is the UK's second major fund management centre and is the sixth largest in Europe.

2.13.6 Securities and currency markets

As well as having a substantial domestic market in **equities** (company shares) and **bonds** (interest-bearing securities), the UK is a major international centre for trading in Eurobond markets, which are the markets for debt issued across borders which is denominated in various non-domestic currencies – not just the euro. Eurobonds account for the majority of all bonds issued and the UK issues 60% of them and has a 70% share of the secondary market.

More **foreign companies** are traded on the London Stock Exchange than on any other exchange. Turnover in these companies' shares in London represents approximately half of global turnover in foreign equities.

The UK has over 30% of the global market in **currency trading**, making London the leading world centre for foreign exchange ('forex') trading.

2.14 London's role as a major financial centre

At the time of the introduction of the euro as a common European currency, it was suggested by many that London could lose its strong position as a leading world financial centre and might lose out to competing European centres such as Frankfurt.

There are a number of aspects favouring London as a major financial centre.

- Its location in time zones: able to deal with US and Asian markets at either end of the day
- A workforce that is English-speaking – the international business language
- A varied pool of relatively well-educated labour
- Non-business activities making the City an attractive place to work
- Transport links (including air) and infrastructure
- A trend towards an increasingly cosmopolitan business environment
- The historical legacy and long tradition of supporting commerce
- Diversity in financial products available and traded
- Market transparency
- 'Fairness' of business environment, with relatively low incidence of corruption
- Government generally responsive to business needs
- Relatively 'light touch' regulatory environment, although being made less so

Against these potentially positive factors, it could be argued that London's institutional financial markets have a generally wholesale mentality.

There are other threats, as well as opportunities, affecting London's future.

- The potential for outsourcing operations to other countries has increased due to technological advances as well as some relaxation in regulatory regimes.

- Financial markets are showing increasing **virtuality**, so that with electronic communication, physical location becomes less significant.

- There are continuing trends towards consolidation in exchanges, clearing houses and central securities depositories.

- Firms are becoming increasingly likely to relocate processing centres and head offices wherever it is most beneficial.

- The financial turmoil of the late 2000s and its aftermath is likely to lead to a markedly changed landscape for the financial sector for the future.

2.15 Aspects of finance in Europe

Germany, which has a large banking and insurance sector, and **Switzerland** both carry a tradition of the **universal bank**. Under this system, any recognised bank can provide a full range of banking services, including retail banking services alongside wholesale and investment banking. This is different from the traditional structure of banking in the **UK**, the **USA** and **Japan**.

Changes such as the repeal of the USA's Glass-Steagall Act in the late 1990s removed some of the restrictions on the range of activities that individual banks could undertake (such as commercial banking alongside investment banking), although forthcoming banking reforms may reverse some of those changes. However, where it appears that a single bank provides such a range of services in the UK and the USA, this is generally managed by setting up separately capitalised subsidiaries with similar names to the parent company.

Spain, **France** and the **Netherlands** have banking traditions somewhere between the universal and segmented models.

Italy's financial system has been more based on banks than on markets, with firms raising funds mainly through the banking system. Equity involvement has been limited, with founding families continuing to play a lead role in firms.

In **Germany** and **France** as well as Italy, relatively little use has been made of equity finance by firms.

Finance for industry in **Germany** often comes directly from the banks, and stock market liquidity is limited, with investment opportunities being more limited than in other advanced economies.

France has a broadly based economy with the Government working closely with industry on major projects. The stock market of France merged with those in Brussels and Amsterdam in 2000 to form Euronext.

The financial systems of the smaller **Northern European (Scandinavian) countries** have been dominated by a few large domestic banks that have evolved into larger Nordic financial groups through cross-border mergers and acquisitions.

2.16 USA

2.16.1 Financial system

The US stock market is the world's largest, with the New York Stock Exchange (**NYSE**) covering major stocks. **NASDAQ** (National Association of Securities Dealers Automated Quotations) is the second largest equity market in the USA.

Fixed interest stocks ('bonds') are issued by government and corporations to create the world's largest bond market. US dollar-denominated fixed interest stocks (including Eurodollar bonds issued by foreign entities) make up around half of total global bond market capitalisation.

Although the USA is often seen as similar to the UK in being a **market-based** financial system, with companies' finance deriving from the issue of securities, at some times the proportion of US company finance coming from bond and equity issues has been lower than in the UK.

Nevertheless, Wall Street, where the NYSE is situated, remains at the centre of the system in people's perceptions. The importance of stocks to the average American grew with the growth of mutual funds (collective investments) and pension plans such as '401(k)' plans.

The size of the US economy and the dominance of the US dollar in international transactions has made the US financial system central to both the US economy and the global economy.

The US banking system is characterised by the large number of deposit-taking banks, which may be either state-chartered or national and federally licensed institutions. Non-depository institutions include securities firms, insurance companies, mutual funds, pension funds and finance companies.

2.16.2 Financial services

The term 'financial services' became more widely used in the USA following the Gramm-Leach-Bliley Act of the late 1990s. This legislation enabled different types of companies operating in the US financial services industry to merge.

For companies in the US, there are broadly two distinct approaches to this form of business.

- One approach is for a bank to buy an insurance company or an investment bank, keep the original brands of the acquired firm, and adds the acquisition to its holding company to diversify its earnings. Outside the USA (for example, in **Japan**), non-financial services companies are permitted within the holding company. Then, each company still appears independent, and has its own customers.

- A second approach is for a bank to create its own brokerage division or insurance division and attempt to sell those products to its own existing customers, with incentives for combining different services with one company.

The US markets are subject to strict regulation by the Securities and Exchange Commission (SEC). The US system is based almost wholly on statute with minimal self-regulation.

2.17 Asia

2.17.1 Key financial centres

Ranking after London and New York, the third and fourth largest financial centres are found in Asia – being **Tokyo** and **Singapore** respectively. Within China, **Shanghai** and **Hong Kong** are also key centres.

2.17.2 China

With a population of around 1.3 billion, **China** comprises approximately 20% of the world population, and so – with continued economic growth – represents substantial buying potential over the longer term. China will come to represent an increasingly significant pool of consumers of services as time goes on.

- China's economic growth (increase in GDP) has averaged around 10% annually since 1978 – approximately four times the UK's growth rate.

- By 2006, China's Gross Domestic Product (GDP) was broadly equivalent to that of the UK, at US$2.5 trillion. By 2011, China's GDP had reached US$7.3 trillion, while the GDP of the USA was $US15 trillion.

- There is increasing foreign investment in China, particularly by European investment funds.

- In recent years, foreign banks and financial institutions have been able to establish a foothold in China through cash and share ownership, in spite of China's traditionally protectionist stance.

In a similar way to **India** and **Malaysia** in recent years, China could become a cost-effective focus for service provision in the **financial sector**. The experience of outsourcing into other emerging markets in recent years shows how security and reliability are key to the expansion of such service provision.

Against these factors in China's favour, it is likely to take some more time for China to build up to the 'critical mass' of other major world financial centres.

2.17.3 Japan

Japan emerged as the most economically developed nation in Asia during the 1960s and 1970s, when the country's real economic growth averaged 7.5% annually. Growth slowed during the 1990s after a bubble in Japanese asset prices. In 2011, Japan's GDP was $US5.9 trillion. The economy is technologically advanced, and has been very successful in international trade, based on efficient manufacturing processes.

The Tokyo Stock Exchange is Japan's largest exchange, accounting for around 80% of total turnover in stocks. The bond market of Japan is the second largest in the world, and both government and corporate bonds are traded.

Accounting standards result in less objectivity than in other jurisdictions, and company information may be less readily available than elsewhere. Private capital investment remains strong.

Key regulatory institutions in Japan are the Ministry of Finance and the Financial Services Agency. The Agency is a Japanese governmental organisation that oversees banking, securities and insurance and reports to the Ministry of Finance.

3 THE ROLE OF GOVERNMENT

Learning objective	1.1.3 **Explain** the role of government including economic and industrial policy, regulation, taxation and social welfare

3.1 Overview

There are various ways in which Government actions impinge on people's lives and on the activities of businesses.

Legislation (laws) introduced by Parliament often gives authority for Government departments to introduce secondary legislation in the form of additional **regulations**.

Government agencies and local authorities affect our lives in many aspects, whether for example, through **taxation** or in the services they provide to us – including roads, and services and benefits to enhance people's **welfare** such as medical services, education, State pensions and elderly services. An argument for public (Government) provision of services such as healthcare and education postulates that these are **merit goods** which, if left to private free market transactions, would be consumed in quantities that would be insufficient for the optimisation of **social welfare**. For example, if the Government did not provide free or subsidised education, it could be argued, many parents would go without educating their children rather than pay fees for education.

The extent to which the Government influences what we do reflects the type of **economic system** we have. The economic system of the UK and of the wider European Union to which the UK belongs can be described as that of the **mixed economy**.

- A **mixed economy** involves some degree of State intervention in economic activity, while mostly markets are allowed to operate as freely as possible so long as intervention is not needed in the public interest. Some goods and services – for example, postal services – may be provided by the State. The government may be seen as playing a role in reducing inequalities in the distribution of income and wealth through the tax system.

- This type of economy stands between the two extremes of a *laissez-faire* **free market economy** in which market forces are allowed to reign, with minimal State intervention, and of a centrally planned **command economy**, such as that of the former Soviet Union and other Communist-ruled States, in which the government controls most industries and regulates many prices and wages, possibly with a rationing system to distribute scarce goods and services.

3.2 The UK and the EU

3.2.1 Overview

The **European Union (EU)**, formerly called the EEC or the European Community (EC), is one of several international economic associations. Its immediate aim is the integration of the economies of the member states. A more long-term aim is political integration. The association dates back to 1957 (the Treaty of Rome) and the EU now has 27 members including the UK.

The European Union has a **common market** combining different aspects, including **a free trade area** and a **customs union**.

- A **free trade area** exists when there is no restriction on the movement of goods and services between countries. This may be extended into a **customs union** when there is a free trade area between all member countries of the union, and in addition, there are common external tariffs applying to imports from non-member countries into any part of the union. In other words, the union promotes free trade among its members but acts as a protectionist bloc against the rest of the world.

- A **common market** encompasses the idea of a customs union but has a number of additional features. In addition to free trade among member countries there are also free markets in each of the **factors of production**. A British citizen has the freedom to work in any other country of the European Union, for example. A common market will also aim to achieve stronger links between member countries, for example by harmonising government economic policies and by establishing a closer political confederation.

3.2.2 UK sovereignty and EU membership

UK Statute law is made by Parliament (or in exercise of law-making powers delegated by Parliament). Until the United Kingdom entered the European Community in 1973, the UK Parliament was completely **sovereign**.

In recent years however, UK membership of the EU has restricted the previously unfettered power of Parliament. There is an **obligation**, imposed by the Treaty of Rome on which the EU is founded, to bring UK law into line with the Treaty itself and with EU Directives. Regulations, having the force of law in every member state, may be made under provisions of the Treaty of Rome.

3.2.3 Status of EU legislation

EU legislation takes the following three forms.

- **Regulations** have the force of law in every EU state without need of national legislation. Their objective is to obtain uniformity of law throughout the EU. They are formulated by the Commission but must be authorised by the Council of Ministers. Regulations are passed by the European Commission, or jointly by the EU Council and European Parliament.

- **Directives** are issued to the governments of the EU member states requiring them within a specified period (usually two years) to alter the national laws of the state so that they conform to the directive. Until a Directive is given effect by a national (UK) statute, it does not usually affect legal rights and obligations of individuals.

- **Decisions** of an administrative nature are made by the European Commission in Brussels. A decision may be addressed to a state, person or a company and is immediately binding, but only on the recipient.

The Council and the Commission may also make recommendations and deliver opinions, although these are only persuasive in authority.

BPP
LEARNING MEDIA

3.3 Monetary policy

3.3.1 Overview

Monetary policy is the area of government economic policy making that is concerned with changes in the **amount of money** in circulation – the **money supply** – and with changes in the **price of money** – **interest rates**. These variables are linked with **inflation** in prices generally, and also with **exchange rates** – the price of the domestic currency in terms of other currencies.

3.3.2 Setting interest rates

Since 1997, the most important aspect of monetary policy in the UK has been the influence over interest rates exerted by the **Bank of England**, the **central bank** of the UK. The **Monetary Policy Committee (MPC)** of the Bank of England was charged with the responsibility of setting interest rates with the aim of meeting the government's current inflation target which currently stands at **2%**, plus or minus 1% as measured by the **Consumer Prices Index (CPI)**, also known as the Harmonised Index of Consumer Prices (HCIP). Inflation below the target of 2% is judged by the Bank of England to be unsatisfactory, as is inflation above the target.

The **UK inflation objective** was originally formalised in the 1998 Bank of England Act. That Act states that the Bank of England is expected 'to maintain price stability, and, subject to that, to support the economic policy of HM Government including its objectives for growth and employment'.

The MPC decides the short-term **benchmark 'repo' rate** at which the Bank of England deals in the money markets. This will tend to be followed by financial institutions generally in setting interest rates for different financial instruments. However, a government does not have an unlimited ability to have interest rates set how it wishes. It must take into account what rates the overall market will bear, so that the benchmark rate it chooses can be maintained. The Bank must be careful about the signals it gives to the markets, since the effect of expectations can be significant.

The monthly minutes of the MPC are published. This arrangement is intended to remove the possibility of direct political influence over the interest rate decision.

The Bank of England **reducing** interest rates is an **easing** of monetary policy.

- Loans will be cheaper, and so consumers may increase levels of debt and spend more. Demand will tend to rise and companies may have improved levels of sales. Companies will find it cheaper to borrow: their lower interest costs will boost bottom-line profits.

- Mortgage loans will be cheaper and so there will be upward pressure on property prices.

- Values of other assets will also tend to rise. Investors will be willing to pay higher prices for gilts (government stock) because they do not require such a high yield from them as before the interest rate reduction.

- Interest rates on cash deposits will fall. Those who are dependant on income from cash deposits will be worse off than before.

The Bank of England **increasing** interest rates is a **tightening** of monetary policy.

- Loans will cost more, and demand from consumers, especially for less essential 'cyclical' goods and services, may fall. Companies will find it more expensive to borrow money and this could eat into profits, on top of any effect from reducing demand.

- Mortgage loans will cost more and so there will be a dampening effect on property prices.

- Asset prices generally will tend to fall. Investors will require a higher return than before and so they will pay less for fixed interest stocks such as gilts.

- Interest rates on cash deposits will rise, and those reliant on cash deposits for income will be better off.

3.4 Exchange rate policy

The **exchange rate** of the national currency (pounds sterling) against other major currencies (such as the US dollar, the euro and the Japanese yen) is another possible focus of economic policy.

The Government could try to influence exchange rates by buying or selling currencies through its central bank reserves. However, Government currency reserves are now relatively small and so such a policy might have to be limited in scope.

Another way the Government might wish to influence exchange rates is through changes in **interest rates**: if UK interest rates are raised, this makes sterling a relatively more attractive currency to hold and so the change should exert upward pressure on the value of sterling. As we have seen, interest rate policy is now determined by the MPC. Interest rate policy is decided in the light of various matters apart from exchange rates, including the inflation rate and the level of house prices.

If the UK joined the **single European currency**, the **euro**, interest rates would effectively be determined at the European level, by the European Central Bank, instead of at the national level as now. It would not be possible for interest rates in different eurozone countries to be much out of line at any one time, since differences would encourage money flows to seek the higher rates available in a particular country, and borrowers would seek the best rates available. The forces of supply and demand would lead to an approximate equalisation of rates.

3.5 Fiscal policy

A government's **fiscal policy** concerns its plans for **spending, taxation and borrowing**.

These aspects of fiscal policy reflect the three elements in public finance.

- **Expenditure**. The government, at a national and local level, spends money to provide goods and services, such as a health service, public education, a police force, roads, public buildings and so on, and to pay its administrative work force. It may also, perhaps, provide finance to encourage investment by private industry, for example by means of grants.

- **Income**. Expenditure must be financed, and the government must have income. Most government income comes from taxation, but some income is obtained from direct charges to users of government services such as National Health Service charges.

- **Borrowing**. To the extent that a government's expenditure exceeds its income, it must borrow to make up the difference. The amount that the government must borrow each year is known as the **Public Sector Net Cash Requirement (PSNCR)** in the UK.

Government **spending is an injection** into the economy, adding to the level of overall demand for goods and services, whereas **taxes are a withdrawal**.

A government's 'fiscal stance' may be **neutral, expansionary** or **contractionary**, according to its overall effect on national income.

- **Spending more money** and financing this expenditure by borrowing would indicate an expansionary fiscal stance. Expenditure in the economy will increase and so national income will rise, either in real terms, or partly in terms of price levels only: the increase in national income might be real, or simply inflationary.

- **Collecting more in taxes** without increasing spending would indicate a contractionary fiscal stance. A government might deliberately raise taxation to take inflationary pressures out of the economy

The impact of changes in fiscal policy is not always certain, and fiscal policy to pursue one aim (eg lower inflation) might for a while create barriers to the pursuit of other aims (eg employment).

Government planners need to consider how fiscal policy can affect savers, investors and companies.

(a) The tax regime as it affects different savings instruments will affect **investors'** decisions.

(b) **Companies** will be affected by tax rules on dividends and profits, and they may take these rules into account when deciding on dividend policy or on whether to raise finance through **debt** (loans) or **equities** (by issuing shares).

The formal planning of fiscal policy usually follows an annual cycle. In the UK, the most important statement is **the Budget**, which takes place in the Spring of each year. The Chancellor of the Exchequer also delivers a Pre-Budget Report each Autumn. The Pre-Budget Report formally makes available for scrutiny the Government's overall spending plans.

3.6 Industrial policy

3.6.1 Overview

While macroeconomic policy-making is concerned with the economy as a while, industrial policy is focused on particular sectors of the economy. The UK government current's approach to industrial policy aims to create an institutional framework that allows businesses to prosper, and individuals and households to improve steadily their living standards.

The institutional framework has the following aims.

- Promoting effective competition
- Flexibility in labour and capital markets
- Maintaining a legal system which gives confidence and trust to market participants
- Providing a stable macroeconomic framework

Other aspects of UK policy concentrate on the advance and commercial application of scientific knowledge, and investment in physical infrastructure, education and health. **Innovation policies** seek to balance the benefits of intellectual property protection with facilitating the widespread exploitation of new knowledge through, among other things, easing barriers to the widespread dissemination and adoption of ideas.

Underpinning this approach is a presumption that, as a whole, the effective operations of markets are a better way of bringing about improvements to business efficiency and the most economically beneficial allocation of capital, knowledge and employment. Government is however seen to have a role where **market failures** arise, for example, in the provision of 'merit goods' in the public interest such as education and healthcare services, in overcoming 'externalities' such as pollution, and through policies on science, skills, innovation and regulation.

Responsibility for the various themes of industrial policy is spread across difference central Government departments, although the **Department for Business, Innovation and Skills** plays a key role.

3.6.2 Industry policy and the European Union

The UK works with the European Commission and other EU Member States to address from the European perspective issues that are confronting all industrialised countries – the challenges laid down by globalisation, including for example the intense competition from growing economies like China and India, the greater fragmentation and wider dispersion of supply chains and increased pressures on industrial and local adjustment in relation to our international competitiveness, and energy and climate change.

Actions under the EU Policy agenda

- A commitment to focus on economic growth and employment

- Shaping policies to allow businesses to create more and better jobs implemented in a way that balances and mutually reinforce economic, environmental and social objectives

- An integrated approach aimed at improving the coherence between different policy dimensions and increasing their relevance to business

- Bringing business directly into the process through the establishment of 'High Level Groups'

These High Level groups bring together members of the various European Commission Directorates General, Member State Governments and relevant stakeholders from industry, consumers/civil society, trade unions, Non-Governmental Organisations and regulators and are mandated to provide advice to policy makers at Community and national levels, industry and civil society organisations on issues effecting European industrial competitiveness.

3.7 Free movement of capital

Free international trade is generally associated with the free movement of goods (and services) between countries. Another important aspect of international trade is the **free movement of capital**.

- If a UK company (or investor) wishes to set up a business in a different country, or to take over a company in another country, how easily can it transfer capital from the UK to the country in question, to pay for the investment?

- Similarly, if a Japanese company wishes to invest in the UK, how easily can it transfer funds out of Japan and into the UK to pay for the investment?

Some countries (including the UK, since the abolition of exchange controls in 1979) have allowed a fairly free flow of capital into and out of the country. Other countries have been more cautious, mainly for one of the following two reasons.

- The free inflow of foreign capital will make it easier for foreign companies to take over domestic companies. There is often a belief that certain key industries should be owned by residents of the country. Even in the UK, for example, there have been restrictions placed on the total foreign ownership of shares in companies such as British Aerospace and Rolls Royce.

- Less developed countries especially, but other more advanced economies too, are reluctant to allow the free flow of capital out of the country. After all, they need capital to come into the country to develop the domestic economy.

3.8 Regulation

3.8.1 Overview

While it is widely accepted that the **market mechanism** enables prosperity, there are aspects of unbridled free markets that can lead to exploitation, abuse of information and dishonest dealing to the detriment of the overall welfare. There is a need, given that such **market failures** have the potential to occur, to have certain protections in place to ensure that markets are conducted in accordance with principles of fairness and consumers in general are dealt with fairly.

Consumer protection in the financial services industry and other consumer markets became an increasingly important aspect of UK Governments' policy from the 1970s onwards. The Financial Services

Act 1986 (FSA 1986) was brought in to replace the system of **self-regulation** which had previously prevailed in the UK financial sector. The FSA 1986 brought a new system of **'self-regulation within a statutory framework'**, with financial services firms authorised by Self-Regulatory Organisations (SROs).

A series of **financial scandals**, including those involving the Maxwell Group, Barings Bank, BCCI and pensions mis-selling, had added weight to the political impetus for change, leading to the establishment of the Financial Services Authority (FSA) as the single statutory regulator of the financial services industry, under the **Financial Services and Markets Act 2000 (FSMA 2000)**.

The **financial crisis of the late 2000s** brought into focus the problems of financial instability affecting some banks and other financial sector institutions. In 2013, the UK's single-regulator system was abolished. The **Prudential Regulation Authority (PRA)** was established to oversee the stability of 'prudentially significant' firms. The regulation of conduct across the sector, including issues surrounding advice given to retail consumers, became the responsibility of the **Financial Conduct Authority (FCA)**, which was formed out of the FSA legal entity.

3.8.2 Voluntary codes and statutory regulation

In some areas and at some times, financial services providers have been subject to **voluntary codes**, which an industry sector develops itself, rather than rules imposed through the law (statutory rules).

Clearly, if the Government chooses and Parliament agrees, it can extend statutory regulation to areas previously governed by voluntary codes. For example, **mortgage advice and selling**, previously governed by the voluntary Mortgage Code, became regulated in 2004. **General insurance** regulation followed in 2005.

The area of banking can be taken as another example. Until 2009, banks and building societies followed a voluntary code (the **Banking Code**) in their relations with personal customers in the UK. In November 2009, responsibility for the regulation of deposit and payment products transferred to the FSA as financial services regulator. A Lending Standards Board (LSB) continues to monitor and enforce compliance with a **Lending Code** that replaces those elements of the Banking Code and Business Banking Code relating to lending.

4 ASSETS AND MARKETS

Learning objectives	**1.2.1 Differentiate** between a financial security and a real asset **1.2.2 Identify** the key features of: a common equity share, a bond, a derivative contract, a unit in a pooled fund, and a foreign exchange transaction

4.1 Types of asset

An asset is an item that has value.

- Tangible assets such as land and buildings (property, or real estate), machinery, oil, sugar and gold, are all **real assets.**

- In a monetary economy, there are claims that may represent the right to a return, such as interest and the eventual repayment of principal (on a **loan**), or dividends payable out of a company's profits (for **shares** in a company). Such claims are **financial assets**.

Loans (**debt**) and shares (**equity**) represent the two main types of financial security. Many companies have both debt and equity in their financing structure.

4.2 Ordinary shares

Ordinary shares are often referred to as **equity shares**, or simply **equities**. The term 'equity' means that each share has an equal right to share in profits. For example, if a company has 10,000 ordinary shares, each share is entitled to $1/_{10,000}$ of the profits made during any period.

The ordinary shareholders of a company are the **owners** of the company. However, it is normal for ordinary shares to possess a **vote**. This means that the holder of any ordinary shares may attend and vote at any meetings held by the company. Whilst the day-to-day control of the company is passed into the hands of the directors and managers, the shareholders must have the right to decide upon the most important issues that affect the business.

Although voting rights may vary for different classes of share, each equity share most typically carries one vote.

Companies legally do not have to declare a **dividend** on ordinary shares, many of them do in order to maintain shareholder loyalty. Companies may pay an interim dividend based on the six-month results, and declare a final dividend based on the year-end results. For public companies, this will not be paid until the shareholders have agreed it at the AGM. Some companies give their shareholders the choice to take their dividend in new shares, rather than cash. New shares are created, but in a way that there will be no significant impact on the share price. The investors are taxed as if they had taken the cash dividend.

Companies may only pay dividends out of post-tax profits – that is, from their **distributable reserves**. In any single year, the dividend paid could exceed the profit for that year, because there may be distributable reserves brought forward from earlier years.

Not only do shares offer income in the form of dividends, they also offer the possibility of **capital growth** when the share price rises.

4.3 Bonds

The term '**bonds**' is used to encompass the asset class of **fixed income securities**.

A **bond** may be defined as a negotiable debt instrument for a fixed principal amount issued by a borrower for a specific period of time, making a regular payment of interest/coupon to the holder until it is redeemed at maturity, when the principal amount is repaid.

Historically, bonds began as very simple negotiable debt instruments, paying a fixed coupon for a specified period, then being redeemed at face value – a 'straight bond'. In the past, bond markets were seen as being investment vehicles that was safe enough for 'widows and orphans'. They were thought to be dull markets with predictable returns and very little in the way of gains to be made from trading.

The bond markets emerged from this shadow during the mid-1970s when both interest rates and currencies became substantially more volatile. Bonds have emerged over the past few decades to be much more complex investments, and there are now a significant number of variations on the basic theme.

Whilst it is perhaps easy to be confused by the variety of 'bells and whistles' that have been introduced into the market in recent years, one should always bear in mind that the vast majority of issues are still straight bonds. The reason for this is that investors are wary of buying investments that they do not fully understand. If an issue is too complex, it will be difficult to market.

Bonds are used by a number of **issuers** as a means of raising finance. Major bond issuers include the following.

- **Sovereign governments** – who need to raise finance to help them cover any national debt or budget shortfall
- **Local authorities** – who need to raise finance to help them cover any local budget shortfall
- **Companies** – who need to raise cash to help them finance business requirements

Regardless of who the issuer is, there are a number of general characteristics that any bond is likely to have which we will examine next.

Negotiability means that it is a piece of paper that can be bought and sold. For certain types of bonds, this is easier than for others. Government bonds tend to be highly liquid, ie very easy to buy or sell, whereas certain corporate bonds are almost illiquid and are usually held to maturity by the initial buyer.

4.4 Pooled funds

In order to minimise the risk involved in investment, it is often a good idea for the investor to spread invested money over a range of instruments, thereby diversifying risk. However, if the individual has a limited amount of money to invest, it will be very difficult to buy a range of individual equities or bonds without incurring relatively high transaction costs.

A way around this problem is for individual investors' investments to be grouped together and form a collective investment vehicle. Here they pool their money in a large fund, which is managed and invested for them by a fund manager.

There are different types of 'pooled' or collective investment vehicle available, the main types being **unit trusts**, **open-ended investment companies (OEICs)** and **investment trusts**. There are also **exchange traded funds (ETFs)**, which are typically designed to track an index.

Authorised unit trusts and OEICs are **Authorised Investment Funds (AIFs)** and are often referred to simply as **funds**.

A unit trust differs from investment trusts and OEICs in the way it is set up, as a unit trust is not a company with shares. A key difference between different pooled investments is the way in which the fund is priced. For unit trusts and OEICs (for example), there is a direct relationship between the value of the underlying investments and the value of units. Units are priced according to Net Asset Value (NAV). Investment trust shares and also ETFs, however, are priced according to supply and demand in the stock market.

Unit trusts are, like OEICs, called **open-ended** funds as there is no limit to the amount of money which can be invested. If no 'second-hand' units are available, the fund is permitted to create more units and expand the fund. Investment trusts, on the other hand, are **closed-ended**: except when new shares are issued – eg, on launch of the trust – the buyer of investment trust shares is buying them from existing holders of the shares.

The advantages and disadvantages of **collective** (or 'pooled') investment, as compared with **direct investment** can be summarised as follows.

Advantages of collective investments

- An individual can invest relatively small amounts, perhaps on a regular basis.

- The pooling of investments enables the fund to make purchases of securities at lower cost than would be possible for an individual.

- The time involved in directly managing one's own portfolio is saved.

- The funds are managed by professional fund managers. A fund manager with a good past performance record may be able to repeat the performance in the future.

- A wide diversification between different shares and sectors can be achieved: this can be impractical and costly in dealing charges for a small portfolio held by an individual.

- Risk is reduced by exposure to a widely diversified spread of investments in the underlying portfolio.

- Specialisation in particular sectors is possible.

- The investor can gain exposure to foreign stocks, which can be costly and inconvenient for an individual who holds shares directly.

- Different funds provide for different investment objectives, such as income or growth, or a combination of both.

Disadvantages of collective investments

- The individual can only choose baskets of investments selected by fund managers, not by himself, and this will not suit all investors.

- Although the individual does not have to pick individual securities, he still has to choose the fund manager, and different managers' performance can vary widely.

- Although 'star' fund managers can have a successful track record with a fund, such 'star' managers may switch jobs, making future management of the fund less certain.

- Larger collective funds find it more difficult to invest in shares of companies with a relatively small capitalisation, because of the small quantities of stock available.

- Successful collective funds investing in smaller companies can become a victim of their own success if more funds are brought in, as a greater fund size can make it more difficult for such a fund to follow their successful strategy.

4.5 Derivative contracts

Derivative contracts is a term encompassing contracts such as **futures, options and swaps** which derive their value from the movement, up or down, in the price of an underlying asset. Derivatives can be used to **speculate** on future price changes, and risks can be high when derivatives are **geared** to be very sensitive to price changes. Derivatives allow both 'long' and 'short' positions to be taken. They may be used to **hedge** or reduce someone's exposure to risks, which can be achieved by taking an opposite position in a derivative relative to an existing risk exposure.

For example, a wheat farmer may sell wheat futures (called a short hedge) to guarantee him a known fixed price for his wheat. If the price of wheat falls between when the farmer buys the contract and its maturity date. The farmer will gain on the futures contract if the wheat price falls, and will lose on the futures contract if the wheat price rises. These gains and losses can respectively be set against the losses and gains that the farmer makes from actually selling his wheat, so that the net effect will be to give him a price that was known in advance.

The FTSE 100 index futures contract could be used to hedge against falls in the share price index over future periods. An investment intermediary, such as a collective (pooled) fund or a pension fund, may use derivative contracts to achieve their objectives. The fund may hold a portfolio of UK shares, and may hedge against a possible fall in the value of its portfolio by selling FTSE 100 index futures. If the market falls while the contract is held, the value of the share portfolio will most probably fall, but this will be compensated for by gains on the futures contract. Having opened the futures contact by selling it, the fund manager will later buy the futures contract in order to crystallise the gain on the contract.

Derivatives contract enable investors to take a position in the price of an asset without actually taking delivery of the underlying asset. For example, a position can be taken on the price of oil, without participants in the related derivative contract taking physical delivery of oil at any point.

Derivatives, including options, can be divided into **exchange-traded** and **over-the-counter (OTC)** types. Exchange-traded derivatives are more standardised and offer greater liquidity than OTC contracts, which are tailor-made to meet the needs of buyers and sellers. Traded options are available on the shares of over 90 major listed UK companies. As they are traded products, they are standardised in terms of expiry dates, quantity of shares per option contract and so on.

4.6 Currency transactions

Currency or foreign exchange trading (or **FOREX** as it is commonly known) is the dealing of the currencies of various countries. London is the biggest centre in the world for FOREX trading, with hundreds of billions in US$ equivalents traded per day. Although some FOREX is required for overseas trade, much of it is traded for speculative purposes, where FOREX traders seek to exploit a particular view on interest rate differentials or exchange rate movements. An investment manager might convert sterling into US dollars, for example, in order to make a purchase of US securities.

There is no formal market place for FOREX trades: in London, trading is **over-the-counter (OTC)**. Prices are advertised on screens and deals are conducted over telephones. The major players are investment banks and specialist currency brokers. This is not a market place where the private investor usually gets directly involved – his currency needs are more often met through specialist money organisations, who themselves have accessed the currency markets through their own specialist broker.

FOREX transactions are described either as spot or forward. **Spot** means the trade is to meet immediate currency needs and will settle in two business days after the trade day (known as T + 2). **Forward** is when an exchange rate is agreed today for settlement at some future date, as agreed by the parties. This is a particularly useful way of eliminating risk from transactions requiring currency (import and export dealings) at some time in the future. Most currencies are quoted against the US dollar.

4.7 Functions of securities markets

Learning objective	1.2.3 **Identify** the functions of securities market in providing price transparency and liquidity

Financial markets mobilise people's savings and put them to use in enabling firms to grow, thus contributing to the wealth of the economy.

An effective securities market will have the following characteristics.

- **Cost efficiency** – in order to maximise volumes and to compete with alternative market venues, the market needs to be cost-effective. Electronic order systems should be the most cost-effective.

- **Liquidity** – liquidity is the ability to enter or exit the market at an acceptable price spread, creating only modest price distortion on a transaction of a reasonable size. Factors contributing to liquidity are effective and efficient IT and settlement systems, stock availability and stock lending facilities and a diverse membership.

- **Price discovery** (the process through which an equilibrium price for a financial instrument is revealed continuously through bid and offer prices, and trading) and **transparency** – it is important that the investor knows the price before, during and after a deal in order to be satisfied that he has a good deal. We discuss this later in this section.

Sophisticated financial markets also fulfil an important role in the **transfer of risk**. We have described, for example, how derivatives markets enable investors, entrepreneurs and market participants to hedge risks as well as to speculate on the prices for assets.

Quote-driven markets depend on the existence of market makers who are prepared to offer two-way quotes in shares. Dealers or 'market makers' are prepared to take risks in meeting orders, and their participation enhances liquidity in the market. In an **order-driven market**, it is buyers' and sellers' respective bids and offers that are matched with one another.

Most shares, futures contracts, and standard options contracts are now traded mainly through an order-driven system. Automated trading, such as the LSE's SETS system, can bypass the need for a human intermediary. Large orders can present a problem, as the broker (or the system) may struggle to find a counterparty at a suitable price. Various order types exist whereby orders may be presented to execute immediately at the prevailing market price, or may be conditional orders depending on price and quantities to match before a trade is achieved.

The **bid** price is the price at which dealers or investors are willing to pay for a stock and the **offer** price is the selling price at which dealers or other investors are willing to sell. In a quote-driven market, the spread or turn – the difference between the bid and the offer – enables dealers to make a profit on transactions. Depending on which securities are being traded, dealers may be working for proprietary trading houses, investment banks, commercial banks, or broker-dealers.

Traders in financial markets are sometimes categorised broadly into **sell-side** and **buy-side**.

- **Sell-side firms** comprise investment banks, brokers, and dealers who provide investment products and transaction services

- **Buy-side firms** are mainly investment managers (including pension funds, mutual funds, hedge funds and insurance companies) who purchase investment products and transaction services

The sell-side / buy-side distinction is not clear-cut, given that a particular firm may encompass market participants on the buy-side as well as the sell-side – for example, many investment banks have subsidiaries or divisions that provide asset management services.

4.8 Transaction costs

Learning objective	**1.2.5 Calculate** round trip transaction costs incorporating bid-ask spreads, dealing commission and transaction taxes, both in percentages and in absolute amounts

The typical costs of a share transaction for a UK investor can be broken down as follows.

- **Purchase cost**. The purchase cost includes a **spread** which is the difference between the bid and offer price of the share. The spread, from which market makers makes their profits, could be 0.5% for a liquid share or 5% or more for a less easily traded share.

- **Broker's commission**. A typical charge could be, say, 1.5% on a deal up to £7,000 and 1.0% above that, with a minimum charge of £25. Execution only services, including online brokers, are generally cheaper than this for individuals, ranging from around £10 per deal upwards. Brokers incur various costs for the resources they employ to fill orders, including costs for market data and order routing systems, exchange memberships and fees, regulatory fees, clearing fees, accounting systems, office space, and staff to manage the trading process.

- **Stamp Duty and SDRT**. Stamp Duty Reserve Tax (SDRT) is payable at 0.5% on the value of purchases of UK equities settled through CREST (ie most transactions), rounded up to the nearest 1p. Stamp Duty is payable on the much less common situation of purchases of UK equities not settled through CREST, at 0.5%, rounded up to the nearest £5. (There is no Stamp Duty if the charge so calculated would be £5 or less.) Stamp Duty on stock registered in Ireland is charged at 0.1%.

- **Panel on Takeovers and Mergers Levy**. The PTM levy is a flat £1 on transactions (sales and purchases) that are in excess of £10,000.

Below is an example of the possible cost of the purchase and sale of shares to the value of £10,001.

Cost of purchase

	£
Shares	10,001.00
Brokerage commission 1.0%	100.00
SDRT at 0.5%	50.01
PTM levy	1.00
Total cost	10,152.01

Cost of sale

	£
Shares	10,001.00
Brokerage commission 1.0%	100.00
PTM levy	1.00
Total cost	10,102.00

Market participants will typically want to make timely trades, often responding quickly to new information about a security or about the wider market, and will typically buy at higher prices than the prices at which they are able to sell, overall. Buyers putting through relatively large buy orders may need to push the price of the security up in order to make the trade. Sellers who want to put through a large sell order quickly may need to accept a lower price than is immediately available to a seller with a small order. The cost effect of this tendency for fluctuating order sizes to move prices is called the **market impact** or **price impact**, and is a **significant component of transaction costs** for large financial institutions.

Limit orders, which will be filled only if the price is better than the stated limit, provide a way of limiting transaction costs, compared with **market orders**, which are filled at whatever prices are available when the order is placed. The **opportunity cost** of using a limit order is that the price may move against the trader before the order is filled. As a rule, a limit order is usually advisable for thinly traded stocks, to avoid the risk of a market order being filled at a possibly very disadvantageous price. For a major stock with relatively deep liquidity, such as BP plc or Microsoft Corporation, bid-ask spreads are generally very small and, given the fiduciary and regulatory duty of the broker to provide best execution, a market order may be more appropriate, depending on the circumstances and the trader's objective.

4.9 Price transparency and liquidity

Learning objectives

1.2.4 Identify the reasons why liquidity and price transparency are thought to be important for the efficient allocation of capital costs when trading in securities markets

1.2.6 Identify the types of securities and the market conditions where price transparency, liquidity and depth are likely to be high / low

1.2.7 Define liquidity risk and identify why it is important

Transparent markets are markets in which data is available to participants on quotes and in real-time (**pre-trade transparency**) and on trades once they occur (**post-trade transparency**). These forms of transparency are required for many securities – particularly equities – by the **Markets in Financial Instruments Directive (MiFID)**. **Over-the-counter (OTC) markets**, such as the market in credit default swaps (CDSs) are typically less transparent.

As we have seen, price discovery is the process through which equilibrium prices for a financial instrument are revealed continuously through bid / offer prices, and trading. An '**efficient market**' would see equilibrium prices change only when new information becomes available. The **efficient markets** hypothesis (EMH) views a market as **informationally efficient** if certain types of information are incorporated into security prices.

For **buy-side** traders, transparency enables the trader to gain knowledge of market values and to estimate potential transaction costs. **Opacity** in markets may be preferred by **sell-side** dealers because they typically have an **informational advantage** over the **counterparties** with whom they trade, such as buy-side market participants.

Liquidity risk or marketability risk has to do with the ease with which an issue can be sold in the market. Smaller issues especially are subject to this risk. In certain markets, the volume of trading tends to concentrate in the 'benchmark' stocks, thereby rendering most other issues relatively illiquid. Some bonds become subject to 'seasoning' as the initial liquidity dries up and the bonds are purchased by investors who wish to hold them to maturity.

The **size of the bid-ask spread** relative to the value of a security is an indication of the **liquidity** of the market in that security. Securities with many daily trades will have more dealers and investors placing orders at any one time, and so it is more likely that the highest bid (sell) price and the lowest ask (buy) prices will be closer. More opaque (less transparent) markets will typically have larger bid-ask spreads because, in opaque markets, dealers will find it more difficult to judge the level of demand for the stock, and so know the equilibrium price.

If a market for a security or securities has many ready and willing buyers and many ready and willing sellers, we can say that the market is **deeply liquid**. The market for US Treasuries (US Federal Government debt) is an example of a deeply liquid market, with the large daily volume of transactions and low bid-ask spreads meaning that **transaction costs** are relatively very low.

However, the level of liquidity for some securities can fluctuate significantly, sometimes in response to wider market sentiments. When the macro-economic environment is relatively benign, liquidity levels may remain relatively high, while in a market downturn when investor sentiment declines, **liquidity may dry up** – particularly for smaller companies such as those on the Alternative Investment Market (AIM), and in order-driven markets where there is no requirement for market makers to maintain two-way quotes at all times –and it may be quite difficult for sellers to find a buyer, particularly for larger orders. Most companies with a larger capitalisation (for example, members of the FTSE 100 Index for UK stocks) are widely held by institutions as well as smaller investors, and are followed closely by large numbers of analysts. These larger companies have a relatively large quantity of stocks in public hands and large numbers of potential buyers and sellers at virtually all times, and so markets for such stocks tend to have a deep level of liquidity.

During the **late 2000s financial crisis** and **housing market downturn**, liquidity in the markets in **mortgage-backed securities** dried up because of widespread uncertainty about the value of the securities. Where such securities relied heavily on sub-prime mortgages, the housing market downturn threatened to bring a spate of foreclosures and the prospect of high levels bad mortgage debt that would not be repaid.

Investors will generally demand a higher expected return from securities where liquidity is low, because they expect compensation for the risk that they may find it difficult to sell the shares quickly during some periods. The price may move adversely while the stockholder Is waiting to sell. Thus, **liquidity risk** – the risk that a lack of liquidity may lead to losses for the investor – will generally be reflected in the price of a security.

4.10 Wider economic effects of well-functioning markets

If markets work well, with reasonable levels of liquidity and low transaction costs (**operational efficiency**), there are various benefits for the investors, for borrowers, and for the wider economy. Firms are better able to take risks and to finance large-scale operations that provide for economies of scale in production if there are willing investors in equities, bringing higher productivity and economic growth. Lenders and borrowers are better able to come together in bond markets to enable debt finance to be available. Governments are able to finance public deficits through markets in which the private sector participates. Through well-developed professional fund markets, individuals are able to enjoy more security in retirement incomes made available through their pension schemes.

In well-developed markets, price transparency improves **informational efficiency**, which describes a situation in which the prices of assets reflect all relevant information about their value. If all investors have access to good quality and timely information about securities, then the prices of stocks will better reflect their fundamental value. This being so, investors' funds will be channelled towards securities yielding the highest expected returns. In a well-functioning economy, backed by a legal environment that protects the rule of law and minimises corruption, the highest returns will tend to be earned on the securities if firms whose assets are the most productive. In an economist's terms, we can then say that greater **allocative efficiency** will have been achieved, because investors' funds are being allocated to the most productive uses.

5 TYPES OF FINANCIAL MARKETS

Learning objectives	**1.3.1 Identify** the main dealing systems and facilities offered in the UK equities market
	1.3.2 Identify the nature of the securities that would be traded on each of the main dealing systems and facilities
	1.3.4 Explain the motivations for, and implications of, dual listing a company
	1.3.7 Distinguish between a quote-driven and order-driven market
	1.3.8 Explain the roles of the various participants in the UK equity market

5.1 The London Stock Exchange

5.1.1 Overview

The **London Stock Exchange** (LSE) is an organised **capital market** which plays an important role in the functioning of the UK economy.

The LSE is a business enterprise. Its primary objective is to establish and run a market place in securities. The LSE provides the main route in the UK for larger companies to raise funds through the issue of **shares** (equity). It makes it easier for large firms and the government to raise long-term capital, by providing a market place for businesses seeking capital and investors to come together. Companies coming to the market may be launching an **initial public offering (IPO)**, or may be coming to the market to obtain further capital, for example for an expansion, through a **secondary offering**.

- Initially, the companies (the borrowers) issue shares to the investing public (savers), and to fund managers who are ultimately investing on behalf of individuals. This is known as the **primary market**.

- Investors would not be willing to invest their money unless they could see some way of releasing it in the future. Consequently, the exchange must also offer a **secondary market** trading in second-hand shares, this allows the investor to convert the shares into cash.

The **Alternative Investment Market** (AIM), which opened in 1995, is a market where smaller companies which cannot meet the more stringent requirements needed to obtain a full listing on the LSE can raise new capital by issuing shares. It is cheaper for smaller company to be on the AIM than to meet the requirements for a full listing. Like the Stock Exchange main market, the AIM is also a market in which investors can trade in shares already issued. The AIM is regulated by the LSE.

5.1.2 Trading methods of The London Stock Exchange

All Stock Exchange members are broker-dealers with **dual capacity**. This means that they can act as agents on behalf of customers or as principals dealing directly with the customers.

Different types of shares, with varying levels of liquidity, trade via different market systems.

System	SETS	SETSqx	SEAQ
Nature	Order driven	Combined order and quote driven	Quote driven
Market makers	**No** market makers	**At least one** market maker per stock	**At least two** market makers per stock
Full list stocks traded	All stocks classified as 'liquid' under MiFID, ie all of FTSE All Share Index, Exchange Traded Funds, Exchange Traded Commodities and the most actively traded Irish stocks	All stocks classified as 'illiquid' under MiFID, ie illiquid equities	None
AIM stocks traded	Most traded AIM stocks	All AIM stocks in AIM EURO sectors not traded on SETS	All remaining AIM stocks

Before the implementation of MiFID, less liquid shares were traded on SETSmm or SEAQ (the LSE historical quote driven system). In October 2007, SETSmm was absorbed into SETS and all SEAQ shares moved to SETSqx in preparation for MiFID. SEAQ is now only used for trading fixed interest products and highly illiquid AIM stocks.

5.1.3 Order-driven v quote-driven markets

Before we look at the detailed mechanics of each of the trading platforms, it is worth considering the fundamental differences between an **order-driven** and a **quote-driven** market.

- Where a market is **order-driven**, the relevant trading system will match buyers and sellers automatically, provided that they are willing to trade at prices compatible with each other. This is essentially the function which SETS performs. Prices of securities which trade on SETS are, therefore, purely driven by the buyers and sellers in the market themselves.

- A **quote-driven** market, such as SEAQ, requires certain market participants (market makers) to take responsibility for acting as buyers and sellers to the rest of the market so that there will always be a price at which a trade can be conducted. For such a market to operate efficiently, up-to-date prices at which market makers are willing to trade need to be made available to other market participants. This is the function performed by SEAQ. Unlike SETS, SEAQ does not provide a mechanism for trades to be executed automatically: transactions are, therefore, normally conducted by telephone.

SETSqx (discussed later in this Section) combines the market making quote-driven model and the order-driven model.

5.1.4 The Stock Exchange Electronic Trading Service (SETS)

The SETS system (known as the Order Book, as it is an order-driven system) is used for the most liquid domestic equities. Since these stocks are highly liquid, an **order matching** system (allowing buyers and sellers to deal with one another directly rather than going through dealers (market-makers) who would charge a spread) provides a cheap market structure for these shares.

The London Clearing House (known as LCH.Clearnet) acts as the central counterparty to all SETS trades.

Novation: all automatically executed trades **'novate'** to LCH.Clearnet such that the buyer buys from LCH.Clearnet and the seller sells to LCH.Clearnet.

5.1.5 The order book

The SETS screen displays limit orders (orders to buy or sell shares with a maximum or minimum price stated). The limit orders are **automatically matched** by the electronic order book. If an order is not matched entirely, the **unmatched portion will remain on the order book**. Orders are prioritised in a strict sequence, with **price** first, then the **time of input** with the earlier orders first.

Below is an example order book for a SETS security.

Buy			Sell		
Time	Volume	Price	Price	Volume	Time
09:03	12,000	174	175	1,100	09:15
10:08	5,000	174	176	1,400	09:12
09:31	11,000	173	176	12,530	09:45
09:32	4,500	173	176	2,721	09:52
09:20	8,350	172	177	12,000	10:00
09:24	12,050	172	177	4,290	10:02
09:40	4,933	172			

In order to trade shares, market participants can then either:

- Match automatically with an order currently displayed on the screen, or
- Place their own order onto the screen and hope someone will match their order at a later time.

5.1.6 SETSqx

SETSqx ('Stock Exchange Electronic Trading Service-quotes and crosses') replaced the Stock Exchange Alternative Trading Service plus (SEATS plus) in June 2007 and in October 2007 it replaced SEAQ for all main market securities.

The SETSqx system combines committed principal quotes with periodic auctions where anonymous limit orders are placed. Market makers and non-market makers can participate in auctions, these auctions take place at 08:00, 11:00, 15:00 and 16:35.

The market makers will provide a ready counterparty to market participants wishing to trade SETSqx shares (and bonds) in return for being able to make profits from a spread between buying and selling prices.

In order to act as a market maker, the relevant firm undertakes **an obligation** to **quote firm, two-way** prices in shares for which they register. Market makers must therefore quote **both buying and selling** prices (two-way prices) at which they **must deal** (firm prices) up to a predetermined transaction size dependent upon historic volumes. This is referred to as the **Exchange Market Size (EMS)**.

Each share is assigned an **EMS**, which is important as this gives the **Minimum Quote Size (MQS)**. This is the minimum amount of shares a market maker must be prepared to buy, or sell, at their quoted price. Market maker obligations – Mandatory Quotation Period from 08:00 until the end of closing auction Obligation to quote up to 1 × EMS.

5.1.7 The Stock Exchange Automated Quotations System (SEAQ)

SEAQ (known as a **quote display system**) is the secondary system used for fixed income securities and less frequently traded AIM stocks.

The SEAQ system is used to disseminate market maker quotes to all market makers simultaneously. Since at least two market makers are required for a share to trade on SEAQ, the system is referred to as a competing market maker system. Some AIM shares are traded on SEAQ, although the majority are traded on SETSqx.

5.2 Dual listed companies

A company may list its shares on more than one exchange – for example, a UK company may list in on the LSE in London while also making its shares available through American Depository Receipts (ADRs) (discussed further later in this Chapter) in New York. This is termed a **cross listing**.

The term **dual listed company (DLC)** describes something different from a cross listing. A DLC involves a corporate structure in which there are two corporations, normally registered in different jurisdictions, which act as a single operating business. The DLC structure involves a **legal equalisation agreement** and **separate stock exchange listings** for each of the corporations.

The two corporations will have different sets of shareholders who agree, through the equalisation agreement, to share the risks and rewards of ownership of the operating business in a specified proportion. The arrangement is broadly similar to a **joint venture**. The agreement will cover matters such as dividends, corporate governance winding up.

Examples of DLCs

- Rio Tinto Group (UK/Australia)
- Tata Motors (India/USA)
- BHP Billiton (UK/Australia)
- Unilever (Netherlands/UK)
- Royal Dutch Shell (Netherlands/UK)

Consequences of dual listing

- The enterprise will have access to a wider pool of investors

- Tax advantages may arise, for example capital gains tax may be saved by choosing a DLC structure instead of a merger

- Increased stock liquidity may reduce bid/offer spreads, lowering transaction costs for investors

- The enterprise will face higher costs in maintaining the dual corporate structure and separate listings

- The business will generally suffer a greater compliance burden, such as the relatively onerous Sarbanes-Oxley Act provisions if there is a listing in the USA

- Investors may find arbitrage opportunities in mis-pricing of the stocks in different jurisdictions

5.3 Fixed interest markets

Learning objective | **1.3.3 Explain** the structure and operation of the primary and secondary UK markets for gilts and corporate bonds

BPP
LEARNING MEDIA

5.3.1 Fixed interest securities

Fixed interest stocks, or 'bonds', are negotiable debt instruments issued by a borrower for a fixed period of time paying interest, known as the **coupon**. The coupon is fixed at the issue date and is paid regularly to the holder of the bond until it is redeemed at maturity when the principal amount is repaid.

Fixed interest securities include **Government bonds** (called gilt-edged stocks, or **'gilts'**, in the case of UK Government issues) and debt instruments issued by companies in the private sector – **corporate bonds**.

Corporate bonds may be sold through an **open offer**, or in a **private placing** to a limited number of professional investors. With an open offer, a syndicate of banks (with one bank as lead manager) will underwrite the issue by buying the bonds and then selling them on to investors. A **bought deal** is where the lead bank buys all the bonds and then sells them to the syndicate. Corporate bonds generally trade in over-the-counter (OTC) markets, with market liquidity being provided by dealers and other market participants.

5.3.2 Gilts

A prime responsibility of the **Debt Management Office (DMO)** of the Treasury is to ensure that the government is able to borrow the money it requires to fund the **Public Sector Net Cash Requirement (PSNCR)**. The most important source of financing open to the government is the gilts market.

Holders of gilts can now receive coupon payments **gross**, unless they opt otherwise. The main investors in gilts are UK pension funds and insurance companies, banks, building societies, overseas investors and private individuals.

The **accrual convention** that is adopted for gilts is not the method used in many other government bond markets. By the accrual method, accrued interest is calculated on the basis of the number of days since the last coupon and the actual number of days in the coupon period.

Gilts prices are quoted on a **decimal** basis (not 32nds of £1, as they were in the past).

The DMO controls the issue of **gilts** into the market place and uses different methods depending upon the circumstances it faces at any time.

5.3.3 Types of gilt issue

Gilts have been most often issued by **auction** in recent years, and this method is also the preferred method for issuing Government stocks in many other countries, including the USA. The alternative **'tap'** **(tender)** method was used more in the past.

Issues by the DMO may be of an entirely new gilt with a coupon/maturity dissimilar to existing issues. Currently, the DMO believes that the range of issues in the market is, if anything, too large and may lead to excessive fragmentation of supply and demand.

In order to avoid the problem above, the DMO may issue a **tranche** of an existing stock. This entails issuing a given amount of nominal value on exactly similar terms to an existing gilt. The DMO refers to this as 'opening up an existing gilt'. The advantages of tranches are that they avoid adding further complexity to the gilt market and increase the liquidity of current issues. When a tranche is issued, it may be identified by the letter 'A' in order to indicate that when the tranche is issued a full coupon may not be paid on the next payment date, to reflect the fact that the gilt has only been in issue for part of the coupon period. A small tranche may be referred to as a **tranchette**.

5.4 The secondary gilts market

5.4.1 Overview

As with the equities market, gilts used to be traded on the floor of the Stock Exchange. However, in 1986 they moved to a telephone-driven market supported by market makers.

The DMO is the lead regulator in the gilts market. Its objective is to ensure that the gilts market remains solvent, liquid and, above all, fair. The reason for this commitment is that the DMO is obliged to issue, on the Government's behalf, gilts to fund the PSNCR. In order to do this, the DMO must have access to the markets. It is the DMO that allows participants to enter the gilts market and, thereafter, it is the DMO that monitors their capital adequacy on a daily basis.

5.4.2 Gilt-Edged Market Makers (GEMMs)

The **Gilt-Edged Market Makers (GEMMs)** are the focus of the market place. Their role is to **ensure that two-way quotes exist at all times** for all gilts. Market makers are allowed to enter the market by the DMO. Once accepted as a gilt-edged market maker, the firm is obliged to make a market in **all conventional gilts**. The **Gilt-Edged Market Makers' Association (GEMMA)** provides end-of-day data for gilts prices to the DMO, and this data is published in the financial press. In return for these services, the DMO makes facilities available to GEMMs that include special dealing arrangements with the DMO, access to Inter-Dealer Brokers (IDBs) and an exclusive right to strip gilts (into their individual cash flows) and to reconstitute them.

For index-linked stocks, because the market is less liquid, the DMO has authorised a more limited list of market makers. GEMMs make use of the LSE's SEAQ (Stock Exchange Automated Quotation system).

5.4.3 Inter-Dealer Brokers (IDBs)

The **Inter-Dealer Brokers (IDBs)** act as an escape valve for GEMMs. If a GEMM was to build up a large position in a particular stock and then decide to unwind it, it might be difficult to achieve without revealing to the rest of the market that he was long or short of a stock. This is obviously a dangerous position and would discourage Gilt-Edged Market Makers from taking substantial positions. The Inter-Dealer Brokers provide an anonymous dealing service, allowing GEMMs to unwind positions. IDBs are only accessible to market makers in the gilts market.

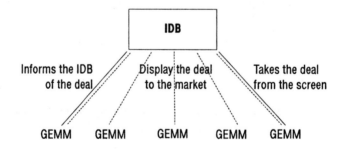

Equity market makers also have access to Inter-Dealer Brokers. The ability to unwind positions anonymously through the IDBs is also viewed as an important mechanism for ensuring equity market liquidity.

5.4.4 Stock Borrowing and Lending Intermediaries (SBLIs)

If market makers wish to take a short position in a stock, ie sell more than they currently have on their books, they will need to have stock in order to settle the trade. The **Stock Borrowing and Lending Intermediaries (SBLIs) provide access to large pools of unused stock**. The institutional investors in the

UK buy large blocks of securities and often hold these blocks for a number of years. The SBLIs borrow stock on behalf of market makers from these dormant positions. The stock is passed to the market maker who uses it to settle the trade, and in effect, to go short.

Eventually, the market maker will be obliged to buy stock to cover the short position, and this stock will then be passed back to the institutional investor. The SBLI charges commission on the trade of around 0.5%. This commission is split between the intermediaries and the institution. This is a facility available to all market participants and provides them with vital access to stock positions enabling them to go short.

The SBLIs also act as a focus for surplus cash, enabling those who are long of funds to deposit money, and market makers who need to borrow money to obtain finance.

5.4.5 Broker-dealers

All member firms of the LSE are **broker-dealers**. Broker-dealers have dual capacity, giving them the choice to either act as agents (broker) on behalf of customers, or to deal for themselves as principal (dealer), dealing directly with customers. Acting as principle involves buying and selling on the firms account.

5.5 Exchange trading and OTC markets

1.3.5 Compare and **contrast** exchange traded and over-the-counter (OTC) markets

Exchanges are centralised markets where the standardisation of financial instruments available enhances liquidity for market participants. An **exchange-traded instrument** is one that is packaged in a standardised way, in respect of the contract size and dates for example, facilitating the creation of a liquid market in the instrument, on an exchange.

OTC (over the counter) markets are decentralised. An 'over the counter' instrument is one that has been specially negotiated with a financial institution, generally to fit the needs of a particular client or group of clients.

5.6 MTFs and 'dark pools'

1.3.6 Distinguish between the following alternative trading venues: Multilateral Trading Facilities, Systematic Internalisers, dark pools

The **Markets in Financial Instruments Directive (MiFID)** has encouraged the development of many new trading and reporting systems that compete with the main exchanges. MiFID introduced the ability to passport **Multilateral Trading Facilities (MTFs)** across borders as a 'core' investment service. MTFs are systems where firms provide services similar to those of exchanges by matching client orders. A firm taking proprietary positions with a client is not running an MTF. There has been debate about the requirements to be imposed on MTFs. The Committee of European Securities Regulators (CESR) has published standards they expect to be met by MTFs, including notifying the home state regulator of activities, fair and orderly trading, price transparency, clarity of systems and reduction of financial crime.

MTFs may be crossing networks or matching engines that are operated by an investment firm or a market operator. Instruments traded on a MTF may include shares, bonds and derivatives. MiFID requires operators of MTFs to ensure their markets operate on a fair and orderly basis. It aims to ensure this by placing requirements on MTF operators regarding how they organise their markets and the information they give to users.

Examples of MTFs include **Turquoise**, **Chi-X**, **PEX** (Portugal) and **Nordic MTF**. **BATS Europe**, operated by the US platform BATS Trading, and **Nasdaq OMX Europe**, an equities platform of the US-based NASDAQ OMX, were both launched in 2008. The European unit of Liffe partnered with HSBC and BNP Paribas to launch **Smartpool**, for large order execution of European stocks. **SIX Swiss Exchange** (formerly SWX Europe) has been in partnership with Nyfix Millennium of the US to create **Swiss Block**, for Swiss blue chip stocks. Nyfix also operates **Euro Millennium™**. **Equiduct** is another MTF.

This new generation of platforms offers the prospect of firms making use of internal crossing networks – more often now called **dark liquidity pools** or **'non-displayed liquidity venues'**, whereby firms can buy and sell blocks of shares off-exchange, away from the public domain. This offers trading anonymity, without prices being displayed on the public order book usually found on exchanges. There are more than 40 dark pools operating in the US, the largest being Goldman Sachs' Sigma X and Credit Suisse's CrossFinder. By mid-2008, dark pools were estimated to account for 12% of US daily stock trading volume. In the past, **stock exchanges** have viewed off-exchange trading as their main source of competition. The moves by **Liffe** and **SIX Swiss Exchange** to form links with dark pools can be seen as a case of 'If you can't beat 'em, join 'em'.

Some exchanges have adapted their technology to handle the need for large orders to be hidden from the market: LSE and Liffe both offer an **iceberg facility** through which only a small part of a large order is displayed at one time. Meanwhile, sell-side brokers have been developing algorithms to help them to detect if an order is being traded away from the market.

More **regulatory attention** could be paid to the growing use of dark pools in the future, in case of any systemic risk that they might present.

5.7 Systematic Internalisers

A **Systematic Internaliser (SI)** is an investment firm which, on an organised, frequent and systematic basis, deals on its own account by executing customer order flow in liquid shares outside a regulated market or a MTF. The SI thus executes orders from its clients against its own book or against orders from other clients.

An SI is effectively treated like a mini-exchange under MiFID, and is subject to pre-trade and post-trade transparency requirements. MiFID requires such firms to publish firm quotes in liquid shares (for orders below 'standard market size') and to maintain those quotes on a regular and continuous basis during normal business hours.

5.8 Order Book for Retail Bonds (ORB)

In 2010, the LSE launched its **Order Book for Retail Bonds (ORB)**. This electronic order-driven trading service offers a select number of **gilts** and **UK corporate bonds**. The launch of ORB introduced continuous two-way pricing for trading in UK gilts and retail-size corporate bonds on-exchange.

RBS was the first issuer, of 5.1% retail bonds with a minimum denomination of £100, on ORB's first day of trading. A number of PIBS (Permanent Interest Bearing Shares of building societies) and former PIBS have been included on ORB.

ORB is not a separate market, but is rather a trading platform designed for gilts and corporate bonds listed on the LSE's main market. ORB was modelled after the established Italian electronic bond market (Borsa Italiana's MOT market), which is the most liquid and heavily traded retail fixed income market in Europe.

Features of ORB

- EU regulations distinguish between 'wholesale' (typically denominations of £50,000 or greater) and 'retail' (usually £1,000, some £5,000 or £10,000)

- Most corporate bonds are wholesale. The secondary market for retail bonds is fragmented, usually over-the-counter (OTC). Therefore, most private investors use corporate bond funds rather than deal directly

- ORB provides a similar facility that for share trading for a select number of gilts, supranational organisations, and UK corporate bonds

- Investors can enter orders on the order book either directly, if a sophisticated investor, or via a broker who offers Direct Market Access (DMA)

- Dedicated market makers also provide two-way prices

- The market operates with an opening auction phase (8.00-8.45am) and closes at 4.30pm

- Settlement is T+1 for gilts and T+3 for corporate bonds

- All bonds are listed on the London Main Market

5.9 High frequency trading

Learning objective 1.3.9 **Explain** high-frequency trading, its benefits and risks

Automated forms of trading have sometimes been blamed for major movements in stock prices. **Program trading** has been defined by the New York Stock Exchange as an order to buy or sell fifteen or more stocks valued at over US$1 million total. In practice, this means that computers are used to enter program trades. Such trades are often made to take advantage of arbitrage opportunities, which seek to exploit small price differences between related financial instruments, such as index futures contracts and the stocks underlying them. **Algorithmic trading** is a form of trading in which orders are entered to an electronic trading platform based on an algorithm which sets criteria for making the trade based on aspects such as timing, price or quantity. Generally, orders will be executed without human intervention.

Studies have found that over half of equity trading volume on major exchanges results from algorithmic trading. A special type of algorithmic trading is **high frequency trading (HFT)** or **'flash' trading**, which seeks to respond to information received electronically before other human traders are able to process the information and place trades. HFT has come to account for approximately 30% of UK equity market transactions, and over 60% in the US.

With trades on exchanges being completed in 2 milliseconds or less, high frequency traders seek to exploit the rapidity of electronic trading, and have sometimes sought to position their servers physically close to an exchange's servers in order to enable data to reach them faster. High frequency traders, it is claimed, can make profits at the expense of institutional investors, by creaming off small amounts from each trade. For example, one possible practice is placing an order, then almost instantaneously cancelling it, and then placing an order for the same stock at the next lower price. By flashing orders quickly, traders may be trying to ascertain where other investors want to buy and sell stocks, and may thus be squeezing slightly better prices from investors.

Exchange Traded Funds (ETFs) have come to be used by high frequency traders as part of complex arbitrage strategies. Such strategies can benefit traders who can place themselves to take advantage of them when they work as intended, but there is the risk that the predominance of HFT can precipitate extreme market volatility which can affect market participants widely. Trading in ETFs accounted for the majority of trades during the 'flash crash' of 6 May 2010, when the DJIA index fell almost 1,000 points in one session.

A further risk arises from the possibility of technical problems in this form of automated trading. In August 2012, Knight Capital Group suffered a significant loss of approximately $440 million after newly installed trading software resulted in the firm sending out large numbers of erroneous orders in NYSE stocks.

The UK Government's **Foresight** programme reported on *The future of computer trading in financial markets* in October 2012. In this report, the UK Government largely rejected proposed European restrictions on HFT, which would be reflected in a revised MiFID 2. The Foresight report was able to find no clear evidence that HFT increased **market volatility**, although HFT had the potential to **increase market illiquidity** periodically. The report finds that there is widespread concern among larger institutional investors that HFT is the cause of **market manipulation**. The Report found no direct evidence of HFT leading to increased market abuse, although there has been little research that would shed light on this issue.

The Report noted that the nature of market making has changed, with high frequency traders now providing the bulk of such activity in both futures and equities. However, unlike designated specialists, high frequency traders typically operate with little capital, hold small inventory positions and have no obligations to provide liquidity during periods of market stress. These factors, together with the ultra-fast speed of trading, create the potential for periodic illiquidity, such as the US Flash Crash.

The Foresight report noted the following beneficial effects of computer-based trading:

- Improved liquidity, as measured by bid-ask spreads and other metrics
- Lower transaction costs for both retail and institutional traders, mainly due to changes in trading market structures stemming particularly from HFT
- Greater efficiency in market pricing, as price discovery is facilitated by how computer-based trading links markets

6 SETTLEMENT PROCEDURES

Learning objective	1.4.1 **Explain** the clearing and settlement procedures for UK exchange traded securities

6.1 Introduction

The usual settlement period in the UK is three business days after the day of the bargain (referred to as T + 3).

Rolling Settlement

Trade date   Settlement date

Three business days settlement period

Settlement of UK equities, corporate bonds, gilts and money market instruments occurs through Euroclear UK & Ireland (also known as CREST), which operates an **electronic dematerialised settlement system**.

Settlement in sterling or euros is made on a **Delivery versus Payment (DVP)** basis, where both parties are ready to settle with each other at the same time, known as real time gross settlement.

6.2 Advanced and delayed settlement

It is possible to negotiate special settlement periods. The ability to have special settlement periods, up to **260 business days** after the day of the trade, gives flexibility to investors.

6.3 Cum and ex status

Shares normally trade on the basis of **cum (with) dividend**. This means that any purchaser of the shares is entitled to expect to receive the next dividend. As a share approaches its dividend payment date, a company sets a **books closed date** (also known as the 'record date' or the 'on register date'). The company pays the next dividend to all shareholders who are on the register of shareholders, on the books closed date. The books closed date will be some time before the dividend payment date to make administration easy for the company.

If a shareholder buys a share cum dividend and fails to have his name entered on the register of shareholders by the books closed date, the company will send the dividend cheque to the previous shareholder. The new shareholder does not lose the dividend, since they are legally entitled to it, but the mechanics of arranging for the old shareholder to remit the dividend to the new shareholder are cumbersome and time consuming.

In order to avoid this problem, the Stock Exchange has developed a system whereby shares will commence trading ex-dividend on the Stock Exchange **two business days prior to the books closed date**. A purchaser of the share ex-dividend is not entitled to receive the next dividend as it belongs to the seller of the share. It is possible, by agreement, to carry out a transaction ex-dividend before the official ex-dividend date. This is only permitted by the Exchange for ten business days before the normal ex-div date.

The idea is that shareholders who buy the shares cum dividend will be able to get on the register of shareholders in time to receive the dividend. Those who buy the shares ex-dividend will not be entered on the register by the books closed date. This means that the appropriate person always receives the dividend from the company.

Marking a Share Ex-Dividend

The **Company Timetable**

Announcement ——— Books Closed ——— Payment

The Stock Exchange

Ex-Dividend Date

Special-Ex Period

10 Business Days | Wed | Fri

2 Business Days

Cum Dividend ——— Ex-Dividend

The **ex-dividend date** will usually be a Wednesday, and books closed date will, therefore, usually be a Friday. Parties may agree bilaterally to trade a share ex-dividend in the **'special ex-dividend' period**, which covers **10 business days** up to the ex-dividend date. For **corporate bonds**, there is a special ex-dividend period of **five business days**. For **gilts**, there is **no special ex- period**.

7 UKLA AND PROSPECTUS REQUIREMENTS

7.1 The LSE and the UKLA

Learning objective

1.5.1 **Explain** the role of the FCA as the UK listing authority

The **London Stock Exchange (LSE)** is a company whose aim is to run an **orderly market place in securities**. The Financial Conduct Authority (FCA) regulates the LSE, and has granted it the status of a Recognised Investment Exchange (RIE). The LSE publishes rules governing the trading in securities in the secondary markets, and to some extent in the primary markets.

The FCA has the statutory role of **Competent Authority**. This obliges the FCA to maintain the **Official List** – the list of companies whose securities are admitted to a UK regulated market such as the LSE. Through a division called the **UK Listing Authority (UKLA)**, it determines which companies may be listed on a UK regulated market, monitors their continuing eligibility, and imposes strict standards of conduct for companies and their advisers in the UKLA Listing Rules.

The UKLA's role also includes the implementation of certain EU Directives and the listing of gilts.

There are two levels of entry into the stock market, namely through the **Official List** and traded on the **main market**, or through the **Alternative Investment Market (AIM)**. Of the two, the Official List (or 'Full List') is the senior market, and membership demands the most onerous responsibilities. While UKLA regulates the Full List, the LSE regulates the AIM, publishing the AIM Rules and monitoring compliance with them.

7.2 Criteria for listing

Learning objectives

1.5.2 **Identify** the listing rules in FSMA 2000, and relevant EU directives
1.5.3 **Explain** the main conditions for listing on the Official List, AIM and ISDX
1.5.4 **Explain** the purpose of the requirement for prospectus or listing particulars

7.2.1 General points

The UKLA's rules for admission to listing are contained in the **Listing Rules**. The Listing Rules are found within the FCA Handbook. These detail the requirements that a company must meet prior to being admitted to the Full List.

There are two tiers of listing:

- **Premium listing** (required for FTSE UK Index membership), involving the UKLA's 'super-equivalent' requirements, which go beyond EU standards

- **Standard listing**, with less stringent requirements that are broadly similar to AIM requirements

A number of entry requirements must be met before a public limited company ('plc') can be admitted to the Official List. (A company must be a plc in order to offer its shares to the public.) In addition to the requirements, the company will be required to pay a fee.

- The expected market value of **shares** to be listed by the company (for a **premium** or a **standard** listing) must be at least **£700,000**. If the company is to issue **debt securities**, the expected market value of the debt is to be at least **£200,000**.

- All securities issued must be **freely transferable**.

- For a **premium listing**, the company must have a trading record of at least **three years**. Its main business activity must have been continuous over the whole three-year period. In addition, there should be three years of audited accounts. This requirement is waived for innovative high growth companies, investment companies and in certain other situations. For a **standard listing**, there is no trading history requirement.

- The shares must be sufficiently marketable. For a **premium listing**, a minimum of **25% of the company's share capital being made available for public purchase** (known as the **free float**) is normally seen to satisfy this requirement. The lower the free float, the fewer shares are available in the market, potentially leading to higher share price volatility. For a standard listing, there is no minimum for the proportion of shares in public hands.

Applicants for a **premium** listing must appoint a UKLA-approved **sponsor** whose role is to:

- Ensure the company and its directors are aware of their obligations
- Ensure the company is suitable for listing and satisfy UKLA of this fact
- Liaise with UKLA and submit documentation to them as required
- Co-ordinate the listing process

7.2.2 Continuing obligations

Applicants for premium listing are bound by the **continuing obligations** of the Listing Rules which require the company to:

- Publish **price-sensitive information**

- Publish information about important transactions undertaken by the company

- Publish changes in the important registers of ownership of the shares, such as notifiable interests and directors' shareholdings

- Publish **annual and half-yearly results**, and details of **dividends**

- Include various specified disclosures and information in its **annual financial report**

Under the FCA's Disclosure and Transparency Rules, a listed company must publish its annual report and accounts within four months of its year-end. Interim reports must be published within two months of the half-year end.

All of the required disclosures must be made through an official **Regulated Information Service (RIS)** or other UKLA-approved **Primary Information Provider (PIP)** service.

Approved RISs include:

- Regulatory News Service (RNS) of the LSE
- PR Newswire Disclose
- Business Wire Regulatory Disclosure

When an announcement is lengthy, guidance is that prominence should be given to **current and future trading prospects**.

If price-sensitive information is inadvertently released to analysts or journalists, a company must take immediate steps to provide the information to the whole market.

A company should correct their public forecasts as soon as it becomes aware that the outcome is significantly different. However, companies are not obliged to tell analysts their forecasts are wrong.

7.2.3 Documentation and advertising

As mentioned above, the applicant's **sponsor** will guide them through the process of applying for a hearing and submitting documentation to the UKLA, the Competent Authority. Documentation in its final form must be submitted **48 hours prior to the hearing** (the '48-hour rule').

Companies are obliged to produce and include in that documentation a statement by the directors confirming that the working capital of the business will be adequate. This letter must be submitted and approved by the sponsor.

Under the Listing Rules, fully listed companies are generally required to produce a **prospectus** containing full details on the company's past and present activities and performance, directors, capital structure and future prospects. This contains detailed information and a report given by the company's accountants on the information produced. The level of detail and the requirement for verification makes a prospectus under the listing rules much more expensive to produce than an ordinary prospectus produced by an unlisted company issuing shares.

7.3 Alternative Investment Market (AIM)

The LSE introduced the second-tier **Alternative Investment Market** in 1995. This forum for trading a company's shares enables companies to have their shares traded through the LSE in a lightly regulated regime. Thus smaller, fast-growing companies may obtain access to the market at a lower cost and with less regulatory burden.

7.3.1 Conditions for admission to AIM

A summary of the main conditions that companies must meet in order to secure admission to AIM is as follows.

- All securities must be **freely transferable**.

- AIM companies must have an LSE-approved **Nominated Advisor (NOMAD)** to advise the directors on their responsibilities, and guide them through the AIM process. The NOMAD is retained to advise the directors once an AIM listing is granted. Should the company lose its NOMAD, it must appoint a new one (otherwise the listing will be suspended).

- AIM companies must also have a **broker** to support trading of the company's shares.

- AIM companies must comply with **ongoing obligations** to publish **price-sensitive information** immediately and to disclose details of **significant transactions**. The NOMAD has a duty to ensure the AIM company meets its ongoing obligations.

- Companies with a track record of less than **two years** must agree to a **'lock-in'**, whereby the directors, significant shareholders and employees with 0.5% or more of their capital, agree **not to sell their shares for a year** following admission.

For AIM companies, there is no minimum level of free float (shares available for purchase by the public), no minimum market value for their securities and no minimum trading history.

However, they must produce a prospectus, which is considerably less detailed than for a full listing, and is known as an **Admission Document**. This document gives details of the company, its shares, financial information, management and future prospects. The prospectus is not examined by the Stock Exchange and investors must make their own judgements as to its contents.

7.3.2 Comparison of requirements

Key requirements for an **AIM** listing, compared with a full (**Premium** or **Standard**) listing on the LSE are compared in the following Table.

Premium Listing	Standard listing	AIM
Three years' trading history required	No trading history requirement	No trading history requirement
£700,000 minimum market capitalisation	£700,000 minimum market capitalisation	No minimum market capitalisation
At least 25% of shares must be held by public	No minimum proportion of shares in public hands	No minimum proportion of shares in public hands

7.4 ISDX (formerly PLUS)

7.4.1 Overview

ISDX (ICAP Securities and Derivatives Exchange) was created after the inter-dealer broker ICAP acquired PLUS Stock Exchange (PLUS-SX) in June 2012 and re-branded it. ISDX (formerly PLUS-SX) has been described as London's third stock market, after the LSE main market and AIM. The market is lightly regulated and was established (as PLUS-SX) to help smaller companies raise capital. PLUS-SX targeted smaller companies needing to raise between £2m (€2.8m) and £3m. The cost of raising finance is lower than on the AIM market. However, PLUS-SX struggled to attract listings thanks, in part, to the success of AIM.

ISDX describes itself as a London-based stock exchange providing UK and international companies with access to European capital through a range of fully listed and growth markets.

7.4.2 ISDX Growth Market

The **ISDX Growth Market** aims to provide growing **small- and medium-sized enterprises (SMEs)** from all industry sectors with a source of equity finance for companies coming to a public market for the first time, as well as being a venue for existing issuers to raise further funds.

ISDX admits companies to its ISDX Growth Market in accordance with the ISDX Growth Market Rules for Issuers, which include its application requirements and continuing obligations requirements. A fast-track admission procedure is available to applicants from the Alternative Investment Market of the London Stock Exchange (AIM), and the Access Market of the Munich Stock Exchange (Bayerische Boerse).

The **market makers** Peel Hunt and Shore Capital make markets in ISDX's major stocks to maintain liquidity provision on the venue and to ensure that it operates as a primary and secondary market.

ISDX faces the prospect of **future competition** as a **listing venue for SMEs** from NYSE Euronext's proposed Entrepreneurial Exchange, and from the LSE, which is believed to be considering possibilities of improving opportunities for SMEs to raise equity.

7.4.3 ISDX Main Board

The **ISDX Main Board** is an **EU Regulated Market** aims to provide companies and other issuers with lower-cost admission to trading through the UKLA's Official List, or other European Competent Authority.

Issuers will be subject to the Listing Rules and the FCA's Disclosure and Transparency Rules. To join the ISDX Main Board, issuers will be required to produce a prospectus approved by the UKLA or other EU body that is a competent authority under the Prospectus Directive.

The application for admission to the ISDX Main Board will be made in conjunction with the issuer's application to the UKLA (or other EU competent authority) for admission to the Official List under a Premium or Standard Listing.

7.5 The Prospectus Directive and cross-border prospectuses

1.5.5 Identify the main exemptions from listing particulars

The **Prospectus Directive** is an EU directive which came into force in December 2003. It was implemented in the UK by the Prospectus Regulations 2005, which amended FSMA 2000, and by the Prospectus Rules in the FCA Handbook.

The Directive requires that a prospectus is produced when there is a public offer of securities or where securities are admitted to trading on an EU regulated market. This provision casts a wider net than listings, since it covers securities traded on 'second' markets and through other trading facilities. The Directive specifies the content of prospectuses and requires that they are approved by the relevant **competent authority** – in the UK, the **FCA**.

These requirements are designed to increase protection of investors by ensuring the quality of prospectuses and to enhance international market efficiency through the issue of single approved prospectuses for use throughout the EEA. Investors must be given 'essential and appropriately structured' information for them to understand the nature of the risks posed by the issuer.

Under the Prospectus Directive, there is a **'single passport'** for issuers, with the result that a prospectus approved by one competent authority can be used across the EEA without any further approval or burdensome administrative procedures in other member states. If the competent authority in the relevant member state approves the prospectus, it will be accepted throughout the EEA.

The overall position is that a prospectus is required in the case of an offer of transferable securities to the public in the EEA, unless an exemption applies. An 'offer' is defined broadly and covers any communication in any form and by any means which presents sufficient information about the terms of the offer and the securities offered such as to enable an investor to decide to buy or subscribe to those securities.

Following **July 2012 amendments** to the Prospectus Directive, the main **exemptions** from the requirement to publish a prospectus are currently follows.

- Offers made only to qualified investors, a category that aligns with the MiFID categorisations of eligible counterparties and professional clients

- Private placements made to fewer than 150 persons in each EEA state other than qualified investors

- Cases where the minimum consideration payable by any person for transferable securities is at least €100,000, or the securities are offered in denominations of at least €100,000

- Cases where the total consideration for the offer in EEA states is less than €100,000

- On admission to trading on a regulated market, there is an exemption for shares representing, over a period of 12 months, less than 10% of the number of shares of the same class already admitted to trading on the same regulated market

8 INFORMATION DISCLOSURE AND CORPORATE GOVERNANCE

Learning objective

1.6.1 Explain the disclosures required under the disclosure and transparency rules relating to directors' interests and major shareholdings

8.1 Dealings by directors and senior executives

In the regulator's **Disclosure and Transparency Rules (DTR)**, DTR3 contains rules on reporting on transactions by **'persons discharging managerial responsibilities' PDMRs** (which includes **directors**) and connected persons in a listed company's securities (and related derivatives).

- PDMRs and connected persons must notify the company within four business days of a transaction

- The company must notify the market via a **Regulated Information Service (RIS)** as soon as possible and no later than the end of the next **business** day

The **Listing Rules (LR)** set out requirements for issuers with a listing or seeking a listing on a UK regulated market. **LR 9 Annex 1** contains the **Model Code**, which restricts dealings on their own account by PDMRs in the company's securities at certain times. The Model Code also governs the approval process and disclosure of such dealings at all times: clearance to deal must be sought from a designated director. The Code is intended to ensure that shareholder-directors demonstrate to other shareholders that they will not abuse their position for unfair advantage. No trades should be undertaken in a listed company by its directors and senior executives in specified **close periods** before the announcement of results.

8.2 Notification requirements: major interests in listed companies

DTR also covers notifications of **major holdings** in a listed company's securities. The rules require those who discharge managerial responsibilities to make notifications to the issuer and the market via a Regulatory Information Service.

DTR requires that, where a person's holding of financial instruments, including interests held through Contracts for Differences (CfDs), in a UK company on the relevant market:

- Reaches or falls below 3% of the **voting rights**, or
- Increases or reduces **across one full percentage point** above 3% (eg 4.9% to 5.2%),

then they must, within **two business days**, notify the company, which must make the notifications public by the end of the following trading day.

For certain voting rights, the thresholds that apply are 5%, 10% and each whole percentage figure above 10%. The holdings involved include holdings of authorised **unit trusts** and **open-ended investment companies,** of EEA qualifying **investment managers**, and of registered US investment managers.

EEA issuers (ie, companies issuing securities) incorporated and with their registered office in another EEA Member State are instead required to comply with their home State's requirements.

There is no longer a requirement for a public company to keep a register of interests in shares (as s211 CA 1985 was repealed when the EU **Transparency Directive** was implemented in 2007).

S793 CA 2006 allows a public company to require persons it believes has or has had during the previous three years an interest in the company's shares to confirm their interest. The company must keep a register of the information received from such investigations.

8.3 Connected parties

For the purposes of the notification rules, a stake includes:

- The stakeholder's own position

- Shares owned by a connected/controlled company: under the Companies Act **a controlled company is one where the stakeholder owns 33⅓% of the capital** (DTR 5.8.1 (2))

- **Concert parties** – meaning an organisational grouping, whether bound by a contract or not, which agrees to act together. For example, five individuals may each obtain a 2% stake in a company which does not in itself require disclosure, however, they are in effect acting as one unit with a 10% stake. (DTR 5.2.1 (a))

8.4 Corporate governance

Learning objectives	**1.6.2 Explain** the purpose of corporate governance regulation and the role of the FRC in promoting good corporate governance
	1.6.3 Explain, in outline, the scope and content of corporate governance standards in the UK
	1.6.4 Explain the London Stock Exchange (LSE) requirements for listed companies to disclose corporate governance compliance

8.4.1 Overview

Issues of **corporate governance** are concerned with how companies are directed and controlled. Institutional shareholders have abandoned their traditional 'back seat' role and show an increasingly pro-active approach to holding directors of the company to account. The change in attitude has been fuelled by some notable corporate failures and the perception that directors may be improving their own pay and conditions at the expense of the shareholders.

8.4.2 The UK Corporate Governance Code

The **2010 UK Corporate Governance Code** was developed from the former 'Combined Code' by the Financial Reporting Council (FRC). The code acknowledges that **corporate governance** is the system by which companies are directed and controlled. Boards of directors are responsible for the governance of their companies. The **shareholders' role** in governance is to appoint the directors and the auditors and to satisfy themselves that an appropriate governance structure is in place. The responsibilities of the board include setting the company's strategic aims, providing the leadership to put them into effect, supervising the management of the business and reporting to shareholders on their stewardship.

In its review of the Code following the financial crisis of the late 2000s, the Financial Reporting Council considered that the impact of shareholders in monitoring the Code could and should be enhanced by better interaction between the boards of listed companies and their shareholders.

The Code takes the stance that satisfactory engagement between company boards and investors is crucial to the health of the UK's corporate governance regime. Companies and shareholders both have responsibility for ensuring that the **'comply or explain'** approach of corporate governance in the UK remains an effective **alternative to a rules-based system**.

The UKLA requires listed companies to **state in their Annual Report**:

- How they have applied the Main Principles set out in the UK Corporate Governance Code 'in a manner that would enable shareholders to evaluate how the principles have been applied'

- Whether it has complied with all relevant provisions of the Code, detailing any that it has not complied with, with the company's reasons for non-compliance

The 'comply or explain' approach has been retained from the earlier Combined Code. The way this operates is widely supported by companies and investors as allowing flexibility while ensuring sufficient information for investors to come to their own conclusions.

The **Main Principles** of the Code are as follows.

Section A: Leadership

Every company should be headed by an **effective board**, which is collectively responsible for the long-term success of the company.

There should be a **clear division of responsibilities** at the head of the company between running the board and the executive responsibility for running the company's business. No one individual should have unfettered powers of decision.

The **chairman** is responsible for leadership of the board and ensuring its effectiveness on all aspects of its role.

As part of their role as members of a unitary board, **non-executive directors** should constructively challenge and help develop proposals on strategy.

Section B: Effectiveness

The board and its committees should have the **appropriate balance of skills, experience, independence and knowledge of the company** to enable them to discharge their duties and responsibilities effectively.

There should be a formal, rigorous and transparent procedure for the **appointment of new directors**.

All directors should be **able to allocate sufficient time** to discharge their responsibilities effectively.

All directors should receive **induction on joining the board** and should regularly **update and refresh** their skills and knowledge.

The board should be **supplied with timely information** to enable it to discharge its duties.

The board should undertake a rigorous formal **annual evaluation** of its own performance and that of its committees and individual directors.

All directors should be **submitted for re-election at regular intervals**, subject to continued satisfactory performance.

Section C: Accountability

The board should present a **balanced and understandable assessment** of the company's position and prospects.

The board is responsible for determining the nature and extent of the significant risks it is willing to take in achieving its strategic objectives. The board should maintain **sound risk management** and **internal control systems**.

The board should establish **formal and transparent arrangements** for considering how they should apply the **corporate reporting and risk management** and **internal control principles** and for maintaining an appropriate **relationship with the company's auditors**.

Section D: Remuneration

Levels of **remuneration** should be **sufficient to attract, retain and motivate directors of the quality required** to run the company successfully, but a company should **avoid paying more than is necessary** for this purpose. A significant proportion of **executive directors' remuneration** should be structured so as to **link rewards to corporate and individual performance**.

There should be a **formal and transparent procedure** for developing **policy on executive remuneration** and for **fixing remuneration packages** of individual directors. No director should be involved in deciding his or her own remuneration.

Section E: Relations with shareholders

There should be a **dialogue with shareholders** based on the mutual understanding of objectives. The board as a whole has responsibility for ensuring that a satisfactory dialogue with shareholders takes place.

The board should use the **AGM to communicate with investors** and to encourage their participation.

8.5 Stewardship Code

The UK **Stewardship Code**, directed at institutional investors who hold voting rights in UK companies and based on the earlier ISC Code, was issued by the Financial Reporting Council in July 2010. It has the aim of making shareholders more active and engaged in corporate governance.

The Code applies to fund managers, but institutional investors are also 'strongly encouraged' to disclose their level of compliance with the principles of the Code.

Adopting the same 'comply or explain' approach as the UK Corporate Governance Code, the Stewardship Code does not require compliance with its principles, but does require fund managers and institutional shareholders who decide not to comply to explain on their websites why they have not complied.

Principles of the Stewardship Code

- **Principle 1:** Institutional investors should publicly disclose their policy on how they will discharge their stewardship responsibilities.

- **Principle 2:** Institutional investors should have a robust policy on managing conflicts of interest in relation to stewardship and this policy should be publicly disclosed.

- **Principle 3:** Institutional investors should monitor their investee companies.

- **Principle 4:** Institutional investors should establish clear guidelines on when and how they will escalate their activities as a method of protecting and enhancing shareholder value.

- **Principle 5:** Institutional investors should be willing to act collectively with other investors where appropriate.

- **Principle 6:** Institutional investors should have a clear policy on voting and disclosure of voting activity.

- **Principle 7:** Institutional investors should report periodically on their stewardship and voting activities.

8.6 Information disclosure and dissemination

Learning objective	**1.6.5 Explain** the continuing obligations of LSE listed companies regarding information disclosure and dissemination

A listed company has a **continuing obligation** to keep holders of securities and the wider market properly informed. The company must also publicise to the market profit announcements, dividend declarations, material acquisitions, changes of directors, and other information to enable holders of securities and members of the public to appraise the company's position and avoid a false market being created in the company's securities. The company's forecasts should be corrected as soon as possible if the actual outcome is significantly different: downward profit revisions in such cases are generally called '**profits warnings**'.

Companies should maintain consistent procedures to determine what information is price-sensitive and should therefore be released. If price-sensitive information is inadvertently released to analysts, journalists or others, the company should take immediate steps to publicise the information to the whole market.

DTR provides that an issuer may **delay** the **public disclosure** of inside information, such as not to prejudice its legitimate interests, provided that the public would not be likely to be misled and the issuer is able to ensure the confidentiality of the information. For example, public disclosure of information may be delayed for a limited period if the firm's financial viability in 'grave and imminent danger' to avoid undermining negotiations to ensure the firm's long-term financial recovery.

The various items of required information described above must be provided through an official **Regulatory Information Service (RIS)** or other UKLA-approved **Primary Information Provider (PIP)** service.

8.7 Company meetings

Learning objectives	**1.6.6 Explain**, in outline, the UK company law requirements regarding the calling of general meetings
	1.6.7 Distinguish annual general meetings and other types of company meetings

8.7.1 General meetings

There are **two types of general meeting** of members of a company:

- Annual General Meeting (AGM)
- General meetings (GMs), held at other times

Companies Act 2006 (CA 2006) changes mean that the concept of an Extraordinary General Meeting (EGM) has been abandoned, and so company meetings are either **AGMs** or **GMs**.

The members of a company in general meeting can exercise **control over the directors**, although only to a limited extent.

- Under normal procedure **one half** of the **directors retire** at each annual general meeting though they may offer themselves for re-election. The company may remove directors from office by **ordinary resolution** (s168).

- **Member approval** in general meeting is required if the directors wish to:

    (a) **Exceed their delegated power** or to use it for other than its given purpose
    (b) **Allot shares** (unless private company with one class of shares)
    (c) **Make a substantial contract** of sale or purchase with a director
    (d) Grant a director a **long-service agreement**

- The **appointment and removal of auditors** is normally done in general meeting

In addition, general meetings are the means by which **members resolve differences** between themselves by voting on resolutions.

The **directors** may have power under the company's Articles of Association ('Articles') to convene a general meeting whenever they see fit.

The removal by CA 2006 of the requirement for private companies to hold an AGM (see below) enables private companies to make many decisions **by written resolution**, although the company will still need to hold meetings to dismiss a director or to remove an auditor before the end of his term of office. The shareholders and directors also still have the power to call a meeting.

Members holding 10% of the paid-up share capital (or 5% in certain limited circumstances for private companies) may demand that a meeting is held.

- A notice conveying the meeting must be set out within **21 days** of the requisition

- The meeting must be held within **28 days** of the notice calling to a meeting being sent out

- If the directors have not called the meeting within 21 days of the requisition, the **members may convene** the meeting for a date within 3 months of the deposit of the requisition at the **company's expense**

Unless the Articles provide otherwise, a **quorum** (the minimum number required in order to proceed) is achieved at a company meeting when two members (shareholders) are present. If **no quorum** is present, the meeting is **adjourned**.

The **court**, on the application of a director or a member entitled to vote, **may order that a meeting shall be held** and may give instructions for that purpose including fixing a quorum of one (s 306 CA 2006). This is a method of last resort to resolve a **deadlock** such as the refusal of one member out of two to attend (and provide a quorum) at a general meeting.

The directors of a **public company** must convene a general meeting if the **net assets fall to half or less of the amount of its called-up share capital** (s656 CA 2006).

8.7.2 Annual General Meeting (AGM)

The **AGM** plays a major role in the life of a **public company (plc)**, although often the business carried out seems fairly routine. For public companies at least, it is a statutorily protected way for members to have a regular assessment and discussion of their company and its management.

A listed company must, under the CA 2006 rules, hold their AGM within **six months of the end of their financial year**.

The AGM will at least consider the following:

- Approving the accounts
- Reappointing directors
- Reappointing auditors and giving power to the directors to fix their remuneration
- Approval or rejection of the dividend

CA 2006 has removed the requirement for **private companies** to hold an **AGM**. However, many existing companies will have been formed under the Companies Act 1985 (CA 1985) and many will have Articles referring to the standard CA 1985 'Table A' which sets out how the company should conduct itself. If a company wishes to amend or replace their Articles of Association, the new Articles will need to be filed at Companies House with a written resolution.

8.7.3 Board meetings

The **board of directors** is the elected representative of the shareholders acting collectively in the management of a company's affairs.

One of the basic principles of company law is that the powers which are delegated to the directors under the articles are given to them as a **collective body**. The **board meeting** is the proper place for the exercise of those powers.

The directors can **unanimously assent** on issues without meeting by a **signed resolution procedure**. Any resolution signed by all the directors entitled to attend a board meeting will be valid, as if it had been decided at a board meeting.

8.7.4 Notice periods for meetings

A company GM must have a minimum notice of **14 days**. In the case of a public company AGM, the minimum is **21 days**, unless the company's Articles specify a **longer** period of notice.

A GM may be called at shorter notice, with a majority of 90% of the voting rights in the case of a private company and 95% in the case of a public company. This does not apply to AGMs of a public company, where unanimity is required. Notices for public company AGMs must state that the meeting is an AGM.

Notice of a meeting can be given:

- In electronic form
- In hard copy form, or
- By means of a website, or
- By a combination of any of the above

The notice must state the time, date and location of the meeting and any resolutions to be agreed.

8.8 Resolutions and voting

8.8.1 Company resolutions

A **resolution** is an agreement or decision made by the directors or members (or a class of members) of a company. A member's (ie, shareholder's) voting power will usually depend on the number of shares the member owns. A resolution is passed when the pre-determined majority is reached, or it fails if the necessary majority is not obtained.

A meeting can pass two types of resolution:

- **Ordinary resolutions** – for most business – carried by a simple majority (more than 50%) of votes cast and requiring 14 days notice

- **Special resolutions** – for major changes – requiring a 75% majority of votes cast and also 14 days notice

Apart from the required size of the majority, the main differences between the types of resolution are as follows.

- The **text** of **special resolutions** must be **set out** in **full** in the notice convening the meeting, and it must be described as a special resolution. This is not necessary for an ordinary resolution if it is routine business.

- A **signed copy** of every **special resolution** must be **delivered** to the **Registrar** for filing within **15 days** of being passed. **Some ordinary resolutions**, particularly those relating to share capital, have to be **delivered** for filing but many do not.

A special resolution is required for **major changes** in the company such as the following.

- A change of name
- Restriction of the objects or other alteration of the articles
- Reduction of share capital
- Winding up the company
- Presenting a petition by the company for an order for a compulsory winding up

Under case law, apart from minor grammatical corrections or clerical errors, the text of a **special resolution** cannot be changed. This is an important distinction between special resolutions and ordinary resolutions.

Subject to anything stated in the company's Articles of Association, a member usually has the same number of votes whether passing a resolution in a **poll** at a general meeting or on a **written** resolution.

In the case of joint holders of shares, the vote of the first-named holder in the register is the one that will be counted, unless the company's Articles state otherwise.

8.8.2 Private companies and resolutions

Following the implementation of CA 2006, for private companies:

- Resolutions may be passed in writing, regardless of a company's Articles, with the same consent as resolutions passed in a general meeting, which are 50% for an ordinary resolution and 75% for a special resolution.

- Written resolutions may be proposed either by the directors or by members holding 5% of voting rights or such lower threshold as the Articles may specify.

- A resolution will automatically lapse after being proposed if it is not passed within 28 days (or such longer period as is specified in the Articles).

Copies of a **written resolution proposed by directors** must be sent to **each member** eligible to vote by hard copy, electronically or by a website. Alternatively, the same copy may be sent to each member in turn. The resolution should be accompanied by a statement informing the member:

- How to **signify their agreement** to the resolution
- The **date** the resolution must be passed by

Written resolutions proposed by members. Members holding **5%** (or lower if authorised by the articles) of the **voting rights** may request a written resolution providing it:

- **Would be effective** (not prevented by the articles or law)
- Is **not defamatory, frivolous** or **vexatious**

A **statement** containing no more than 1,000 words on the subject of the resolution may accompany it.

- Copies of the resolution, and statements containing information on the subject matter, how to agree to it and the date of the resolution must be sent to each member within **21 days** of the request for resolution.

- **Expenses** for circulating the resolution **should be met by the members** who requested it unless the company resolves otherwise. The company may **appeal to the court** not to circulate the 1,000 word statement by the members if the rights provided to the members are being abused by them.

8.8.3 Public companies and resolutions

Following CA 2006, a **public** company (plc) can only pass a resolution by a vote being taken at a meeting of the members, which may be the Annual General Meeting (AGM). A public company can no longer pass a written resolution.

8.8.4 Resolutions: record-keeping

The company must keep minutes of all proceedings at general meetings. They must also keep copies of all resolutions of members passed other than at general meetings. These records must be kept for 10 years and need to be available for inspection by members on request.

8.8.5 Proxies

If the member is unable to be present at the meeting, they may appoint a **proxy** to vote for them.

When sending out proxy forms, companies usually suggest the names of directors of the company who can be appointed by the member to act as a proxy, voting as they see fit unless otherwise instructed. The maximum period of time before a meeting that a company may specify for the deposit or revocation of a proxy is 48 hours.

There are two different types of proxy.

- A **general proxy** is used to appoint another person to vote as he thinks fit, considering anything that is discussed at the meeting.

- A **special proxy** (or '**two-way proxy**') is used to appoint another person to vote in a particular way, either for or against a resolution.

A proxy is valid for the **meeting and any adjournment**.

The Companies Act 2006 provides that a proxy has the **right to speak** and **to vote on a show of hands and on a poll**, regardless of any provisions in the company's Articles. (See below on voting methods.) Thus, following CA 2006 changes, proxies may exercise all the powers the member would have if they were present in person (s324(1)).

8.8.6 Voting methods

The vote on a resolution in a general meeting (or in a meeting of a class of members) is by a **show of hands**, unless a **poll** is legitimately called for. A declaration by the chairman that the resolution is carried on a show of hands is all that is required for a resolution to be passed: but this does not apply if a poll is called for. The number of votes for or against on a show of hands need not be counted. In a poll, the votes will reflect the number of shares held.

There is a common law duty on the chairman to demand a poll on a vote if he considers that the outcome would be different from that reached on a show of hands. Many companies – particularly quoted companies – count all votes on a poll as a matter of practice. An appropriate requirement is usually set out in the company's articles. Some companies still allow meeting participants – whether members attending in person or by proxy – to demonstrate their feelings on a resolution through a show of hands.

In general, on a show of hands, each member present is entitled to one vote. In the case of a **proxy** however, on a show of hands, a proxy will have one vote for and one vote against the resolution, if the proxy has been appointed by multiple members some of whom have instructed the proxy to vote for and some of whom have instructed the proxy to vote against the resolution (s285(2) CA 2006, as amended). This provision in s285(2) is subject to any provision in the company's articles.

A member can appoint different proxies in respect of different shares that member holds (s324(2)), and these multiple proxies will have multiple votes on a show of hands, subject to the company's articles.

By s321 CA 2006, any five or more members, or the holders of at least 10% of the voting rights, can demand a poll, except on resolutions to elect a chair or adjourn.

If members want an independent scrutiny of a poll, they must make their request up to one week after the meeting.

9 INTERNATIONAL MARKETS

9.1 Government bonds comparison

Government bonds of other countries share some of the features of gilts. Below is a summary of the major foreign government bonds and their key features.

	Japan (JGB)	US T-Bond	French bonds**	German Bund	Eurobonds	UK Corporates	UK Gilt
Coupon Frequency	Semi-annual	Semi-annual	Annual	Annual	Annual	Annual	Semi-annual
Settlement	3 business days	Same/ Next day	Varies**	3 business days	3 business days	3 business days	Same/ Next day
Registered or bearer	R or B	R	B	B	B	R	R
Normal life	10 years, some super-longs 40 yrs	Life of over 10 years	Lives of between 6 and 30 years	Mostly 10 years	Varied		Varied
Withholding tax	25%, but bilateral agreement reduces to 10%	None	None	None	None	20%	None
Medium-term debt	–	T-Note life of 2 to 10 years*	BTAN life of 2 to 5 years	BOBLs (lives up to 5 yrs); Schatz (2 to 6 yrs)	–	–	–
Settlement agencies	Japanese Government Bond Clearing Corporation	Federal Reserve	Relit, Sicovam, Euroclear and Clearstream	Euroclear and Clearstream	Euroclear and Clearstream	CREST	CREST, Clearstream, Euroclear and Bank of New York
Accrued interest convention	$\frac{\text{Actual}}{365}$	$\frac{\text{Actual}}{\text{Actual}}$	$\frac{\text{Actual}}{\text{Actual}}$	$\frac{\text{Actual}}{\text{Actual}}$	$\frac{\text{Actual}}{\text{Actual}}$	$\frac{\text{Actual}}{\text{Actual}}$	$\frac{\text{Actual}}{\text{Actual}}$

*   All types of US government bond are issued by Dutch Auction.

**   In the secondary market, the BTAN settles T + 1, whereas the OAT settles T + 3. The French government also has an inflation-linked bond, the OATi.

9.2 ADRs and GDRs

American Depositary Receipts (ADRs) are the conventional form of trading UK and other countries' equities in the US on the NYSE. In order to encourage US investors to buy UK shares, the shares are lodged with an American bank which then issues a receipt for the shares. This receipt is in bearer form and denominated in dollars.

It is possible to trade ADRs in what is known as **pre-release form**. Here, the holding bank releases the receipt to the dealer prior to the deposit of shares in its vaults. The dealer may then sell the ADRs in the market. However, the cash raised through this trade must then be lodged with a holding bank as collateral for the deal. This situation may exist for a maximum of three months, at the end of which the broker must purchase shares in the cash market and deposit them with the holding bank which then releases the collateral.

ADRs, whilst being designated for the American market, also trade in London. These securities are traded through the **International Order Book**. In line with the domestic American markets, settlement for ADRs takes place in three business days.

The ADR holder has all the transferability of the American form document with no stamp duty, other than a one-off fee on creation of 1½%. Dividends are received by the bank which holds the shares. They are then converted into dollars and paid to the holders. The holder of the ADR has the right to vote at the company's meeting in the same way as an ordinary shareholder.

The only right which they do not possess is that of participation in rights or bonus issues. In the case of such an issue, the bank holding the shares will sell the bonus shares or rights nil paid and distribute the cash proceeds to the ADR holders. Any ADR holder who wishes to participate in the rights issue will have to convert their ADR back into share form.

A **Global Depositary Receipt (GDR)** is very similar to an ADR. Like an ADR, a GDR is a security, which bundles together a number of shares of a company listed in another country. It is a term used to describe a security primarily used to raise dollar-denominated capital either in the US or European markets. The name GDR is a generic term describing structures deployed to raise capital either in dollars and/or euros.

9.3 Markets: USA

9.3.1 Equities

The United States is home to the world's largest stock market with its constituent parts being the New York Stock Exchange (NYSE), the American Stock Exchange, NASDAQ OMX, the Philadelphia Stock Exchange, the Boston Stock Exchange, the Chicago Stock Exchange, the Cincinnati Stock Exchange and the Pacific Exchange.

The **NYSE** was established in 1792 and is an order-driven floor dealing market. **NASDAQ** OMX is a screen-based, quote-driven market which is owned and operated by NASDAQ OMX group, the stock of which was listed on its own stock exchange in 2002, and is monitored by the Securities and Exchange Commission.

Trading on the NYSE revolves around **specialists** who receive and match orders via a limit order book. Specialists will also act as market makers where an order cannot be matched via the order book to ensure continuous liquidity in a stock. The primary regulator of the US equities market is the SEC.

Orders are processed through the **Super Display Book System**, the NYSE's primary order processing system. Exchange member firms input orders in a similar way to SETS and these reach specialists via the **trading post**, where the security is traded. The user, who may be an investor or a broker, receives a confirmation report of the transaction in real time as soon as the order is executed.

Settlement is T+3 (three business days) and the central clearing house is the **Depository Trust Company (DTC)**. For dividends paid to overseas investors, a default 30% **withholding tax** is applied, which may be halved if a **double taxation treaty** is in force.

9.3.2 US Government bond market

The **US Government bond market** is the largest Government bond market in the world. This size is evident in both the quantity of issuance in the primary market and volumes of activity in the secondary market.

The US Treasuries market is not dissimilar in structure from the UK gilts market. This is due to the UK reforms that have been designed to bring the two markets into line. Indeed, the general direction of all government bond markets has been towards greater '**fungibility**' or similarity, with the US being seen as the role model.

The key player in the market is the **Federal Reserve** (the 'Fed'). As the US central bank, it operates in much the same way as the Bank of England in the UK.

The **US Treasury** is part of government and responsible for the issuance of debt in order to fund the deficit.

Central to the operation of the market are the **primary dealers**. These firms are the market makers. They are authorised to conduct trades by the Fed and are obliged to make markets in all issues. As with the UK, there are inter-dealer brokers (IDBs) to facilitate the taking and unwinding of large positions. There are no money brokers, but there is a full repo market.

While the stocks are listed on the New York Stock Exchange, the market is effectively an over-the-counter market. The market operates 09:00 to 16:00 locally, but is perhaps the most truly global market. The market has deep liquidity across the maturity range.

There are three main types of instrument issued.

- **Treasury bills (T-bills)** – with a maturity of 3 - 12 months, at a discount to face value
- **Treasury notes (T-notes)** – coupon securities, issued with initial maturities of 2 -10 years
- **Treasury bonds (T-bonds)** – coupon securities, issued with an initial life of over 10 years

The **US Treasury** is responsible for the **issuance** of new securities. Issuance takes place on a regular calendar with weekly issues of three or six-month Treasury bills, monthly issues of one-year bills and two and five-year notes, and quarterly issues in set cycles of longer dated stocks.

The **competitive auction** in the US is basically the system that was introduced into the UK in 1987. The principal differences are that, in the US, the primary dealers are obliged to bid for stock and bids are on a yield basis (rather than price in the UK).

9.3.3 US domestic corporate bond markets

Unlike the UK, the US corporate sector has been able to borrow substantial sums via the issue of debt securities. In part, this has been forced upon them by the highly fragmented nature of the domestic banking market. Equally, however, investors are willing to hold corporate debt as part of their portfolios in a way in which UK investors are not.

Under **rule 144A**, corporates are allowed to issue bonds into the **private placement market** without seeking full SEC registration. This access to the market is not restricted to overseas issuers, and the market is dominated by US domestic issuers who have chosen not to enter the public market.

9.3.4 Yankee bondss

Ever since 1945, the dollar has been the key international currency. Prior to the emergence of the Eurodollar market (and to a limited extent after this), there has been substantial interest from non-US firms in raising dollar finance. A **Yankee bond** is a dollar-denominated bond issued in the US by an overseas borrower. Given that Eurodollar bonds may not be sold into the US markets until they have **seasoned** (a period of 40 days), there is still a divide between the Euromarket and the domestic market.

9.4 Markets in Japan

9.4.1 Equities

The Tokyo Stock Exchange is order-driven through the CORES dealing system. Settlement is on T+3 by book entry transfer through the JSCC (Japanese Securities Clearing Corporation). Withholding tax of 20% on dividends may be reduced if a double taxation treaty applies.

9.4.2 JGBs

The **bond market** in **Japan** is dominated by Government bonds. This domination is not in terms of volume, where **Japanese Government Bonds (JGBs)** account for only half of the market, but in the secondary market where they account for over 80% of the secondary market trading. Within this, there tends to be a strong focus on the 'benchmark' bond. This has in the past caused wide discrepancies between the benchmark and other 'side issues'.

The **issue process** is complex with a monthly auction/syndicate issue. In Japan, the syndicate (still dominated by the large investment banks) is allocated 40% of the issue, with 60% sold via public auction. The terms of the issue are set by the Ministry of Finance having taken soundings in the market from the syndicate.

JGBs trade on both the Tokyo Stock Exchange (**TSE**) and the Broker-Broker (OTC) market. The market does tend to focus on the 'benchmark' issues, with occasionally 90% of the volume taking place in that stock. However, any issues that are deliverable into the JGB future will possess a fair degree of liquidity.

TSE transactions settle after three days (T+3) with the OTC taking nine days or more, following a complicated settlement timetable. Settlement is conducted through book entry systems.

9.4.3 Other markets in Japan

In Japan, there are a number of important issuers other than the government. In the form of 'quasi-government' there are the agencies and municipal stocks.

International borrowers are able to access the domestic pool of savings through the issue of Samurai (publicly issued yen bonds) and Shibosai (yen bonds issued via private placement).

9.5 Markets in France

9.5.1 Equities

There is one stock market in France: Euronext. It operates a computerised order book known as the NSC. Settlement is on T+3 through the systems of Euroclear France, the central securities depository.

9.5.2 Bonds

The French bond market developed into one of the key international bond markets, mainly due to the economic transformation that took place since the introduction of the 'Franc fort' policy in 1985. In 1993, plans were announced to move towards a more independent central bank in line with the obligations of the Maastricht Treaty. This commitment made the French market the most efficient bond market within the first wave of European Economic and Monetary Union (EMU), with a transparent, liquid and technologically strong market.

The development of MATIF (the French financial futures market, now part of Euronext) and the trading of the 'Notional' future into the French long bond were also a vital component in the reform of the market.

The French Government issues the following **types of bond**, each with a different maturity.

- **Bons du Trésor à Taux Fixe (BTFs)** are the French T-bills, issued at a discount to face value and with maturities of 13, 26 and 52 weeks.

- **Bons du Trésor à Taux Fixe et Intéret Annuel (BTANs)** are fixed rate Treasury notes issued with maturities of between two and five years and an annual coupon. New issues are made on a six-monthly basis and, in between these new issues, existing issues are reopened on a monthly basis.

- **Obligations Assimilables du Trésor (OATs)** are the conventional Government bonds that have become the key funding instruments used by the Government. They are issued with maturities of between 6 and 30 years. OAT strips are permitted. **OATis** are 'inflation-linked OATs that pay a fixed real coupon annually, with the principal being guaranteed at par plus indexation against inflation.

All French Government issues are now in book entry form with no physical delivery. The settlement period is T + 1 and the bonds can be settled through Clearstream and Euroclear.

Over half the market is made up of debt issues from the **public corporations**. These stocks are not, for the most part, guaranteed by the Government, but the corporations concerned do possess strong credit ratings. They have established their own market structure in order to facilitate trading in their stocks. All issues are by way of a placing through a syndicate of mainly local banks.

9.6 Markets in Germany

9.6.1 Equities

The Deutsche Börse is a fierce competitor with the LSE. Trading takes place through a computerised order book called XETRA. Settlement is normally T+2. Clearing, settlement and custody take place through Clearstream.

9.6.2 Bonds

The German bond market, including Government bonds, domestic bonds and Eurobonds, is the third largest in the world and one of the largest in Europe (the second largest after Italy).

Unlike the UK, Germany has a strong **corporate debt market** and a relatively weak equity market. The bulk of finance for industry is provided through the banks, either as lenders or shareholders, with debt securities other than Eurobonds being less significant. Within the context of debt issuance, it is the banks that issue bonds and then lend on the money to the corporate sector.

The German financial markets have undergone a process of liberalisation and modernisation. These have gradually removed the residual capital controls and allowed the development of a market in futures and options. With the adoption of the Euro, the German bond market emerged as the benchmark for Government bonds of the Eurozone.

The bulk of the banking sector bond issuance comes in the form of Pfandbriefe. These are effectively bonds collateralised against portfolios of loans. Offenliche Pfandbriefe are backed by loans to the public sector and Hypotheken Pfandbriefe are backed by mortgages.

There is a variety of **types of issue**:

- **(Bundesanleihen)** are the conventional bonds in the market, with normal maturities of ten years. Special bonds have been issued to fund the reunification process and are referred to as unity bonds.

- **Bobls (Bundesobligationen)** are medium-term issues with lives of up to five years.

- **Bundesschatzanweisungen (Schatze) and Kassenobligationen** are a second type of medium-term finance: these were issued with maturities of between two and six years.

- **BU-Bills** are six-month bills issued by the Bundesbank.

Settlement date for domestic bond deals is three banking days after the day of dealing. This now matches to the Eurobond three-day settlement period, allowing Government or bank bonds held outside Germany to settle via Euroclear and Clearstream.

9.7 Emerging markets

There are various **bond and equity markets in growing and emerging markets**, each with its own unique characteristics.

In many of these markets, bond and equity trading is OTC and is restricted to locally registered participants. Settlement systems in such markets tend to be run by central banks with no counterparty guarantees. In addition, non-electronic settlement systems and physical delivery are not uncommon. These characteristics make participation both difficult and risky for the UK investor.

In an effort to achieve some international harmonisation, the larger (G30) economies have published some recommendations of good practice including T + 3 settlement for equities.

9.8 Eurobonds

Learning objective	1.7.2 **Explain** the structure and operation of the primary and secondary markets for Eurobonds

9.8.1 The market

The Eurobond market is, in effect, an international market in debt. Companies issuing debt in the Eurobond market have their securities traded all around the world and are not limited to one domestic market place.

The market only accepts highly rated companies, since Eurobonds themselves are unsecured debt.

9.8.2 The instruments

In essence, a Eurobond is simply a debt instrument issued by a borrower (typically a government or a large company) normally or predominantly **outside of the country in whose currency it is denominated**. For example, a US dollar Eurobond could be issued anywhere in the world except for the US. As such, a better name for it might be an 'international bond'. As mentioned above, Eurobonds frequently carry no security other than the high name and credit rating of the issuer. Another important feature of bonds issued in this market is that, for the most part, they are issued in **bearer form**, with no formal register of ownership held by the company.

For a number of pragmatic reasons, the clearing houses in the Euromarkets do maintain a form of register of ownership, but this register is not normally open either to government or tax authorities. Combined with the feature of being bearer documents, a vital aspect of the Eurobond is that, unlike most government bonds, it does not attract withholding tax. **Eurobonds pay coupons gross and usually annually**.

Most Eurobonds are issued in **bullet form**, redeemed at one specified date in the future. However, a number of issues have alternative redemption patterns. Some bonds are redeemed over a number of years with a proportion of the issue being redeemed each year. Whilst Eurobonds are not issued in registered form, each will have an identifying number. A **drawing** of numbers is made every year from the pool of bonds in issue, the numbers drawn are published and the bonds are called in and redeemed. This redemption process is known as a drawing on a Eurobond.

9.8.3 Dealing and settlement

There is no formal market place for Eurobond trading. The market is telephone driven and the houses are based in London. The market is regulated by the **International Capital Market Association (ICMA)** which operates rules regulating the conduct of dealers in the market place.

Settlement is conducted for the market by two independent clearing houses, **Euroclear and Clearstream**. These clearing houses immobilise the stocks in their vaults and then operate electronic registers of ownership.

Settlement in the Eurobond market is based on a **three business day** settlement system. Once again, the important feature about the registers maintained by the two clearing houses is that they are not normally available to any governmental authority, thereby preserving the bearer nature of the documents.

9.8.4 Eurobond issuance

New Issues in the Eurobond Market

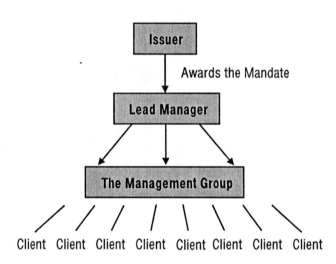

The most common form of issue used in the Eurobond market is a **placing**. A traditional method of issuing a Eurobond is for an issuer to appoint a lead manager and award them the mandate. The mandate gives the lead manager the power and responsibility to issue the bond on the issuer's behalf. The lead manager may then create a management group of other Eurobond houses. Each house then receives a portion of the deal and places it with its client base. The lead manager may elect to run the entire book alone, and miss out the other members of the management group.

In normal issues, the lead manager has the ability to amend the terms of the issue as market conditions dictate. It is also common for the lead manager to place the entire deal themselves in these circumstances without forming a syndicate.

There are a number of variations on these methods of issue. Under a **fixed price reoffer**, the members of the management group are prohibited from selling the bonds in the secondary market at below the issue price until the syndicate has been broken. The syndicate will break when the lead manager believes the bulk of the issue has been placed.

9.9 International settlement and clearing

Learning objective   **1.7.3 Explain** the settlement and clearing procedures overseas, including the role of international central securities depositories, and the different settlement cycles and challenges in managing global assets

9.9.1 International markets settlement

	Order or quote driven	Settlement period: equities	Settlement period: Govt. bonds	Settlement agency
USA	NYSE – order* NASDAQ – quote	T + 3	T + 0	DTC DTC
Japan	TSE – order	T + 3	T + 3	TSE
Germany	Xetra – order	T + 2	T + 2	Clearstream
France	Order	T + 3	T + 3	Euroclear
UK	SETS – order SETSqx – quote and order SEAQ – quote	T + 3	T + 1	Euroclear UK & Ireland

* International trading on the NYSE is largely made up of American Depository Receipts (ADRs). ADRs will help facilitate the trading of non-US company shares within the US. ADRs settle T+3, are dominated in dollars and pay a dollar dividend.

9.9.2 Central securities depositories (CSDs)

In 1989, the Group of 30 (G30) recommended that each domestic market should establish a **Central Securities Depository (CSD)** to hold securities. The fundamental objectives for the establishment of a CSD are for gains in efficiencies and for reduction in risk. Efficiency gains are achieved through the elimination of manual errors, lower costs and increased speed of processing through automation, which all translate into lower risks. Most markets that did not already have established CSDs in 1989 have organised one or more CSDs and centralised local settlement through them.

9.9.3 Alternative holding systems

Almost all countries have some form of central depository where the securities are either immobilised or dematerialised.

- In a **'dematerialised' system**, there is no document which physically embodies the claim. The system relies on a collection of securities accounts, instructions to financial institutions which maintain those accounts, and confirmations of account entries.

- **Immobilisation** is common in markets that previously relied on physical share certificates, but the certificates are now immobilised in a depository, which is the holder of record in the register. Access by investors to the depository is typically through financial institutions which are members of the depository.

Through the establishment of CSDs, investors are able to reduce risks of loss, theft and illiquidity costs substantially by holding securities through one or more tiers of financial intermediaries such as banks or brokers.

There can be several types of holding systems. For example, some professional investors and financial intermediaries have direct contractual relationships with CSDs. They hold interests in securities through accounts on the records of the CSDs. Other investors, particularly retail investors, generally hold their interests through brokers or other financial intermediaries at a lower tier in the multi-tiered structure.

9.9.4 ICSDs and CSDs

International Central Securities Depositories (ICSDs) have established linkages with several domestic **CSDs** and have created a sub-custodian network.

The roles of ICSDs and CSDs are distinguished in the following Table.

ICSDs	CSDs
International client base	Domestic/local client base
Cross-border activity	Domestic activity only
All securities	Local securities only
Settlement	Settlement
Custody	Custody
Collateral management	
Other services	
Securities lending	

The principal ICSDs – **Euroclear** and **Clearstream** – have traditionally provided clearance and custody of Eurobonds and other Euromarket instruments. In recent years however they have increasingly become involved in settlement and custody of international equities.

10 THE PRINCIPAL-AGENT PROBLEM

Learning objectives

1.8.1 Explain how capital markets allow the beneficial ownership and the control of capital to be separated

1.8.2 Distinguish between beneficial owners (principals) and the various agents involved in the capital allocation process

1.8.3 Explain how conflict between the interests of agents and principals gives rise to the 'agency' or 'principal-agent' problem

1.8.4 Identify examples of agency costs such as: expropriation, perquisites, self-dealing, and higher cost of capital, which arise when the agency problem is known to exist

1.8.5 Identify the main reasons why it is argued that reducing the agency problem benefits the investment profession and society as a whole

10.1 The separation of ownership and control

A small company or firm typically has a strong alignment between the company's **ownership** and its **control**. The company will typically be run by owner-managers, who are perhaps within the same family. The managers will typically be the major shareholders. It is in the interests of the owner-managers for the company to succeed, and for shareholder wealth to be maximised.

A company that seeks to expand may seek capital market finance by floating on a stock market. It will offer its shares to outside investors whose many will provide an injection of funds for the company. In larger companies, professional managers may be hired who may have little or no shareholding in the company.

There is then a separation of ownership and control. The shareholders, as owners (or **principals**) are investing with the hope of increasing their wealth or generating dividends. The managers who work for the company (as **agents**) may have different objectives, such as gaining benefits (perks) for themselves, dealing on their own account (in a financial firm), pursuing pet projects or 'empire-building' for themselves in ways that often do not align with shareholders' interests. Directors or senior managers might misuse the company's resources is to benefit themselves at the expense of stockholders.

The misalignment of objectives that arises from this separation of ownership and control is known as the **agency problem**.

10.2 The agency problem

Agency theory sees employees of businesses, including managers, as individuals, each with his or her own objectives. Various people are involved as agents. Within a department of a business, there are departmental objectives. If achieving these various objectives leads also to the achievement of the objectives of the organisation as a whole, there is said to be **goal congruence**. Goal congruence is accordance between the objectives of agents acting within an organisation and the objectives of the organisation as a whole.

Agency problems arise from the misalignment of goals, and this can make clients, including individuals, more reluctant to provide finance intermediaries in the investment industry: they might tend to prefer keeping their assets as cash, for example. This will limit market liquidity and makes it more difficult for firms to grow, potentially hurting growth prospects in the economy.

10.3 Moral hazard

Moral hazard is the prospect that a party insulated from risk may behave differently from the way it would behave if it were fully exposed to the risk. The classic example is often deemed to originate from the insurance industry, where coverage against a loss might increase the risk-taking behaviour of the insured. The fact that the loss is protected in some tangible way means that the risk appetite of the insured is skewed. When applied to the behaviour of **managers and executives in a financial trading firm**, one can infer how the issue of moral hazard may *increase* the likelihood of irrational behaviour towards **risk-taking**. If managers have an incentive, perhaps through their remuneration structure, to take risks in order to meet short-term targets, the long-term objectives and even the viability of the firm may be compromised if some of those risks turn bad. This is seen by many analysts as one of the key problems leading to the late 2000s financial crisis, and it is partly for this reason that regulators have sought, with only some success, to impose standards on the remuneration process in larger financial firms.

In 2008, during the bailout of AIG, Fannie Mae and Freddie Mac in the US, the phrase 'moral hazard' became commonly used. The problem, according to many observers, was that the rescue of the banks (including those in the UK which were saved by the UK Government) echoed the case of Long Term Capital Management (LTCM), the collapsed US hedge fund in 1998, as these rescues increased moral hazard, or the risk that investors would enter into contracts in bad faith. Knowing that the government was there to help them, banks and other investors were free to make irresponsible commitments. **Financial bail-outs** of lending institutions by governments, central banks or other institutions can encourage risky lending in the future, if those that take the risks come to believe that they will not have to carry the full burden of losses. Systematically significant (so-called '**too big to fail**') lending institutions can make risky loans that will pay handsomely if the investment turns out well but will result in the firm being bailed out by the taxpayer if the investment turns out badly.

10.4 Reducing the agency problem through pay and shares

One strategy sometimes used to enhance goal congruence and to mitigate the 'agency problem' is giving managers some profit-related pay, or providing incentives which are related to profits or share price. The costs of such arrangements can be viewed as **agency costs**.

Examples of such remuneration incentives are:

- **Profit-related/economic value-added pay**. Pay or bonuses related to the size of profits or economic value-added.

- **Rewarding managers with shares**. This might be done when a private company 'goes public' and managers are invited to subscribe for shares in the company at an attractive offer price. In a management buy-out or buy-in (the latter involving purchase of the business by new managers; the former by existing managers), managers become owner-managers.

- **Executive Share Options Plans (ESOPs)**. In a share option scheme, selected employees are given a number of share options, each of which gives the holder the right after a certain date to subscribe for shares in the company at a fixed price. The value of an option will increase if the company is successful and its share price goes up.

Such measures might however merely encourage management to adopt 'creative accounting' methods which will distort the reported performance of the company in the service of the managers' own ends.

10.5 Other ways to reduce the agency problem

Separation of roles is another way in which the agency problem might be mitigated. The agency theory suggests that not too much power should accrue to a single individual within an organisation. The role of the Chairman and the Chief executive for example should be split.

Accounting standards. The financial statements of a company are the main vehicle of corporate information to the shareholders. Agency theory suggests that audited accounts of limited companies are an important source of 'post-decision' information, potentially minimising investors' agency costs.

Corporate governance. An alternative approach to attempt to monitor managers' behaviour is through the adoption of a corporate framework of decision making that restricts the power of managers and increases the role of independent external parties in the monitoring of their duties. This can be achieved for example by establishing 'management audit' procedures, by introducing additional reporting requirements, or by seeking assurances from managers that shareholders' interests will be foremost in their priorities.

Regulation. In the regulated **financial services industry**, rules and principles designed to ensure that financial services firms deal properly with conflicts of interest and treat customers fairly should help to reduce the agency issues that can arise in the industry. The ban on investment advisers receiving commission from product providers, implemented at the end of 2012 following the **Retail Distribution Review (RDR)**, aims to align the interests of the adviser more closely with those of the customer. The RDR seeks to make a clear distinction between advice and sales in the retail financial sector. Other practices that are against customers' interests and which regulatory rules seek to stop include excessive **churning** of accounts, and **front-running of orders**, where a broker, on receiving a large order, might place an order himself in advance, in order to take advantage of an anticipated price rise resulting from the large order.

CHAPTER ROUNDUP

- Financial intermediaries such as banks and building societies take deposits from savers and re-lend to borrowers. Financial intermediation brings benefits from aggregation and maturity transformation.

- Financial services products can help people manage risk, for example by pooling risks (insurance) and by offering access to diversified portfolios of assets at relatively low cost.

- Capital markets, such as the London Stock Exchange, are markets for long-term capital. Money markets are shorter term debt markets in which banks and other financial institutions deal mainly with each other, on a wholesale basis.

- The financial services industry is a key sector of the UK economy. Key areas are banking, life insurance, general insurance, pensions, fund and asset management, currency markets and securities markets. London has various advantages which have enabled it to maintain its position as a leading global financial centre.

- The Government plays a role in economic and industrial policy, regulation, taxation and social welfare. Regulatory interventions seek to avoid or provide remedies for cases of market failure, thus protecting consumers and providing free and fair markets. Economic policy encompasses monetary policy (particularly through interest rates), fiscal policy (public spending and taxation) and exchange rate policy (occasional intervention in currency markets).

- Financial markets mobilise people's savings and put them to use in enabling firms to grow, thus contributing to the wealth of the economy. An effective securities market has characteristics of cost-efficiency, liquidity and price discovery, which is enhanced by transparency.

- In many European countries, the financial system has been more based on banks than on markets, with firms raising funds mainly through the banking system. In Germany and France as well as Italy, for example, relatively little use has been made of equity finance by firms.

- The size of the US economy and the dominance of the US dollar in international transactions has made the US financial system central to both the US economy and the global economy.

- Ranking after London and New York, the third and fourth largest financial centres are found in Asia – being Tokyo and Singapore respectively. Within China, Shanghai and Hong Kong are also key centres.

- The financial crisis of the late 2000s highlighted severe strains in the global financial system. Policy steps taken in different countries included monetary and fiscal stimulus, central bank liquidity operations, policies to promote asset market liquidity and actions to resolve problems at specific institutions.

- Equities may be listed on the primary markets (such as the LSE), and may be dual-listed in more than one country. The Alternative Investment Market (AIM) is the UK's less regulated second-tier market.

- The Debt Management Office (DMO) takes responsibility for issuing gilts on behalf of the Treasury.

- Secondary markets now include new competition from various Multilateral Trading Facilities (MTFs).

- Where a market is order-driven, the relevant trading system will match buyers and sellers automatically, provided that they are willing to trade at prices compatible with each other. A quote-driven market requires certain market participants (market makers) to take responsibility for acting as buyers and sellers to the rest of the market so that there will always be a price at which a trade can be conducted.

- On the LSE, the SETS system (known as the Order Book, as it is an order-driven system) is used for the most liquid domestic equities. The London Clearing House (known as LCH.Clearnet) acts as the central counterparty to all SETS trades.

- SETSqx ('Stock Exchange Electronic Trading Service-quotes and crosses') has replaced SEAQ for all main market securities. SETSqx combines the market making quote-driven model and the order-driven model.

- In the gilts market, Gilt-Edged Market Makers (GEMMs) have the role of ensuring that there are two-way quotes at all times for all gilts.

- A Systematic Internaliser (SI) is an investment firm which deals on its own account by executing client orders outside a regulated market or a MTF.

- Settlement of UK equities, corporate bonds, gilts and money market instruments occurs through Euroclear UK & Ireland (EUI), which operates an electronic dematerialised settlement system.

- Operating an investment exchange is a regulated activity (arranging deals in investments) and therefore requires regulatory approval.

- The most important London market for financial futures and options is NYSE Liffe.

- Companies must release required information to the market through an official Regulatory Information Service (RIS) or other UKLA-approved Primary Information Provider (PIP) service.

- The Prospectus Directive requires that a prospectus is produced when there is a public offer of securities or where securities are admitted to trading on a regulated market. Some exemptions apply. The Directive specifies the content of prospectuses and requires that they are approved by the relevant competent authority (the FCA).

- The UK Corporate Governance Code aims to promote confidence in corporate reporting and governance, and to promote good governance. Companies must 'comply or explain'.

- Companies legislation makes provisions on the conduct and structure of company meetings which will apply in the absence of any provisions to the contrary in the company's Articles of Association.

- The markets in major developed economies internationally share many features of the UK equity and bond markets. In many emerging economy markets however, bond and equity trading is OTC and is restricted to locally registered participants. Settlement systems in such markets tend to be run by central banks with no counterparty guarantees.

- The Eurobond market is an international market in debt. Companies issuing debt in the Eurobond market have their securities traded all around the world and are not limited to one domestic market place.

- Domestic markets have established Central Securities Depositories (CSDs) to hold securities. In a 'dematerialised' system, the system relies on a collection of securities accounts, instructions to financial institutions which maintain those accounts, and confirmations of account entries. With the alternative of immobilisation, certificates are immobilised in a depository, which is the holder of record in the register. International Central Securities Depositories (ICSDs) have established linkages with several domestic CSDs and have created a sub-custodian network.

- The separation of ownership and control that is typical in a larger enterprise gives rise to the principal-agent problem. There are different ways in which the objectives of principals and agents may be more closely aligned, which result in agency costs, but help to enable financial markets to work and the economy to grow.

TEST YOUR KNOWLEDGE

1. Outline the benefits of financial intermediation.

2. What is meant by securitisation of debt?

3. Explain the status of an EU Directive in relation to national law.

4. What is meant by 'market impact' (or 'price impact") in the context of transaction costs?

5. What role does the LCH.Clearnet play in SETS orders?

6. What is a GEMM?

7. Identify two risks of high frequency trading.

8. What is the standard settlement period for UK equities?

9. When do equities go ex-dividend?

10. Explain the role of a NOMAD.

11. Outline the main principles of Section E (Relations with shareholders) of the UK Corporate Governance Code.

12. Explain what is meant by 'immobilisation' in the context of central depositories.

TEST YOUR KNOWLEDGE: ANSWERS

1. Financial intermediation has the following benefits.

    - Intermediaries provide ways in which a lender can deposit money to spend in the future, together with a ready source of funds for borrowers.

    - Financial intermediaries aggregate or 'package' the amounts lent by savers and lend on to borrowers in different amounts.

    - Financial intermediaries provide for maturity transformation: intermediation bridges the gap between the wish of many lenders for liquidity and the desire of many borrowers for loans over longer periods.

    - Risk is reduced by pooling. Since financial intermediaries lend to a large number of individuals and organisations, losses suffered through default by borrowers or capital losses are pooled.

    (See Section 1.4)

2. Securitisation of debt means creating tradable securities which are backed by less liquid assets such as mortgages and other long-term loans.

    (See Section 2.7)

3. EU Directives are issued to the governments of the EU member states requiring them within a specified period (usually two years) to alter the national laws of the state so that they conform to the directive. Until a Directive is given effect by a UK statute it does not usually affect legal rights and obligations of individuals.

    (See Section 3.2.3)

4. Buyers putting through relatively large buy orders may need to push the price of the security up in order to make the trade. Sellers who want to put through a large sell order quickly may need to accept a lower price than is immediately available to a seller with a small order. The effect of this tendency for fluctuating order sizes to move prices is known the market impact or price impact.

    (See Section 4.8)

5. The LCH.Clearnet acts to guarantee all trades and so remove counterparty risk. This process is known as novation.

    (See Section 5.1.4)

6. GEMMs – gilt-edged market makers – provide liquidity for the gilt market.

    (See Section 5.4.2)

7. Firstly, automated trading such as HFT can precipitate extreme volatility in markets, which could have significant effects on a trader's position. Secondly, software glitches may lead to errors in automated trades, resulting in possible unpredictable losses.

    (See Section 5.9)

8. T + 3.

    (See Section 6.1)

9. Two business days before the books closed date.

    (See Section 6.3)

10. AIM companies must have an LSE-approved Nominated Adviser (NOMAD) to advise the directors on their responsibilities, and guide them through the AIM process. The NOMAD is retained to advise the directors once an AIM listing is granted. Should the company lose its NOMAD, it must appoint a new one (otherwise the listing will be suspended).

   (See Section 7.3.1)

11. Section E of the Code has the following Main Principles.

   There should be a dialogue with shareholders based on the mutual understanding of objectives. The board as a whole has responsibility for ensuring that a satisfactory dialogue with shareholders takes place.

   The board should use the AGM to communicate with investors and to encourage their participation.

   (See Section 8.4)

12. Immobilisation is common in markets that previously relied on physical share certificates. The certificates are now immobilised in a depository, which is the holder of record in the register. Access by investors to the depository is typically through financial institutions which are members of the depository.

   (See Section 9.9.3)

2

Ethics and investment professionalism

INTRODUCTION

Ethical conduct is a matter of continuing debate. There have been many examples of misbehaviour at all levels of large organisations in recent years, including for example the frauds associated with Enron. All professional bodies are alarmed by these events and what they say about ethical standards in everyday life.

What do individuals, firms and the financial sector stand to lose if there are slips in professional standards, even if those slips are put right? Probably the most significant thing at stake is the reputation of the individuals and firms involved, which can have implications for the reputation of the whole sector. In business as in other areas of life, reputation must typically be built up by small steps over a long time, but it can be lost in a moment.

1 ETHICAL AND COMPLIANCE-DRIVEN BEHAVIOUR

Learning objectives	**2.1.1 Describe** the need for ethics in the investment industry
	2.1.2 Identify the ethical obligations to clients, prospective clients, employers and co-workers
	2.1.3 Identify positive and negative behavioural indicators
	2.1.4 Critically evaluate the outcomes which may result from behaving ethically – for the industry, individual advisers, and consumers
	2.1.5 Critically evaluate the outcomes which may result from limiting behaviour to compliance within the rules – for the industry, individual advisers, and consumers

1.1 Introduction

Firms have to follow **the law** and **regulations**, or else they will be subject to fines and their officers might face similar charges. **Ethics** in organisations relates to **social responsibility** and **business practices.**

People who work for organisations bring their own **values** into work with them. Organisations encompass a variety of ethical frameworks.

- **Personal ethics** deriving from a person's upbringing, religious or non-religious beliefs, political opinions, personality and so on.

- **Professional ethics**, for example the CFA's Code of Ethics.

- **Corporate culture** (eg 'Customer first'). Culture, in denoting what is normal behaviour, also denotes what is the right behaviour in many cases.

- **Organisation systems**. Ethics might be contained in a formal code, reinforced by the overall statement of values. A problem might be that good ethics does not always save money, and there is a real cost to ethical decisions. Equally, there can be substantial risk, and costs, if poor ethics results in loss of reputation for the firm.

Business ethics are relevant to competitive behaviour. This is because a market can only be free if competition is, in some basic respects, fair. There is a distinction to be drawn between competing aggressively and competing unethically.

1.2 Values – personal, corporate, societal

Beyond merely developing rules, human groups and individuals have formulated **values** which, if followed by all, result in a better outcome than if individuals acted only out of their own **self-interest**. For example, a commonly espoused **personal value** is that of **concern for others**, or acting towards others in the way that you would wish them to act towards you. Some have associated the rules, principles and values they have personally sought to live by with **religion**, while others have seen the rules, principles and values as having a **rational** basis.

The concept of **societal values** is of values that are generally agreed by reasonable people or that are widely accepted. At a corporate level, reference to values or the corporate culture suggests that particular ways of acting can become prevalent throughout a firm, whether by design or not. A 'culture' of pursuing short-term profit or revenue even if customers are misled ('having the wool pulled over their eyes') may pervade through a firm, either at the instigation of an aggressive if short-sighted and unethical senior management team, or as the unintended consequence of mis-judged target-setting incentive structures for employees.

1.3 The ethical environment

Whereas the political environment in which an organisation operates consists of laws, regulations and government agencies, the social environment consists of the customs, attitudes, beliefs and education of society as a whole, or of different groups in society; and the ethical environment consists of a set (or sets) of well-established rules of personal and organisational behaviour.

The ethical environment refers to justice, respect for the law and a moral code. The conduct of an organisation, its management and employees will be measured against ethical standards by the customers, suppliers and other members of the public with whom they deal.

An example of unethical behaviour is to **present misleading information** to a customer which wrongly claimed that they would be likely to be better off transferring from a work-based pension scheme to a personal pension, when this is not the case. Such pension transfers led to the widespread pensions mis-selling scandal in recent years.

More recently, excessively zealous selling of 'sub-prime' and 'undocumented' or 'self-certified' mortgages to those who lacked the resources to meet future payments has been seen by many as a root cause of the financial crisis on of the late 2000s, particularly in the US housing market. However, views vary about which behaviours are unethical in such a situation, and attributing 'blame' for such a crisis is complex.

- Were consumers to blame for over-committing themselves?

- Were mortgage brokers to blame for selling mortgages to those who were likely to default?

- Were lenders to blame for making the funds available, while knowing that the mortgages could be 're-packaged' and sold on to investors in securitised form?

Because of differences about where to draw the line between ethical and unethical behaviour, there is much to be said for formulating clearly stated **principles** and **codes** that will apply to particular professional groups or to particular regulated activities.

1.4 Self-interest in the organisational context

The **free market model** of society is based on the idea that individuals act to maximise their own utility. They seek to do this by making decisions to enter into transactions based on the utility gained compared with the opportunity cost on the transaction: the opportunity cost is typically the utility to be gained from spending the same amount of money on the next best alternative. The basic economic model assumes that the economic actor makes decisions out of **self-interest**, as well as being in possession of full **information**.

By and large, we can expect that people will act to better their own interests. But how is this best achieved?

The *Harvard Business Review* reported that the US retailer, Sears Roebuck was deluged with complaints that customers of its car service centre were being charged for unnecessary work: apparently this was because mechanics had been given targets of the number of car spare parts they should sell. The mechanics were seeking to advance their own self-interest in trying to meet the targets set by the organisation.

When targets are set, the key consideration may be to enhance revenues, in the interests of shareholders of the firm. Sales targets for the sale of financial products might, for example, encourage advisers, acting out of self-interest, to advise unnecessary **switching** of client's investments in order to generate commission.

- As well as attracting regulatory sanctions, excessive switching of customers' investments by a firm may, as soon as it becomes known to customers or the media, damage the **firm's reputation**. A poorer reputation could hit sales significantly, thus hurting the business and shareholders' profits that the targets were originally seeking to enhance.

- The adviser responsible for unnecessary switching of customer investments is also liable to damage **his or her own reputation** as a professional. Through the practice of excessive switching having been discovered, the adviser has in fact damaged the self-interest he or she was seeking to promote.

Such examples illustrate how the interaction of self-interest with motivation and with a firm's rules can be complex. Self-interest can be a powerful motivator, encouraging employees to do a better job, but the wrong incentives can lead to sub-optimal outcomes arising.

There remains a debate about whether consumers should be protected by a comprehensive set of rules with the objective of making sure that they do not enter into bad deals or transactions, or whether the rule of **caveat emptor** ('let the buyer beware') should guide all transactions.

Ethical implications of financial incentives

The following is an extract from the regulator's *Guidance Consultation: Risks to customers from financial incentives* (September 2012).

'We know that the way sales staff are paid influences how and what they sell to consumers and can encourage a culture of mis-selling. For example, we have seen a sales person intentionally lie about the price of a product to increase his bonus; another adviser cut corners to rush through six sales in the last few days of a quarter to avoid his pay being reduced; and, staff able to double their bonuses even if they were mis-selling. Incentives may also be used to skew sales to more profitable products, for example we have seen advisers at one firm earn a significantly higher incentive for the more profitable products. This culture must change.

'This programme will be taken forward by the Financial Conduct Authority (FCA), which will have the objective of making sure markets work well so that consumers can get a fair deal. This work aligns with the FCA's new supervisory approach of intervening earlier to reduce the underlying causes of consumer detriment.'

The regulator developed guidance to help firms identify and manage the risks from incentive schemes.

In summary, the regulator expects firms to:

- Properly consider if their incentive schemes increase the risk of mis-selling and, if so, how

- Review whether their governance and controls are adequate

- Take action to address any inadequacies – eg, changing governance, controls, or the schemes themselves

- Where risks cannot be mitigated, take action to change their schemes, and

- Where a recurring problem is identified, investigate, take action and pay redress to consumers who have suffered detriment

---

1.5 Reasons for unethical behaviour

Unethical behaviour can arise for a number of different reasons. **Discussion Paper 18** *An ethical framework for financial services* (FSA, 2002) suggested some of them, as outlined below.

- The pressure of short-term gain could be seen to encourage undesirable behaviour. Staff bonus payments may often seem to be geared to pure bottom line success. How risks and tensions can be identified is a constant issue – eg truth versus loyalty, one person versus the many? In all of this, it is usual for the values and actions of senior management to influence employee levels.

- Some individuals behave unethically because they think it is worth the risk. This may be related to a short-termist agenda, or may simply be personally selfish. People weigh up the pros and cons and take a chance. It is a deliberate risk/reward trade off. Others may believe they are behaving ethically but come to operate by a different yardstick to that used by others. They might do something which is deemed unethical, but which seems acceptable from their own perspective.

- Others (and some of these groups are not mutually exclusive) may be unaware of the values embedded in existing regulatory standards. So, they comply (or don't comply!) blindly with the 'letter of the law', rather than thinking about the wider effects their behaviour might have.

1.6 Two approaches to business ethics

Lynne Paine (*Harvard Business Review*, March-April 1994) suggests that ethical decisions are becoming more important as penalties, in the US at least, for companies which break the law become tougher. Paine suggests that there are two approaches to the management of ethics in organisations.

- Compliance-based (or 'rules-based')
- Integrity-based

1.6.1 Compliance-based approach

A rules-based compliance approach is primarily designed to ensure that the company **acts within the letter of laws and regulations**, and that violations are prevented, detected and punished. Some organisations, faced with the legal consequences of unethical behaviour take legal precautions such as those below.

- Compliance procedures to detect misconduct
- Audits of contracts
- Systems for employees to report criminal misconduct without fear of retribution
- Disciplinary procedures to deal with transgressions

1.6.2 Integrity-based programmes

An integrity-based approach combines a concern for the law with an **emphasis on managerial responsibility** for ethical behaviour. Integrity strategies strive to define companies' guiding values, aspirations and patterns of thought and conduct. When integrated into the day-to-day operations of an organisation, such strategies can help prevent damaging ethical lapses, while tapping into powerful human impulses for moral thought and action.

The integrity-based approach, as compared with a rules-centred or compliance-based approach, echoes the **principles-based approach** to financial services regulation that is followed by the FCA. The principles-based approach requires firms to act with integrity and to treat customers fairly, for example. Unlike rules, such principles require senior management to apply higher-level professional values in how they run their business.

A compliance-based approach suggests that bureaucratic control is necessary; an integrity-based or principles-based approach relies on cultural control.

Basing our professional work on integrity, instead of asking 'Show me where it says we can't...', we ask 'How can we improve our standards and conduct our business with integrity?'.

1.7 Professional integrity

1.7.1 The principle of integrity

Financial services is an important industry, affecting the lives of most people. The industry needs not simply to provide the necessary expertise, but to do so with integrity.

The regulators' first Principle for Businesses is **Integrity**:

'A firm must conduct its business with integrity.'

The first Statement of Principle for Approved Persons is also **Integrity**:

'An approved person must act with integrity in carrying out his controlled functions.'

What do we mean by professional integrity? Among the attributes that contribute to integrity are:

- **Honesty** – which will mean that the person will not deliberately mislead another

- **Reliability** – meaning that the person can be relied upon to maintain appropriate levels of competence and skill in practice

- **Impartiality** – this means treating different people fairly, where the people involved could be customers, or employees

- **Openness** – which implies transparency, where appropriate and where justifed confidentiality is not breached

1.7.2 Professional integrity and ethics in financial services

Professional integrity and ethical issues within financial services can be demonstrated in various ways.

- **The workings of financial markets**. There are various wrongs that can occur. Trading on inside information is an offence and corrodes confidence in markets. If investors believe that price movements may be caused by such practices, then they perceive that the market is rigged against them, and they may suffer financial losses as a result. Research analysis firms are showing lack of integrity if they or their employees deal ahead of publication of research, which could take an unfair advantage of price movements caused by publication of research.

- **The operation of institutions**. Organisations need to make arrangements that ensure as far as possible that employees, and the firm, will operate with integrity. These arrangements can take various forms, and should include training in matters of ethics. Conflicts of interest should be avoided, wherever possible, before they become a problem.

- **Personal conduct of finance professionals and representatives**. Professional employees, and appointed representatives who may be acting as **agents**, should act with integrity, and there should be transparency: they should be *seen* to act with integrity, to encourage **consumer** confidence. As individuals, they must play their part in complying with conduct of business rules of the regulator, and also rules set out by the firm.

1.8 Responsibilities to stakeholders

The various groups with an interest of some kind in the business and its activities are termed **stakeholders** in the business and include shareholders, employees, customers and suppliers. Large organisations tend to be more often held to account over this duty than small ones.

In the FSA **Discussion Paper 18** *An ethical framework for financial services* (2002), the regulator commented on how the highest ethical standards can generate significant benefits for all stakeholders, for example with the following potential benefits.

- **Market confidence.** High ethical standards offer the potential of differentiating the UK financial services sector as being renowned for good ethical practice. A good ethical track record for the sector could help it (and its regulator) to absorb some 'shocks'.

- **Consumer protection.** Improved ethical standards might include a better relationship between firms and consumers which would be reflected in, for example, improved financial promotions.

- **Financial crime.** High ethical standards could change the perception that it is easy to launder money in the UK, and reduce the scope for our firms and markets to be targeted by criminals in the first place. This can be done by developing individual responsibility and a sense of involvement by all staff.

- **Public awareness and confidence.** Higher business and individual standards of behaviour promote the integrity and the general probity of all working in financial services, enhancing public perceptions and trust in the firms and individuals concerned.

2 CFA CODE OF ETHICS AND PROFESSIONAL STANDARDS

Learning objectives	2.2.1 **Identify** the elements of the CFA Code of Ethics 2.2.2 **Explain** the professional principles and values on which the CFA Code of Ethics is based 2.2.3 **Apply** the CFA Code of Ethics to a range of ethical dilemmas

2.1 Overview

The **CFA Institute** has set out a **Code of Ethics** and **Standards of Professional Conduct** for CFA members and candidates.

The Institute states: 'High ethical standards are critical to maintaining the public's trust in financial markets and in the investment profession'.

Institute members (including holders of the Chartered Financial Analyst® [CFA®] designation) and CFA candidates must abide by the Code and Standards and are encouraged to notify their employer of this responsibility.

- Violations may result in disciplinary sanctions by CFA Institute.

- Sanctions can include revocation of membership, revocation of candidacy in the CFA Program, and revocation of the right to use the CFA designation.

The **Standards of Practice Handbook** (Tenth edition, 2010) explains the Standards of Professional Conduct in greater detail, with accompanying case studies, and is available on the CFA Institute web site **www.cfainstitute.org**.

2.2 The Code

Members of CFA Institute (including CFA charterholders) and **Candidates** for the CFA designation must:

- Act with integrity, competence, diligence, respect, and in an ethical manner with the public, clients, prospective clients, employers, employees, colleagues in the investment profession, and other participants in the global capital markets

- Place the integrity of the investment profession and the interests of clients above their own personal interests

- Use reasonable care and exercise independent professional judgment when conducting investment analysis, making investment recommendations, taking investment actions, and engaging in other professional activities

- Practice and encourage others to practice in a professional and ethical manner that will reflect credit on themselves and the profession

- Promote the integrity of and uphold the rules governing capital markets

- Maintain and improve their professional competence and strive to maintain and improve the competence of other investment professionals

2.3 Standards of Professional Conduct

The CFA Standards of Professional Conduct are as follows. [**Notes** about the standards are shown in **square brackets**.]

I. Professionalism

*A. **Knowledge of the Law**. Members and Candidates must understand and comply with all applicable laws, rules, and regulations (including the CFA Institute Code of Ethics and Standards of Professional Conduct) of any government, regulatory organization, licensing agency, or professional association governing their professional activities. In the event of conflict, Members and Candidates must comply with the more strict law, rule, or regulation. Members and Candidates must not knowingly participate or assist in and must dissociate from any violation of such laws, rules, or regulations.*

[Note that members and candidates practising in **different countries** must abide by all relevant regulatory requirements, whether of their own country or of foreign jurisdictions. It follows that, as investment professionals, CFA members and candidates need to keep up-to-date on the regulations affecting them. If they are in doubt, they should **consult** compliance staff.]

*B. **Independence and Objectivity**. Members and Candidates must use reasonable care and judgment to achieve and maintain independence and objectivity in their professional activities. Members and Candidates must not offer, solicit, or accept any gift, benefit, compensation, or consideration that reasonably could be expected to compromise their own or another's independence and objectivity.*

[Investment professionals may sometimes be under pressure to accept free trips or other gifts that could influence their recommendations or their research. They should only accept **modest gifts**, and should avoid situations in which there could be, or could appear to be, a conflict of interest.]

*C. **Misrepresentation**. Members and Candidates must not knowingly make any misrepresentations relating to investment analysis, recommendations, actions, or other professional activities.*

[A misrepresentation is an untrue statement or omission of a fact, or any statement that is otherwise false or misleading. '**Knowingly**' means that the member or candidate either knows or should have known that the misrepresentation was being made. Members and candidates must not misrepresent any aspect of their practice, including: their or their firm's qualifications or credentials; their or their firm's performance record; or the characteristics of an investment, including guaranteeing returns on a risky investment product. This Standard also prohibits **plagiarism** in the preparation of material, such as research reports. Such plagiarism may have taken place in oral communication, such as in client meetings: it does not only apply to written material.]

*D. **Misconduct**. Members and Candidates must not engage in any professional conduct involving dishonesty, fraud, or deceit or commit any act that reflects adversely on their professional reputation, integrity, or competence.*

[This Standard covers compliance with regulations and professional integrity. Dishonesty in personal behaviour will reflect badly on the person's profession.]

II. Integrity of capital markets

A. Material Non-public Information. Members and Candidates who possess material non-public information that could affect the value of an investment must not act or cause others to act on the information.

[The meaning of '**material**' is that disclosure of the information is likely to result in a change in the price of the security, or that a reasonable investor would want to know the information before making an investment decision. Information is '**non-public**' if it has not yet been communicated to the market generally, and so investors have not had the opportunity to react to it. If a group of analysts has received information from a company, the information is not public until it has been disseminated to other investors. In accordance with **mosaic theory**, it is acceptable for an analyst to link together and analyse public information and non-material non-public information in order to predict events, in such a way that the conclusion is the same as from material non-public information.

Many investment firms set up **firewalls**, often called **Chinese walls**, which are designed to contain sensitive information. These 'walls' are administrative and physical barriers and other internal arrangements, commonly used to separate sales and research departments from corporate finance departments, which often have confidential, sometimes inside, information.]

B. Market Manipulation. Members and Candidates must not engage in practices that distort prices or artificially inflate trading volume with the intent to mislead market participants.

[Market manipulation could involve taking a large position in a security in order to distort the price of a related **derivative**. Dissemination of **false or misleading information** in order to distort prices may also amount to market manipulation.]

III. Duties to clients

A. Loyalty, Prudence, and Care. Members and Candidates have a duty of loyalty to their clients and must act with reasonable care and exercise prudent judgment. Members and Candidates must act for the benefit of their clients and place their clients' interests before their employer's or their own interests. In relationships with clients, members and candidates must determine applicable fiduciary duty and must comply with such duty to persons and interests to whom it is owed.

[This Standards accords with the **FCA's rule** that firms must act honestly, fairly and professionally in accordance with the best interests of the client: this is the regulator's '**client's best interests rule**'.

A **fiduciary** is an individual or institution that is in a position of **trust**: that is, they have the duty of acting for the benefit of another party in respect of matters that come within the scope of the relationship between them.

Investment professionals must ensure that clients get the best execution for trades. In the case of **dealing commission ('soft' commission)** being used to purchase research for the benefit of client portfolios, the investment professional must accept that the commission 'belongs' to the client and so must be directed to the client's benefit. (We discuss the use of dealing commission further when we consider the regulator's rules, in Chapter 3 of this Study Text.)

Proxy voting is another instance of a fiduciary relationship. The investment manager should always vote on a proxy issue that have an economic benefit to the client, unless the client instructs otherwise.]

B. Fair Dealing. Members and Candidates must deal fairly and objectively with all clients when providing investment analysis, making investment recommendations, taking investment action, or engaging in other professional activities.

[The investment professional should **not favour** one client over another when making recommendations or taking actions on investments: this is 'fair dealing'. Discretionary and non-discretionary clients must be treated equally. **New issues** should be offered to all clients for whom the security is an appropriate investment. Block trades, or over-subscribed issues, should be distributed among clients on a *pro rata* basis.

The FCA rules on client order handling – covered in Chapter 3 of this Study Text – are also relevant here.]

C. Suitability.

1. When Members and Candidates are in an advisory relationship with a client, they must:

a. Make a reasonable inquiry into a client's or prospective client's investment experience, risk and return objectives, and financial constraints prior to making any investment recommendation or taking investment action and must reassess and update this information regularly.

b. Determine that an investment is suitable to the client's financial situation and consistent with the client's written objectives, mandates, and constraints before making an investment recommendation or taking investment action.

c. Judge the suitability of investments in the context of the client's total portfolio.

2. When Members and Candidates are responsible for managing a portfolio to a specific mandate, strategy, or style, they must make only investment recommendations or take only investment actions that are consistent with the stated objectives and constraints of the portfolio.

[A basic principle is that of 'KYC' – Know Your Client, before making any investment recommendation. To comply with this Standard, the investment professional should carry out a documented '**fact find**' for the client. The fact find will establish: the type and nature of the client; the client's attitude to risk; the client's investment objectives, taking into account the trade-off between risk and expected returns; constraints on investment, including liquidity constraints, legal requirements, the time horizon, and the client's tax position.]

D. Performance Presentation. When communicating investment performance information, Members and Candidates must make reasonable efforts to ensure that it is fair, accurate, and complete.

[Statements of performance must be complete, fair, and accurate. The CFA Institute has developed the **Global Investment Performance Standards (GIPS)** – an accepted set of common standards for the investment management industry. Compliance is voluntary, but investment professionals and their firms are encouraged to adopt the standards, which are becoming increasingly widely used.]

E. Preservation of Confidentiality. Members and Candidates must keep information about current, former, and prospective clients confidential unless:

1. The information concerns illegal activities on the part of the client or prospective client,
2. Disclosure is required by law, or
3. The client or prospective client permits disclosure of the information

[Investment professionals should generally avoid disclosing information about a client except to authorised fellow employees of the firm who are working for the client's benefit.]

IV. Duties to employers

A. Loyalty. In matters related to their employment, Members and Candidates must act for the benefit of their employer and not deprive their employer of the advantage of their skills and abilities, divulge confidential information, or otherwise cause harm to their employer.

[Although **independent practice** is not expressly prohibited, investment professionals should not enter into independent practice where it is in conflict with their employers' interests. Where preparations are made to undertake independent practice before leaving an employer, the investment professional should take care to ensure that the employer's interests are maintained. The investment professional has a duty to act in the employer's best interests until the effective time of their resignation. The investment professional must take care not to misappropriate trade secrets or client lists, misuse confidential information, or solicit the employer's clients.]

B. Additional Compensation Arrangements. Members and Candidates must not accept gifts, benefits, compensation, or consideration that competes with or might reasonably be expected to create a conflict of interest with their employer's interest unless they obtain written consent from all parties involved.

[**Additional compensation** may include payments from clients or from third parties. The employer has a right to know about such arrangements. An example would be where an investment professional newly employed by a firm is continuing to advise clients whom he has been advising in an independent capacity, separately from his work for the firm: the employer's written consent should be sought.]

C. Responsibilities of Supervisors. Members and Candidates must make reasonable efforts to detect and prevent violations of applicable laws, rules, regulations, and the Code and Standards by anyone subject to their supervision or authority.

[A supervisor is responsible for the ethical behaviour of subordinates, whether or not they are CFA Institute members or candidates. You may be supervising a large number of employees, so that you will not be able to evaluate the conduct of each of them. You will then need to delegate supervisory responsibilities, but this delegation does not remove your supervisory responsibilities. A supervisor can rely on the effectiveness of reasonable **compliance procedures**, and should not accept a supervisory appointment unless such reasonable procedures are in place. The supervisor must respond promptly to any violations, carry out a thorough investigation and place appropriate limits on relevant employees' activities until the investigation is completed.

The compliance procedures in place should:

- Be set out in a clearly written and readily understood manual
- Designate a compliance officer and define his responsibilities and authority clearly
- Outline the scope of compliance procedures
- Outline what is permissible conduct
- Set out procedures for reporting violations and sanctions
- Be communicated to all employees and updated regularly]

V. Investment analysis, recommendations, and actions

A. Diligence and Reasonable Basis. Members and Candidates must:

1. Exercise diligence, independence, and thoroughness in analyzing investments, making investment recommendations, and taking investment actions.

2. Have a reasonable and adequate basis, supported by appropriate research and investigation, for any investment analysis, recommendation, or action.

[Investment professionals must make reasonable and diligent efforts to ensure that **research** is sound, whether it is primary research, secondary research (conducted by someone else in the same firm), or third party research. Information that is suspected of being inaccurate should not be used.

B. Communication with Clients and Prospective Clients.

Members and Candidates must:

1. Disclose to clients and prospective clients the basic format and general principles of the investment processes they use to analyze investments, select securities, and construct portfolios and must promptly disclose any changes that might materially affect those processes.

2. Use reasonable judgment in identifying which factors are important to their investment analyses, recommendations, or actions and include those factors in communications with clients and prospective clients.

3. Distinguish between fact and opinion in the presentation of investment analysis and recommendations.

[Information sent to clients, by whatever means of communication, should be readily comprehensible by clients, so that they can make informed decisions. Analysts must communicate to clients the basic features or **characteristics of the investment**, and should set out the key **factors that support any recommendation**. Opinion (eg, on the future prospects of an investment) must be differentiated from fact.]

C. Record Retention. Members and Candidates must develop and maintain appropriate records to support their investment analyses, recommendations, actions, and other investment-related communications with clients and prospective clients.

[The hard copy or electronic files maintained by investment professionals should include sources of **information** and the **methodology** through which conclusions and recommendations were reached. Such files remain the property of the firm, not of the employee. The CFA Standard does not set down a minimum holding period, and local regulatory provisions should be followed. (See Chapter 3.)]

VI. Conflicts of interest

A. Disclosure of Conflicts. Members and Candidates must make full and fair disclosure of all matters that could reasonably be expected to impair their independence and objectivity or interfere with respective duties to their clients, prospective clients, and employer. Members and Candidates must ensure that such disclosures are prominent, are delivered in plain language, and communicate the relevant information effectively.

[This Standard emphasises full **disclosure** of conflicts of interest. This will enable the parties who are potentially affected to come to their own judgement about the objectivity of the advice and of the investment actions being taken. A conflict of interest could be present where the investment professional has a beneficial interest in a security; or where a firm has consultancy, underwriting and broker-dealer relationships in relation to an issuer that could conflict.

Investment professionals should report to their employer beneficial ownership that they have in securities, and any directorships or similar positions that might reasonably be considered to involve a conflict of interest. If in doubt, they should consult the matter with a supervisor or compliance officer.]

B. Priority of Transactions. Investment transactions for clients and employers must have priority over investment transactions in which a Member or Candidate is the beneficial owner.

[Conflicts may arise with IPOs (Initial Public Offerings) of stock where a price rise is expected on listing of the stock, or in respect of private placements. Conflicts will be avoided if investment professionals do not participate. Those involved in investment decision making should comply with a restricted period before trading for clients, to avoid '**front-running**' of client trades. The FCA rules on investment research are relevant here – see Chapter 3.]

BPP
LEARNING MEDIA

C. Referral Fees. Members and Candidates must disclose to their employer, clients, and prospective clients, as appropriate, any compensation, consideration, or benefit received from or paid to others for the recommendation of products or services.

[Disclosure should include the nature of the benefit and an estimate of the monetary value, and should take place before any arrangement is commenced. Investment professionals should consult a supervisor and legal counsel concerning such prospective arrangements.]

VII. Responsibilities as a CFA Institute Member or Candidate

A. Conduct as Members and Candidates in the CFA Program. Members and Candidates must not engage in any conduct that compromises the reputation or integrity of CFA Institute or the CFA designation, or the integrity, validity, or security of the CFA examinations.

B. Reference to CFA Institute, the CFA Designation, and the CFA Program. When referring to CFA Institute, CFA Institute membership, the CFA designation, or candidacy in the CFA Program, Members and Candidates must not misrepresent or exaggerate the meaning or implications of membership in CFA Institute, holding the CFA designation, or candidacy in the CFA program.

CHAPTER ROUNDUP

- Ethics is about rules, principles and standards to be observed, by people, by firms, and in society generally.

- The conduct of an organisation, its management and employees will be measured against ethical standards by the customers, suppliers and other members of the public with whom they deal. Perceptions of its conduct will determine the reputation of the organisation, which can take time to build up, while it can be reduced quickly.

- Ethical conduct by all team members should be a major concern for management. Inside the organisation, a compliance-based approach highlights conformity with the law. An integrity-based approach suggests a wider remit, incorporating ethics in the organisation's values and culture. Organisations sometimes issue codes of conduct to employees. Many employees are bound by professional codes of conduct.

- The CFA Code of Ethics covers placing the integrity of the profession and the interests of clients above your own interests; acting with integrity, competence, and respect; and improving and maintaining your professional competence.

- The CFA Standards of Professional Conduct cover: professionalism, integrity of the capital markets, duties to clients, duties to employers, investment analysis and recommendations, and conflicts of interest.

Test Your Knowledge

Check your knowledge of the chapter here, without referring back to the text.

1. How do Principle for Businesses 1 and Statement of Principle 1 relate to professional standards?

2. How could high ethical standards in financial services firms help in the fight to stop financial crime?

3. Theodore is a Chartered Financial Analyst and works for a City of London firm. His role is as an investment analyst, and he is based in a developing country. The country where he works is modernising rapidly but does not yet have laws prohibiting insider dealing. Theodore becomes aware of a takeover of a local firm which he expects to take place at a substantial premium, making a purchase of shares in the local firm potentially very attractive.

    Comment on whether Theodore has relevant obligations under the CFA Standards of Professional Conduct.

4. Scott Hambling is a CFA member and private client adviser who has been intensifying his marketing efforts recently in order to increase his client base. Scott presents a seminar at a golf club, to which selected club members have been invited. He discusses the recent performance of the stock market and explains that he has developed a method to predict future movements in stock market indices through identifying patterns in historical data. This method, he tells his audience, shows that there is certain to be an uplift in the main UK indices over the next six months.

    Comment on what Scott has told his audience with regard to the CFA Standards of Professional Conduct.

5. Gabriel is a Candidate in the CFA programme. He has spent eight weeks as an intern, without pay, at Renfrew Burton Advisers. In the course of the internship, Gabriel played a major role in drafting a compliance manual for the firm, as part of its efforts to prepare for the Retail Distribution Review. Towards the end of his internship, Gabriel accepts a paid position with Forward Point plc, another company which is seeking to prepare for implementation of the RDR. Gabriel makes copies of his work at Renfrew Burton, before his internship has ended, for use in his new role.

    Comment on Gabriel's actions with regard to the CFA Standards of Professional Conduct.

6. Scott Blair is an analyst at Ice Investment Company. He is currently working closely with Volcano Inc, a chocolate company that is in the process of preparing for a secondary equity offering. Scott is taking part in a conference call with Volcano, who are discussing the failed launch of a new product. The failed launch will result in a significant drop in earnings. Throughout the call, members of the Ice sales team are wandering in and out of Scott's office and hear the information about the failed launch and earnings fall. As a result, they sell stock from client, proprietary and employee accounts. Which of the following statements is most appropriate?

    A   Scott has breached Standard II.A Material Non-public Information by allowing the sales team in his office, but the sales team has not breached Standard II.A Material Non-public Information because they did not misappropriate the information

    B   Scott has not breached Standard II.A Material Non-public Information because he did not trade on the information or encourage the sales team to do so, but the sales team has breached Standard II.A Material Non-public Information by trading on the information

C   Scott has not breached Standard II.A Material Non-public Information because he did not trade on the information or encourage the sales team to do so, and the sales team has not breached Standard II.A Material Non-public Information because they did not misappropriate the information

D   Scott has breached Standard II.A Material Non-public Information because he did not prevent the transfer of the information and the sales team has breached Standard II.A Material Non-public Information by trading on the information

7.   Adam Long, an equity analyst, has got a one-off freelance assignment with Caspian, a fund management firm, whose CEO he knows from previous employment. The assignment is a report on Agala Inc, which was agreed over a meal and sealed with a handshake. Just before completing the task he is offered an interview for a full-time analyst position at a leading equity house. To impress them with the quality of his work, he is thinking of showing them the work he has done on Agala. Which of the following statements is most appropriate?

A   Adam cannot show the work he has done on Agala to his prospective employer as this would be a breach of Standard II B – Market Manipulation

B   Adam can show his work to his prospective employer because it is his work which he has not yet shown to Caspian and he has no written contract with Caspian

C   Adam must disclose his work to his prospective employer as not to do so would be a breach of Standard VI A – Disclosure of Conflicts, which requires disclosure of all matters of potential interest to potential employers

D   Adam should not disclose his work even though he has no written contract with Caspian. To do so would be a likely breach of Standard IV A – Loyalty

8.   Paula Yavy, a senior equity analyst at Hollander, has recently completed some research into Casco Inc and concluded that the stock should go on Hollander's buy list. Following well documented internal procedures she calls a team meeting and notifies her subordinates of her decision. One of her team, knowing it is against the firm's rules, buys stocks in Casco for their own account. Paula does not become aware of this action. Which of the following statements is most appropriate?

A   Paula has breached Standard VI A – Responsibilities of Supervisors as she should not have allowed one of her team to trade the stock based on her buy recommendation

B   Paula has not breached Standard VI A – Responsibilities of Supervisors as she was following well documented procedures to prevent what happened from happening

C   Paula has breached Standard VI A – Responsibilities of Supervisors as she failed to supervise reasonably and adequately the actions of those she supervises

D   Paula has not breached Standard VI A – Responsibilities of Supervisors as even the best designed compliance procedures cannot prevent all breaches from occurring

9.   Fred Connor is a precious metals analyst for Alpha Securities and has just finished a report on Gamma Gold mining Inc. In the report he has included an estimate of the gold reserves of Gamma's mines. Connor arrived at his estimation based on sample drilling information released by the company. In his opinion, the company has large reserves. On the back of his estimation he has made a buy recommendation. Which of the following standards is most likely to have been breached?

A   Standard III A – Loyalty, Prudence and Care
B   Standard IV C – Responsibilities of Supervisors
C   Standard V A – Diligence and Reasonable Basis
D   Standard V B – Communication with Clients and Prospective Clients

TEST YOUR KNOWLEDGE: ANSWERS

1. The regulators' first Principle for Businesses is Integrity: 'A firm must conduct its business with integrity.'

   The first Statement of Principle for Approved Persons is also Integrity: 'An approved person must act with integrity in carrying out his controlled functions.'

   (See Section 1.7.1)

2. High ethical standards could change the perception that it is easy to launder money in the UK, and reduce the scope for our firms and markets to be targeted by criminals in the first place. This can be done by developing individual responsibility and a sense of involvement by all staff.

   (See Section 1.8)

3. In the event of any conflict, Members and Candidates must comply with requirements and standards that are more strict than those of the country in which he is based. Theodore has received material non-public information and must abide by Standard II A. He must not act nor cause others to act on the information.

   (See Section 2.3)

4. Scott has contravened Standard III B, *Fair dealing*, which states that Members and Candidates must deal fairly and objectively with all clients when providing investment analysis, making investment recommendations, taking investment action, or engaging in other professional activities. The future course of stock market indices is uncertain and cannot be known with certainty.

   (See Section 2.3)

5. Although Gabriel's internship is unpaid, he has used resources of the firm in drafting the manual and he would be considered an employee because of the work experience and knowledge he is able to gain through the internship. By copying the material, Gabriel is in violation of his duties to an employer under Standard IV A.

   (See Section 2.3)

6. **D.** Standard II A – Material Non-public Information.

   (See Section 2.3)

7. **D.** Standard IV A – Loyalty. Even though Adam has no written contract he has an obligation to let Caspian act on the work he has done and should not disclose it to a prospective employer unless he obtains permission from Caspian to do so.

   (See Section 2.3)

8. **C.** Paula has failed in her supervisory role, not because her recommendation was acted upon as there were adequate procedures in place to prevent this, but because there were no procedures in place to review or record trading in a recommended stock .

   (See Section 2.3)

9. **C.** Connor should base his recommendation on more information that a drilling estimate.

   (See Section 2.3)

3

The regulation of financial markets and institutions

INTRODUCTION

Following the re-structuring of financial services regulation, the Financial Conduct Authority (FCA) and the Prudential Regulation Authority (PRA) are regulators of the financial services sector in the UK. The Bank of England now has much wider regulatory powers than before the 2013 re-structuring of regulation.

The regulators' strategy on supervision has been undergoing some change following the financial crisis of the late 2000s, with a more 'intrusive' approach being adopted.

The regulator has a duty to address financial crime, and we will examine in this Chapter how the financial services industry must keep in place measures to help prevent and stop such crime.

1 EU FINANCIAL SERVICES HARMONISATION

1.1 The single European market concept

Passporting for firms operating across borders is an important concept in the creation of the single market but is only one of various tools in trying to encourage cross-border activities. In recognition of the need for a co-ordinated approach to the creation of a single market in Europe, the EU convened the Lisbon Conference which led, in 1999, to the announcement of the aim of creating a single market in financial services, they had hoped, by 2005. This process is known as the **Financial Services Action Plan (FSAP)**.

The stated aims of the FSAP are to create a single wholesale market, an open and secure retail financial services market and state-of-the-art prudential rules and regulation. The longer-term aim at that time was that Europe would be the world's most competitive economy by 2010.

In order to achieve this, a committee of 'wise men' was set up, chaired by Alexandre Lamfalussy who is a senior European academic and adviser. This committee was charged with identifying targets for completing the single market for the investment industry by making the implementation of Directives more efficient and effective.

The 'wise men' proposed a **four-level approach** which has evolved, after **2011 changes** with the replacement of the former Level 3 committees with new **European Supervisory Authorities (ESAs)**, into the following form.

- **Level 1:** Framework legislation is proposed by the Commission and adopted by the European Council and the European Parliament, generally under the ordinary legislative procedure, otherwise through special legislative procedures. This legislation (Directive or Regulation) specifies in individual articles whether legislative power is delegated to the Commission to adopt Level 2 measures.

- **Level 2:** Secondary legislation is drafted and adopted by the Commission in line with the delegation of legislative competence in the Level 1 text. The Commission does this with the assistance of specialist committees of finance ministry experts.

    The Commission submits its draft measure to the relevant committee for discussion and receives its opinion. Oversight by the Council and Parliament of the exercise of delegated Commission power depends on the committee system (the so-called 'comitology procedure') specified in the Level 1 text.

    The Commission will often seek advice from the relevant ESA on the implementing measures, using this as it sees fit.

- **Level 3:** The **ESAs** advise the Commission when it prepares detailed Level 2 requirements.

    Where time permits, there is extensive consultation between the ESAs (comprising the **European Banking Authority (EBA), European Securities and Markets Authority (ESMA),** and **European Insurance and Occupational Pensions Authority (EIOPA))** and providers and users of financial services.

    The ESAs are also empowered to adopt guidance, which is to be treated on a comply-or-explain basis by national supervisors. The ESAs are required to consult and undertake cost benefit analysis on this 'where appropriate'.

BPP
LEARNING MEDIA

- **Level 4 Enforcement:** The Commission, as the guardian of the Treaties, is responsible for ensuring that directives are properly transposed and that EU legal requirements are then applied, pursuing enforcement action where required. The Commission has tended to concentrate its resources on the first of these. The ESAs provide an additional resource and opportunity to investigate alleged breaches of EU law. In the event that a breach is ascertained, the ESA may recommend a course of action to the competent authority concerned. If the competent authority fails to respond, the matter may be escalated. This may lead to the Commission issuing a formal opinion and, if certain conditions are met, a decision addressed to an individual financial institution.

While the aims of Lamfalussy may be applauded, the practicalities of creating a complete single market remain questionable. Arguably a large number of barriers have stood in the way of full and meaningful integration, including the following.

- Lack of proper implementation of Directives by some member states
- Delay in implementation of Directives by some member states
- Lack of real censures for non-compliant member states
- Lack of consumer desire to deal with foreign service providers
- Lack of integration of cross-border settlement and clearing services
- Lack of full coverage of the FSAP measures
- Protectionism in some member states, eg requiring market-makers to have a local presence
- Differences in law, language and culture throughout the EU
- Lack of a clear view as to what a single market might ultimately look like

1.2 The late 2000s financial markets crisis and its consequences

The **Financial Stability Forum (FSF)** was a body made up of authorities from various major countries and international institutions. After the April 2009 G20 Summit in London, the FSF became the **Financial Stability Board (FSB)**. In April 2008, the FSF reported on the recent turmoil in financial markets.

The FSF's report noted that the turmoil that broke out in the summer of 2007 followed an exceptional boom in **credit growth** and **leverage** in the financial system. A long period of **benign economic and financial conditions** had increased the amount of risk that borrowers and investors were willing to take on. Institutions responded, expanding the market for securitisation of credit risk and aggressively developing the **'originate and distribute' model**: institutions originating loans then distributed them as packaged securities. The system became increasingly dependent on originators' underwriting standards and the performance of credit rating agencies.

By the summer of 2008, accumulating losses on US **subprime mortgages** were triggering widespread disruption to the global financial system. Large losses were sustained on complex structured securities. Institutions reduced leverage and increased demand for liquid assets. Many credit markets became illiquid, hindering credit extension.

Eight months after the start of the market turmoil, many financial institutions' balance sheets were burdened by assets that have suffered major declines in value and vanishing market liquidity. Market participants were reluctant to transact in these instruments, adding to increased financial and macroeconomic uncertainty.

To re-establish confidence in the soundness of markets and financial institutions, the FSF authorities began to take exceptional steps with a view to facilitating adjustment and **dampening the impact on the real economy**. These steps have included **monetary and fiscal stimulus**, **central bank liquidity operations**, policies to **promote asset market liquidity** and actions to **resolve problems at specific institutions**. Financial institutions have taken steps to rebuild capital and liquidity cushions.

The turmoil in markets heightened focus on the debate about how European regulatory initiatives are organised. Changes the EU has agreed to the structure of regulatory and supervisory cooperation include the new **European Systemic Risk Board (ESRB)** that was set up at the beginning of 2011.

Operating at arm's length from the European Central Bank (ECB), the **ESRB** has powers to issue warnings and recommendations on threats to economies and financial systems. The ESRB's voting members include the EU member countries' central bank governors, the ECB President and ECB Vice-President, and the chairmen of the three **European Supervisory Authorities (ESAs)** covering banking, insurance and securities markets, which replace the earlier Lamfalussy Level 3 committees.

1.3 Role and powers of ESMA

1.3.1 ESMA's role

As stated in its official material, ESMA is an independent EU Authority that contributes to safeguarding the stability of the European Union's financial system by:

- Ensuring the integrity, transparency, efficiency and orderly functioning of securities markets, and
- Enhancing investor protection

ESMA aims to foster supervisory convergence among **securities regulators**, and also **across financial sectors** by working closely with the other ESAs competent in the field of **banking (EBA)**, and insurance and **occupational pensions (EIOPA)**.

ESMA's work on **securities** legislation contributes to the development of a single rule book in Europe, with two purposes:

- To ensure the consistent treatment of investors across the EU, enabling an adequate level of protection of investors through effective regulation and supervision

- To promote equal conditions of competition for financial service providers

As part of its role in standard setting and reducing the scope of regulatory arbitrage, ESMA strengthens international supervisory co-operation. Where requested in European law, ESMA supervises certain pan-European entities.

Finally, ESMA also contributes to the financial stability of the EU, in the short, medium and long-term, through its contribution to the work of the ESRB, which seeks to identify potential risks to the financial system and to provide advice to diminish possible threats to the financial stability of the EU. ESMA is also responsible for coordinating actions of securities supervisors or adopting emergency measures when a crisis situation arises.

1.3.2 ESMA's competences and powers

Although ESMA continues the work of the former Committee of European Securities Regulators (CESR), the Authority has new competencies and powers, including the following:

- The ability to draft legally binding technical standards in EU Member States

- The ability to launch a fast-track procedure to ensure consistent application of EU law

- Powers in resolving disagreements between national authorities

- Additional consumer protection responsibilities, including the ability to prohibit financial products that threaten financial stability or the orderly functioning of financial markets for a period of three months

- Emergency powers

- Participation in Colleges of Supervisors and on-site inspections

BPP LEARNING MEDIA

- Monitoring systemic risk of cross-border financial institutions

- A new supervisory role, in particular for credit rating agencies

- The ability to enter into administrative arrangements with supervisory authorities, international organisations and the administrations of third countries

1.3.3 ESMA and the 4-level legislative procedure

The Authority explains its role within the revised 4-level legislative procedure as follows.

- Level 1 Directives and regulations continue to set out the high level political objectives on the area concerned by the legislation. Occasionally, at this early stage, ESMA may be asked for technical advice by the Commission as it develops its legislative proposal.

- However, ESMA has been given a greater role in Level 2 in drafting what can be considered as subordinate acts (known as delegated acts and implementing acts). Delegated acts are concerned more with the substantive content of the legislative requirement, for example setting out what authorisation information firms must provide to competent authorities, whilst implementing acts are similar to executive measures giving effect to the substantive requirements, this might include for example, standard forms, templates and procedures for communicating information or processes between competent authorities.

- At Level 3, ESMA will develop guidelines and recommendations with a view to establishing consistent, efficient and effective supervisory practices within the European System of Financial Supervision, and to ensure the common, uniform and consistent application of Union Law. The guidelines and recommendations are addressed to competent authorities or financial market participants. Whilst not legally binding, these have been strengthened under ESMA and competent authorities must now make every effort to comply and must explain if they do not intend to comply. Financial market participants can also be required to report publically whether they comply. ESMA will also take other steps under Level 3 to ensure supervisory convergence.

- At Level 4, a fast track procedure has been introduced by the Regulation establishing ESMA. On this basis, ESMA now has a new role. At the request of a national competent authority, the European Parliament, Council, Commission or the Stakeholder Group, ESMA can be requested to launch an enquiry and can issue a recommendation addressed to the national authority, within two months of launching its investigation. ESMA will also be able to launch investigations on its own initiative. The Commission will also be able to follow its usual procedures for referring a case against the Member State to the Court of Justice.

1.4 Markets in Financial Instruments Directive

Learning objective — 3.1.3 **Explain** the purpose and scope of the Markets in Financial Instrument Directive (MiFID) with respect to: passporting, roles of the home and host state, core and non-core investment services, financial instruments covered by the legislation

1.4.1 Overview

The **Markets in Financial Instruments Directive (MiFID)** was adopted by the European Council in April 2004 and is part of the European **Financial Services Action Plan**. MiFID was originally due for implementation in April 2006. However, due to the number of changes that MiFID requires the industry to make, the deadline was deferred twice, delaying its effective date until **1 November 2007**.

MiFID replaces the previous Investment Services Directive (ISD), and it applies to all **investment firms**, eg investment and retail banks, brokers, assets managers, securities and futures firms, securities issuers and hedge funds. For more detail on the criteria for establishing whether a firm is subject to MiFID, see 'Scope of MiFID', later in this Section.

EU Directives require the law in each country to be changed by Parliament in accordance with the Directive.

1.4.2 Passporting within the EEA

The idea of a **'passport'**, which already existed under the ISD, enables firms to use their domestic authorisation to operate not only in their **home state**, but also in other **host states** within the **European Economic Area** (EEA) (EU plus Norway, Iceland and Liechtenstein).

An important aspect of MiFID is that, to make cross-border business easier, the home country principle has been extended. Under MiFID, investment firms which carry out specified investment services and activities (a wider range than under the ISD, as detailed below) are authorised by the member State in which they their registered office is located (the **home state**).

Where a **branch** is set up, **host state** rules will continue to apply. A **tied agent** established in the EEA will be able to act on behalf of a firm instead of the firm needing to set up a branch. (A **'tied agent'**, similarly to an **appointed representative** under FSMA 2000, acts on behalf of and under the authority of an investment firm and as a result does not require authorisation.)

Where a firm makes use of a passport:

- **Organisational matters** will be regulated by the **home state**: these include authorisation, fitness and propriety, capital adequacy, Principles for Businesses, senior management arrangements, systems and controls, client assets including client money, conflicts of interest, personal account dealing (as covered in the conduct of business rules, COBS), investment research (COBS), transaction reporting and transparency, and compensation arrangements.

- **Operational matters**, for example conduct of business rules which are not 'organisational matters' will be regulated by:

    - The **host state**, for activities of a branch 'within its territory'
    - The **home state**, for cross-border services

1.4.3 Scope of MiFID

MiFID applies to a specified range of 'core' **investment services and activities** in relation to specified categories of **financial instruments**, as summarised below.

- **Investment firms** are firms which provide such services or engage in such activities.

- Investment firms are also regulated in respect of various 'non-core' **ancillary services** they may provide (as also listed below).

- **Credit institutions** (which includes banks and building societies, in the UK) are regulated by the Banking Consolidation Directive. MiFID provisions will however apply, including organisational and conduct of business requirements, when EEA credit institutions provide investment services to clients, perform investment activities (PERG 13.2, Q5).

Investment services and activities

- Receiving and transmitting orders
- Execution of orders on behalf of clients
- Dealing on own account
- Managing portfolios on a discretionary basis
- Investment advice

- Underwriting of financial instruments
- Placing of financial instruments
- Operating a Multilateral Trading Facility (MTF)

Ancillary services

- Safekeeping and administration of financial instruments, including: custodianship; collateral and cash management

- Granting credit or loans to an investor to enable him to carry out a transaction in which the firm is involved

- Advising undertakings on capital structure, industrial strategy

- Advising on mergers and acquisitions

- Foreign exchange services connected with providing investment services

- Investment research, financial analysis or other general recommendations relating to transactions in financial instruments

The broad range of UK firms falling under the rules as MiFID firms comprises: dealing and managing firms, MTFs, corporate finance firms, venture capital firms, commodity firms, oil and energy market participants, credit institutions carrying on MiFID business, exchanges, UCITS investment firms, and certain advisers and professional firms.

1.4.4 MiFID exclusions

Although MiFID has extended regulation beyond what was regulated under the ISD, there are a number of exclusions. These exclusions mean that a significant part of the **retail financial services sector** falls outside the scope of MiFID, as explained below.

MiFID's overall scope is narrower than the UK regulatory regime. However, a UK exclusion (in the Regulated Activities Order) will not apply if it conflicts with MiFID.

The following are **excluded** from the scope of MiFID.

- **Insurance companies** including reinsurers

- **Pension funds** and **collective investment schemes**, and their depositories or managers, although UCITS managers who provide advice or discretionary management to clients who are not funds will generally be subject to MiFID requirements

- **Group treasury activities**

- **Persons administering their own assets**

- **Professional investors** investing only for themselves

- **Commodity producers and traders**

- Investment services relating to administration of **employee share schemes**

- **Incidental business in the course of professional activity** bound by legal, ethical or regulatory provisions

- **Firms not providing investment services** or involved in investment activities

MiFID **Article 3** allows Member States **to exclude** from MiFID the activities of the firms whose investment services are limited to receiving and transmitting orders in transferable securities or collective investment schemes, plus related advice. (The UK exercised this exemption.) Such firms may not hold client money or securities, nor put themselves in debt to the client. Orders must be transmitted only to investment firms, credit institutions, EEA-regulated collective investment schemes or closed-ended funds traded on a regulated market in the EEA. Many firms of **financial advisers** and other **retail investment product**

distributors will meet these criteria, and the UK has enabled them to be excluded from MiFID regulation. Such firms may alternatively opt in, in order to benefit from **passporting**.

1.4.5 The 'common platform'

The organisational and systems and controls requirements of **MiFID** and the **Capital Requirements Directive (CRD)** are implemented through a single set of organisational requirements in the FCA's Handbook (SYSC Chapters 4-10), known as the '**common platform**'. The common platform applies to firms which are subject to either or both of CRD. Additionally, the common platform was extended beyond MiFID firms with effect from 1 April 2009. Now, most firms come within the common platform, and the only firms outside it are insurers, managing agents and the Society of Lloyd's.

1.5 UCITS Directives

Learning objective	**3.1.4 Explain** the purpose and scope of the Undertakings for Collective Investment in Transferable Securities (UCITS) Directives

1.5.1 EU provisions on collective investment schemes

The EU has enacted a number of directives relevant to collective investment schemes (CISs). These are known as the **UCITS Directives. UCITS** stands for **Undertakings for Collective Investment in Transferable Securities**.

The aim of UCITS was to create a type of passport throughout the EEA for collective investment schemes that meet the UCITS criteria. The idea was to promote the free movement of services in the same way as investment firms can passport their services throughout the EEA.

The CIS must be authorised in its home State and receive confirmation from its home State regulator that the CIS complies with UCITS criteria. That confirmation is then provided to the host State regulator, who the fund manager notifies that they wish to market the fund in that EEA state. Although UCITS aims to make cross-border sales of CIS easier, the CIS must comply with the marketing rules of the host state and the documentation requirements of the directive.

The first **UCITS Directive** contained a number of limitations. The main limitation was that the definition of **permitted investments** was very narrow. This meant that generally schemes wanting to use UCITS to sell cross-border could only invest in transferable securities. Initially the permitted investments included securities funds (containing for example shares and bonds), warrant funds and umbrella funds, where each sub-fund is either a securities fund or a warrant fund. In addition, the first UCITS Directive contained various categories of scheme, eg a securities fund and an umbrella fund, with separate investment rules for each category.

UCITS was updated in 2002 by the **UCITS III Product Directive,** which expanded the range of assets which UCITS funds are able to invest in. It also made provision for a single UCITS scheme to replace all of the previous categories of fund which had separate rules.

UCITS IV, implemented in July 2011, enhances the UCITS regime with:

- A simplified notification procedure for funds
- Procedures for fund mergers
- Cross-border 'master-feeder' structures
- A new standardised 'key investor information' (KII) document

1.5.2 UCITS schemes

As a result of the **UCITS Product Directive**, UCITS schemes are now able to invest in the following types of **permitted investment**.

- Transferable securities (see below)
- Money market instruments
- Forward contracts and financial derivatives
- Deposits
- Units in other Collective Investment Schemes

Transferable securities comprise shares, instruments creating or acknowledging indebtedness (eg debentures, loan stock, bonds, government and public securities) and certificates representing certain securities.

Although **commodity derivatives** are excluded, it would appear that derivatives based on commodity indices could be eligible as financial derivatives.

1.6 European Market Infrastructure Regulation (EMIR)

Learning objective	3.1.5 **Explain** the purpose and scope of the European Market Infrastructure Regulation (EMIR)

The **European Market Infrastructure Regulation (EMIR)** has the purpose of enhancing stability in the over-the-counter (OTC) derivatives markets of the EU.

EMIR implements a G20 commitment to have all EU **standardised OTC derivatives** cleared through a CCP.

EMIR comprises a set of standards for regulation of OTC derivatives, central counterparties (CCPs) and trade repositories.

Aspects of EMIR

- **Reporting obligations for OTC derivatives**. Counterparties to all derivatives contracts are required to report post-trade contract details to a registered trade repository. This requirement will capture all exchange and OTC derivative trades, intragroup trades, and trades with non-financial counterparties.

- **Clearing obligations for eligible OTC derivatives to be cleared through CCPs**. This will apply to contracts between any combination of financial counterparties or non-financial counterparties (NFCs) that are above the clearing threshold.

  The clearing thresholds for firms are:

  - €1bn in gross notional value for OTC credit and equity derivatives (individual thresholds)
  - €3bn in gross notional value for interest rate and foreign exchange (individual thresholds)
  - €3bn in gross notional value for commodities and others (combined threshold)

  Transactions designed to reduce risks to commercial activity or treasury financing activity are exempted from the clearing threshold. The European Securities and Markets Authority (ESMA) will determine the classes of OTC derivatives that must be cleared and ESMA will maintain a register showing which CCPs are permitted to clear derivatives of each class.

- **New risk mitigation requirements for all OTC derivative trades that are not centrally cleared**. These requirements are concerned with timely confirmation, dispute resolution, reconciliation and portfolio compression. (Portfolio compression replaces existing contracts so as to reduce the overall notional size and number of outstanding contracts without changing the risk profile or present value of portfolios.) For counterparties subject to the clearing obligation, there will be additional requirements concerning initial and variation margin and daily valuation for their uncleared trades.

- **Common rules for CCPs and for trade repositories**. All derivative contracts are to be reported, by both financial and non-financial counterparties, to a trade repository by the following working day. Trade repositories include TriOptima and DTCC.

- **Rules on the establishment of interoperability between CCPs**.

The EMIR came into force in mid-2012, but full implementation is expected to occur over a series of dates during 2013 and 2014. Under the new rules, all standardised OTC derivative contracts should be traded on exchanges or electronic trading platforms, where appropriate, and cleared through CCPs.

In the UK, EMIR has been implemented through the **Financial Services and Markets Act 2000 (Over the Counter Derivatives, Central Counterparties and Trade Repositories) Regulations 2013**.

2 UK FINANCIAL SERVICES REGULATION

2.1 Statutory regulation of financial services

The creation of the **Financial Services Authority (FSA)** as the UK's main **statutory regulator** for the industry brought together regulation of investment, insurance and banking.

With the implementation of FSMA 2000, the FSA took over responsibility in 2001 for:

- Prudential supervision of all regulated firms, which involves monitoring the adequacy of their management, financial resources and internal systems and controls, and

- Conduct of business regulations. This involves overseeing firms' dealings with investors to ensure, for example, that information provided is clear and not misleading

Arguably, the FSA's role as rule-maker was diminished by the requirements of EU Single Market Directives – in particular, the far-reaching **Markets in Financial Instruments Directive (MiFID)**, implemented in November 2007 – as the FSA increasingly needed to apply rules which have been formulated at the **European level**.

2.2 The new UK regulatory structure

The regulation of the UK financial services industry has continued to evolve and react to new circumstances as they develop. There was criticism of the FSA for failing to be aware of the weakness of banks such as **Northern Rock**, which required emergency assistance and had to be nationalised. The financial turmoil of the late 2000s stemmed in large part from excessive lending by banks, particularly to sub-prime borrowers, and from the 'securitisation' or packaging of mortgages by lenders for selling on to investors who were insufficiently aware of the risks attached to the securities, This period of turmoil has highlighted the need for continuing review and reform of regulatory arrangements.

In **June 2010**, with a new Conservative-Liberal Democratic coalition Government in power, it was announced that the Financial Services Authority in its current form would be abolished.

- The changes bring a sweeping increase in the powers of the **Bank of England**, which has a new remit of preventing a build-up of risk in the financial system. At the top of the regulatory structure, a new subsidiary of the Bank based on the FSA's Prudential Business Unit (which was formed in

April 2011), the **Prudential Regulation Authority (PRA)** has become the prudential regulator responsible for ensuring the safe operation of over 1,000 deposit-taking institutions, as well as insurers, investment banks and some other institutions.

- The FSA legal entity became the **Financial Conduct Authority (FCA)**, which will be responsible for consumer protection in financial services, the regulation of conduct of business (including in firms regulated by the new PRA) and market conduct. The European Supervisory Authorities (ESAs) have the task of drawing up European standards including rules for consumer protection and financial innovation. The FCA will be the lead UK authority in ESMA and will be active with the other ESAs, EBA and EIOPA, in consumer protection activity.

The **re-structuring of the regulator into the PRA and FCA** – with the so-called 'twin peaks' regulatory structure – was implemented on 1 April 2013. The FSA had moved to a 'twin peaks' operating model in advance of the re-structuring, in April 2012.

2.3 Dual regulation

Firms that are '**dual regulated**', such as banks, insurers and major investment firms, will be supervised by two independent groups for **prudential** and **conduct** regulation. These groups will work to different objectives and act separately with firms, but will coordinate internally to share information and data.

All other firms will be supervised by one supervision area for both conduct and prudential issues.

The FCA and PRA will operate separate **authorisation** functions, but there will be a single authorisation process for dual-regulated firms. Dual-regulated firms will apply to the PRA unless they are directed to apply to the FCA. In applications from dual-regulated firms for authorisation, variation of permission and **approval of persons** carrying out controlled functions, the FCA will either give or refuse consent. If the FCA does not give its consent, the PRA must reject the application. In cases of a change in control, passporting to operate in different EEA countries, or a cancellation of permission, the PRA must consult the FCA but it is not bound by the FCA's response.

The FCA and the PRA will operate different sets of **threshold conditions** that firms must meet in order to be authorised.

Before taking **enforcement action** against a dual-regulated firm, the FCA will consult the PRA. The regulators will then decide whether to carry out an investigation jointly, or separately.

The supervision models will be different for the PRA and FCA:

- **Prudential supervision** will continue to have dedicated resources supervising firms, and
- **Conduct supervision** will focus more on thematic work, and less on firm-specific work

2.4 Financial Conduct Authority (FCA)

As an '**integrated conduct**' regulator, the **FCA** will look across the whole financial services sector, not only in **investment and capital markets** but also in **banking and wholesale insurance markets**. The FCA can be expected to be more interventionist than the FSA was. For example, the FCA has been given a product intervention power, which will give it the 'flexibility to intervene quickly and decisively where it considers that a product or product feature is likely to result in significant consumer detriment. The FCA will seek to deal with the root of the problem, rather than reacting to the effects, when it is already too late. Product approval by firms is sometimes referred to as **New Product Due Diligence (NPDD)**, a process which will become of more importance under the regulator's new product intervention policy.

The FCA (and the PRA) will be able to make public certain information relating to **enforcement** investigations at the warning notice stage, instead of when the Final Notice is published, as is presently the case. The financial services industry has argued that earlier publication could lead to significant reputational damage and could undermine consumer confidence.

2.5 Prudential Regulation Authority (PRA)

The PRA will be responsible for the prudential regulation of banks, insurance companies and large investment firms. Only these firms will be subject to '**dual regulation**' (see the diagram *New UK regulatory architecture*).

The PRA has a single **general objective** is fundamentally different from that of earlier regulatory regimes and is:

Promoting the safety and soundness of PRA-authorised persons (s2B FSMA 2000)

The new Authority is to meet this objective primarily by seeking to minimise any adverse effects of firm failure on the UK financial system and by ensuring that firms carry on their business in a way that avoids adverse effects on the stability of the system.

Regarding insurance, the PRA has a more specific **insurance objective** of: contributing to the securing of an appropriate degree of protection for those who are or may become policyholders (s2C FSMA 2000).

The purpose of the PRA is to focus on the stability of the system overall, albeit through the mechanism of the supervision of individual firms. This will require close coordination with the new **Financial Policy Committee**, whose role it will be to manage the risks in the system as a whole. The PRA will be a key contributor to the information and analysis on which the Financial Policy Committee (FPC) will base its judgements.

Given the PRA's statutory objective to contribute to financial stability, supervisory efforts will focus on **large international banks**. In the case of UK subsidiaries of overseas banks, links of the UK entity with the group as a whole as well as the group's viability need to be an integral part of the PRA's supervisory assessment.

Regarding insurance, the PRA will have the more specific **insurance objective** of contributing to securing an appropriate degree of protection for policyholders.

In order to deliver its objective of stability of the financial system, the PRA will use a new framework to assess **risks to financial stability**.

Risks to a firm will be identified using:

- Baseline monitoring
- Investigation and assurance
- The macroeconomic and business context

The PRA will take a forward-looking and **judgment-based approach to supervision**. Baseline monitoring will be undertaken for all firms, including those that can be resolved with minimal disruption to the financial system (eg credit unions and small deposit-takers). This monitoring will include a review of a firm's resolvability (at least) once a year, analysis of a firm's financial position, discussions with senior management and ensuring compliance with minimum prudential standards for capital, liquidity and large exposures, as well as early interventions (where necessary) driven by a **Proactive Intervention Framework (PIF)**.

UK regulatory architecture

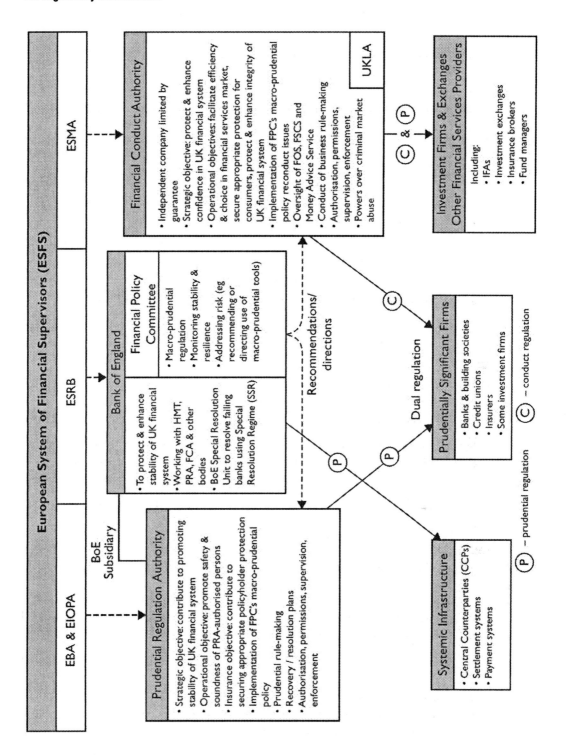

2.6 The Bank of England

The responsibility of the **UK's central bank**, the **Bank of England**, for banking supervision was transferred to the **FSA** – the previous regulator – as part of the **Bank of England Act 1998**. Despite losing responsibility for banking supervision, the Bank of England ('the Bank') gained the role in 1998 of **setting official UK interest rates**, a role carried out by the Bank's **Monetary Policy Committee (MPC)**.

The Bank of England ('the Bank') – the central bank of the United Kingdom – plays an important role in the regulatory system. The Bank's **Financial Policy Committee (FPC)** plays a key regulatory role, and the **PRA** is a subsidiary of the Bank.

The Bank has two core purposes: to **ensure monetary stability** and to **contribute to financial stability**.

- **Monetary stability** means stable prices and confidence in the currency. Stable prices are defined by the Government's inflation target, which the Bank seeks to meet through the decisions delegated to the Monetary Policy Committee (which sets benchmark interest rates), explaining those decisions transparently and implementing them effectively in the money markets.

- **Financial stability** entails detecting and reducing threats to the financial system as a whole. This is pursued through the Bank's financial and other operations, including lender of last resort, oversight of key infrastructure and the surveillance and policy roles delegated to the Financial Policy Committee (FPC).

The Bank is able to make **interventions in the currency markets**, to the extent that its currency reserves enable it to do so.

The Bank of England also undertakes **open market operations** in the money markets to implement monetary policy. (including **'quantitative easing'**, termed more colloquially **'printing money'**, although it generally refers to creating balances rather than actually printing banknotes). In addition, the Bank operates the wholesale payments system, the real-time gross settlements system.

The Bank is also the financial system's '**lender of last resort**', being ready to provide funds in exceptional circumstances, as occurred when the bank Northern Rock got into financial difficulties in 2007.

2.7 Financial Policy Committee (FPC)

The would-be functions of the Council for Financial Stability and the Bank of England's Financial Stability Committee have been merged into the **Financial Policy Committee (FPC)** of the Bank. In common with the existing Councils, the new FPC has representatives from prudential regulators and from HM Treasury. Additionally, the 11-member FPC also has external representation and will meet four times annually and at times of crisis.

The FPC will address issues of financial stability and resilience at the 'macro' level – that is, at the level of the economy and the financial services sector and sub-sectors. These are referred to as **macro-prudential** risks, while risks at the level of the firm are **micro-prudential** risks.

The absence of an effective macro-prudential agency was considered to have been a major failing in the UK, EU and US before the recent financial crisis. This lack was highlighted with the inability of the authorities to deal with asset price bubbles, especially in the property market, and the accumulation of debt and leverage across the financial system.

S9C Bank of England (BoE) Act 1998 (as amended by FSA 2012) provides that the FPC is to exercise its functions with a view to:

- Contributing to the achievement by the Bank of England of the **Financial Stability Objective**, and

BPP
LEARNING MEDIA

- Subject to that, supporting the economic policy of the Government, including its objectives for growth and employment

The Bank's **Financial Stability Objective** is stated in s2A Bank of England Act 1998 (as amended by FSA 2012), which states that an objective of the Bank shall be: **To protect and enhance the stability of the financial system of the UK.**

The responsibility of the Committee in relation to the achievement by the Bank of the Financial Stability Objective relates primarily to the identification of, monitoring of, and taking of action to remove or reduce, **systemic risks** with a view to protecting and enhancing the resilience of the UK financial system (s9C(2) BoE Act 1998). Systemic risk here means a risk to the stability of the UK financial system as a whole or of a significant part of that system, whether the risk arises in the UK or elsewhere.

Those **systemic risks** include, in particular:

- Systemic risks attributable to structural features of financial markets, such as connections between financial institutions

- Systemic risks attributable to the distribution of risk within the financial sector, and

- Unsustainable levels of leverage, debt or credit growth (s9C(3) BoE Act 1998)

The legislation does not require or authorise the FPC to exercise its functions in a way that would in its opinion be likely to have a significant adverse effect on the capacity of the financial sector to contribute to the growth of the UK economy in the medium or long term.

The **FPC** will have the following **tools** at its disposal:

- Setting system-wide cyclical capital requirements, reducing capital buffers required in a crisis while toughening them in more favourable economic times

- Altering risk weights, enabling the Bank to force banks to hold more capital against specific classes of assets in apparently frothy markets

- Setting limits on leverage as a backstop against excessive lending where changing risk weights might not be effective

- Requiring forward-looking loss provisioning to prepare for future losses when lending growth is strong

- Setting limits on borrowing, eg with maximum loan-to-value ratios for mortgages

- Setting limits on lending through regulation

Although these functions might work better if implemented at the international level, Deputy Governor of the Bank Paul Tucker has expressed the view that they should also work if put into effect only in the UK.

2.8 Systemic financial crisis management

Under the 2013 re-structuring of regulation, the Bank of England has primary operational responsibility for **financial crisis management**.

When it is clear that **public funds may be put at risk,** the Governor of the BoE will have a statutory duty to notify the Chancellor.

A crisis management **memorandum of understanding (MoU)** underpins the process.

The MoU addresses:

- The responsibilities of the Bank and HM Treasury in a crisis
- The duty of the BoE to notify the Treasury of a risk to public funds
- The Chancellor's exercise of a power of direction over the Bank in a crisis

This process will now be backed up by a **statutory duty** to coordinate the exercise of these functions in a crisis.

As a power of last resort, the Treasury can direct the Bank:

- To provide liquidity support during a crisis, and
- To exercise its powers under the special resolution regime

A January 2012 '**New Approach**' paper stresses that this power is exercisable only where there is a real risk to financial stability, or public funds have already been used, and that the BoE retains operational autonomy when managing threats to stability in which public funds are not at risk.

2.9 HM Treasury

The **Treasury** is the United Kingdom's economics and finance ministry. It is responsible for formulating and implementing the UK Government's financial and economic policy. The Chancellor of the Exchequer has overall responsibility for the work of the Treasury.

The Treasury's aim is to raise the rate of sustainable growth and achieve rising prosperity and a better quality of life, with economic and employment opportunities for all.

It has various objectives and performance targets including maintaining a stable macroeconomic environment with low inflation and sound public finances. It is the Treasury that have determined that the Bank of England should target at inflation level of 2%, as measured by the 12 month increase in the Consumer Price Index.

The Debt Management Office is an agency of the Treasury. The DMO takes responsibility for issuing government debt.

2.10 HM Treasury and the FCA

The minister with overall responsibility for the Treasury, the Chancellor of the Exchequer, is ultimately responsible for the regulatory system for financial services under FSMA 2000.

HM Treasury, to which the **FCA is accountable**, will judge the regulator against the requirements laid down in FSMA 2000 which includes a requirement to ensure that the burdens imposed on the regulated community are proportionate to the benefits it will provide.

Accountability of the FCA to HM Treasury

- HM Treasury has the power to **appoint or to dismiss the Board and Chairman of the FCA**.

- HM Treasury requires that the FCA submit an **annual report** covering such matters as the discharge of its functions and the extent to which the regulatory objectives have been met.

- HM Treasury also has powers to commission and publish an independent review of the **economy, efficiency and effectiveness** of the FCA's use of resources and to commission official enquiries into serious regulatory failures.

2.11 Other bodies

Learning objectives

3.2.6 Explain the function of the following bodies / persons: the Panel for Takeovers and Mergers, the Department for Business Innovation and Skills, the Office of Fair Trading, the Competition Commission, and the Information Commissioner

3.2.7 Explain the make-up of the Panel on Takeovers and Mergers (the Takeover Panel) and how it is financed

2.11.1 The Office of Fair Trading (OFT)

The **Office of Fair Trading (OFT)** has the goal of helping make markets work well for consumers. Markets work well, the OFT states, 'when fair-dealing businesses are in open and vigorous competition with each other for custom'.

The OFT offers advice, support and guidance to businesses on competition issues and on consumer legislation. It also seeks to promote good practice in business by granting 'approved status' to Consumer Codes of Practice meeting set criteria. The OFT will pursue businesses that rig prices or use unfair terms in contracts.

The OFT also regulates the consumer credit market with the aim of ensuring fair dealing by businesses in the market. It operates a **licensing system** through which checks are carried out on consumer credit businesses and issues guidelines on how the law will be enforced.

2.11.2 The OFT and the FCA and PRA

The OFT has specific responsibilities under FSMA 2000.

It is part of the role of the OFT to keep under review the activities and rules of the regulators with respect to competition issues.

If the OFT believes that regulatory rules will impact adversely on competition, then it will report this to the FCA, the Treasury and the **Competition Commission (CC)** (see above).

A **Memorandum of Understanding (MOU)** covers procedures in areas of common interest between the OFT and the FCA and PRA, to foster co-operation and to avoid duplication.

The Government has announced that the **regulation of the consumer credit market** will be transferred from the OFT to the FCA on 1 April 2014. The regulator plans to work with consumers, the industry and Government to develop proposals for effective regulation that helps the market to work well and seeks to ensure fair treatment for consumers. Proposals include an interim permission for OFT licence holders to continue to carry on regulated consumer credit activities.

2.11.3 The Competition Commission

The **Competition Commission (CC)** has a general function in ensuring that the operation of the regulatory regime set up under FSMA 2000 and the exercise by the FCA of its powers under the Act cannot be considered anti-competitive and that there are no adverse effects on competition.

More specifically, the CC has the following two roles under FSMA 2000.

- The first role (under **s162** FSMA 2000) concerns the FCA's rules, guidance and statements of principle, which the **Office of Fair Trading (OFT)** is responsible for keeping under review.

- The second role (under **s306** FSMA 2000) relates to the regulatory provisions and practices of **Recognised Investment Exchanges** and **Recognised Clearing Houses**. The OFT is also required to keep these regulatory provisions and practices under review.

In both cases, the **OFT** must make a **report** if it considers that rules, guidance and principles, or regulatory provisions and practices, have a significantly adverse effect on competition. The OFT may also make a report if it considers that there is no such effect on competition.

Any such report made by the OFT must be sent to the CC. The **CC** must **investigate** the subject matter of the OFT's report. If that report concludes that there is a significant adverse effect on competition and the OFT has asked the CC to consider the report, the CC must make its own report, unless it considers – giving reasons – that no useful purpose would be served by a report.

If the CC makes a report and concludes that there is an adverse effect on competition, it must also state whether it considers that the effect is justified and if not, state what action the Treasury ought to direct the FCA to take. The Treasury will then consider whether to direct to the regulators to take action.

2.11.4 Overview of competition regulation

Statutory Merger Control

Office of Fair Trading

Looks at current takeovers and mergers
to ascertain if there has been a
substantial lessening of competition

May clear (i.e. bid can go ahead) or refer
the bid to Competition Commission

Competition Commission

Commission investigates the bid and
recommends whether there has been a
substantial lessening of competition

Bid is block   **Bid is cleared**

UK competition regulations are designed to ensure mergers and acquisitions are not going to result in uncompetitive practices or a **substantial lessening of competition**.

Competition investigations have a two-tier approach involving Office of Fair Trading (OFT) investigation followed by possible reference to the Competition Commission for a second-stage, in-depth investigation where necessary.

The only exception to this is where **Secretary of State for Business, Innovation and Skills** intervenes in cases of national security. The Secretary of State is head of the Department for Business, Innovation and Skills (BIS).

The main statutory rules on competition are within the **2002 Enterprise Act**.

As guidance, the following scenarios will qualify for OFT investigation.

- The combined enterprise **controls at least 25%** of the goods or services in the sector in the UK (the **share of supply test**), or
- The UK turnover of the entity being acquired **exceeds £70 million** (the **turnover test**)

The OFT can investigate **four months** from when the transaction is made public. Cases referred to the CC must normally be investigated **within 24 weeks** of the date of reference.

The CC has the power to **impose fines** for failure to comply with any request for information.

The CC will publish preliminary findings prior to its final decision and will consult on, and give reason for, its conclusion. Appeals against this decision may be made to the **Competition Appeal Tribunal,** a separate judicial body.

2.11.5 The Information Commissioner

Under the **Data Protection Act 1998 (DPA 1998)**, where persons process personal data, whether electronically or manually, they must (unless exempt) be registered with the **Information Commissioner** (who maintains a **public registry of data controllers**) and must comply with the DPA provisions. The requirements apply to most organisations and cover all personal data about living persons, including for example clients and employees, or any other person. Failure to register is a criminal offence.

If the Information Commissioner considers that a data controller is in contravention of any of the data protection principles, the Commissioner can serve an **enforcement notice**. If the data controller fails to comply with the enforcement notice, he is committing an offence and could be subject to a **fine** of **£5,000**.

2.11.6 Data protection obligations

There are various obligations for any organisation that keeps personal information, as follows.

- The organisation must have a **data protection policy**.

- **Personal data** must have been **obtained lawfully and fairly** and shall not be processed unless at least one of the **Schedule 2 conditions** is met (see below).

- In the case of **sensitive personal data** (eg, regarding racial or ethnic origin, religious or political beliefs, health, or sexual orientation), the data subject's explicit consent is normally required.

- Data must be **held and used** only for **lawful purposes**.

- Data should be used only **for the purposes for which it was originally obtained**.

- The data must not exceed what is **necessary** for the purpose for which it was obtained.

- Data must be **accurate** and must be **updated regularly**.

- Data must **not be kept longer than is necessary** for its lawful purpose.

- The person whose data is held is entitled to ask for **access** to that information (called a **subject access request**)and has the right to correct it where appropriate. The **data subject** may be charged a **maximum fee of £10 for access** to their records, with a **maximum fee of £2** in the case of credit reference agency records. The person is also entitled to be told the source, purposes and recipients of the data. The 1998 Act requires **subject access requests** to be dealt with 'promptly' and, in any event, within **40 days** of the request (along with any fee) being received.

- The data must be **protected** by appropriate technical and organisational measures against unauthorised or unlawful access and against accidental loss, destruction or damage.

- Personal data must not be transferred outside the European Economic Area unless to a country or territory that ensures an adequate level of protection for the rights and freedoms of data subjects in respect of processing of personal data.

The **Schedule 2 conditions** (see above) are that:

(a) The data subject has given consent to the processing of the data

(b) The processing is necessary in connection with a contract entered into by the data subject

(c) The processing is necessary for the data controller to comply with legal obligations

(d) The processing is necessary for public functions exercised in the public interest

(e)   The processing is necessary in pursuing the data controller's legitimate interests, provided that the processing does not prejudice the data subject's rights, freedoms or legal interests

The Information Commissioner can serve an **enforcement notice** if it considers a data controller to be in breach of any of the data protection principles. Failure to comply with such an enforcement notice is an offence, carrying a fine of up to £500,000.

2.11.7 The Panel for Takeovers and Mergers and the City Code

Learning objectives	**3.2.8 Explain** the regulatory status of the City Code on Takeovers and Mergers
	3.2.9 Explain the main provisions of the City Code including the bid timetable

The **Panel on Takeovers and Mergers** (or **Takeover Panel**) is an independent body whose main functions are to issue and administer the **City Code on Takeovers and Mergers** (the **Takeover Code**) and to supervise and regulate takeovers and other matters to which the Code applies. Its central objective is to ensure fair treatment for shareholders in takeover bids.

The Panel has **powers** under the **Companies Act 2006** to make rules on takeover regulation, to require disclosure of information, and to impose sanctions on those who breach its rules. The Panel is funded by a flat £1 levy on all transactions dealt on the LSE above £10,000, plus document charges and exemption charges.

The Panel's Takeover Code (or 'City Code') applies to all offers for public companies, and for private companies in some cases (eg if recently listed), where the company has registered offices or central control in the UK, if any of their securities are admitted to trading on a UK regulated market.

Under **CA 2006**, which implemented the EU **Takeovers Directive**, the City Code has **statutory effect** with regard to transactions to which it applies, except in the Channel Islands and the Isle of Man where the Takeover Panel claims jurisdiction on a non-statutory basis.

The City Code applies to all takeover and merger transactions, including partial offers for less than 100% of a company's shares and situations where control of a company is to be obtained or consolidated. However, it does not usually relate to offers for non-voting, non-equity shares.

The Code is intended to ensure fair treatment for all shareholders. It is recognised that it is impossible to devise rules that cover every situation.

Key points of the City Code

■   All holders of the securities of an offeree company of the same class must be afforded equivalent treatment. If a person acquires control of a company, the other holders of securities must be protected.

■   The holders of the securities of an offeree company must have sufficient time and information to enable them to reach a properly informed decision on the bid.

■   The board of an offeree company must act in the interests of the company as a whole and must not deny the holders of securities the opportunity to decide on the merits of a bid.

■   When a person or group acquires interests in shares carrying 30% or more of the voting rights of a company, they must make a cash offer to all other shareholders at the highest price paid in the 12 months before the offer was announced (30% of the voting rights of a company is treated by the Code as the level at which effective control is obtained, even though a controlling interest is achieved at 50%).

■   When interests in shares carrying 10% or more of the voting rights of a class have been acquired by an offeror in the offer period and the previous 12 months, the offer must include a cash alternative for all shareholders of that class at the highest price paid by the offeror in that period.

Further, if an offeror acquires for cash any interest in shares during the offer period, a cash alternative must be made available at that price at least.

- If the offeror acquires an interest in shares in a target company at a price higher than the value of the offer, the offer must be increased accordingly.

- Any offer must stay open for at least 21 days. If the company has reached its acceptance level it must declare that the offer has gone 'unconditional with regard to acceptances'. Any offer will then remain open for 14 days to allow those shareholders who have been resisting the takeover to take the opportunity to sell their shares and leave the company.

- Once a bid has lapsed, a bidding company may not launch a further bid for at least 12 months.

- For an offeror company achieving an acceptance level of 90% or above, Companies Act procedures enable it to force any minority shareholders to sell their shares to the offer company.

2.12 FSMA 2000

3.2.3 Explain the scope of the Financial Services and Markets Act 2000 (as amended by the Financial Services Act 2012)

3.2.4 Explain the scope of the Regulated Activities Order 2001 (as amended) in terms of: regulated activities, specified investments

2.12.1 Overview

The Financial Services and Markets Act 2000 (FSMA 2000) is the legislation under which the statutory regulation of investment business in the UK was established. FSMA 2000 was amended by the Financial Services Act 2012 in order to establish the revised regulatory framework that came into effect on 1 April 2013.

FSMA 2000 set up a framework in which anyone undertaking investment business in the UK must either be authorised to do so, or must qualify for an exemption from authorisation.

Section 19 FSMA 2000 contains what is known as the **general prohibition**.

- The general prohibition states that no person can carry on a regulated activity in the UK, nor purport to do so, unless they are either **authorised or exempt**.

- The definition of person here includes both **companies and individuals**. The list of exemptions and exclusions are set out in the regulations. There is no right to apply for an exemption from S19 if you do not fall into the existing categories.

- The sanctions for breaching S19 are fairly severe, namely: criminal sanctions (up to two years' imprisonment and an unlimited fine), unenforceability of agreements, compensation, and actions by the regulators to restrain such activity, including injunctions and restitution orders.

Broadly speaking, a person will be covered by **FSMA 2000** if they carry on the activity:

- In the UK, eg has an establishment in the UK.

- Into the UK from overseas, eg providing cross-border dealing services (subject to certain limited exclusions for overseas persons).

- In another European Economic Area (EEA) state, if his registered office is in the UK and he is passporting services into that state under one of the single market directives.

- In another EEA state, if his registered office is in UK and the day-to-day management of the activity is the responsibility of that UK office.

2.12.2 Authorisation by FCA or PRA?

A firm will apply to either the Financial Conduct Authority (FCA) or the Prudential Regulation Authority (PRA), depending on the type of firm.

- **Dual-regulated firms** (banks and building societies, credit unions, insurers and some investment firms) are authorised by the PRA but only with FCA approval. In this process, the FCA will focus on **conduct** issues, while the PRA will be more concerned with the **financial soundness** of the firm.

- **FCA-only regulated firms** (including independent financial advisers, investment exchanges, insurance brokers and fund managers) are authorised by the FCA.

2.12.3 Exempt persons

The following are the most important types of person that are **exempt** from the requirement to seek authorisation under FSMA 2000.

- **Appointed representative.** In markets such as life assurance, the bulk of sales takes place through self-employed individuals who act on behalf of the companies. The exemption removes such appointed representatives from the scope of authorisation so long as they act solely on behalf of one firm and that firm takes complete responsibility for their actions.

- **Members of professions.** Some of the investment business activities of certain members of professions, including lawyers, accountants and actuaries enjoy an exemption for the requirement for authorisation. Member firms of **Designated Professional Bodies' (DPBs)** – including the Institute of Chartered Accountants in England and Wales (ICAEW), the Law Society, the Institute of Actuaries, the Council for Licensed Conveyancers, and the Royal Institution of Chartered Surveyors – require authorisation if they recommend the purchase of specific investments such as pensions or listed company shares to clients, approve financial promotions or carry out corporate finance business. If the firms' activities are 'non-mainstream' investment business, only assisting clients in making investment decisions as part of other professional services, they are exempt from authorisation but must obtain a licence from the DPB, under which they are subject to a lighter form of regulation.

- **Members of Lloyd's.** The requirement to seek authorisation is disapplied for members of Lloyd's writing insurance contracts. The Society of Lloyd's, however, is required to be authorised. This exemption covers **being** a Lloyd's member but does not cover the activities of **advising** on Lloyd's syndicate participation or **managing** underwriting activities.

- **Recognised Investment Exchanges (RIEs), Recognised Overseas Investment Exchanges (ROIEs)** and **Recognised Clearing Houses (RCHs)**.

2.12.4 Regulated activities

What range of activities are **regulated activities**? The activities regulated by FSMA 2000 are set out in the **Regulated Activities Order** (as amended).

Regulated activities

- **Accepting deposits.** These must be accepted by way of business to be covered.

- **Issuing electronic money.** Some banks and building societies issue 'e-money' which is a form of electronic money that can be used (like notes and coins) to pay for goods and services.

- **Effecting or carrying out contracts of insurance as principal.** From the end of November 2001, the FSA took responsibility for regulating all insurers for capital adequacy purposes and life insurance firms for Conduct of Business Rules. From January 2005, sales and administration of general insurance became regulated, as well as life insurance.

- **Dealing in investments as principal or agent**. This covers buying, selling, subscribing for or underwriting investments.

- **Arranging deals in investments**. This covers making, offering or agreeing to make any arrangements with a view to another person buying, selling, subscribing for or underwriting investments.

- **Arranging regulated mortgage contracts**. This covers most mortgages, but generally does not cover buy-to-let or second charge loans.

- **Arranging home reversion plans**. Home reversion plans are one of two types of equity release product, the other being lifetime mortgages.

- **Arranging home purchase plans**. A home purchase plan serves the same purpose as a normal mortgage, in that it provides consumers with finance to buying a home. But it is structured in a way that makes it acceptable under Islamic law. As interest is contrary to Islamic law, a home purchase plan is in essence a sale and lease arrangement. The plan provider buys the property, which is then sold to the home purchaser by instalments.

- **Operating a multilateral trading facility (MTF)**. An MTF is a system which may be operated by an investment firm that enables parties, who might typically be retail investors or other investment firms, to buy and sell financial instruments.

- **Managing investments**. Managing investments belonging to another person where there is exercise of discretion by the manager.

- **Assisting in the administration and performance of a contract of insurance** (see above).

- **Safeguarding and administering investments** or arranging such activities.

- **Sending dematerialised instructions**. This relates to the electronic transfer of title to securities set up by the Uncertificated Securities Regulations (1995) – currently operated by Euroclear UK & Ireland.

- **Establishing a collective investment scheme.** This would include the roles of the trustee and the depository of schemes.

  Sections 235 and 236 FSMA 2000 define 'Collective Investment Schemes' to mean arrangements regarding property of any description where the participants and profits or income are pooled and the property in the scheme is managed by an operator.

- **Establishing, operating or winding-up a personal pension scheme or a stakeholder pension scheme**. Personal pension schemes include Self-Invested Personal Pensions (SIPPs), as their name implies. A stakeholder pension scheme follows similar rules to a personal pension plan, with caps on charges in addition.

- **Advising on investments**.

- **Advising on regulated mortgages, home reversion plans, home purchase plans and regulated sale and rent back agreements**.

- **Lloyd's market activities**. Lloyd's is the UK's largest insurance market.

- **Entering funeral plan contracts**.

- **Entering into and administering regulated mortgages, home reversion plans, home purchase plans and regulated sale and rent back agreements**.

- **Agreeing to carry on most regulated activities**. This is itself a regulated activity and so a firm must get the appropriate authorisation before agreeing to undertake business such as dealing or arranging for clients.

- **Bidding in emissions auctions.**

- **Operating dormant accounts for meeting repayment claims and managing dormant accounts.**

As you can see from the above list, the activities regulated cover the investment industry, banking, insurance and mortgage lending industries, and Lloyd's.

2.12.5 Activities carried on 'by way of business'

Note that the regulated activity must be carried on '**by way of business**' for the regulations to apply. Whether something is carried on by way of business is, ultimately, a question of judgement: in general terms it will depend on the degree of continuity and profit. HM Treasury has also (via secondary legislation) made explicit provisions for certain activities, such as accepting deposits. This will not be regarded as carried on by way of business if a person does not hold himself out as doing so on a day-to-day basis, ie he only accepts deposits on particular occasions. An example of this would be a car salesman accepting a down payment on the purchase of a car.

2.12.6 Excluded activities

The **Perimeter Guidance Manual (PERG)** in the FCA Handbook gives guidance about the activities which are regulated under FSMA 2000 and the exclusions which are available.

As set out in the Regulated Activities Order and reiterated in PERG, the following activities are **excluded** from the requirement for authorisation.

- **Dealing as principal** where the person is not holding themselves out to the market as willing to deal. The requirement to seek authorisation does not apply to the personal dealings of unauthorised individuals for their own account, ie as customers of an authorised firm. It would also exclude companies issuing their own shares.

- **Trustees, nominees and personal representatives**. These persons, so long as they do not hold themselves out to the general public as providing the service and are not separately remunerated for the regulated activity, are generally excluded from the requirement to seek authorisation.

- **Employee share schemes**. This exclusion applies to activities which further an employee share scheme.

- **Media**, eg TV, radio and newspapers. Many newspapers and other media give investment advice. However, provided this is not the primary purpose of the newspaper, then under the exceptions granted within FSMA 2000, it need not seek formal authorisation. On the other hand, the publication of '**tip sheets**' (written recommendations of investments) will require authorisation.

- **Overseas persons**. Overseas persons are firms which do not carry on regulated activity from a permanent place within the UK. This exception covers two broad categories: first, where the activity requires the direct involvement of an authorised or exempt firm and, second, where the activity is carried on as a result of an unsolicited approach by a UK individual. Thus, if a UK individual asks a fund manager in Tokyo to buy a portfolio of Asian equities for them, the Japanese firm does not need to be authorised under FSMA 2000.

2.12.7 Specified investments

Only activities relating to **specified investments** are covered by FSMA 2000. Specified investments are also defined in the **Regulated Activities Order** (as amended).

Specified investments

- **Deposits**. Simply defined, this is a sum of money paid by one person to another under the terms that it will be repaid on a specified event (eg on demand).

- **Electronic money**. This is defined as monetary value, as represented by a claim on the issuer, which is stored on an electronic device, is issued on receipt of funds and is accepted as a means of payment by persons other than the issuer.

- **Rights under a contract of insurance**. Included in this category are general insurance contracts (such as motor insurance, accident or sickness), long-term insurance contracts (such as life and annuity) and other insurance contracts (such as funeral expense contracts).

- **Shares** or stock in the capital of a company wherever the company is based.

- **Debentures, loan stock and similar instruments**, eg certificate of deposit, Treasury bills of exchange, floating rate notes, bulldog bonds and unsecured loan stock (but not cheques or other bills of exchange, banker's drafts, letters of credit, trade bills or Premium Bonds).

- **Government and public securities**, eg gilts, US Treasury bonds (not National Savings & Investments products, such as Premium Bonds and Savings Certificates).

- **Warrants**. A warrant gives the right to buy a new share in a company.

- **Certificates representing certain securities**, eg American Depository Receipts.

- **Units in a Collective Investment Scheme** including shares in, or securities of, an Open-ended Investment Company (OEIC). A collective investment scheme is a specified investment whatever underlying property the scheme invests in.

- **Rights under a personal pension scheme or a stakeholder pension scheme**. These are pension plans which are not employment-based (occupational) schemes. As indicated above, a SIPP is a personal pension scheme.

- **Options** to acquire or dispose of any specified investment or currencies, gold, silver, platinum or palladium.

- **Futures** on anything for investment purposes. This differs from the treatment of options as it will cover all futures regardless of the underlying investment, provided it is for investment purposes.

  The definition of 'investment purposes' is complex. In general terms, any futures contract traded either on an exchange, or in an over-the-counter market or form similar to that traded on an exchange, will constitute an investment. The type of future, in effect, excluded by this definition would be a short-term contract between a producer and a consumer of a good to purchase that good in the future, eg a wheat buyer buying from a farmer. This can sometimes be referred to as a 'commercial purpose future'.

Exam tip

> As a rule of thumb, unless the examiner indicates otherwise, you should assume that a future *is* for investment purposes.

- **Contracts for differences (CfDs)**. A CfD is a contract whose price tracks the price of an underlying asset, while the CfD holder does not take ownership of the asset. The underlying asset might be a company's shares, a bond, a currency, a commodity or an index. Investors can use CfDs to take a short position – and thus gain from price declines, but lose if the price rises.

- **Lloyd's syndicate capacity and syndicate membership**. Lloyd's is an insurance institution specialising in risks such as aviation and marine insurance. Insurance is provided by members and syndicates.

- **Rights under a funeral plan contract**. These are contracts whereby someone pays for their funeral before their death.

- **Rights under a regulated mortgage contract, a home reversion plan or a home purchase plan**. Note that not all mortgages are covered, only regulated mortgages. In a regulated mortgage, the loan is secured by a first legal mortgage or property located in the UK, which will be occupied (at least 40% of the time) by the borrower or their family.

- **Emissions allowances**
- **Rights to or interests in anything that is a specified investment listed** (excluding 'Rights under regulated mortgage contracts'). 'Repos' (sale and repurchase agreements) in relation to specified investments (eg a government bond) are specified investments.

Spot currency ('forex') trades, general loans (eg car loans), property deals and National Savings & Investments products are *not* specified investments.

When applying for authorisation to carry out a regulated activity regarding a specified investment, the firm will specify on the application form which regulated activities relating to which specified investments it wishes to conduct.

2.13 Senior Management Arrangements, Systems and Controls

Learning objective	3.2.5 **Explain** the purpose and scope of the FCA's rules regarding Senior Management Arrangements, Systems and Controls (SYSC)

2.13.1 Overview

The FCA's **PRIN 3** (Principle for Businesses 3) states as follows.

Management and control
A firm must take reasonable care to organise and control its affairs responsibly and effectively, with adequate risk management systems.

This emphasis comes from a desire to avoid a repetition of the collapse of Barings Bank, where it was clear that management methods and the control environment were deficient.

The regulator suggests that, in order to comply with its obligation to maintain appropriate systems, a firm should carry out a regular review of the above factors. However, it would not be a breach of the Management and Control Principle if the firm failed to prevent unforeseeable risks.

There is a section of the *FCA Handbook* called **Senior Management Arrangements, Systems and Controls (SYSC)**. As the name suggests, the main purpose of this part of the Handbook is to encourage directors and senior managers of authorised firms to take appropriate responsibility for their firm's arrangements and to ensure they know their obligations.

The purposes of SYSC are:

- To encourage firms' directors and senior managers to take appropriate practical responsibility for their firms' arrangements on matters likely to be of interest to the regulator because they impinge on the regulators' functions under FSMAS 2000

- To increase certainty by amplifying Principle 3, under which a firm must take reasonable care to organise and control its affairs responsibly and effectively, with adequate risk management systems

- To encourage firms to vest responsibility for effective and responsible organisation in specific directors and senior managers

- To create a **common platform** of organisational and systems and controls requirements for firms (Note that most firms now come within the common platform requirements, and the only firms outside them are insurers, managing agents and the Society of Lloyd's.)

BPP
LEARNING MEDIA

2.13.2 Organisational requirements

A firm must have robust **governance arrangements**, which include a clear **organisational structure** with well defined, transparent and consistent lines of responsibility, effective processes to identify, manage, monitor and report the risks it is or might be exposed to, and **internal control mechanisms**, including sound administrative and accounting procedures and effective control and safeguard arrangements for information processing systems.

Firm must establish, implement and maintain an adequate **business continuity policy**.

Firm must establish, implement and maintain **accounting policies and procedures** that enable it, at the request of the regulator, to deliver in a timely manner to the regulator financial reports which reflect a true and fair view of its financial position and which comply with all applicable accounting standards and rules.

Firm must **monitor and evaluate** the adequacy and effectiveness of its systems, internal control mechanisms and arrangements established and take appropriate measures to address any deficiencies.

Depending on the nature, scale and complexity of its business, it may be appropriate for a firm to form an audit committee with formal terms of reference. An **audit committee** could typically examine management's process for ensuring the appropriateness and effectiveness of systems and controls, examine the arrangements made by management to ensure compliance with requirements and standards under the regulatory system, oversee the functioning of the internal audit function (if applicable) and provide an interface between management and external auditors.

The senior personnel of a common platform firm must be of sufficiently good repute and sufficiently experienced as to ensure the sound and prudent management of the firm.

A common platform firm, when allocating functions internally, must ensure that senior personnel and, where appropriate, the supervisory function, are responsible for ensuring that the firm complies with its obligations under the regulatory system. In particular, senior personnel and, where appropriate, the supervisory function must assess and periodically review the effectiveness of the policies, arrangements and procedures put in place to comply with the firm's obligations under the regulatory system and take appropriate measures to address any deficiencies.

2.13.3 Employees, agents and other relevant persons

Firm must employ personnel with the **skills, knowledge and expertise** necessary for the discharge of the responsibilities allocated to them.

Firm must have arrangements concerning the **segregation of duties** within the firm and the prevention of conflicts of interest. The effective segregation of duties is an important element in the internal controls of a firm in the prudential context.

Firm must ensure that its relevant persons are **aware of the procedures** which must be followed for the proper discharge of their responsibilities.

The systems, **internal control mechanisms** and arrangements established by a firm must take into account the nature, scale and complexity of its business and the nature and range of investment services and activities undertaken in the course of that business.

The firm must monitor and, on a regular basis, evaluate the adequacy and effectiveness of its systems, internal control mechanisms and arrangements established, and take appropriate measures to address any deficiencies.

2.13.4 Compliance, internal audit and financial crime

A common platform firm must establish, implement and maintain **adequate policies and procedures** sufficient to ensure compliance of the firm including its **managers, employees and appointed representatives** (or where applicable, tied agents) with its obligations under the regulatory system and for countering the risk that the firm might be used to further financial crime.

A common platform firm must, where appropriate and proportionate in view of the nature, scale and complexity of its business and the nature and range of investment services and activities undertaken in the course of that business, establish and maintain an internal audit function which is separate and independent from the other functions and activities of the firm.

A common platform firm must ensure the policies and procedures established include systems and controls that:

- Enable it to identify, assess, monitor and manage money laundering risk
- Are comprehensive and proportionate to the nature, scale and complexity of its activities

2.13.5 Conflicts of interest

A common platform firm must establish, implement and maintain a written conflicts of interest policy and ensure that it:

- Takes all reasonable steps to identify conflicts of interest
- Details arrangements to prevent conflicts of interest
- Discloses any conflicts where they may remain

2.13.6 Other requirements

Other SYSC requirements include the following.

- A common platform firm to have effective processes to identify, manage, monitor and report the risks it is or might be exposed to

- Management cannot delegate responsibility where operational functions are outsourced

- A firm must ensure record keeping is adequate to ensure that the regulator can monitor its regulatory compliance

- Management and prudential requirements relating to **banks and insurance companies** relating to risk management systems for liquidity risk, operational risk, group risk, credit risk, market risk, insurance risk and prudential requirements.

Furthermore, the **compliance function** must be designed for the purpose of complying with regulatory requirements and to counter the risk that the firm may be used to further financial crime.

Depending on the nature, scale and complexity of the business, it may be appropriate for the firm to have a separate compliance function although this is not an absolute requirement. The organisation and responsibilities of the compliance department should be properly recorded and documented and it should be staffed by an **appropriate number of persons** who are sufficiently **independent** to perform their duties objectively. The compliance function should have unfettered access to relevant records and to the governing body of the firm.

2.13.7 Whistleblowing

SYSC also sets out guidance on **whistleblowing** where an employee blows the whistle on breaches of regulations or laws by their employer. This guidance reflects general legislation set out in the **Public Interest Disclosure Act 1998 (PIDA)**.

SYSC suggests that authorised firms should have appropriate internal procedures to implement PIDA. Under PIDA, firms may not exclude contractually an employee's right to 'blow the whistle'. PIDA also protects employees from unfair dismissal in such circumstances.

In addition, if the firm or member of staff of an authorised firm were to discriminate against an employee who made a disclosure in any way, the FCA would regard this as a serious matter. In particular, the regulator would probably question the firm's '**suitability**'– one of the '**threshold conditions**' for authorisation – and the individual's **fitness and propriety**. In serious cases, the regulator could withdraw the firm's authorisation and an individual's approval.

2.14 Trustee Act 2000

Learning objective **3.2.10 Explain** the purpose and scope of the Trustee Act 2000: the rights and duties of the parties involved, the nature of the trust deed and the investment powers of trustees

The main aim of the **Trustee Act 2000** was to widen the investment powers and powers of delegation for trusts. Trustees and their advisers need to follow the Act **unless the trust deed overrules the Act**.

The earlier Trustee Investment Act 1961 authorised trustees to invest in certain permitted investments and obliged them to split trust funds between different types of investments. Under the Trustee Act 2000, trustees can make any investment of any kind that they could as if the funds were their own, except for investment in overseas land. Trustees are however subject to a fundamental duty to act in the best interests of all the beneficiaries. They are subject to a **statutory duty of care** in exercising their investment powers, and under the Trustee Act 2000 must also:

- Keep aware of the need for diversification and suitability of the investments of the trust
- Obtain and consider 'proper advice' when making or reviewing investments
- Keep investments under review

The investment provisions of the Trustee Act 2000 do not apply to occupational pension schemes (which are governed by the Pensions Act 1995), authorised unit trusts or to some schemes under the Charities Act 1993.

2.15 Pensions regulation

Learning objective **3.2.11 Explain** the significance of the Pensions Act 2004: scheme-specific funding requirement, the Pensions Regulator, the Pension Protection Fund

2.15.1 Types of pension scheme

Pension schemes invest money during a person's working life in order to provide a source of income when that person retires.

Schemes may be categorised into two types:

- Defined contribution or money purchase schemes
- Defined benefit or final salary schemes

Defined contribution schemes will tend to collect a stable amount of money or stable proportion of an employee's salary each month for investment. However, whilst the contributions into the scheme may be defined, the eventual amount available as a pension is not known. The ultimate pension benefits will depend on, amongst other things, the amount of money contributed and the investment performance.

Defined benefit schemes aim to provide a known benefit for employees. This will typically be a pre-specified proportion of final salary on retirement, with the proportion being dependent on the number of years' service an employee has provided to their employer. While the amount to be received by way of pension is therefore defined, the required level of contributions into the scheme cannot be known in advance. For example, if investments perform poorly, contributions may have to be increased in order to ensure sufficient funds will be available to pay the pension as originally promised.

Approved pension schemes receive tax relief on contributions made.

2.15.2 The Pensions Regulator

The **Pensions Regulator** is the regulatory body for work-based pension schemes in the UK. It replaced OPRA as the regulator in 2005. A **work-based pension scheme** is any scheme that an employer makes available to employees. This includes all occupational schemes, and any stakeholder and personal pension schemes where employees have direct payment arrangements.

The Pensions Regulator has a defined set of statutory objectives, and wide **powers** to investigate schemes and to take action where necessary. The Regulator takes a proactive, risk-focused approach to regulation.

The **Pensions Act 2004** gave the Pensions Regulator a set of specific objectives.

- To protect the benefits of members of work-based pension schemes

- To promote good administration of work-based pension schemes

- To reduce the risk of situations arising that may lead to claims for compensation from the Pension Protection Fund (PPF)

2.15.3 The Pension Protection Fund

The **Pensions Act 2004** introduced the **PPF** to protect employees in the event their company scheme is not able to meet its obligations. Where a sponsoring employer becomes insolvent and unable to pay its liabilities, the PPF will provide compensation up to 100% of benefits to existing pensioners and up to 90% of benefits to those who have not yet retired. The PPF is funded by a levy on all defined benefit pension schemes. The greater the deficit of a company's pension fund between the present value of its future liabilities and the current fund size, the greater the amount that must be contributed into the scheme. This works as an incentive to firms to reduce down their deficits.

The funding provisions of this new scheme requires trustees to:

- Prepare a **statement of funding principles** specific to the circumstances of each scheme, setting out how the statutory funding objective will be met. (This statement must be reviewed every three years.)

- Obtain periodic actuarial valuations and actuarial reports

- Prepare a schedule of contributions

- Put in place a recovery plan where the statutory funding requirement is not met

2.15.4 Statement of Investment Principles

Learning objective	3.2.12 **Explain** the purpose of a Statement of Investment Principles

Members of work-based pension schemes must be given specific information regarding the investment of money held within the pension scheme and the investment returns received. This will be set out in the **Statement of Investment Principles (SIP)** which must be provided to members, generally each year, and which must include specific information required by legislation and regulations.

The **SIP** sets out the trustees' view on a number of issues, including:

- The scheme-specific funding requirement
- The nature of investments held by the fund
- The risk of the fund

It is good practice for the trustee boards to have an investment sub-committee to provide appropriate focus.

Trustees should set out an overall investment objective for the fund that:

- Represents their best judgement of what is necessary to meet the fund's liabilities
- Takes account of their attitude to risk

Objectives for the overall fund should not be expressed in terms that which have no relation to the fund's liabilities, such as performance relative to other pension funds, or to a market index.

A strengthened Statement of Investment Principles, followed best practice guidelines, should set out:

- Who is taking which decisions and why this structure has been selected

- The fund's investment objective

- The fund's planned asset allocation strategy, including projected investment returns on each asset class, and how the strategy has been arrived at

- The mandates given to all advisers and managers

- The nature of the fee structures in place for all advisers and managers, and why this set of structures has been selected.

3 REGULATION OF FINANCIAL CONDUCT

Learning objective	3.3.1 **Explain** the role and statutory objectives of the Financial Conduct Authority (FCA)

3.1 Overview of the FCA

The **Financial Conduct Authority (FCA)** is the conduct regulator for the UK financial services industry. The FCA also has responsibility for the prudential regulation of investment exchanges, many investment firms and other financial services providers.

Although set up by statute, the FCA is not regarded as acting on behalf of the Crown. Its members, officers and staff are, therefore, not Crown or civil servants. Like its predecessor – the FSA – the FCA is structured as a **company limited by guarantee**, and is given its powers by FSMA 2000.

The FCA is **accountable to the Treasury** and, through the Treasury, to **Parliament**.

The FCA is governed by a **Board** that is appointed by the Treasury. The majority of the Board members are non-executive. One of the non-executive members is a senior non-executive.

The FCA's Board sets the policy of the Authority. Day-to-day decisions and staff management are the responsibility of the FCA's **Executive Committee**.

The Authority is operationally independent of Government and is funded entirely by the firms it regulates.

Under Schedule 1ZA and 1ZB FSMA 2000, the FCA and the PRA have **statutory immunity** from prosecution other than where it can be shown to be acting in bad faith, or in breach of human rights legislation.

3.2 The FCA's statutory objectives

3.2.1 Strategic objective

The Financial Services Act 2012 (FSA 2012) gives the **Financial Conduct Authority (FCA)** a single **strategic objective**:

> **'Ensuring that the relevant markets function well'** (s1B(2) FSMA 2000, as amended by FSA 2012)

The '**relevant markets**' comprise (s1F FSMA 2000):

- The financial markets

- Markets for regulated financial services (as defined in FSMA 2000), and

- The markets for services that are provided by non-authorised persons in carrying on regulated activities without contravening the general prohibition

3.2.2 Operational objectives

This strategic objective is supported by three **operational objectives**:

- **The consumer protection objective**: securing an appropriate degree of protection for consumers

- **The integrity objective:** protecting and enhancing the integrity of the UK financial system

- **The competition objective**: promoting effective competition in the interests of consumers in the market for regulated financial services and for services provided by a recognised investment exchange

The Authority also has a duty to **address financial crime** (broadly, following the existing approach to tackling such crime).

In an October 2012 speech, a spokesperson for the regulator explained that the FCA was being set up to work with firms with the aim of ensuring that they put **consumers at the heart of their business**. Underlining this are three **outcomes**:

- Consumers get financial services and products that meet their needs from firms they can trust

- Firms compete effectively with the interests of their customers and the integrity of the market at the heart of how they run their business

- Markets and financial systems are sound, stable and resilient with transparent pricing information

3.2.3 Consumer protection objective

In considering what degree of **protection for consumers** may be appropriate, the FCA must have regard to (s1C FSMA 2000):

- The differing degrees of risk involved in different kinds of investment or other transaction

- The differing degrees of experience and expertise that different consumers may have

- The needs that consumers may have for the timely provision of information and advice that is accurate and fit for purpose

- The general principle that consumers should take responsibility for their decisions

- The general principle that those providing regulated financial services should be expected to provide consumers with a level of care that is appropriate having regard to the degree of risk involved in relation to the investment or other transaction and the capabilities of the consumers in question

- The differing expectations that consumers may have in relation to different kinds of investment or other transaction

- Any information which the consumer financial education body has provided to the FCA in the exercise of the consumer financial education function

- Any information which the scheme operator of the ombudsman scheme has provided to the FCA

3.2.4 Integrity objective

Regarding this objective, the **integrity of the UK financial system** includes (s1D FSMA 2000):

- Its soundness, stability and resilience
- Its not being used for a purpose connected with financial crime
- Its not being affected by behaviour that amounts to market abuse
- The orderly operation of the financial markets, and
- The transparency of the price formation process in those markets

3.2.5 Competition objective

The matters to which the FCA may have regard in considering the **effectiveness of competition** include:

- The needs of different consumers who use or may use those services, including their need for information that enables them to make informed choices

- The ease with which consumers who may wish to use those services, including consumers in areas affected by social or economic deprivation, can access them

- The ease with which consumers who obtain those services can change the person from whom they obtain them

- The ease with which new entrants can enter the market, and

- How far competition is encouraging innovation

3.3 The FCA Handbook

Learning objective	3.3.2 **Identify** and distinguish among the blocks of the FCA Handbook

The Handbooks of the FCA and PRA are based on the Handbook of the previous regulator, the FSA. As well as separate FCA and PRA Handbooks being developed, a combined Handbook is being maintained during the transition to the new regulatory arrangements. There are some common parts of the FCA and PRA Handbooks – for example, the Principles for Businesses. Your syllabus does not require you to know the blocks of the PRA Handbook.

The FCA derives its power to make rules in the *FCA Handbook* from FSMA 2000. The FCA Handbook includes the over-arching **Principles for Businesses** as well as various detailed rules such as those contained in the **Conduct of Business Sourcebook**.

At the legal cutover (1 April 2013), the FSA Handbook was split between the FCA and the PRA to form the two new Handbooks – one for the PRA and one for the FCA. Most provisions in the FSA Handbook are incorporated into the **PRA Handbook**, the **FCA Handbook**, or both, in line with each new regulator's set of responsibilities and objectives.

The new Handbooks reflect the new regulatory regime (for example, references to the FSA are replaced with the appropriate regulator), and in some areas more substantive changes have been made to reflect the existence of the two regulators, their roles and powers.

The *FCA Handbook* is split into seven main blocks, as follows.

High Level Standards	Prudential Standards
Principles for Businesses (PRIN)	General Prudential Sourcebook (GENPRU)
Statements of Principle and the Code of Practice for Approved Persons (APER)	Prudential Sourcebooks for Banks, Building Societies and Investment Firms (BIPRU), for Insurers (INSPRU), for UCITS Firms (UPRU) and for Mortgage and Home Finance Firms and Insurance Intermediaries (MIPRU)
Threshold Conditions (COND)	
Senior Management Arrangements, Systems and Controls (SYSC)	
Financial Stability and Market Confidence (FINMAR)	Interim Prudential Sourcebooks (for Friendly Societies, Insurers and Investment Businesses) (IPRU)
Training and Competence (TC)	
Fit & Proper Test for Approved Persons (FIT)	
General Provisions (GEN)	
Fees Manual (FEES)	

Business Standards
Conduct of Business (COBS)
Banking Conduct of Business (BCOBS)
Insurance: New Conduct of Business Sourcebook (ICOBS)
Mortgages and Home Finance: Conduct of Business (MCOB)
Client Assets (CASS)
Market Conduct (MAR)

Regulatory Processes	Redress
Supervision (SUP)	Dispute Resolution: Complaints (DISP)
Decision Procedure and Penalties Manual (DEPP)	Compensation (COMP)

Specialist Sourcebooks
Collective Investment Schemes (COLL)
Credit Unions (CREDS)
Professional Firms (PROF)
Recognised Investment Exchanges (REC)
Regulated Covered Bonds (RCB)

Listing, Prospectus and Disclosure
Listing Rules (LR)
Prospectus Rules (PR)
Disclosure Rules and Transparency Rules (DTR)

Handbook Guides point particular kinds of firm in the direction of material relevant to them in the Handbook. These include guides for Energy Market Participants, for Oil Market Participants, and for Service Companies.

There are also **Regulatory Guides** on certain topics, including the Enforcement Guide (EG), and the Perimeter Guidance Manual (PERG) which gives guidance about the circumstances in which authorisation is required or exempt person status is available.

3.4 Principles for Businesses

Learning objectives

3.3.3 Identify the FCA's Principles for Businesses (PRIN 2.1.1 & 4)

3.3.4 Explain the application and purpose of the FCA's Principles for Businesses (PRIN 1.1.1 & 2)

3.4.1 The Principles and their application

The **High Level Standards** known as the **Principles for Businesses** apply (in whole or, in some cases, in part) to every **authorised firm** carrying out a regulated activity. Approved persons are subject to a separate set of principles, known as **Statements of Principle** – see later in this Chapter.

The eleven *Principles for Businesses* are adopted by both the FCA and the PRA, and are as follows.

Principles for Businesses
1. Integrity A firm must conduct its business with integrity.
2. Skill, care and diligence A firm must conduct its business with due skill, care and diligence.
3. Management and control A firm must take reasonable care to organise and control its affairs responsibly and effectively, with adequate risk management systems.
4. Financial prudence A firm must maintain adequate financial resources.
5. Market conduct A firm must observe proper standards of market conduct.
6. Customers' interests A firm must pay due regard to the interests of its customers and treat them fairly.
7. Communications with clients A firm must pay due regard to the information needs of its clients and communicate information to them in a way that is clear, fair and not misleading.
8. Conflicts of interest A firm must manage conflicts of interest fairly, both between itself and its customers and between a customer and another client.
9. Customers: relationships of trust A firm must take reasonable care to ensure the suitability of its advice and discretionary decisions for any customer who is entitled to rely upon its judgement.
10. Clients' assets A firm must arrange adequate protection for clients' assets when it is responsible for those assets.
11. Relations with regulators A firm must deal with its regulators in an open and co-operative way and must disclose to the appropriate regulator appropriately anything relating to the firm of which that regulator would reasonably expect notice.

3.4.2 Scope of the Principles

Some of the principles (such as Principle 10) refer to **clients**, while others (such as Principle 9) refer to **customers**. This difference affects the scope of the relevant principles.

- **'Client'** includes everyone from the smallest retail customer through to the largest investment firm. It therefore includes, under the terminology of MiFID, eligible counterparties, professional customers and retail customers.

- **'Customer'** is a more restricted term that includes professional and retail clients but excludes 'eligible counterparties'. 'Customers' are thus clients who are not **eligible counterparties**. Principles 6, 8 and 9, and parts of Principle 7, apply only to **customers**.

3.4.3 Breaches of the Principles

Learning objective	**3.3.5 Explain** the consequences of breaching the FCA's Principles for Businesses (PRIN 1.1.7-9; DEPP 6.2.14 & 15)

Breaching a Principle makes the firm liable to **enforcement or disciplinary sanctions**. In determining whether a Principle has been breached it is necessary to look to the standard of conduct required by the Principle in question. Under each of the Principles, the onus will be on the regulator to show that a firm has been at fault in some way.

The definition of 'fault' varies between some of the different Principles.

- Under **Principle 1 (Integrity)**, for example, the regulator would need to demonstrate a lack of integrity in the conduct of a firm's business.

- Under **Principle 2 (Skill, care and diligence)** a firm would be in breach if it was shown to have failed to act with due skill, care and diligence in the conduct of its business.

- Similarly, under **Principle 3 (Management and control)** a firm would not be in breach simply because it failed to control or prevent unforeseeable risks, but a breach would occur if the firm had failed to take reasonable care to organise and control its affairs responsibly or effectively.

S150 FSMA 2000 creates a right of action in damages for a **private person** who suffers loss as a result of a contravention of certain **rules** by an authorised firm. However, a private person may not sue a firm under S150 FSMA 2000 for the breach of a **Principle**.

3.5 Approved Persons and Statements of Principle

Learning objective	**3.3.7 Explain** the application and purpose of the Statements of Principle and Code of Practice for Approved Persons (APER)

3.5.1 Approved persons

Section 59 FSMA 2000 states that a person (an individual) cannot carry out certain **controlled functions** unless that individual has been approved by the relevant regulator (FCA or PRA). This requirement gives rise to the term **'approved person'**, and the Supervision Manual (SUP) covers the approval process.

3.5.2 Statements of Principle and Code of Practice for Approved Persons

The regulators' **Statements of Principle** apply generally to **approved persons** (ie, to relevant employees of regulated firms) when they are performing a **controlled function** – see later in this Chapter.

The Statements of Principle will not apply where it would be contrary to the UK's obligations under EU Single Market Directives. Under **MiFID** rules, the requirement to employ personnel with the necessary knowledge, skills and expertise is reserved to the firm's **Home State**. As a result, the UK regulators do not have a role in assessing individuals' competence and capability in performing a controlled function in relation to an **incoming EEA firm** providing MiFID investment services.

Under the Financial Services Act 2012 (FSA 2012), the Statements of Principle relate not only to an individual's conduct in relation to the **controlled functions** they perform, but also to any **other regulated activities** functions they perform which relate to the firm within which they hold their approved person status. The term **accountable functions** is used in the Statements of Principle to cover both controlled functions and the other regulated activities an approved person performs.

There are seven **Statements of Principle**.

- The first four Principles apply to all approved persons (which includes those performing a **significant-influence function** as well as those not performing a significant-influence function).

- As noted in the Table below, the final three Principles only apply to approved persons performing a significant-influence function.

Statements of Principle for Approved Persons	
1. An approved person must act with integrity in carrying out his accountable functions.	**Apply to all approved persons**
2. An approved person must act with due skill, care and diligence in carrying out his accountable functions.	
3. An approved person must observe proper standards of market conduct in carrying out his accountable functions.	
4. An approved person must deal with the FCA, the PRA and other regulators in an open and co-operative way and must disclose appropriately any information of which the FCA or the PRA would reasonably expect notice.	
5. An approved person performing an accountable significant-influence function must take reasonable steps to ensure that the business of the firm for which he is responsible in his accountable function is organised so that it can be controlled effectively.	**Apply only to those with a significant-influence function**
6. An approved person performing an accountable significant-influence function must exercise due skill, care and diligence in managing the business of the firm for which he is responsible in his accountable function.	
7. An approved person performing an accountable significant-influence function must take reasonable steps to ensure that the business of the firm for which he is responsible in his accountable function complies with the relevant requirements and standards of the regulatory system.	

As required under FSMA 2000, the **Code of Practice for Approved Persons** helps approved persons to determine whether or not their conduct complies with the Statements of Principle. It sets out descriptions of conduct which, in the regulators' opinion, does not comply with the Statements of Principle, and factors which will be taken into account in determining whether or not an approved person's conduct does comply with the Statements of Principle. These descriptions have the status of **evidential provisions**. Thus, the Code is not conclusive – it is only evidential towards indicating that a Statement of Principle has been breached.

Either the FCA or the PRA have the power to discipline an approved person who has breached a Statement of Principle, regardless of whether that regulator approved the person.

3.6 Authorisation of firms

Learning objective   **3.3.6 Explain**, in outline, the procedures for authorisation for firms, including knowledge of the threshold conditions and liaison with the PRA where relevant

3.6.1 Overview

A firm may be authorised by one of the following routes:

- Authorisation by the FCA or PRA, or
- Passporting under the Markets in Financial Instruments Directive (MiFID)

A firm seeking authorisation may need to apply to either the FCA or the PRA, depending on the type of firm. Dual-regulated firms (banks and building societies, credit unions, insurers and some investment firms) are authorised by the PRA, but subject to FCA approval. FCA-only regulated firms (including independent financial advisers, investment exchanges, insurance brokers and fund managers) are authorised by the FCA.

Passporting under MiFID – as described earlier in this Chapter – is a further authorisation route, enabling a firm to conduct business throughout the EEA.

3.6.2 Authorisation by the regulators

The most common route to authorisation is to obtain permission from one of the regulators to carry out one or more regulated activities.

Bear in mind that a firm will apply to either the FCA or the PRA, depending on the type of firm.

- Dual-regulated firms are authorised by the PRA, with FCA approval
- FCA-only regulated firms are authorised by the FCA

The permission that a firm receives will play a crucial role in defining the firm's business scope. This permission is sometimes referred to as **Part 4A permission** as it is set out in Part 4A of FSMA 2000 (as amended by FSA 2012).

Where a firm wishes to obtain permission from the regulator to do a regulated activity, it must show that it is **fit and proper**.

- The applicant must satisfy the **threshold conditions** (see the next Section)

- The regulator will also need to be satisfied that the applicant firm is ready, willing and able to comply with the regulatory requirements applicable to authorised firms

Where a firm obtains permission to do one or more regulated activities, it is then authorised to do those activities. In the application, the applicant must set out which regulated activities and specified investments it requires permission for. The permission will set out what activities and investments are covered and any limitations and requirements that the regulator wishes to impose.

It is not a criminal offence for a firm to go beyond its permission but doing so may give rise to claims from consumers. Furthermore, the regulator will be able to use the full range of disciplinary sanctions, such as cancelling or varying permission.

3.7 Threshold conditions

3.7.1 Introduction

Before it grants permission, the relevant regulator must be satisfied that the firm meets the '**threshold conditions**' for the activity concerned in order to be deemed fit and proper. The regulator must ensure that a firm meets the threshold conditions when agreeing an application by the firm to vary a permission, or when varying or imposing requirements on a firm.

The FCA and the PRA each have their own set of **threshold conditions**, but a number of the conditions are common to both regulators.

The FCA and the PRA have the power to create '**threshold condition codes**'. These will elaborate on the conditions and how they will apply to different categories of firm.

3.7.2 General conditions

The following threshold conditions apply under the FCA/PRA structure.

- For **dual-regulated firms**, the applicant must have the **legal status** to carry on certain regulated activities.

- The regulator will consider the **location of the offices** of the applicant. If the applicant is a UK company, its head and registered offices must be located in the UK. For an applicant that is not a company, if it has its head office in the UK, then it must carry on business in the UK.

- Firms will need to ensure that no impediment to their **effective supervision** arises from: the nature and complexity of regulated activities undertaken, products offered, and the business organisation. This condition also covers the effect of close links of the applicant with other entities, eg other members of the same group, and whether these have an effect on effective supervision by the regulator.

- An applicant for FCA authorisation must have **appropriate resources** for the activities they seek to undertake. Such resources would not only include capital, but also non-financial resources such as personnel. Adequacy of resources will be determined by reference to the scale and nature of business, risk to the continuity of services, and the effect of a firm's membership of a group if applicable. Dual-regulated firms will need to take account of the operational objectives of the FCA and of the skills and experience of the firm's management.

- Another threshold condition relates to the **suitability** of the applicant. The firm must be considered to be 'fit and proper', ie it must have integrity, be competent and have appropriate procedures in place to comply with regulations. Suitability to carry on one regulated activity does not mean that the applicant is suitable to carry on all regulated activities. FCA-authorised firms must ensure that their affairs are conducted in an appropriate manner with regard to the interest of consumers and the integrity of the UK financial system. Those responsible for managing the affairs of a firm are to act with probity, in order to satisfy the regulators that the firm is fit and proper – in making their assessments, the regulators will consider the entirety of a firm's board and non-board senior management. Management will be required to minimise the extent to which their business could be used for financial crime.

The FCA will refuse applications at an earlier stage if it does not think that the proposed offering of products or services is in the interests of consumers or, more broadly, if it poses a significant risk to regulatory objectives.

3.7.3 FCA's Business Model Threshold Condition

The FCA will apply the **Business Model Threshold Condition**, which refers to the risk that might be posed for a firm, for its customers and for the integrity of the UK financial system.

The FCA has stated that this new threshold condition demonstrates the importance that the FCA will place on a firm's ability to put forward an appropriate, viable and sustainable business model, given the nature and scale of business it intends to carry out. The regulator will expect firms to demonstrate adequate contingency planning in their business models. Firms will be expected to make clear how their business model meets the needs of clients and customers, not placing them at undue risk, or placing at risk the integrity of the wider UK financial services industry.

3.7.4 PRA's Business to be Conducted in a Prudent Manner Threshold Condition

The PRA's **Business to be Conducted in a Prudent Manner Threshold Condition** is closely equivalent to the FCA's appropriate resources and business model conditions, which we have described above. PRA-authorised firms must hold appropriate financial and non-financial resources. Appropriate resources are evaluated by reference to complexity of activities, the liabilities of the firm, effective management, and the ability to reduce risks to the safety and soundness of the firm.

3.8 Approved persons and controlled functions

3.8.1 Overview

Learning objectives	3.3.8 **Define** an approved person 3.3.11 **Identify** the main assessment criteria in the FCA's Fit and Proper Test for approved persons (FIT)

Certain **individuals** within an authorised firm will require **approval** from the relevant regulator because they carry out **controlled functions**. We explain what the controlled functions are below.

It is important to appreciate that the process of an **individual** obtaining **approved person** status is different from the process of a **firm** obtaining **authorisation**.

To obtain approval, a person must satisfy the regulator that they are **fit and proper** to carry out the controlled function. The suitability of a member of staff who performs a controlled function is covered in the **Fit and Proper Test for Approved Persons** (included in the High Level Standards section of the FCA Handbook).

3.8.2 Obtaining approval

The most important criteria for obtaining approval are as follows.

- **Honesty, integrity and reputation.** The regulator will examine whether the person's reputation might have an adverse impact on the firm they are doing a controlled function for. This will include looking at a number of factors including whether they have had any criminal convictions, civil claims, previous disciplinary proceedings, censure or investigations by any regulator.

- **Competence and capability.** The regulator will examine whether the Training and Competence requirements in the FCA Handbook have been complied with and whether they have demonstrated by training and experience that they are able to perform the controlled function.

- **Financial soundness.** The regulator will look at whether the applicant has any outstanding judgement debts, has filed for bankruptcy or been involved in any similar proceedings.

It is the **obligation of the authorised firm** for which the person works to apply to the relevant regulator for approval for each controlled function to be undertaken.

3.9 Controlled functions

Learning objectives
3.3.9 Define a controlled function

3.3.10 Identify the types of controlled function defined within the FCA Handbook (SUP 10A)

3.3.12 Explain the application procedure for approved persons (SUP 10A) and how the PRA may also be involved

3.3.13 Explain the procedure for an approved person moving within a group and how the PRA may also be involved (SUP 10A)

Section 59 FSMA 2000 and the **Supervision Manual (SUP)** state that a person cannot carry out a **controlled function** in a firm unless that individual has been **approved** by the relevant regulator.

Note that we are now referring to the individual members of staff of an authorised firm, and appointed representatives of firms. When such an individual is performing a controlled function and is not approved, there is a breach of statutory duty, and a private person has the right to sue their firm for damages if they have suffered loss, using s71 FSMA 2000.

The **FCA** may specify a function as a **controlled function** if the individual performing it is:

- Exerting a significant influence on the conduct of the firm's affairs
- Dealing directly with customers, or
- Dealing with the property of customers

In **dual-regulated firms**, the 'significant-influence functions' (SIFs) are divided between the PRA and the FCA, so as to reduce the duplication of approvals by each of the regulators.

The **PRA** may specify a function as a **controlled function** if, in relation to carrying on a regulated activity by a PRA-authorised firm, it is a SIF.

For an individual who performs **both PRA and FCA-related SIFs**, application for approval may need only to be made to the PRA, provided that there is a single application for both roles. The PRA approval will cover the approval of the FCA functions. In such a case, the PRA must get the consent of the FCA before granting approval. Where a person ceases to perform a controlled function, the firm must notify the regulator within seven business days.

The specific controlled functions are split into groups as shown in the following Table. (The numbering is discontinuous because of past re-categorisations of functions.)

As shown in the Table, there are:

- FCA-controlled functions for FCA-authorised firms (**FCAcont FCAauth** below)
- FCA-controlled functions for PRA-authorised firms (**FCAcont PRAauth**), and
- PRA-controlled functions for PRA-authorised firms (**PRAcont PRAauth**)

Individuals who fall within all of the categories in the Table **except** *CF30 Customer functions* would be considered to be exerting a **significant influence** on the conduct of the firm's affairs. The previous regulator (the FSA) strengthened its approach to 'significant-influence' functions (**SIFs**) by ensuring that those likely to exert a significant influence on a firm fall within the scope of the approved persons regime.

Group	Function (CF)	FCAcont FCAauth	FCAcont PRAauth	PRAcont PRAauth
Governing functions	1. Director	•		•
	2 (PRA). PRA firm Non-executive Director			•
	2 (FCA). FCA firm Non-executive Director	•		
	3. Chief executive	•		•
	4. Partner	•		•
	5. Director of unincorporated association	•		•
	6. Small Friendly Society	•		•
Required functions	8. Apportionment and oversight	•	•	
	10. Compliance oversight	•	•	
	10a. CASS operational oversight	•	•	
	11. Money laundering reporting	•	•	
	12. Actuarial			•
	12A. With-profits actuary			•
	12B. Lloyd's actuary			•
	40. Benchmark submission	•	•	
	50. Benchmark administration	•	•	
Systems and controls function	28. Systems and controls	•		•
Significant management function	29. Significant management	•	•	
Customer functions	30. Customer function	•	•	

Note the following points about particular functions.

- **Governing functions**. A firm will have one or more approved persons responsible (eg the Board of Directors) for directing its affairs.

- **Required functions: Apportionment and oversight function**. A director or senior manager will be responsible for either or both of the functions of apportionment of responsibilities, and oversight of systems and controls.

- **Systems and controls function**. This is the function of acting in the capacity of an employee of the firm with responsibility for reporting to the governing body of a firm, or the audit committee (or its equivalent) in relation to (1) its financial affairs, (2) setting and controlling its risk exposure, and (3) adherence to internal systems and controls, procedures and policies.

- **Significant management function**. It is expected that only a few firms will need to seek approval for an individual to perform this function. In most firms, those approved for the governing functions, required functions and the systems and controls function are likely to exercise all the significant influence at senior management level.

- **Customer function**. This applies to activities carried on from a UK establishment and has to do with giving advice on, dealing and arranging deals in and managing investments. (It does not apply to banking business such as deposit-taking and lending.)

3.10 Training and competence

3.10.1 Overview

Principle 3 of the **Principles for Businesses** requires firms to take reasonable care to organise and control its affairs responsibly and effectively, with adequate risk management systems. This implies having appropriate systems of control, including ensuring that **employees maintain and enhance competence**.

SYSC states that a firm's systems and controls should enable it to satisfy itself of the suitability of anyone who acts for it. A requirement under **MiFID** is that firms must employ personnel with the skills, knowledge and expertise necessary for the discharge of the responsibilities allocated to them.

The **Training and Competence (TC)** sourcebook within the FCA Handbook applies only to firms whose employees advise **retail clients**, **customers or consumers**.

Appropriate examination requirements no longer apply to **wholesale business** in the financial services sector.

3.10.2 The competent employees rule

Competence means having the skills, knowledge and expertise needed to discharge the responsibilities of an employee's role. This includes achieving a good standard of **ethical behaviour**.

- The **competent employees rule** is now the main Handbook requirement relating to the competence of employees. The purpose of the TC Sourcebook is to support the FCA's supervisory function by supplementing the competent employees rule for **retail activities**.

- The **competent employees rule** is that firms must employ personnel with the skills, knowledge and expertise necessary for the discharge of the responsibilities allocated to them..

3.10.3 Assessment of competence and supervision

A firm must not assess an employee as competent to carry on an activity until the employee has demonstrated the necessary competence to do so and passed, where required, each module of an **appropriate examination** approved by the regulator. This assessment need not take place before the employee starts to carry on the activity. However, if the employee carries on the activity, the firm must ensure that the employee gains an appropriate qualification **within 30 months** of starting to carry on that activity. If the adviser does not complete the qualification within 30 months, they must stop carrying out the activity until they have passed.

A firm must not allow an employee to carry on an activity without appropriate **supervision**.

A firm must ensure that an employee –such as a trainee adviser – does not carry on an activity (other than an overseeing activity) for which there is an examination requirement without first passing the relevant **regulatory module** of an appropriate examination.

3.10.4 Ongoing assessment

Firms should ensure that their employees' training needs are assessed at the outset and at regular intervals (including if their role changes). Appropriate training and support should be provided to ensure that training needs are satisfied. The quality and effectiveness of such training should be reviewed regularly.

Firms must review regularly and frequently employees' competence and take appropriate action to ensure that they remain competent for their role.

An employee is, of course, additionally subject to the **fit and proper test** on becoming an **approved person**.

A firm should ensure that employees **maintain their competence**, for example through a formal programme of **Continuing Professional Development (CPD)**.

3.10.5 Specialist examinations

Specialist examinations must be completed in addition for giving advice in the areas shown below. (Activity numbers are as listed in TC Appendix 1.)

Pensions transfer specialists and broker fund advisers must attain the specialist examinations before acting in those roles. For other specialist roles listed below, advisers must be monitored by a competent person until an appropriate exam is passed.

- Regulated mortgage contracts advice (Activity number 20)
- Equity release (Activity number 21)
- Long-term care insurance contracts (Activity number 7)
- Pension transfer specialist (Activity number 11)
- Broker fund adviser (Activity number 10)

3.10.6 The Retail Distribution Review (RDR)

Since January 2013, there has been a new landscape for retail financial advice in the UK. The changes result from the extensive Retail Distribution Review that was launched in 2006, to address recurring problems and low consumer trust in the retail financial services market.

The following provisions cover required **initial and ongoing knowledge** for all **investment advisers**. Standards must be met whether advisers are engaged in providing **independent advice** or **restricted advice**.

3.10.7 General RDR requirements

RDR rules apply to firms advising **retail clients** on **retail investment products (RIPs)**, a broader term than what are called, elsewhere in the regulator's rules, packaged products. In particular, investment trust securities, as well as structured 'capital-at-risk' products, are included in the definition of RIPs and so are covered by the new advice rules.

If an individual performs any of the RDR TC activities and so acts as a **retail investment adviser (RIA)** – even if this is only on one occasion – then they still need an **appropriate RDR qualification** and need to be approved to carry out the controlled function: **CF30 Customer Function**.

Appropriate Qualification Tables in the regulator's **Training and Competence Sourcebook** (TC, Appendix 4E) detail which are the appropriate qualifications for the various activities requiring qualifications.

Some advisers may choose to reach the required standards (eg, if they do not want to take the exam route) by undertaking an alternative assessment available from some providers.

3.10.8 Notification requirements for firms

As part of the regulator's **risk-based supervisory strategy for individuals,** since **July 2011** firms have been required to notify the FCA of adviser competence issues.

A firm must notify the FCA as soon as they become aware, or have information that suggests any of the following has occurred, or **may have** occurred, in relation to any of its advisers:

BPP
LEARNING MEDIA

- An adviser who has been assessed as competent is no longer considered competent
- An adviser has failed to attain an appropriate qualification within the prescribed time limit
- An adviser has failed to comply with a Statement of Principle in carrying out his/her controlled function
- An adviser has performed an activity to which the training and competence (TC) requirements apply before having demonstrated the necessary competence and without appropriate supervision

Why does the regulator need this information? The information gathered will be fed, along with data from other sources, into an adviser database that has the objective of **identifying the highest risk advisers**.

3.10.9 Maintaining competence

Continuing Professional Development (CPD) is a term used to describe the process an individual needs to go through to keep their knowledge and skills up to date.

The FCA Handbook (TC2.1.13G) states that a firm should ensure that **maintaining competence** for an employee takes into account such matters as:

- Technical knowledge and its application
- Skills and expertise
- Changes in the market and to products, legislation and regulation

These aspects may vary, for example according to whether an individual is independent or tied, is a general financial planner or specialist, or whether they have any managerial responsibilities within the firm. For example, a supervisor attending a coaching course could reasonably use this as CPD – it is not restricted just to technical knowledge.

Firms should have systems in place to be able to monitor an individual's competence. This is likely to focus on either the activities undertaken to maintain competence, eg **CPD records**, or **tests** used to ensure that knowledge is acceptable at any point. In practice, both methods are likely to be used.

Under the **RDR requirements**, **retail investment advisers (RIAs)** need to carry out at least **35 hours** of **CPD** annually, of which **21 hours** must be structured. **Structured CPD** is an activity that has a defined learning outcome and must take a **minimum of 30 minutes**. Both structured and unstructured CPD must be capable of being **independently verified**.

3.10.10 T&C record-keeping

A firm must make appropriate records to demonstrate compliance with the rules in TC and keep them for the following periods after an employee stops carrying on the activity:

- At least five years for MiFID business
- Three years for non-MiFID business, and
- Indefinitely for a pension transfer specialist

3.11 Professionalism requirements for retail advisers

Learning objective	3.3.15 **Explain** the professionalism requirements that have to be met by retail advisers and investment managers (TC 1-3)

3.11.1 Overview

The regulator has declared that it aims to deliver standards of professionalism that inspire consumer confidence and build trust so that, in time, financial advice is seen as a profession on a par with other professions. Achievement of this objective is linked closely to the wider package of Retail Distribution Review (RDR) proposals, which include major changes to adviser charging.

3.11.2 Statement of Professional Standing (SPS)

Retail investment advisers are required to hold a **Statement of Professional Standing (SPS)** if they want to give independent or restricted advice since the end of 2012, when the RDR changes came into effect.

The SPS will provide customers with evidence that the adviser subscribes to a **code of ethics**, is qualified, and has kept their knowledge up to date. The SPS must be issued by an FCA-accredited body that will be subject to oversight by the regulator in relation to their investment adviser members' activities.

3.11.3 Accredited body requirements

The **FCA-accredited bodies** issuing SPSs must satisfy the following criteria:

- They act in the public interest and further the development of the profession
- They carry out effective verification services
- They have appropriate systems and controls in place and provide evidence to us of continuing effectiveness, and
- They cooperate with the regulator on an ongoing basis

The **accredited bodies** is subject to **FCA oversight** in relation to their investment adviser members' activities, and must ensure that all advisers who use their services:

- Are appropriately **qualified**. (The body must check 100% of any required 'gap-fill' qualifications to meet RDR standards.)
- Have made an annual written declaration that they have complied with the **Statements of Principle** and Code of Conduct for Approved Persons **(APER)** and subscribe to a **code of ethics**
- Have completed **Continuing Professional Development (CPD)** requirements. (The body must carry out random CPD sample checks in at least 10% of cases.)

4 INVESTMENT EXCHANGES AND DERIVATIVES MARKETS

Learning objectives

3.4.1 Explain the role of an investment exchange

3.4.2 Explain the need for, and relevance of, investment exchanges needing to be recognised by the FCA

3.4.3 Explain how the Bank of England regulates clearing houses in the UK

3.4.4 Identify the recognised investment exchanges and clearing houses in the UK

3.4.5 Identify and distinguish the roles of LSE, NYSE Liffe, and LCH.Clearnet

4.1 Recognised Investment Exchanges (RIEs)

The FCA recognises and supervises a number of **Recognised Investment Exchanges (RIEs)**. The act of running an investment exchange is, in itself, a regulated activity (arranging deals in investments) and therefore requires regulatory approval. However, **RIE** status exempts an exchange from the requirement. This status assures any parties using the exchange that there are reasonable rules protecting them.

Membership of an RIE does not confer authorisation to conduct regulated activities. Many firms are members of an RIE and are also required to be authorised and regulated by the FCA. Membership of an

RIE gives the member privileges of membership associated with the exchange, such as the ability to use the exchange's systems.

To gain recognised status, an investment exchange must satisfy requirements set out in the **FSMA 2000 (Recognition Requirements for Investment Exchanges and Clearing Houses) Regulations 2001**. The FCA Specialist Sourcebook named **REC** within the FCA's Handbook also sets out the requirements.

RIE requirements include:

- **Financial resources** 'sufficient for the proper performance of its functions'

- **Suitability**: the exchange must be a fit and proper person, taking due account of all the circumstances, including connections with other persons

- **Systems and controls** that are adequate and appropriate for the scale and nature of the business, including those related to risk management, transmission of information, and safeguarding of assets

- **Safeguards for investors**, with business being conducted in an orderly manner, dealings limited to investments in which there is a proper market, and measures to reduce the likelihood of financial crime or market abuse

- Rules regarding **disclosure by securities issuers** enabling, in the event of a failure by the issuer, suspension of trading and publication of the non-compliance

- **Promotion and maintenance of standards**

- **Complaints** investigation and resolution arrangements

- Effective **discipline** arrangements, for monitoring and enforcing compliance

- **Rules covering default** by an exchange member

Exchanges with RIE status:

- ICE Futures Europe
- LIFFE Administration and Management (NYSE Liffe)
- London Stock Exchange plc
- ICAP Securities and Derivatives Exchange Limited (ISDX) (formerly PLUS Stock Exchange)
- The London Metal Exchange Limited (LME)

As well as the UK exchanges that are permitted to operate under the RIE status, certain **Recognised Overseas Investment Exchanges (ROIEs)** are permitted to operate in the UK.

4.2 NYSE Liffe

The most important London market for financial futures and options is **NYSE Liffe**, formerly Euronext.liffe, and before that the London International Financial Futures and Options Exchange (LIFFE).

Euronext was formed in 2000 by the merger of the Amsterdam, Brussels and Paris securities and derivatives exchanges. In 2001 Euronext purchased Liffe. Trading takes place on an electronic order matching system known as Liffe.Connect. Only NYSE Liffe members are able to trade and clear contracts.

Once a trade has been matched it is registered with the LCH.Clearnet which becomes the central counterparty. To protect itself from the risk that firms default, LCH Clearnet requests margin is posted.

Initial margin is payable on opening a contact. It is a returnable good faith deposit required from all those entering 'risky' positions. The amount required by the LCH.Clearnet is usually linked to the worst probable (not possible) one-day loss that a position could sustain. Initial margin is payable in cash and various acceptable collateral. This amount will be returned as long as the investor honours his contractual obligations. However, should the investor default, this initial margin will be used by the LCH to offset the effect of default.

In addition to initial margin, variation margin is payable based on the profits and losses incurred on each position during the day. At the end of each day the positions are 'marked-to-market' to the daily settlement price, and profits and losses are calculated. Variation margin is essentially 'pay as you go' profits and losses on a daily basis. Variation margin is normally payable in cash only.

The day-to-day supervision of the rules on Euronext.liffe is carried out by the Market Supervision Department.

NYSE Liffe members are subject to a comprehensive set of **membership rules** that focus particularly on trading conduct. As such, they focus primarily on the relationship between members rather than between members and customers. It should be remembered that membership of NYSE Liffe does not convey any kind of authorisation to conduct investment business in the UK. It allows access to the market place.

Infringements of the rules will lead initially to an investigation by the Market Supervision Department, which may ultimately lead to a disciplinary hearing for the member concerned. Penalties may be imposed on its members by NYSE Liffe, such as fines, trading suspensions and, ultimately, expulsion from exchange membership.

4.3 Recognised Clearing Houses (RCHs)

Recognised clearing houses (RCHs), along with recognised payments systems and securities settlement systems, are known collectively as **Financial Market Infrastructures (FMIs)**. Following the changes introduced in the Financial Services Act 2012 (FSA 2012), the **Bank of England (BoE)** has responsibility for supervising FMIs.

Recognition of a RCH by the BoE permits the organisation to carry out the clearing and settlement functions for an exchange.

At present there are the following **RCHs**:

- CME Clearing Europe Limited
- Euroclear UK & Ireland Limited
- European Central Counterparty Ltd
- ICE Clear Europe Limited
- LCH.Clearnet Limited
- Liffe Administration and Management

4.4 Designated Investment Exchanges (DIEs)

In addition to those RIEs in the UK and overseas which the FCA recognises, there are also overseas exchanges that have been given a form of approval yet are not able to conduct regulated activities in the UK.

The term 'designated' does not indicate exemption from the requirement to seek authorisation. **Designated Investment Exchange (DIE)** status assures any UK user of the overseas market that the FCA believes there are appropriate forms of local regulation that guarantee the investor's rights.

There are currently around thirty **Designated Investment Exchanges** and they include, for example:

- Tokyo Stock Exchange
- New York Stock Exchange
- New York Futures Exchange
- Euronext Amsterdam Commodities Market
- Hong Kong Exchanges and Clearing Limited

(A full list is shown in the **Financial Services Register** on the regulators' website, and also in the Glossary of the **FCA Handbook**.)

4.5 Regulation of derivatives markets

4.5.1 Introduction

The UK **derivatives exchanges**, which include NYSE Liffe and the London Metals Exchange, are Recognised Investment Exchanges. Accordingly, the exchanges mainly regulate the market, with the FCA being responsible for the financial soundness and conduct of business of exchange members.

4.5.2 MiFID

In Europe the most important source of regulation for the derivatives market is the Markets in Financial Instruments Directive (MiFID). MiFID harmonised the day-to-day regulation of dealings in the securities and derivatives markets, making it easier for firms to conduct their business in financial instruments all around the European Economic Area (EEA) without having to seek specific authorisation in each state.

MiFID applies to investment firms who are carrying out activities in relation to the following derivative instruments:

- Derivatives relating to securities, currencies, interest rates and yields, financial indices and financial measures settled either physically or in cash, including: options, futures, swaps and forward rate agreements

- Commodity derivatives capable of being settled in cash, commodity derivatives capable of being physically settled on a regulated market or multilateral trading facility, and certain other commodity derivatives which are not for commercial purposes, and thus **MiFID introduced commodity derivatives into the list of regulated investments**

- Derivative instruments for transferring credit risk

- Financial contracts for differences (CfDs)

- Derivatives relating to climatic variables, freight rates, emission allowances, inflation rates or other official economic statistics capable of being settled in cash

A UK-based firm would normally receive its authorisation to trade in derivatives from the relevant regulator (FCA or PRA, depending on the type of firm). There are similar bodies in other EEA states.

4.5.3 USA

In the USA, there are two main relevant regulatory bodies, the **Securities and Exchange Commission (SEC)** and the **Commodity Futures Trading Commission (CFTC)**. US regulations governing derivatives trading originally stem from the Wall Street crash of 1929 and are contained in the **Commodity Exchange Act 1936** which have been updated through the **Commodity Futures Modernization Act 2000**. The SEC primarily regulates derivatives on securities whereas the CFTC primarily regulates commodities.

4.5.4 International Accounting Standard 39

Under International Accounting Standard 39 (IAS 39), derivatives must be recognised in the **balance sheet at fair value** (except those that are used as a hedge). Fair value is defined as the value at which a contract could be exchanged, or a liability settled between two parties in an arm's length transaction. All (non-hedge) derivatives must, therefore, be 'marked to market' and stated at their current market value.

The treatment of gains and losses depends on whether or not the derivative can be recognised as a hedging instrument. However, assuming this is not the case (ie usual situation), **gains and losses from changes in market value will be recognised as income or expenses** in the company's income statement.

4.5.5 Market transparency

Learning objective	**3.4.9 Explain** the arrangements for market transparency and transaction reporting in the main derivative markets

Trading on a derivatives exchange is subject to transparency rules of the exchange, as governed by regulatory provisions. MiFID is backed up by the **Transparency Directive** in its efforts to create a single capital market for the EEA. The Transparency Directive requires pre- and post-trade transparency in the markets so that investors can easily compare execution venues and therefore select the best market to trade financial instruments in, rather than having to use their own monopolistic national exchange.

4.6 Trading systems for derivatives

Learning objectives	**3.4.6 Identify** the featuresof trading systems for derivatives **3.4.8 Identify** the main features of clearing and settlement for trading on derivatives exchanges, and when trading over-the-counter (OTC)

4.6.1 Exchange trading

For the **London International Financial Futures and Options Exchange (NYSE Liffe)**, the main international derivatives exchange of the NYSE Euronext group, trading is undertaken on LIFFE CONNECT, an electronic order matching system.

LCH.Clearnet (LCH) acts as a **central counterparty** on behalf of Liffe for all trades. LCH receives a feed from Liffe of trades from its LIFFE CONNECT trading system. These are agreed trades and the Trade Registration System (TRS) and the Clearing Processing System (CPS) permit clearing members to confirm business into the correct clearing accounts.

The LCH then acts as principal to all trades which have been transacted. Hence every exchange member who buys or sells a contract ends up with a position with the LCH either directly, if they themselves are clearing members, or indirectly through the clearing member of the exchange who clears their trades.

The LCH thus takes all the risk of counterparties failing to honour obligations. The LCH reduces its risk by requiring cash or collateral deposits (initial margins) for the clearing members' positions.

Only NYSE Liffe members can trade on Liffe and anyone else wishing to trade a Liffe contract must do so through such a member who takes responsibility for the registration, margining and settlement of the trade.

Individuals using the services of NYSE Liffe members

- **Traders** – people seeking a profit on their own behalf, known as 'locals', or on their company's behalf

- **Brokers** – people acting for a third party and making profits by charging commission

Day-to-day supervision on Liffe is carried out by the Market Supervision Department (MSD) of the exchange.

4.6.2 OTC derivatives

Since 2009, there have been moves in both the USA and Europe to have **over-the-counter (OTC) derivatives** cleared through **clearing houses**. These changes are being introduced with **European Market Infrastructure Regulation (EMIR)**. This should increase transparency and reduce the risk of counterparty default, and may thus help to reduce systemic risks arising from OTC derivatives trading.

Before implementation of EMIR, settlement of OTC derivatives was direct with the counterparty rather than through an exchange or clearing broker. Confirmations then needed to be sent out by counterparties, who would need to make the necessary amendments for corporate actions, instead of this being dealt with by a broker.

5 FCA BUSINESS STANDARDS

5.1 Client classification

Learning objective	3.5.1 **Explain** the purpose of client categorisation

5.1.1 Levels of protection for clients

Classifying clients into different types allows different regulatory rules to be applied to each type of client, who may therefore be afforded different degrees of protection under the regulatory system. The main corpus of rules affected by the categorisation of any particular client is that found in the **Conduct of Business Sourcebook (COBS)** in the FCA Handbook.

Within any cost-effective regulatory system, protection provided ought to be **proportionate** to the need for protection. This is because there is not only a cost element to protection but also an inverse relationship with freedom. It is desirable that those who do not require high protection are given more freedom to trade without the restrictions that the rules inevitably bring.

The **size** and **financial awareness** of **clients** will determine the level of protection. As the size/knowledge increases, protection will decrease. A system of categorising clients can help determine that the level of protection is appropriate to the client.

While this would ideally be a continuous process, gradually moving from full protection to no protection, in practical terms this is an impossibility.

5.2 The client categories

Learning objectives

3.5.2 Distinguish between a retail client, a professional client and an eligible counterparty (COBS 3.4, 3.5 & 3.6)

3.5.3 Apply the rules relating to treating a client as an elective professional client (COBS 3.5.3)

3.5.4 Apply the rules relating to treating a client as an elective eligible counterparty (COBS 3.6.4)

3.5.5 Apply the rules relating to providing clients with a higher level of protection (COBS 3.7)

5.2.1 Overview

The terms used to classify clients has changed following the implementation of MiFID created three client categories:

- **Eligible counterparties** – who are either **per se** or **elective** eligible counterparties
- **Professional clients** – who are either **per se** or **elective** professional clients
- **Retail clients**

As well as setting up criteria to classify clients into these categories, MiFID provides for clients to **change** their initial classification, on request.

A client who is not an eligible counterparty is a **customer**.

5.2.2 Clients

A **client** is a person to whom an authorised **firm** provides a service in the course of carrying on a **regulated activity** or, in the case of MiFID or equivalent third country business, a person to whom a firm provides an **ancillary service**.

The scheme of categorisation is summarised in the following diagram.

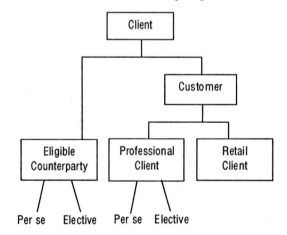

5.2.3 Retail clients

Retail clients are defined as those clients who are not professional clients or eligible counterparties.

5.2.4 Professional clients

Some undertakings are automatically recognised as **professional clients**. Accordingly, these entities may be referred to as **per se** professional clients. (An **undertaking** is a company, partnership or unincorporated association.)

Clients who are *per se* **professional clients** are as follows.

- Entities that **require authorisation or regulation** to operate in the financial markets, including: credit institutions, investment firms, other financial institutions, insurance companies, collective investment schemes and pension funds and their management companies, commodity and commodity derivatives dealers, 'local' derivatives dealing firms, and other institutional investors

- In relation to **MiFID** or equivalent third country business, a **large undertaking** – meaning one that meets two of the following size requirements:

  - €20,000,000 Balance sheet total
  - €40,000,000 Net turnover
  - €2,000,000   Own funds

- In relation to business that is not **MiFID** or equivalent third country business, a **large undertaking** meeting **either** of the following requirements:

  - Called up share capital or net assets of at least £5,000,000 or equivalent, or

  - Two of the three following size tests:

    - €12,500,000 balance sheet total
    - €25,000,000 net turnover
    - 250 average number of employees in the year

  Trusts with assets of at least £10m and partnerships or unincorporated associations with net assets of at least £5m are also per se professional clients for non-MiFID business.

- Central banks, international institutions, and national and regional government bodies

- Institutional investors

A firm may treat a retail client as an **elective professional client** if the following tests are met.

- **Qualitative test.** The firm assesses adequately the client's **expertise**, **experience** and **knowledge** and thereby gains reasonable assurance that, for the transactions or services envisaged, the client is capable of making his own investment decisions and understanding the risks involved.

- **Quantitative test.** In the case of **MiFID** or equivalent third country business, at least **two** of the following three criteria must apply.

  - The client has carried out at least ten 'significant' transactions per quarter on the relevant market, over the last four quarters

  - The client's portfolio, including cash deposits, exceeds €500,000

  - The client has knowledge of the transactions envisaged from at least one year's professional work in the financial sector

Additionally, for opting up to professional client status to apply:

- The client must agree in writing to be treated as a professional client

- The firm must give written warning of the protections and compensation rights which may be lost

- The client must state in writing, separately from the contract, that it is aware of the consequences of losing protections

It is the responsibility of the professional client to keep the firm informed about changes (eg in portfolio size or company size) which could affect their categorisation.

COBS states that an elective professional client should not be presumed to have market knowledge and experience comparable to a *per se* professional client.

5.2.5 Eligible counterparties

In relation to MiFID or equivalent third country business, a client can only be an eligible counterparty (ECP) in relation to eligible counterparty business. This limits the **ECP regime**, which is a **'light touch'** level of protection, to executing orders on behalf of clients, dealing on own account, and receiving and transmitting orders.

The following, and their non-EEA equivalents, are **per se eligible counterparties** (ie they are automatically recognised as eligible counterparties).

- Insurance companies, investment firms and credit institutions
- UCITS collective investment schemes, and their management companies
- Pension funds, and their management companies
- Other EEA-authorised financial institutions
- National governments, central banks and supranational organisations

A firm may treat an undertaking as an **elective eligible counterparty** if the client:

- Is a *per se* professional client (unless it is such by virtue of being an institutional investor), or

- Is an elective professional client and requests the categorisation, but only in respect of the transactions and services for which it counts as a professional client, and

- In the case of MiFID or equivalent third country business, provides 'express confirmation' of their agreement (which may be for a specific transaction or may be general) to be treated as an eligible counterparty

If the prospective counterparty is established in another EEA state, for MiFID business the firm should defer to the status determined by the law of that other State.

5.2.6 Providing a higher level of protection to clients

Firms must allow **professional clients** and **eligible counterparties** to re-categorise in order to get more protection. Such clients are themselves responsible for asking for higher protection if they deem themselves to be **unable** to assess properly or manage the risks involved.

Either on its own initiative or following a client request or written agreement:

- A **per se eligible counterparty** may be re-categorised as a **professional client** or **retail client**
- A **per se professional client** may be re-categorised as a **retail client**

The **higher level of protection** may be provided through re-categorisation:

- On a general basis
- Trade by trade
- In respect of specified rules
- In respect of particular services, transactions, transaction types or product types

The client should (of course) be notified of a re-categorisation.

Firms must have written internal policies and procedures to categorise clients.

5.3 Client agreements

Learning objective	3.5.6 **Apply** the rules relating to client agreements (COBS 8.1)

If a firm carries on **designated investment business**, other than advising on investments, for a **new retail client,** the firm must enter into a **basic agreement** with the client. Thus, for example, there should be a client agreement when discretionary investment management services are provided. Although little guidance is given in the rules as to the contents, the agreement will set out the essential rights and obligations of the firm, and must be in writing – on paper or other durable medium. For a **professional client**, there is no requirement for an agreement, although most firms will wish there to be one.

In good time, normally **before** the client is bound by any agreement relating to designated investment business or ancillary services, the firm must provide to the retail client – either in a durable medium or on a website, if the website conditions are satisfied:

- The terms of the agreement

- Information about **the firm and its services**, including information on communications, conflicts of interest and authorised status

The agreement and information may be provided **immediately after** the client is bound by the agreement if the agreement was concluded using a means of distance communication (eg telephone).

Relevant material changes to the information provided must be notified to the client in **good time**.

A **record** of the client agreement should be kept for five years, or for the duration of the relationship with the client if longer. For pension transfers or opt-outs, or FSAVCs, the record should be kept indefinitely.

5.4 Financial promotions and communications

Learning objective   **3.5.7 Explain** the purpose and scope of the financial promotions rules and the exemptions from them (COBS 4.1)

5.4.1 Introduction

A **financial promotion** is an **invitation** or **inducement** to **engage** in investment activity. The term therefore describes most forms and methods of marketing financial services. It covers traditional advertising, most website content, telephone sales campaigns and face-to-face meetings. The term is extended to cover **marketing communications** by MiFID.

The purpose of regulation in this area is to create a regime where the quality of financial promotions is scrutinised by an authorised firm who must then comply with lengthy rules to ensure that their promotions are **clear**, **fair and not misleading** (Principle 7) and that customers are treated **fairly** (Principle 6).

The **financial promotions rules** within COBS apply to a firm:

- Communicating with a **client** in relation to **designated investment business**

- **Communicating** or **approving** a **financial promotion** (with some exceptions in respect of: credit promotions, home purchase plans, home reversion schemes, non-investment insurance contracts and unregulated collective investment schemes (UCIS))

Firms must also apply the rules to promotions issued by their **appointed representatives**.
For financial promotions, the **general application rule** applies. This indicates that the rules apply to a firm in respect of designated investment business carried out from an establishment maintained by the firm or its appointed representative in the UK. Additionally, in general the rules apply to firms carrying on business with a client in the UK from an establishment overseas.

The financial promotions rules also apply to:

- Promotions communicated to a person in the UK

■ Cold (unsolicited) calling to someone outside the UK, if the call is from within the UK or is in respect of UK business

The financial promotions rules do **not** apply to incoming communications in relation to **MiFID business** of an investment firm **from another EEA state** that are, in its home state, regulated under MiFID.

5.4.2 Fair, clear and not misleading

Learning objective	3.5.8 Explain the fair, clear and not misleading rule (COBS 4.2)

A firm must ensure that **a communication or financial promotion is fair, clear and not misleading**, and is **appropriate and proportionate** considering the means of communication and the information to be conveyed.

This rule applies to financial promotions communicated by the firm except:

■ Communications directed at professional clients or eligible counterparties (ie 'non-retail')
■ Excluded communications (see below)
■ Third party prospectuses in respect of designated investment business

The **fair, clear and not misleading rule** is specifically interpreted in COBS as it applies to financial promotions in some aspects, as follows.

■ If a product or service places a client's capital at risk, this should be made clear

■ Any yield figure quoted should give a balanced impression of both short-term and long-term prospects for the investment

■ Sufficient information must be provided to explain any complex charging arrangements, taking into account recipients' needs

■ If either of the regulators' names is used, any non-regulated aspects should be made clear

■ A fair, clear and not misleading impression should be given of the producer for any packaged product or stakeholder products not produced by the firm

5.4.3 Identifying promotions as such

A firm must ensure that a **financial promotion** addressed to a **client** is clearly **identifiable as such**.

■ This rule does not apply to a third party prospectus in respect of **MiFID** (or equivalent third country) business.

■ There are also some exceptions in respect of **non-MiFID** business, including prospectus advertisements, image advertising, non-retail communications, deposits and pure protection long-term care insurance (LTCI) products.

5.4.4 Excluded communications

A firm may rely on one or more of the following aspects which make a communication into an **excluded communication** for the purposes of the rules.

■ A financial promotion that would benefit from an exemption in the Financial Promotion Order (see below) if it were communicated by an unauthorised person, or which originates outside the UK and has no effect in the UK

■ A financial promotion from outside the UK that would be exempt under the Financial Promotion Order (Overseas communicators) if the office from which the financial promotion is communicated were a separate unauthorised person

- A financial promotion that is subject to, or exempted from, the Takeover Code or to the requirements relating to takeovers or related operations in another EEA state

- A personal quotation or illustration form

- A **'one-off' financial promotion** that is not a cold call. The following conditions indicate that the promotion is a 'one-off', but they need not necessarily be present for a promotion to be considered as 'one-off'.

    (i)   The financial promotion is communicated only to one recipient or only to one group of recipients in the expectation that they would engage in any investment activity jointly

    (ii)   The identity of the product or service to which the financial promotion relates has been determined having regard to the particular circumstances of the recipient

    (iii) The financial promotion is not part of an organised marketing campaign

5.4.5 Financial Promotions Order

Section 21 FSMA 2000 makes it criminal for someone to undertake a financial promotion, ie invite or induce another to engage in investment activity, unless they are either:

- An **authorised firm** (ie **issuing the financial promotion**), or
- The content of the communication is **approved** by an authorised firm

There are a number of exemptions from s21 set out in the **Financial Promotions Order**. The effect of being an **exemption** is that the promotion would **not** need to be issued or approved by an authorised firm. It would therefore not have to comply with the detailed financial promotion rules.

The main examples are as follows. (Other exemptions cover certain one-off and purely factual promotions.)

Exemption	Comments
1. Investment professional	A communication to an authorised or exempt person.
2. Deposits and insurance	Very limited application of COBS.
3. Certified high net worth individuals	Anyone may promote **unlisted securities** to persons who hold certificates of high net worth (normally signed by their accountant or employer, however, these can now be self-certified by an individual) and who have agreed to be classified as such. Requirements for a certificate are that a person must have a net income of £100,000 or more, or net assets (excluding principal property) of £250,000 or more. Note that, if applicable, the financial promotion should not invite or induce the recipient to engage in business with the firm that signed the certificate of high net worth.
4. Associations of high net worth individuals	Anyone can promote non-derivative products to associations of high net worth investors.
5. Sophisticated investors	Anyone can promote products to a person who holds a certificate indicating that they are knowledgeable in a particular stock (normally signed by an authorised firm, however, individuals can now self-certify themselves as sophisticated in relation to unlisted securities) and who have signed a statement agreeing to be such. Note that the financial promotion should not invite or induce the recipient to engage in business with the authorised firm that signed the certificate.
6. Takeover Code	Promotions subject to the Takeover Code.

5.4.6 Communicating with retail clients

Learning objective | **3.5.9 Explain** the rules relating to communications with retail clients (COBS 4.5)

The general rule on **communicating with retail clients** in relation to **designated investment business** states that firms must ensure that the information:

- Includes the **name of the firm** (which may be the **trading name** or **shortened name**, provided the firm is identifiable)

- Is accurate and does not emphasise potential benefits of investment without also giving a **fair and prominent indication of relevant risks**

- Is **sufficient** for and presented so as to be **likely to be understood** by the **average member** of the group to whom it is directed or by whom it is likely to be received

- Does **not disguise, diminish** or **obscure** important **items, statements** or **warnings**

In deciding whether and how to communicate to a target audience, the firm should **consider**: the nature of the product/business, risks, the client's commitment, the average recipient's information needs and the role of the information in the sales process.

The firm should consider whether omission of a relevant fact will result in information being **insufficient, unclear, unfair** or **misleading**.

Information comparing business / investments / persons must

- Present **comparisons** in a meaningful, fair and balanced way

- In relation to MiFID or equivalent third country business, specify **information sources**, key facts and assumptions

If **tax treatment** is referred to, it should be stated prominently that the tax treatment depends on the individual circumstances of the client and may be subject to change in future. (One of a couple of exceptions to this rule is that it does not apply to deposits other than cash ISAs or CTFs.)

The firm should ensure that information in a financial promotion is **consistent** with other information provided to the retail client. (**Deposits** are an exception to this rule.)

5.4.7 Past, simulated past and future information

Learning objective | 3.5.10 **Explain** the rules relating to past, simulated past and future performance (COBS 4.6)

Rules on **performance information** apply to information disseminated to retail clients, and to financial promotions. In the case of non-MiFID business, the rules do not apply to deposits generally nor to pure protection long-term care insurance (LTCI) contracts.

Past performance information must:

- **Not** be the most prominent feature of the communication (although it could be, in a periodic statement for managed investments)

- Include appropriate information covering at least the **five preceding years**, or the whole period the investment/service has been offered/provided or the whole period the financial index has been established, if less than five years

- Be based on and must show complete **12-month periods**

- State the **reference period** and **source of the information**

- Contain a **prominent warning** that the figures refer to the past and that past performance is not a reliable indicator of future results

- If denominated in a foreign **currency**, state the currency clearly, with a warning that the return may increase or decrease as a result of currency fluctuations

- If based on gross performance, disclose the effect of **commissions**, fees or other charges

The above provisions are to be interpreted in a way that is '**appropriate and proportionate**' to the communication.

Simulated past performance information must:

- Relate to an investment or a financial index

- Be based on actual past performance of investments/indices which are the same as, or underlie, the investment concerned

- Contain a **prominent warning** that figures refer to simulated past performance and that past performance is not a reliable indicator of future performance

Future performance information must:

- **Not** be based on nor refer to simulated past performance
- Be based on **reasonable assumptions** supported by **objective data**
- If based on gross performance, disclose the effect of **commissions**, fees or other charges
- Contain a **prominent warning** that such forecasts are not a reliable indicator of future performance
- Only be provided if **objective data** can be obtained

5.4.8 Financial promotions containing offers or invitations

Learning objective	3.5.11 **Explain** the rules relating to direct offer promotions (COBS 4.7)

A **direct offer financial promotion** is a form of financial promotion which enables investors to purchase investments directly 'off the page' without receiving further information.

A direct offer financial promotion to retail clients must contain whatever **disclosures** are relevant to that offer or invitation (such as information about the firm and its services, and costs and charges) and, for non-MiFID business, additional appropriate information about the relevant business and investments so that the client is reasonably able to understand their nature and risks, and consequently to take investment decisions on an informed basis.

5.4.9 Unwritten promotions and cold calling

Learning objective	3.5.12 **Explain** the rules relating to cold calls and other promotions that are not in writing (COBS 4.8)

These rules apply for **retail clients**.

An **unwritten financial promotion** outside the firm's premises may only be initiated if the person communicating it:

- Does so at an appropriate time of day

- Identifies himself and his firm, and makes his purpose clear

- Clarifies if the client wants to continue or terminate the communication, and terminates it on request at any time

- If an appointment is arranged, gives a contact point to a client

Firms may only make **cold (unsolicited) calls** if:

- The recipient has an established client relationship with the firm, such that the recipient envisages receiving them, or

- The call is about a generally marketed packaged product (not based on a high volatility fund), or

- The call relates to controlled activities by an authorised person or exempt person, involving only readily realisable securities (not warrants)

5.4.10 Approving financial promotions

Learning objective	3.5.13 **Explain** the rules relating to systems and controls in relation to approving and communicating financial promotions (COBS 4.10)

The rules in **SYSC** require that a firm which communicates with a client regarding designated investment business, or communicates or approves a financial promotion, puts in place **systems and controls** or **policies and procedures** in order to comply with the COBS rules.

As we have seen, FSMA 2000 prohibits an unauthorised person from communicating a financial promotion, unless either an exemption applies or the financial promotion is approved by an authorised firm. Approval of a financial promotion by an **authorised firm** enables it to be communicated by an **unauthorised firm**.

A firm **approving** a financial promotion must confirm that it **complies** with the **financial promotion rules**. The firm must withdraw its approval, and notify anyone it knows to be relying on its approval, if it becomes aware that it no longer complies with the financial promotion rules.

5.4.11 Record keeping requirements relating to financial promotions

Learning objective	3.5.14 **Explain** the record keeping requirements relating to financial promotions (COBS 4.11)

A firm must make an adequate record of any financial promotion it communicates or approves. The record must be retained for:

- An indefinite period, for a pension transfer, opt-out or FSAVC

- Six years for a life policy, occupational pension scheme, SSAS, personal pension scheme or stakeholder pension scheme

- Five years for MiFID or equivalent third country business

- Three years for other cases

5.4.12 Distance marketing communications

Learning objective	3.5.15 **Explain** the rules relating to distance marketing communications (COBS 5.1)

The EU **Distance Marketing Directive (DMD)** covers the distance marketing of financial services and has been enacted in the UK via the **Financial Services (Distance Marketing) Regulations 2004**.

COBS Chapter 5 on *Distance communications* includes provisions conforming to the DMD. COBS clarifies how the **Distance Marketing Directive (DMD)** and the Regulations should be interpreted by authorised firms. It requires that certain product disclosures are given to **consumers** who conclude contracts at a distance.

The regulator has taken the view that responsibility for the DMD requirements applies to the Home State except in the case of a branch, in which case responsibility rests with the EEA State in which the branch is located. This means that the relevant COBS rules will apply to branches in the UK, including branches of foreign (EEA or non-EEA) firms.

A **distance contract** is one which is concluded under an **organised distance sales or service-provision scheme** directly or through an intermediary with exclusive use of one or more **means of distance communication**.

Concluding a contract by **means of distance communication** includes by post, telephone, fax or the internet.

The DMD introduced requirements to provide consumers with certain **detailed information** before a contract is concluded, including information about:

- The identity of the supplier (including geographical address)
- Product details (including price and fees), and
- Particulars of the contract (including rights of cancellation)

During **voice telephony** communications, only specified abbreviated distance marketing information needs to be provided. However, the standard distance marketing information must still be provided on a durable medium in good time before the customer is bound by any distance contract or offer.

5.4.13 Information about the firm

Learning objective | **3.5.16 Explain** the rules relating to providing information about the firm and compensation information (COBS 6.1)

Information about a firm and its services which must be provided to a **retail client** comprises the following general information.

- The firm's **name and address** (permanent place of business), and **contact details** which allow effective communication

- For MiFID and equivalent third country business, the **languages** the firm uses for documents and other communication

- **Methods of communication with clients** which are used by the firm, including those for sending and receiving orders where relevant

- Statement that the firm is **authorised**, and the name of the authorising **competent authority** (eg the Financial Conduct Authority) – with the authority's contact address, in the case of MiFID business

- If the firm is acting through an **appointed representative or tied agent**, a statement of this fact specifying the EEA State in which the representative/agent is registered

- The nature, frequency and timing of **performance reports** provided by the firm (in accordance with rules on reporting to clients)

- For a MiFID or common platform firm or a third country (non-EEA) investment firm, the firm's **conflicts of interest policy** (or a summary of it)

- For other firms, details of **how the firm will ensure fair treatment** of clients when material interests or conflicts of interest arise

5.4.14 FCA financial promotions power

The FCA has a **power** – new under the Financial Services Act 2012 –to **ban misleading financial promotions** (s137R FSMA 2000, as amended).

- The regulator will be able to give a **direction** to firms requiring them immediately to withdraw or to modify promotions which it deems to be misleading, and to publish such decisions.

- The firm will be able to make **representations** to the FCA to challenge the Authority's decision. The FCA may then decide to amend or revoke its decision, or it may confirm its original decision. After having given the firm the opportunity to challenge the decision, the FCA can publish: (1) Its direction, (2) A copy of the promotion, and (3) The regulator's reasons for banning it. The FCA may publish details even if it has decided to revoke its decision.

5.5 Suitability

Learning objective	3.5.19 **Explain** the rules relating to assessing suitability (COBS 9.2)

5.5.1 Assessing suitability

Suitability rules apply when a firm makes a **personal recommendation** in relation to a **designated investment** (but not if the firm makes use of the rules on basic scripted advice for stakeholder products).

The firm has obligations regarding the assessment of **suitability**: the firm must take reasonable steps to ensure that, in respect of designated investments, a personal recommendation or a decision to trade is **suitable for its client**.

To meet this obligation, the firm must **obtain necessary information** regarding the client's:

- **Knowledge and experience** in the relevant investment field (including: types of investment or service with which the client is familiar; transactions experience; level of education and profession or former profession; understanding of risks)

- **Investment objectives** (including: length of time he wishes to hold the investment; risk preferences; risk profile; purposes of the investment)

- **Financial situation** (including: extent and source of regular income; assets including liquid assets; investments and real property; regular financial commitments) (Is he able to bear any investment risks, consistent with his investment objectives?)

The firm is entitled to **rely on information provided by the client**, unless it is aware that the information is out of date, inaccurate or incomplete.

A **transaction** may be **unsuitable** for a client because of

- The risks of the designated investments involved
- The type of transaction
- The characteristics of the order
- The frequency of trading
- It resulting in an unsuitable portfolio (in the case of **managing investments**)

For non-MiFID business, these rules apply to business with **retail clients**. When making personal recommendations or managing investments for **professional clients**, in the course of MiFID or equivalent third country business, a firm is entitled to assume that the client has the necessary experience and knowledge, in relation to products and services for which the professional client is so classified.

5.5.2 Suitability report

A firm must provide a **suitability report** to a retail client if the firm makes a personal recommendation and the client:

- Buys or sells shares/units in a regulated collective investment scheme
- Buys or sells shares through an investment trust savings scheme or investment trust ISA
- Makes or changes contributions to a personal or stakeholder pension scheme
- Elects to make income withdrawals from a short-term annuity
- Enters into a pension transfer or pension opt-out

A suitability report is required for all personal recommendations in relation to **life policies**.

A suitability report is **not** required:

- If the firm acts as investment manager and recommends a regulated collective investment scheme
- If a non-EEA resident is not in the UK when acknowledging consent to the proposal form
- For small life policies (not > £50 p.a.) recommended by friendly societies
- For recommendations to increase regular premiums on an existing contract
- For recommendations to invest further single contributions to an existing packaged product

The suitability report must generally be provided to the client **as soon as possible after the transaction is effected**. For personal or stakeholder pension schemes requiring notification of cancellation rights, the report must be provided no later than 14 days after the contract is concluded.

The suitability report must, at least

- Specify the client's **demands and needs**

- Explain the firm's **recommendation** that the transaction is suitable, having regard to information provided by the client

- Explain any possible **disadvantages** of the transaction to the client

The firm should give details appropriate to the **complexity** of the transaction.

For **income withdrawals** from a **short-term annuity**, the explanation of possible disadvantages should include **risk factors** involved in income withdrawals or purchase of a short-term annuity.

5.6 Appropriateness – for non-advised sales

Learning objectives

3.5.20 **Explain** the rules relating to assessing appropriateness (COBS 10.2)

3.5.21 **Explain** the rules relating to warning a client about the appropriateness of their instructions (COBS 10.3)

3.5.22 **Identify** circumstances when assessing appropriateness is not required (COBS 10.4, 10.5 & 10.6)

The central aim of the appropriateness rules – which were introduced under **MiFID** – is to prevent complex products from being sold on an **execution only** basis (that is, without advice) to **retail clients** who do not have the experience and/or the knowledge to understand the risks of such products.

The **appropriateness** rules apply to a firm providing **MiFID investment services**, **other than** making a personal recommendation and managing investments ('non-advised sales'). (As we have seen, the **suitability** rules apply where there is a personal recommendation.) The rules thus apply to '**execution only**' services which are available in the UK, where transactions are undertaken at the initiative of the customer without advice having been given.

Additionally, for both MiFID and non-MiFID business, the appropriateness rules apply to arranging or dealing in **derivatives** or **warrants** for a **retail client**, when in response to a **direct offer financial promotion**. The FCA Handbook Glossary defines **derivatives** as comprising **contracts for differences (CfDs), futures and options**.

Except for the case of direct offer business, the appropriateness test is not required for non-MiFID business: therefore, it does not apply to non-MiFID products such as insurance policies, deposits (including structured deposits) and pension plans.

To **assess appropriateness**, the firm must ask the client to provide information on his knowledge and experience in the relevant investment field, to enable the assessment to be made.

The firm will then:

- Determine whether the client has the necessary **experience and knowledge** to understand the **risks** involved in the product/service (including the following aspects: nature and extent of service with which client is familiar; complexity; risks involved; extent of client's transactions in designated investments; level of client's education and profession or former profession)

- Be entitled to assume that a **professional client** has such experience and knowledge, for products/services for which it is classified as 'professional'

Unless it knows the information from the client to be out-of-date, inaccurate or incomplete, the firm may rely on it. Where reasonable, a firm may infer knowledge from experience. One firm may rely on another MiFID firm's assessment of appropriateness, in line with the general rule on reliance on other investment firms.

The firm may seek to increase the client's level of understanding by providing appropriate information to the client.

If the firm is satisfied about the client's experience and knowledge, there is **no duty to communicate** this to the client. If the firm concludes that the product or service is **not appropriate** to the client, it must **warn** the client. The warning may be in a standardised format.

If the client provides insufficient information, the firm must **warn** the client that such a decision will not allow the firm to determine whether the service or product is appropriate for him. Again, the warning may be in a standardised format.

If a client who has received a warning asks the firm to go ahead with the transaction, it is for the firm to consider whether to do so 'having regard to the circumstances'.

Records relating to appropriateness must be kept for at least **five years**.

A firm **need not assess appropriateness**:

- For an execution-only service in listed shares, funds and other non-complex financial instruments provided on the initiative of the client, if the client is warned that there will be no suitability assessment and the firm meets conflict of interest requirements

- If it is receiving or transmitting an order in relation to which it has assessed suitability

- If it is able to rely on a recommendation made by an investment firm

- On each occasion, in new dealings with a client engaged in a course of dealings

5.7 Referring to specialists

Learning objective **3.5.23 Identify** circumstances where own authority or expertise is limited and there is the need to refer to specialists

Very few financial advisers have extensive or sufficient knowledge in all areas of financial planning. If dealings with a client involve actions that are beyond the authority of the adviser, either as a result of the firm's rules or the regulator's requirements and rules, then the adviser should seek authority from an appropriate person.

The adviser should be able to refer to other specialists within the firm, and should be willing to do so if necessary. Advisers may also need to refer to specialists outside their business in certain areas of advice and should explain to the client when it would be necessary.

5.8 Best execution

Learning objective **3.5.25 Explain** the rules relating to best execution (COBS 11.2)

The basic COBS rule of **best execution** is as follows.

> A firm must take all reasonable steps to obtain, when executing orders, the best possible result for its clients taking into account the **execution factors**. The execution factors are price, costs, speed, likelihood of execution and settlement, size, nature or any other consideration relevant to the execution of an order.

In determining the relative importance of the execution factors, firms must take into account **best execution criteria** which comprise characteristics of the:

- Client, including categorisation as retail or professional
- Client order
- Financial instruments
- Execution venues

The '**best possible result**' must be determined in terms of **total consideration** – taking into account any costs, including the firm's own commissions in the case of competing execution venues, and not just quoted prices. (However, the firm is not expected to compare the result with that of clients of other firms.) Commissions structure must not discriminate between execution venues.

When a firm is **dealing on own account with clients**, this is considered to be execution of client orders, and is therefore subject to the best execution rule.

If a firm provides a best quote to a client, it is acceptable for the quote to be executed after the client accepts it, provided the quote is not manifestly out of date.

The obligation to obtain best execution needs to be interpreted according to the particular type of financial instrument involved, but the rule applies to **all types of financial instrument**.

5.9 Order execution policy

5.9.1 Policy requirements

The firm must establish and implement an **order execution policy**, and it must monitor its effectiveness regularly. The policy must include, for each class of financial instruments, information on different execution venues used by the firm, and the factors affecting choice of execution venue.

The firm should choose venues that enable it to obtain on a consistent basis the best possible result for execution of client orders. For each client order, the firm should apply its execution policy with a view to achieving the best possible result for the client.

If orders may be executed outside a regulated market or multilateral trading facility, this must be disclosed, and clients must give prior express consent.

A firm must be able to demonstrate to clients, on request, that it has followed its execution policy.

5.9.2 Client consent and clients' specific instructions

The firm must provide a **retail client** with details on its execution policy before providing the service, covering the relative importance the firm assigns to execution factors, a list of execution venues on which the firm relies, and a clear and prominent warning that **specific instructions** by the client could prevent the firm from following its execution policy steps fully.

If the client gives **specific instructions**, the firm has met its best execution obligation if it obtains the best result in following those instructions. The firm should not induce a client to gives such instructions, if they could prevent best execution from being obtained. However, the firm may invite the client to choose between execution venues.

The firm must obtain the **prior consent** of clients to its execution policy, and the policy must be **reviewed annually** and whenever there is a material change in the firm's ability to achieve the best possible result consistently from execution venues.

5.10 Client order handling

Learning objective **3.5.26 Explain** the rules relating to client order handling (COBS 11.3)

The general rule on **client order handling** is that firms must implement procedures and arrangements which provide for the prompt, fair and expeditious execution of client orders, relative to other orders or the trading interests of the firm.

These procedures and arrangements must allow for the execution of otherwise comparable orders in accordance with the time of their reception by the firm.

When carrying out **client orders**, firms must:

- Ensure that orders are promptly and accurately recorded and allocated
- Carry out otherwise comparable orders sequentially and promptly, unless this is impracticable or not in clients' interests
- Inform a retail client about any material difficulty in carrying out orders promptly, on becoming aware of it

Where it is not practicable to treat orders sequentially eg because they are received by different media, they should not be treated as 'otherwise comparable'.

Firms must not allow the **misuse of information** relating to pending client orders. Any use of such information to deal on own account should be considered a misuse of the information.

When overseeing or arranging **settlement**, a firm must take reasonable steps to ensure that instruments or funds due are delivered to the client account promptly and correctly.

Aggregation (grouping together) of client orders with other client orders or a transaction for own account is not permitted unless the following apply.

- It is unlikely to work to the disadvantage to any of the clients

- It is disclosed to each client that the effect of aggregation may work to its disadvantage

- An **order allocation policy** is established and implemented, covering the fair allocation of aggregated orders, including how the volume and price of orders determines allocations, and the treatment of partial executions

5.11 Use of dealing commission

Learning objective **3.5.27 Explain** the rules relating to the use of dealing commission (COBS 11.6)

The practice of using dealing commission (previously called **soft commission**) dates back many years. The practice developed from brokers effectively **rebating** part of the commission paid by large fund management clients, to be used to cover the costs of services such as equity research. The effect was to reduce the 'real' commission paid for the execution of the trade. It is therefore necessary to control these arrangements to ensure that customers who ultimately pay the commissions, namely the fund managers' clients, are protected from abuse.

The rules on the use of dealing commission aim to ensure that an investment manager's arrangements, in relation to dealing commissions spent on acquiring services in addition to execution, are transparent and demonstrate accountability to customers so that customers are treated fairly.

The rules therefore ensure firms comply with Principle 1 (Integrity), Principle 6 (Customers' Interests) and Principle 8 (Conflicts of Interest).

The rules on the use of dealing commission apply to investment managers when executing customer orders through a broker or another person in shares or other investments which relate to shares, eg warrants, hybrids (ADRs and options) and rights to, or interests in, investments.

When the investment manager passes on the broker's or other person's charges (whether commission or otherwise) to its customers and in return arranges to receive goods or services **the rules require the investment manager to be satisfied that the goods or services:**

- Relate to the execution of trades, or
- Comprise the provision of research

This is subject to a clause that the goods or services will reasonably assist the investment manager in the provision of services to its customers and do not impair compliance with the duty of the investment manager to act in the best interests of its customers.

In relation to goods or services relating to the execution of trades, the regulator has confirmed that post-trade analytics, eg performance measurement, is not going to be an acceptable use of dealing commission.

Where the goods or services relate to research, the investment manager will have to be satisfied that the research:

- Is capable of **adding value** to the investment or trading decisions by providing **new insights** that inform the investment manager when making such decisions about its customers' portfolios

- In whatever form its output takes, represents **original thought**, in the critical and careful consideration and assessment of new and existing facts, and does not merely repeat or repackage what has been presented before

- Has **intellectual rigour** and does not merely state what is commonplace or self-evident, and

- Involves analysis or manipulation of data to reach **meaningful conclusions**

Examples of goods or services that relate to the execution of trades or the provision of research that are **not** going to be **acceptable** to the FCA include the following.

- Services relating to the valuation or performance measurement of portfolios
- Computer hardware
- Dedicated telephone lines
- Seminar fees
- Subscriptions for publications
- Travel, accommodation or entertainment costs
- Office administration computer software, such as word processing or accounting programmes
- Membership fees to professional associations
- Purchase or rental of standard office equipment or ancillary facilities
- Employees' salaries
- Direct money payments
- Publicly available information
- Custody services relating to designated investments belonging to, or managed for, customers

Investment managers must make **adequate prior disclosure** to customers about receipt of goods and services that relate to the execution of trades or the provision of research. This should form part of the summary form disclosure under the rule on inducements. **Periodic disclosures** made on an annual basis are recommended.

5.12 Inducements

For MiFID business, inducements rules apply to all fees, other payments and non-monetary benefits, which must enhance the quality of the service provided to clients, in accordance with the client's best interests. Firms within the scope of MiFID must disclose to clients the essential details or the existence, nature and amount of fees, payments or non-monetary benefits. The disclosure must be made before services are provided and must be clear, comprehensive and accurate.

The inducements rules supplement Principles 1 and 6 of the *Principles for Businesses*. They seek to ensure that firms do not conduct business under arrangements that may give rise to conflicts of interest.

In relation to the sale of **retail investment products**, the following are among the list provided at COBS 2.3.15 as broadly deemed to be **reasonable non-monetary benefits**.

- Gifts, hospitality and promotional prizes of reasonable value, given by product provider to the firm
- Assistance in promotion of retail investment products
- Generic product literature which enhances client service, with costs borne by the recipient firm
- Generic technical information
- Training facilities
- Reasonable travel and accommodation expenses, eg to meetings or training

If a product provider makes benefits available to one firm but not another, this is more likely to impair compliance with the **client's best interests rule**. Most firms deliver against the inducements requirements by drafting detailed '**gifts policies**' (although the rule does **not** explicitly require firms to have a gifts policy). These contain internal rules regarding disclosure, limits and clearance procedures for gifts.

5.13 Personal account dealing

Learning objective	3.5.28 **Explain** the rules on personal account dealing (COBS 11.7)

Personal account dealing relates to trades undertaken by the staff of a regulated business for themselves, or by those providing outsourced services for the firm. Such trades can create **conflicts of interest** between staff and customers. As a matter of good practice, a firm's policy on personal account dealing should generally be extended to immediate family members.

A firm conducting **designated investment business** must establish, implement and maintain adequate **arrangements** aimed at preventing employees who are involved in activities where a conflict of interest could occur, or who has access to inside information, from:

- Entering into a transaction which is prohibited under the **Market Abuse Directive**, or which involves misuse or improper disclosure of confidential information, or conflicts with an obligation of the firm to a customer under the regulatory system

- Except in the course of his job, advising or procuring anyone else to enter into such a transaction

- Except in the course of his job, disclosing any information or opinion to another person if the person disclosing it should know that, as a result, the other person would be likely to enter into such a transaction or advise or procure another to enter into such a transaction

The **firm's arrangements** under these provisions must be designed to ensure that:

- All relevant persons (staff involved) are aware of the personal dealing restrictions

- The firm is informed promptly of any personal transaction

- A service provider to whom activities are outsourced maintain a record of personal transactions and provides it to the firm promptly on request

- A record is kept of personal transactions notified to the firm or identified by it, including any related authorisation or prohibition

The rule on personal account dealing is **disapplied** for personal transactions:

- Under a discretionary portfolio management service where there has been no prior communication between the portfolio manager and the person for whom the transaction is executed

- In UCITS collective undertakings (eg OEICs and unit trusts) where the person is not involved in its management

- In life policies

- For successive personal transactions where there were prior instructions in force, nor to the termination of the instruction provided that no financial instruments are sold at the same time

5.14 Churning and switching

'**Churning**' of investments and excessive **switching** between products are similar wrongs. They involve the cynical **overtrading** of customer accounts for the purpose of generating commission. This would clearly contravene the **client's best interests rule**.

Churning or switching will often be difficult to isolate, unless blatant. Much would depend upon the market conditions prevailing at the time of dealing.

The **COBS rules** on churning and switching state that:

- A series of transactions that are each suitable when viewed in isolation may be unsuitable if the recommendations or the decisions to trade are made with a frequency that is not in the best interests of the client

- A firm should have regard to the client's agreed investment strategy in determining the frequency of transactions. This would include, for example, the need to switch within or between packaged products

5.15 Conflicts of interest

Learning objective | **3.5.29 Explain** the purpose of the principles and rules on conflicts of interest, including: identifying, recording and disclosing conflicts of interest and managing them to ensure the fair treatment of clients (PRIN 2.1.1, Principle 8, SYSC 10.1.1-7, 10.1.8/9 & 10.2)

5.15.1 Overview

Principle 8 of the Principles for Businesses requires that a firm must manage conflicts of interest fairly, both between itself and its customers and between a customer and another customer. **SYSC 4 and SYSC 10** require the firms' boards of directors to establish effective frameworks to identify, control and review conflicts of interest. The **Conduct of Business Sourcebook (COBS)** contains detailed rules governing the purchase of goods and services using customers' money and the allocation of investment opportunities between customers.

SYSC 10 applies to firms carrying on regulated activities or providing MiFID ancillary services, where a service is provided to any category of client.

- Under MiFID, firms are required to keep a conflicts of interest policy in writing which identifies the circumstances which may give rise to a conflict of interest with material risk of damage to clients. This policy should specify the measures adopted to manage conflicts and require that necessary records of conflicts are kept.

- The MiFID conflicts of interest rules will apply to **all clients**: retail, professional and eligible counterparties.

5.15.2 SYSC 10 general provisions

The firm must take all **reasonable steps** to **identify conflicts of interest** between the firm, its managers, employees and appointed representatives or tied agents, or between clients, which may arise in providing a service.

The firm must take into account, as a minimum:

- Likely financial gains, or avoidance of losses, at the expense of a client

- Interests in the outcome of a service which are different from the client's interest

- Financial incentives to favour some clients or groups of client, and

- Whether the firm carries on the same business as the client, or receives inducements in the form of monies, goods and services other than the standard commission or fee for that service

Regularly updated records must be kept of where conflicts of interest have or may arise.

The firm must maintain and operate effective **organisational and administrative arrangements** to prevent conflicts of interest from giving rise to material risk of damage to clients' interests.

Where conflicts are not preventable, the firm must **disclose** them to clients – in a durable medium, in sufficient detail for the client to take an informed decision – before undertaking business.

Firms should aim to **identify** and **manage** conflicts under a **comprehensive conflicts of interest policy**. That firms actively manage conflicts is important: over-reliance on disclosure without adequate consideration of how to manage conflicts is not permitted.

5.15.3 Conflicts policy (SYSC 10.1)

A firm must maintain an effective **conflicts of interest policy**, in **writing** and appropriate to the size and type of firm and its business.

The conflicts of interest policy must:

- Identify circumstances constituting or potentially giving rise to conflicts materially affecting clients
- Specify procedures and measures to manage the conflicts

The procedures and measures must:

- Be designed to ensure that activities are carried on an appropriate **level of independence**

- As and where necessary, include procedures to **prevent and control exchange of information** between persons involved, to **supervise persons separately**, to remove **links in remuneration** producing possible conflicts, to prevent exercise of **inappropriate influence**, and to **prevent and control simultaneous and sequential involvement** of persons in separate services or activities

In drawing up its conflicts policy, the firm must pay **special attention** to the following **activities** (in particular, where persons perform a combination of activities): investment research and advice, proprietary trading, portfolio management and corporate finance business, including underwriting or selling in an offer of securities, and advising on mergers and acquisitions.

5.15.4 Managing conflicts of interest

Firms must manage conflicts of interest fairly between itself and customers and also between customers, under PRIN 8. SYSC rules combine with COBS rules in directing how a firm can manage conflicts.

A potential conflict of interest might be dealt with by one or more of the following methods.

- **Declining to act**. This can ensure that the conflict does not arise, or is removed in the future.

- **Chinese Walls**. These are administrative and/or physical barriers, and other internal arrangements, which are designed to contain sensitive information and to reduce the likelihood of it spreading between departments of the firm.

- **Independence policy**. This is a written policy of a firm, requiring that the firm and its employees follow a policy of independence in their business.

- **Disclosure**. Following MiFID, disclosure is now only to be used as a measure of last resort under SYSC 10, when all other reasonable steps to manage a conflict fail.

5.16 Retail advice and charging

Learning objectives

3.5.17 **Explain** the rules on adviser charging and remuneration (COBS 6.3 & 6.4)
3.5.24 **Distinguish** between independent and restricted advice (COBS 6.2A)
3.5.36 **Distinguish** between packaged products and retail investment products

5.16.1 Introduction

The rules arising from the **Retail Distribution Review (RDR)** have applied **since 31 December 2012**. The regulator considers that removing the potential for commission to bias product recommendations means that consumers can be more confident that they are being sold the product that best fits their needs. The RDR rules represent a fundamental change and ware leading to many firms re-thinking their business models.

5.16.2 Key points of the RDR

Under the RDR rules, **independent advice** and **restricted advice** are distinguished. In making the distinction between **independent advice** and **restricted advice**, the regulator wants to set a new standard for independent investment advice and to improve clarity for consumers about the different types of advice on offer.

If an adviser declares themselves to offer **independent advice**, they will need to consider a broader range of **retail investment products (RIPs)**, a wider category than packaged products.

The definition of a **packaged product** (a pre-RDR category that still has some relevance) encompasses units in regulated collective investment schemes (CISs) (such as unit trusts and open-ended investment companies (OEICs)), investment trust savings schemes, personal pensions, stakeholder pensions and life policies. Packaged products are products that can be bought 'off-the-shelf', with the terms and conditions and price identical for all potential investors. The product will be a packaged product regardless of whether it is wrapped in an ISA.

Advice which is not independent must be labelled as **restricted advice**, for example as advice on a limited range of products or providers.

Under the new regime, a firm making a personal recommendation to a retail client to **invest in a retail investment product**, or providing **related services** can no longer receive commission from the product provider. The firm will instead receive an **adviser charge** that has been agreed with the client in advance.

5.16.3 Independent advice and restricted advice

All advisers must inform their clients, before providing advice, whether they provide 'independent' or 'restricted' advice.

- If an adviser declares themselves to offer **independent advice**, they will need to consider a broader range of products beyond the existing definition of 'packaged products'. (See below on retail investment products or RIPs.)

- Advice which is not independent must be labelled as **restricted advice**, for example as advice on a limited range of products or providers. Restricted advisers are still required to meet the regulator's suitability requirements even if they offer restricted advice.

5.16.4 The standard for independent advice

The RDR standard for **independent advice** is intended to ensure that such advice is genuinely free from bias towards particular solutions or any restrictions that would limit the range of solutions that firms can recommend to their clients. In providing independent advice, a firm should not be restricted by product provider, and should also be able to objectively consider all types of retail investment products which are capable of meeting the investment needs and objectives of a retail client.

Advice that does not meet the standard for independent advice is **restricted advice**. Restricted advice will come in many different forms. While a firm needs to describe the nature of its restricted advice service to clients, it is free to choose the words that are appropriate for its service.

Independent advice is defined in the Handbook as 'a personal recommendation to a retail client in relation to a RIP where the personal recommendation provided meets the requirements of the **rule on independent advice** ('the **standard for independent advice**') (COBS 6.2A.3R), which requires that the personal recommendation is:

- **Based on a comprehensive and fair analysis of the relevant market**, and
- **Unbiased and unrestricted**

It will be clear that a firm must not hold itself out to a retail client as **acting independently** unless it meets the standard for independent advice. We now define the key terms in the definition of independent advice in detail.

The term **retail investment product (RIP)** is defined in the FCA Handbook Glossary as a product that is one of the following, whether or not held within an ISA or Child Trust Fund:

- Life policy

- Unit (in an authorised unit trust or OEIC)

- Stakeholder pension scheme (including group schemes)

- Personal pension scheme (including group schemes)

- Interest in an investment trust savings scheme

- Security in an investment trust

- Any other designated investment which offers exposure to underlying financial assets, in a packaged form which modifies that exposure when compared with a direct holding in a financial asset – this could include an Exchange Traded Fund (ETF)

- Structured capital-at-risk product (SCARP)

The definition of a RIP is intentionally broad to ensure that all comparable investment products sold to retail clients on an advised basis, including those developed in the future, are subject to the same relevant selling standards, for example the requirement to be remunerated by adviser charges.

Examples of financial instruments that are **not** RIPs would include a share in an individual company whose primary business is not investing in two or more financial assets, an individual fixed interest security, and an individual derivative, where the exposure to the relevant asset is not modified in any way.

Note the use of the term 'relevant market' in the standard for independent advice above. COBS 6.2A.11G states that a **relevant market** should 'comprise all retail investment products which are capable of meeting the investment needs and objectives of a retail client'.

- For example, if a client indicates that they are only interested in ethical and socially responsible investments (SRI), it is clear that there is a range of products that would never be suitable for them, namely non-ethical investments. Their relevant market would exclude non-ethical investments, and an adviser would not need to consider these products when forming independent advice for such a client.

- So, a relevant market in the context of the standard for independent advice is defined by a client's investment needs and objectives and not, for example, by product or service types.

What are the implications of the terms **'comprehensive and fair analysis'** and **'unbiased and unrestricted'** as used in the standard? The regulator gives the following guidance.

- If a firm cannot or will not advise on a particular type of retail investment product, and that product could potentially meet the investment needs and objectives of its new and existing clients, then its advice will not meet the standard for independent advice.

- In other words, the justification for a firm excluding types of retail investment products from its range needs to be **centred on the client**. As an example, the fact that a firm's professional indemnity insurance policy specifically excludes certain products would not be a valid reason for never advising on such products. However, firms may consider **Unregulated Collective Investment Schemes (UCIS)** too risky for the clients they usually deal with, and the regulator would not expect a firm to recommend these just to prove they are offering independent advice.

The regulator expects that UCIS will be suitable for very few retail clients, if any. (COBS 4.12 already limits the categories of investors to whom UCIS can be marketed.) Where the regulator has identified high-risk products and recommended that they should not reach UK retail investors in the UK, a firm does not need to consider them for its clients to meet the standard for independent advice.

Providing unbiased and unrestricted advice might include considering **financial products that are not RIPs**, such as National Savings & Investments products or cash ISAs, if they could meet the client's needs and objectives (COBS 6.2A.14-17G).

5.16.5 Restricted advice

Restricted advice is defined (in the Handbook Glossary) as:

- A personal recommendation to a retail client in relation to a retail investment product which is not independent advice, or

- Basic advice (on stakeholder products, using pre-scripted questions)

In other words, if a personal recommendation on a retail investment product does not meet the standard for independent advice, then it is restricted advice.

Restricted advice must meet the same suitability, inducement, adviser charging and professionalism standards as independent advice. The key difference in the requirements is in **disclosure**.

- In its **written disclosure**, a firm that provides restricted advice must explain the nature of the restriction (COBS 6.2A.6R).

- A firm must also provide **oral disclosure** if it engages in spoken interaction with a retail client (COBS 6.2A.9R).

The rules allow firms **flexibility** in how they **describe** their restricted advice services, so long as they are being **fair, clear and not misleading** in their communications.

- A firm can, for example, explain that it reviews the whole market for the particular products on which it gives advice, if this is an accurate description of its service.

- A firm should not, however, give the impression that it has restricted its product range to those products that are most suitable for a particular client.

5.16.6 Adviser charging

An important element of the RDR **adviser charging** rules is a **ban on firms receiving or paying commission** in relation to personal recommendations to retail customers on retail investment products (RIPs) or providing related services. '**Related services**' in this context covers arranging or administering recommended transactions, and managing the relationship between the client and a discretionary investment manager (DIM).

A firm making a personal recommendation to a retail client to **invest in a retail investment product**, or providing **related services**, no longer receives commission from the product provider. The firm will instead receive an **adviser charge** that has been agreed with the client in advance.

- The **adviser** must not solicit or accept commission, remuneration or benefit of any other kind, even if the intention is to pass it on to the client.

- The **product provider** must not offer or pay commission, remuneration or benefits of any kind in connection with advice or related services. However, product providers may facilitate the payment of adviser charges from the client's investment and is not barred from paying administrative or other charges to third parties, such as fund supermarkets.

This charging regime will apply for both independent advice and restricted advice, but **not** for **basic advice** (using **pre-scripted questions**) on stakeholder products. (For this kind of basic advice, advisers are still able to earn commission on individual sales, post-RDR.)

5.16.7 Charging structure

Adviser charges could be tailored for the particular client or may be structured as a standardised **price list**. The **charging structure** is a matter for the firm, and could be based on fixed fees, hourly rates or on a percentage of funds invested, for example, subject to the requirement to act in the client's best interests.

The charging structure must be **disclosed to the client** in writing and in clear and plain language, 'in good time' before any advice or related services are provided. Material **discrepancies** between actual charges and the disclosed charging structure must be disclosed to the client as soon as practicable.

There should only be **ongoing charges** if the firm is providing an ongoing value-added service and if this is disclosed to the client.

The total adviser charge payable by the client, in cash or cash-equivalents, and in what amounts and at what times, must be agreed with and disclosed to the client as soon as is practicable in a durable medium or via a website. Consequences of **cancellation** must be stated, where payments are to be made over time, for example in instalments.

5.16.8 Records

Firms must keep **records** of:

- The charging structure
- The total adviser charge payable for each client
- Reasons for any material difference between the adviser charge and the charging structure

5.16.9 Product providers

The new adviser charging regime will also apply to **product providers** who advise clients directly on their own products, based on the following rules.

- Product providers' adviser charges must be 'at least reasonably representative' of adviser services provided and should thus not include costs of creating and administering the product. Amounts charged should be such as would be appropriate if the advice and related services were offered by an unconnected firm.

- Product costs should not be structured so that they mislead or conceal the distinction between product costs and adviser charges. The regulator is seeking to end product providers' past practice of offering to allocate over 100% of a client's investment without indicating clearly that higher charges will apply.

5.16.10 Legacy (pre-RDR) assets

Guidance from the regulator states that a firm may continue to accept commission after 30 December 2012 if there is a clear link between the commission payment and an investment in a retail investment product that was made by the retail client following a personal recommendation made, or a transaction executed, on or before 30 December 2012. Thus, **trail commission** on advice given before the RDR rules come into effect can continue, and even transferred to a new adviser or firm, until the product matures or is terminated.

Trail commission (or 'renewal commission') comprises annual payments to a financial adviser, normally by deduction from the value of investments, over the years after an investment contract has been commenced.

5.16.11 Disclosure of charges – non-advised sales

Under the RDR, rules on the disclosure of charges and commission apply to a firm selling or arranging packaged products for retail clients, where **no personal recommendation** is given. The firm must disclose, in cash terms, any **commission receivable** by it or its associates. (RDR rules have not changed the commission arrangements for **non-advised sales**.)

5.17 FCA's Product intervention power

Learning objective	3.5.18 **Explain** the FCA's approach to Temporary Product Intervention

5.17.1 Product intervention

An initiative of the previous regulator, the FSA, that will be taken forward by the FCA concerns identifying consumer detriment problems at an earlier stage through **product intervention**.

The FCA's product intervention power gives it the 'flexibility to intervene quickly and decisively' where it considers that a product or product feature is likely to result in significant consumer detriment. The FCA will seek to deal with the root of the problem, rather than reacting to the effects, when it is already too late.

5.17.2 Temporary product intervention rules (TPIRs)

The FCA gets its power to make product intervention rules under s137D FSMA 2000 (as amended by FSA 2012) aiming to tackle issues relating to specific products (or types of products), product features or marketing practices.

Normally, the FCA must **consult the public** before making any rules. However, s138L FSMA 2000 provides a general exemption from this requirement if the FCA considers that the delay involved in complying with the requirement would be prejudicial to the interests of consumers.

S138M makes a more specific exemption for making **temporary product intervention rules (TPIRs)**, where the FCA considers it necessary or expedient in order to advance its objectives. Such TPIRs, made **before consultation** (under s138M FSMA 2000), are limited to a maximum duration of 12 months. TPIRs will offer protection to consumers in the short term while allowing either the FCA or industry to develop a more permanent solution to address the source of detriment. They may also be made in response to competition or (if applicable) market integrity issues.

Rules may range from requiring certain product features to be included, excluded or changed, requiring amendments to promotional materials, to imposing restrictions on sales or marketing of the product or, in more serious cases, a ban on sales or marketing of a product in relation to all or some types of customer.

In a December 2012 Consultation Paper, the regulator set out the following examples of the kind of scenarios in which TPIRs might be used by the FCA.

- Products that would be acceptable but for the inclusion or exclusion of particular features

- Products where there is a significant incentive for inappropriate or indiscriminate targeting of consumers

- Markets where firms restrict their product range or access to their product range in ways designed to increase profitability by restricting consumer choice, reducing competition, or creating barriers to search, switching, or entry

- Products which may bring about significant detriment as a result of being inappropriately targeted; or

- In particularly serious cases, a product considered to be inherently flawed – for example, a product that has such disadvantageous features that the majority of consumers, or specified types of consumer, are unlikely to benefit.

5.18 Investment research

5.18.1 Investment research and conflicts of interest

Learning objective	3.5.30 **Explain** the rules relating to investment research produced by a firm and disseminated to clients (COBS 12.2)

There have been concerns that analysts have been encouraged to write favourable research on companies in order to attract lucrative investment banking work. There have also been concerns about firm's employees recommending particular securities while privately trading contrary to the recommendation.

COBS rules on investment research apply to MiFID business carried on by a MiFID investment firm. Rules on disclosure of research recommendations apply to all firms.

There are rules covering investment research which is intended or likely to be disseminated to clients or to the public.

Firms must ensure that its measures for **managing conflicts of interest** cover the **financial analysts** who produce its investment research, and any other relevant staff.

The firm's arrangements must ensure that:

- The financial analysts and other staff involved do not undertake personal transactions or trade on behalf of other persons, including the firm (unless they are acting as a market maker in good faith), in financial instruments to which unpublished investment research relates, until the **recipients** of the research have had a **reasonable opportunity** to act on it

- In other circumstances, personal transactions by financial analysts and other staff in financial instruments related to investment research they are producing which is **contrary to current recommendations** must only occur in **exceptional circumstances** and with **prior approval** of the firm's legal or compliance function

- The firm and its staff must not **accept inducements** from those with a material interest in the subject matter of investment research, and they must not **promise issuers favourable research coverage**

- Issuers and persons other than financial analysts must not be allowed to **review pre-publication drafts** of investment research for any purpose **other than to verify compliance** with the firm's legal obligations, if the draft includes a recommendation or a target price

There is an exemption from the rules in this section where a firm distributes investment research **produced by a third party** which is not in the firm's group, provided that the firm does not alter the recommendations and does not present the research as produced by the firm. The firm is required to verify that the independent producer of the research has equivalent arrangements in place to avoid conflicts of interest.

5.18.2 Non-independent research

Learning objective | **3.5.31 Explain** the rules relating to the publication and dissemination of non-independent research (COBS 12.3)

Investment research is research which Is described as investment research or in similar terms, or is otherwise presented as an objective or independent explanation of the matters contained in the recommendation. Research not meeting this requirement falls within the definition of **non-independent research**.

Non-independent research must:

- Be clearly identified as a **marketing communication**

- Contain a clear and prominent statement that it does not follow the requirements of independent research and is not subject to prohibitions on dealing ahead of dissemination of research

Financial promotions rules apply to non-independent research as if it were a marketing communication.

Firms must take **reasonable care** to ensure that research recommendations are fairly presented, and to disclose its interests or indicate conflicts of interest.

Situations where conflicts can arise include:

- Employees trading in financial instruments which they know the firm has or intends to publish non-independent research about, before clients have had a reasonable opportunity to act on the research (other than where the firm is acting as a market maker in good faith, or in the execution of an unsolicited client order)

- Non-independent research intended first for internal use and for later publication to clients

5.18.3 Research recommendations

Learning objective | **3.5.32 Explain** the disclosure requirements relating to the production and dissemination of research recommendations (COBS 12.4)

The **identity** (name, job title, name of firm, competent authority) of the person responsible for the research should be disclosed clearly and prominently.

The research should meet certain **general standards** for example to ensure that facts are distinguished from interpretations or opinions. Projections should be labelled as such. Reliable sources should be used, and any doubts about reliability clearly indicated. The substance of the recommendations should be possible to be substantiated by the regulator on request.

Additionally, the firm must take reasonable care to ensure **fair presentation**, broadly covering the following aspects.

- Indication of material sources, including the issuer (if appropriate)
- Disclosure of whether the recommendation was disclosed to the issuer and then amended
- Summary of valuation basis or methodology
- Explanation of the meaning of any recommendation (eg 'buy', 'sell', 'hold')
- Risk warning if appropriate
- Planned frequency of updates
- Date of release of research, and date and time of prices mentioned
- Details of change over any previous recommendation in the last year

Firms must make **disclosures** in research recommendations broadly covering the following areas.

- All **relationships and circumstances** (including those of affiliated companies) that may reasonably be expected to impair the objectivity of the recommendation (especially, financial interests in any relevant investment, and a conflict of interest regarding the issuer)

- Whether employees involved have **remuneration** tied to investment banking transactions

- **Shareholdings** held by the firm (or an affiliated company) of over 5% of the share capital of the issuer

- **Shareholdings** held by the issuer of over 5% of the share capital of the firm (or an affiliated company)

- Other **significant financial interests**

- Statements about the **role of the firm** as market maker, lead manager of previous offers of the issuer in the last year, provider of investment banking services

- Statements about **arrangements** to prevent and avoid conflicts of interest, prices and dates at which employees involved acquired shares

- **Data** on the proportions of the firm's **recommendations** in different categories (e. g. 'buy', 'sell', 'hold'), on a quarterly basis, with the proportions of relevant investments issued by issuers who were investment banking clients of the firm during the last year

- Identification of a **third party** who produced the research, if applicable, describing also any alteration of third party recommendations and ensuring that any summary of third party research is fair, clear and not misleading

For shorter recommendations, firms can make reference to many of the relevant disclosures, eg by providing a website link.

5.19 Disclosure requirements

Learning objectives	**3.5.33 Explain** the obligations relating to preparing product information (COBS 13.1 & COLL 4.7) **3.5.34 Explain** the rules relating to the form and content of a key features document and a key investor information document (COBS 13.2, 13.3, 14.2 & COLL 4.7)

5.19.1 Key features documents and illustrations

A firm selling a packaged product (other than UCITS funds) must provide a **key features document** and a **key features illustration** to the client.

The **key features illustration** sets out **projected performance** and the **effect of charges**. It must normally include a **standardised deterministic projection**, which will be either a **generic projection** or a **personal projection**.

A **single document** may be used as the key features document for **different schemes**, if the schemes are offered through a **platform service** and the document clearly describes the difference between the schemes.

A **key features document** must:

- Be produced / presented to **at least** the quality / standard of **sales and marketing material** used to promote the product

- Display the **firm's brand** as prominently as any other

- Include the **keyfacts logo** prominently at the top

- Include the following **statement**, in a prominent position:

  'The Financial Conduct Authority is a financial services regulator. It requires us, [provider name], to give you this important information to help you to decide whether our [product name] is right for you. You should read this document carefully so that you understand what you are buying, and then keep it safe for future reference.'

- Not include anything that might reasonably cause a retail client to be **mistaken** about the **identity** of the firm that produced, or will produce, the product

Post-RDR, a rule is added to require that **changes to adviser charges** for packaged products are explained to retail clients.

5.19.2 Contents of key features document

Required headings in a **key features document** are as follows. (The **order** shown below must be followed.)

- *Title:* '**key features of the [name of product]**'

- *Heading:* '**Its aims**' – followed by a brief description of the product's aims

- *Heading:* '**Your commitment**' or '**Your investment**' – followed by information on what a retail client is committing to or investing in and any consequences of failing to maintain the commitment or investment

- *Heading:* '**Risks**' – followed by information on the material risks associated with the product, including a description of the factors that may have an adverse effect on performance or are material to the decision to invest

- *Heading:* '**Questions and answers**' – (in the form of questions and answers) about the principal terms of the product, what it will do for a retail client and any other information necessary to enable a retail client to make an informed decision

The **key features document** must:

- Include **enough information** about the nature and complexity of the product, any minimum standards / limitations, material benefits / risks of buying or investing for a retail client to be able to make an **informed decision** about whether to proceed

- Explain arrangements for handling **complaints**

- Explain the **compensation** available from the FSCS if the firm cannot meet its liabilities

- Explain whether there are **cancellation / withdrawal rights**, their duration and conditions, including amounts payable if the right is exercised, consequences of not exercising, and practical instructions for exercising the right, including the address to which any notice must be sent

- For personal pension schemes, explain clearly and prominently that **stakeholder pension schemes** are available and might meet the client's needs as well as the scheme on offer

5.19.3 Key investor information document

Managers of authorised UCITS funds must prepare in English a short document containing **key investor information (KII)**, so as to enable retail investors to understand the nature and risks of the investment product and therefore take decisions on an informed basis.

The **KII document** must contain:

- Identification of the scheme, and the words 'key investor information'
- A short description of the investment objectives and policy

BPP
LEARNING MEDIA

- Past performance presentation or scenarios
- Costs and charges
- The risk/reward profile of the investment, with any guidance and risk warnings
- Details of how to obtain additional information

Marketing communications for UCITS schemes must specify how the prospectus and KII may be obtained.

5.20 Cancellation and withdrawal rights

Learning objective   **3.5.35 Explain** the rules relating to cancellation rights (COBS 15)

5.20.1 Introduction

Cancellation and withdrawal rights apply to firms that enter into a cancellable contract, which means most providers of retail financial products, including distance contracts, based on deposits or designated investments.

5.20.2 Cancellation periods

A consumer has a right to cancel within the following minimum **cancellation periods**.

- Life and pensions contracts: 30 calendar days
- Cash deposit ISAs: 14 calendar days
- Non-life and non-pensions contracts (advised non-distance contracts): 14 calendar days
- Non-life and non-pensions contracts (distance contracts): 14 calendar days

The **cancellation period begins**:

- **Either:** From the day the contract is concluded (but, for life policies, when the consumer is informed that the contract has been concluded),

- **Or:** From the day when the consumer receives the contract terms and conditions, if later

5.20.3 Disclosure of rights to cancel or withdraw

Where the consumer would not already have received similar information under another rule, the firm must **disclose** – in a durable medium and in good time or, if that is not possible, immediately after the consumer is bound – the right to cancel or withdraw, its duration and conditions, information on any further amount payable, consequences of not exercising the right, practical instructions for exercising it, and the address to which notification of cancellation or withdrawal should be sent.

5.20.4 Exercising a right to cancel

A consumer's notification of exercise of a right to cancel is deemed to have observed the deadline if it is **dispatched**, in a durable medium, before the deadline expires.

The consumer does **not** need to give any **reason** for exercising the right to cancel.

5.21 Record keeping and reporting information

Learning objectives

3.5.37 Explain the rules relating to record keeping for client orders and transactions (COBS 11.5)

3.5.38 Apply the rules relating to occasional reporting to clients (COBS 16.2)

5.21.1 Record keeping

Firms are required to arrange for orderly records to be kept, which must be sufficient to enable the FCA (or other competent authority) to:

- Monitor compliance with the requirements under the regulatory system
- Ascertain that the firm has complied with all obligations with respect to clients and potential clients

A firm must take reasonable care to make and retain adequate records of matters and dealings (including accounting records) which are the subject of requirements and standards under the regulatory system.

Records should be capable of being reproduced in English, on paper, or alternatively in the official language of a different country for records relating to business done there.

MiFID requires firms to keep records for **five years**, for MiFID business generally.

For **non-MiFID business**, a retention period of five years also commonly applies, but there are the following exceptions.

Record retention periods

- Indefinitely, for pension transfers, pension opt-outs and FSAVCs (Free-Standing Additional Voluntary Contributions arrangements, for pensions)

- Six years for financial promotions for life policies and pension contracts

- Three years for non-MiFID suitability records for products other than pension transfers, pension opt-outs, FSAVCs, life policies and personal and stakeholder pension contracts

- Three years, for copies of confirmations and periodic statements, in respect of non-MiFID business

- Three years, for periodic statements provided to participants in collective investment schemes

- Six months for records of telephone conversations and electronic communications

5.21.2 Reporting executions (trade confirmations)

In respect of **MiFID** and equivalent third country business, a firm must ensure that clients receive **adequate reports** on the services provided to it by the firm and their costs.

A firm must provide promptly in a durable medium the **essential information** on **execution of orders** to clients in the course of **designated investment business** (except where it is **managing** the investments ie, under a **discretionary management agreement**). The information may be sent to an agent of the client, nominated by the client in writing.

For retail clients, a notice confirming execution (a confirmation) must be sent as soon as possible and no later than the first business day following receipt of confirmation from the third party.

Copies of confirmations dispatched must be **kept** for at least **five years**, for MiFID and equivalent third country business, and for at least **three years** in other cases.

Information to be included in trade confirmations to a retail client

- Reporting firm identification
- Name / designation of client

BPP
LEARNING MEDIA

- Trading day and time
- Order type (eg limit order / market order)
- Venue identification
- Instrument identification
- Buy / sell indicator (or nature of order, if not buy / sell)
- Quantity
- Unit price
- Total consideration
- Total commissions and expenses charged with, if requested, itemised breakdown
- Currency exchange rate, where relevant
- Client's responsibilities regarding settlement, including time limit for payment or delivery
- Details if client's counterparty was in firm's group or was another client, unless trading anonymous

For **derivative transactions**, the essential information includes maturity, delivery or expiry date; for options, the last exercise price, whether it can be exercised before maturity, and the strike price. For **transactions closing out a futures position**, it includes details of each contract in the open position, and each contract that was closed out, and the profit or loss arising to the client (**difference account**). For the **exercise of an option**, it includes the date of exercise, the time of exercise (or that the client will be notified of the time on request), whether the exercise creates a sale or purchase in the underlying asset, the strike price of the option, and any consideration from or to the client.

5.21.3 Periodic reporting to clients

Learning objective	3.5.39 **Apply** the rules relating to periodic reporting to clients (COBS 16.3)

A firm **managing investments** on behalf of a client must provide a periodic statement to the client in a durable medium, unless such a statement is provided by another person. The statement may be sent to an agent nominated by the client in writing.

Information to be included in a periodic report

- Name of the firm

- Name / designation of retail client's account

- Statement of contents and valuation of portfolio, including details of:

    - Each designated investment held, its market value or, if unavailable, its fair value
    - Cash balance at beginning and end of reporting period
    - Performance of portfolio during reporting period

- Total fees and charges, itemising total management fees and total execution costs

- Comparison of period performance with any agreed investment performance benchmark

- Total dividends, interest and other payments received in the period

- Information about other corporate actions giving rights to designated investments held

For a **retail client**, the **periodic statement** should be provided once every **six months**, except that:

- In the case of a leveraged portfolio, it should be provided at least **once a month**.

- It should be provided every **three months** if the client requests it. (The firm must inform clients of this right.)

- If the retail client elects to receive information on a transaction-by-transaction basis and there are no transactions in derivatives or similar instruments giving rise to a cash settlement, the periodic statement must be supplied at least once every **twelve months**.

A firm managing investments (or operating a retail client account that includes an uncovered open position in a contingent liability transaction – involving a potential liability in excess of the cost) must report to the client any **losses** exceeding any **predetermined threshold** agreed with the client.

Periodic statements for **contingent liability transactions** may include information on the **collateral value** and **option account valuations** in respect of each option written by the client in the portfolio at the end of the relevant period.

For **non-MiFID business**, a firm need not provide a periodic statement to a client habitually resident outside the UK if the client does not wish to receive it, nor in respect of a **CTF** if the annual statement contains the periodic information.

5.21.4 Reporting to fund investors

Learning objective

3.5.40 **Explain** the rules relating to reporting on the progress of an authorised fund to unitholders (COLL 4.5)

The **manager of an authorised fund** – ie, either a unit trust, or an OEIC (referred to in FCA rules as an ICVC – an Investment Company with Variable Capital) – must report to the unitholders with regular and relevant information about the progress of the fund.

A **short report** and a **long report** must be prepared half-yearly and annually. The short report is to be sent to all unitholders, and the long report is to be made available to unitholders on request.

The reports must be available within four months of the year-end and within two months of the end of the half-year.

Short report contents

- Investment objectives, policy and strategy
- Brief assessment of risk profile
- For UCITS schemes, the synthetic risk and reward indicator (SRRI) – a risk indicator for investors, on a scale of 1 (low risk / low reward) to 7 (high risk / high potential reward)
- Review of investment activities and performance
- Performance record
- Details of the portfolio at the period-end, and the extent of changes in the period
- Any other significant information, such as scheme changes and charges

Long report contents

- Half-yearly or annual accounts, as applicable
- Report of the manager (half-yearly)
- Comparative table (annually), setting out performance for the last five calendar years, and the net asset value (NAV) per unit at the end of each of the last three years
- Report of the depositary (annually)
- Report of the auditor (annually)

5.22 Client assets and client money rules

Learning objectives
3.5.41 Explain the concept of fiduciary duty

3.5.42 Explain the application and purpose of the rules relating to custody of client assets held in connection with MiFID business (CASS 6.1)

5.22.1 Introduction

The rules in this section link to Principle 10 of the *Principles for Businesses*. The rules aim to restrict the commingling of client's and firm's assets and minimise the risk of client's investments being used by the firm without the client's agreement or contrary to the client's wishes, or being treated as the firm's assets in the event of its **insolvency**.

Fiduciary duty is an obligation that a person (including a firm) has to act in the best interests of another.

■   An investment manager has a fiduciary duty his or her clients
■   The director of a company has a duty to the company's shareholders
■   A trustee has a fiduciary duty to the beneficiaries of a trust

A firm has a fiduciary duty – a duty of care – to look after **client assets** and **client money**. The focus therefore is on two main issues, namely custody of investments, and client money. A firm should keep accurate records distinguishing client money and assets from the money or assets of other clients or of the firm, and should keep these records for five years.

The client assets rules (contained in the **Client Assets (CASS)** section of the FCA Handbook) have a broader coverage than the rules contained in COBS, the Conduct of Business Sourcebook, in that they afford protection not only to retail and professional clients, but also to **eligible counterparties**.

Under MiFID, client assets are regulated by the **home state**. Therefore, for example, if a French firm is **passporting** into the UK, it will adhere to French client assets rules.

5.22.2 Holding client assets

Learning objectives
3.5.43 Explain the rules relating to the protection of clients' assets and having adequate organisation arrangements (CASS 6.2)

3.5.44 Explain the rules relating to depositing assets with third parties (CASS 6.3)

3.5.45 Explain the purpose of the rules relating to the use of clients' assets (CASS 6.4)

Firms sometimes hold investments on behalf of clients in physical form, eg bearer bonds, or may be responsible for the assets but not physically holding them as they are held elsewhere, eg with another custodian or via CREST.

Firms which hold financial instruments belonging to clients must make arrangements to **safeguard clients' ownership rights**, especially in the event of the firm's insolvency. Firms are not permitted to use financial instruments which are held for clients **for their own account** unless they have the express consent of the client. Additionally, a firm must not enter into arrangements for securities financing, such as stock lending or repurchase agreements, without the client's express prior consent.

The firm must have **adequate organisational arrangements** to minimise risk of loss or diminution of clients' financial instruments or of rights over them resulting from misuse, fraud, poor administration, inadequate record-keeping or other negligence.

As far as practicable, the firm must effect registration or recording of legal title to financial instruments, normally in the name of

- The client, or
- A nominee company

For nominee companies controlled by the firm, the firm has the same level of responsibility to the client regarding custody of the assets.

In the case of **overseas financial instruments**, where it is in the client's best interests, the instruments may be held by

- Any other party, in which case the client must be notified in writing

- The firm, subject to written consent (if a retail client) or notification of the client (for professional clients)

5.22.3 Requirement to protect client money

Learning objectives	3.5.47 **Explain** the application and general purpose of the client money rules (CASS 7.2) 3.5.48 **Explain** the rules relating to the segregation of client money (CASS 7.4)

A firm must make adequate arrangements to safeguard clients' rights over **client money** the firm holds, and to prevent the use of client money for the firm's own account.

As with financial instruments, the firm must have **adequate organisational arrangements** to minimise risk of loss or diminution of clients' money or of rights over such money resulting from misuse, fraud, poor administration, inadequate record-keeping or other negligence.

If a firm leaves some of its own money in a client money account, this will be referred to as a '**pollution of trust**' and, if the firm fails, the liquidator will be able to seize all the money held in the client account for the general creditors of the firm.

5.22.4 Client accounts

Client money must be deposited with

- A central bank
- An EEA credit institution
- A bank authorised in a third country, or
- A qualifying money market fund

A firm should undertake adequate **due diligence** before placing any client assets or client money with third parties. The due diligence should amount to more than simply checking the credit rating of the institution. Appropriate due diligence might assess a bank's market reputation, assess legal requirements or market practices, and consider risk diversification as well as credit ratings on an ongoing basis, The due diligence review carried out should be documented.

5.22.5 Intra-group client money deposits

Following the collapse of Lehman Brothers, it transpired that 50% of Lehman Brothers International (Europe)'s had placed 50% of its client money with a group bank that became insolvent.

From 1 June 2011, firms are subject to a **20% maximum limit on intra-group client money deposits** in client bank accounts. Firms which already exceed the 20% limit before that date must conduct suitable due diligence and diversify their client money deposits over the next few months.

The regulator has stated that it will pursue its credible deterrence strategy aggressively in relation to firms which breach this rule.

5.22.6 Financial instruments: reconciliations with external records

3.5.46 **Explain** the rules relating to records, accounts and reconciliations of clients' assets (CASS 6.5)

The firm should ensure that any **third party** holding clients' **financial instruments** provides regular statements.

To ensure accuracy of its records, the firm must carry out regular reconciliations between its own records and those of such third parties

- As regularly as is necessary, and
- As soon as possible after the date to which the reconciliation relates

The person, who may be an employee of the firm, carrying out the reconciliation should, whenever possible, be someone who is independent of the process of producing and maintaining the records. (This type of control is called **segregation of duties**.)

5.22.7 Financial instruments: reconciliation discrepancies

Any **discrepancies** revealed in the reconciliations – including items recorded in a suspense or error account – must be corrected promptly.

Any unreconciled shortfall must be made good, if there are reasonable grounds for concluding that the firm is responsible. If the firm concludes that someone else is responsible, steps should be taken to resolve the position with that other person.

If a firm has not complied with the reconciliation requirements 'in any material respect', then it must inform the regulator without delay.

5.22.8 Client money: reconciliations with external records

3.5.49 **Explain** the rules relating to records, accounts and reconciliations of clients' assets (CASS 7.6)

Broadly, if a firm holds money that belongs to someone else, then that money is client money.

As with financial instruments, to ensure accuracy of its records, the firm must carry out regular reconciliations between its own client money records and those of third parties, such as a bank, holding **client money**

- As regularly as is necessary, and
- As soon as possible after the date to which the reconciliation relates

In determining the **frequency** of reconciliations, the firm should **consider relevant risks**, such as the nature, volume and complexity of the business, and where the client money is held.

The regulator recommends that reconciliations should compare and identify discrepancies between

- The balance of each **client bank account** as recorded by the firm, *and* the balance shown on the bank's statement, and

- The balance as shown in the firm's records, currency by currency, on each **client transaction account** – for **contingent liability investments**, which includes certain derivatives, spot forex trades, spread bets and contracts for difference (CFDs) – *and* the balance shown in the third party's records.

Any **approved collateral** held must be included in the reconciliation.

5.22.9 Client money: reconciliation discrepancies

The **reason** for any **discrepancy** must be identified, unless it arises solely from timing differences between a third party's accounting systems and those of the firm.

Any **shortfall** must be paid into (or any **excess** withdrawn from) the client bank account by the close of business on the day the reconciliation is performed.

If a firm cannot resolve a difference between its internal records and those of a third party holding client money, the firm must pay its own money into a relevant account to make up any difference, until the matter is resolved.

As with financial instruments held, If a firm has not complied with the reconciliation requirements in respect of client money 'in any material respect', then it must inform the regulator without delay.

5.22.10 Discharge of fiduciary duty

Money **ceases to be client money** if it is paid:

- To the client or his authorised representative

- Into a bank account of the client

- To the firm itself, when it is due and payable to the firm, or is an excess in the client bank account

- To a third party, on the client's instruction, unless it is transferred to a third party to effect a transaction – for example, a payment to an intermediate broker as initial or variation margin on behalf of a client who has a position in derivatives. In these circumstances, the firm remains responsible for that client's equity balance held at the intermediate broker until the contract is terminated and all of that client's positions at that broker closed

5.22.11 Mandated accounts

Learning objective	3.5.50 **Explain** the rules relating to mandated accounts (CASS 8)

CASS also contains rules that apply where a firm '**controls**' rather than holds client assets, for example via a **direct debit mandate** or by holding **credit card details**.

In the case of such mandated accounts, the firm must maintain adequate records and internal control procedures regarding the mandates, conditions attached to them, and any transactions done under them. This is to try to avoid any misuse of the client's assets.

The mandate must be obtained from the client **in writing** and **retained by the firm**.

6 FCA SUPERVISION

Learning objective	3.6.1 **Explain** the FCA's risk-based approach to supervision and the enforcement and disciplinary powers of the FCA

6.1 The FCA's risk-based approach to supervision

Bear in mind that the FCA supervises the conduct of both FCA-regulated and dual-regulated firms, and also has the task of prudential regulation of FCA-regulated firms. The PRA is responsible for prudential regulation of dual-regulated firms.

6.2 Powers of the regulators

The **powers** of the new regulators – the FCA and the PRA – include the following. (Note that the term '**firm**' is used generally in the regulations to apply to an authorised person, whether the person is an individual, a partnership or a corporate body.)

- Granting **authorisation** and **permission** to firms (under **Part 4A** of FSMA 2000) to undertake regulated activities
- **Approving** individuals to perform controlled functions
- Issuing (under **Part 9A FSMA 2000**):
    - (In the case of the FCA) general **rules** for authorised firms which appear to be necessary or expedient to advance the FCA's operational objectives (such as the **Conduct of Business** rules, and rules on firms holding clients' money)
    - (In the case of the PRA) general **rules** for PRA-authorised firms which appear to be necessary or expedient to advance the PRA's objectives
- **Supervision** of authorised firms to ensure that they continue to meet the regulators' authorisation requirements and that they comply with the regulatory rules and other obligations
- Powers to take **enforcement action** in the criminal courts, in respect of offences that include:
    - Carrying on a **regulated activity** while **not being authorised or exempt**
    - **Falsely claiming** to be **authorised or exempt**
    - **Contravening the financial promotions restrictions** in communicating an invitation to engage in investment activity
    - **Misleading the FCA**
    - **Giving false information** to, or **failing to co-operate** with, an **investigator** appointed by the FCA
    - Breaching **money laundering regulations**
- Powers to **discipline** authorised firms and approved persons

The **FCA** has powers to:

- Take action against any person for **market abuse** or **insider dealing** (under Part V of the Criminal Justice Act 1993)
- **Recognise** investment exchanges
- As the **UK Listing Authority**, approve companies for stock exchange listings in the UK

If a person or firm wishes to appeal against a decision made by the regulator, that party may appeal to the **Tax and Chancery Chamber of the Upper Tribunal** (often referred to just as the **Upper Tribunal**) – a body that is independent of the FCA, with its rules being determined by the Lord Chancellor.)

The FCA oversees the **Financial Ombudsman Service (FOS)** and the **Money Advice Service**.

The FCA and PRA jointly oversee the **Financial Services Compensation Scheme (FSCS)**.

6.3 Investigatory powers

The regulator has wide **investigatory powers** under ss165–176 FSMA 2000.

- **Information and documents.** The power to require an authorised firm (or any person connected with it), appointed representatives or certain other persons, eg RIEs, to provide it with information, reports or other documents it needs to carry out its duties.

- **Investigators.** The regulator may appoint investigators to investigate possible regulatory breaches. This power covers authorised firms, approved persons, appointed representatives and, in some cases such as market abuse, all persons.

- **Entry to premises.** The regulator may seek access to an authorised firm's premises on demand. Where this is refused, a court warrant may be obtained.

6.4 Disciplinary measures

Under s45 FSMA 2000, the regulator has a general power to **vary or cancel a firm's Part 4A permission** to undertake a regulated activity or withdraw authorisation entirely. More commonly, the regulator will vary a firm's permission by placing tailored requirements on the firm. For example, the regulator may use the power to stop the firm seeking a particular class of client or selling particular investments. Such action is typically taken to protect consumers.

Variation or withdrawal of approval applies to certain individuals who work within an authorised firm and require approval. Approval to perform a **controlled function** may be removed if the individual is no longer fit and proper to conduct that controlled function. To withdraw approval, the regulator must refer the matter to the Regulatory Decisions Committee (RDC), which will give the individual (copied to their employer) a warning notice followed by a decision notice.

Section 56 FSMA 2000 allows the regulator to prohibit individuals from carrying out specified functions in relation to regulated activities within the investment industry. A **Prohibition Order** may be issued in respect of anyone whether they are approved or not: such an order could be imposed on a trader, a director, an IT staff member or a secretary, for example.

The regulator may discipline firms or approved persons for acts of misconduct. **Disciplinary measures** available include private warnings, public statements of misconduct or censures and fines.

There are two types of **restitution powers** available to the regulator – those that require a court order, and those the regulator can impose itself.

- The regulator can apply to the court to require any person who has breached a rule or other requirement of FSMA 2000 to provide compensation or restitution to those who have suffered loss as a result, for example in cases such as market abuse against non-authorised persons.

- Where an authorised firm has breached a rule or other requirement of FSMA 2000, the regulator may require the firm to provide compensation or restitution without a court order.

- Where there is evidence of industry-wide rule breaches (such as that seen in the pensions mis-selling scandal) the regulator may ask HM Treasury to make an order authorising an industry-wide review or enquiry.

The regulator may also (under s380 FSMA 2000) apply to a court for an **injunction** to restrain or prohibit persons from breaking a rule or other requirement of FSMA 2000.

6.5 Supervisory tools

The supervisory tools available to the regulators are of four types:

- **Diagnostic** – designed to identify, assess and measure risk
- **Monitoring** – to track the development of risks
- **Preventative** – to reduce or limit identified risks and prevent risks from crystallising
- **Remedial** – to address risks that have crystallised

In the supervisory process, the regulators may use a broad range of **tools**, including the following.

- Desk-based reviews
- Liaison with other agencies or regulators
- Meetings with the management and representatives of the firm
- On-site inspections
- Reviews and analysis of periodic returns and notifications
- Reviews of past business
- Transaction monitoring
- Use of auditors
- Use of skilled persons reports*

* Under s166 FSMA 2000, the regulator can require a firm to appoint an independent skilled person who will review a specified aspect of the business of the firm.

6.6 The FCA's risk assessment process

The FCA is a risk-based regulator and has declared that its risk framework will be the 'engine room' of the business, providing support to the key activities, namely: supervision, policy, enforcement and authorisation.

- Given its broad remit, the FCA will need to consider **detriment** when carrying out its risk assessments.

- In quantifying detriment, the FCA will assess **probability** and **impact**.

- Impact will be further broken down into **incidence** (for example, the number of consumers affected or potentially affected) and **severity** (for example, the amount of welfare or detriment involved per consumer).

Such assessments will be based on current understanding of the risk or opportunity as well as reasonable expectations of how they will develop under a variety of scenarios. This type of analysis will help to support the FCA's aim of intervening earlier and more swiftly to prevent detriment, by evaluating the costs and benefits of the timing of any action.

6.7 The FCA's Firm Systematic Framework

The statutory objectives of the FCA will drive what the organisation will do.

As we have seen, the FCA's single **strategic objective** is, in summary, **'Making markets work well'**. The FCA's three operational objectives are: ensuring consumer protection, market integrity, and competition in the interests of consumers. Of these, the newest for the FCA is the latter. As a primary statutory objective, we will be obliged to consider the role of competition (or lack of it) as a driver of poor outcomes in markets and work out how to address these problems.

The starting point for the FCA's supervision process will be the **categorisation of firms** into four new categories – C1, C2, C3 or C4 – according to their impact on consumers and the market, while recognising that there is not a one-size-fits-all approach. So, for example, C1 firms are those likely to be the largest, most complex firms with very large client assets or trading bases, whereas C4 firms are likely to be those smaller firms with simpler business models and products.

Overall, the new categorisation means that the FCA will have supervisors allocated to firms with the greatest potential to cause risks to consumers or market integrity. Given limited resources, **supervisors will be deployed flexibly to deal with problems** that arise and specific issues and products that have potential to or are already causing consumer harm.

Alongside this approach is the way in which firms will be supervised on a day-to-day basis. The **FCA supervision model** will be based on three key pillars – **FSF**, **Event Driven**, and **Issues & Products**.

The FCA's forward-looking assessment of a firm's conduct risks will be undertaken within a new **Firm Systematic Framework (FSF)** – the **first pillar** of the supervision model. This is designed to answer the key question of 'Are the interests of customers and market integrity at the heart of how the firm is run?'

The FSF will involve:

- Analysing firms' business models and strategies so that the FCA can form a view of the sustainability of the business from a conduct perspective and where future risks might lie, and

- Assessment of how the fair treatment of customers and ensuring market integrity is embedded in the way in which the firm runs its business, from the 'tone from the top', through how culture is embedded across the firm, to how the firm manages and controls its risks.

The approach will be differentiated depending on the categorisation of the firm into one of four conduct supervision categories, which broadly are as follows.

- **C1**: Universal banks or investment banks with very large trading operations and substantial client assets; banking and insurance groups with large numbers of retail customers

- **C2**: Large wholesale firms; firms from different sectors having a substantial number of retail customers

- **C3**: Firms across different sectors with a significant wholesale presence and/or retail customers

- **C4**: Smaller firms, including almost all intermediaries

Broadly, C1 and C2 firms will experience the most intensive focus and shorter, two-year regulatory cycles. C3 and C4 firms will too have their business models evaluated, but this will be done on a four-year cycle and through a combination of risk profiling, which will determine which firms will be interviewed.

The **second pillar** is based on dealing with **issues that are emerging** or have happened and are unforeseen in their nature. This is termed '**event-driven work**' and will cover matters from mergers and acquisitions, to whistleblowing allegations, to spikes in reported complaints at a firm. The FCA will seek to secure customer redress, where applicable.

The **final pillar** is broadly termed '**issues and products**' and will be largely driven by the analysis made of each sector by the regulator's sector teams. These teams will produce Sector Risk Assessments of conduct risks across all sectors. This will determine whether there are cross-firm and/or product issues driving poor outcomes for consumers or endangering market integrity, the degree of potential detriment, and whether the regulator should be undertaking any thematic pieces of work to assess or mitigate these risks.

The FCA will adopt a differentiated approach depending on how it prudentially categorises a firm. Firms will, in addition to the C1 to C4 categorisation, also be allocated one of three **prudential categories**. **CP1** firms are those whose failure would have a significant impact on the market in which they operate, but where the FCA is not yet confident that orderly wind-down can be achieved. These will still be supervised on a going-concern basis with the aim of minimising the probability of failure. Firms that have a significant market impact but for which an orderly wind-down can be achieved, will be categorised as **CP2** and supervised on a proactive 'gone-concern' basis.

Those where failure, even if disorderly, is unlikely to have significant impact, will be categorised as **CP3** and supervised on a reactive gone-concern basis.

For the vast majority of firms, the focus will be on managing failure when it happens, rather than focusing on reducing its probability.

7 REDRESS

7.1 Complaints

| Learning objective | 3.6.2 **Explain** the FCA rules relating to handling of complaints (DISP 1.3) |

7.1.1 General points

Firms carrying on regulated activities may receive **complaints** from their clients about the way the firm has provided financial services or in respect of failure to provide a financial service. This could include allegations of financial loss whether or not such losses have actually yet occurred: for example, in the case of a mis-sold pension contract, future losses may be involved. Under the FCA's rules, a firm must have **written procedures** to ensure complaints from eligible complainants are properly handled.

A **complaint** is defined as 'any **oral or written** expression of dissatisfaction, whether justified or not, from or on behalf of, a person about the provision of, or failure to provide, a financial service, which alleges that the complainant has suffered (or may suffer) financial loss, material distress or material inconvenience'.

The rules on how firms must handle complaints apply to **eligible complainants**. An eligible complainant is a person eligible to have a complaint considered under the Financial Ombudsman Service.

An eligible complainant must be:

- A **consumer**
- A smaller business – that is, with fewer than 10 employees and turnover or annual balance sheet not exceeding €2 million (called a '**micro-enterprise**')
- A **charity** with annual income of less than £1 million, or
- A **trust** with net asset value of less than £1 million

The rules do not apply to **authorised professional firms** (such as firms of accountants or solicitors) in respect of their **non-mainstream regulated activities**.

For **MiFID business**, the **complaints handling and record rules** apply to:

- Complaints from **retail clients**, but not those who are not retail clients
- Activities carried on from a **branch** of a UK firm in another EEA state, but not to activities carried on from a branch of an EEA firm in the UK
- If a firm takes responsibility for activities **outsourced** to a third party processor, the firm is responsible for dealing with complaints about those activities

7.1.2 Consumer awareness rule

To aid **consumer awareness** of the complaints protection offered, firms must:

- Publish a **summary** of their internal processes for dealing with complaints promptly and fairly.
- Refer eligible customers in writing to this summary at, or immediately after, the point of sale.
- Provide the summary on request, or when acknowledging a complaint.

7.1.3 Complaints handling

Firms, and UK firms' branches in the EEA, must establish procedures for the reasonable handling of complaints which

- Are effective and transparent

- Allow complaints to be made by any reasonable means (which might include email messages, or telephone calls, for example)

- Recognise complaints as requiring resolution

In respect of non-MiFID business, firms must ensure that they identify any **recurring or systemic problems** revealed by complaints. For MiFID business, the requirement is that firms must use complaints information to detect and minimise risk of '**compliance failures**'.

7.1.4 Complaints resolution

Learning objective	3.6.6 **Explain** the procedure and time limits for the resolution of complaints (DISP 1.4, 1.5 & 1.6)

For all complaints received, the firm must:

- Investigate the complaint **competently, diligently and impartially**

- Assess **fairly, consistently and promptly**:

  - whether the complaint should be upheld

  - what remedial action and/or redress may be appropriate

  - whether another respondent may be responsible for the matter (in which case, by the **complaints forwarding rule**, the complaint may be **forwarded** to that other firm, promptly and with notification of the reasons to the client)

- Offer any redress or remedial action

- Explain the firm's assessment of the complaint to the client, its decision, including any offer of redress or remedial action made – in a fair, clear and not misleading way

Factors relevant to assessing a complaint

- All the available evidence and circumstances
- Similarities with other complaints
- Guidance from the FCA, FOS, or from other regulators

The firm should aim to resolve complaints as early as possible, minimising the number of unresolved complaints referred to the FOS – with whom the firm must cooperate fully, complying promptly with any settlements or awards.

Complaints **time limit, forwarding and reporting rules** do not apply to complaints which are **resolved by the next business day** after the complaint is made.

7.1.5 Time limit rules

On receiving a complaint, the firm must

- Send to the complainant a prompt written acknowledgement (no time limit is specified) providing 'early reassurance' that it has received the complaint and is dealing with it, and

- Ensure the complainant in kept informed of progress on the complaint's resolution thereafter.

By the end of **eight weeks** after receiving a complaint which remains unresolved, the firm must send:

- A final response, or

- A holding response, which explains why a final response cannot be made and gives the expected time it will be provided, informs the complainant of his right to complain directly to the FOS if he is not satisfied with the delay, and encloses a copy of the FOS explanatory leaflet

The regulator expects that, within eight weeks of their receipt, almost all complaints will have been substantively addressed.

7.1.6 Time barring

Complaints received outside the FOS **time limits** (see below) may be rejected without considering their merits in a final response, but this response should state that the FOS may waive this requirement in exceptional circumstances.

7.1.7 Complaints record-keeping

Learning objective	3.6.7 **Apply** the rules relating to record keeping and reporting concerning complaints (DISP 1.9 & 1.10)

Records of complaints and of the measures taken for their resolution must be retained for:

- **Five years**, for MiFID business
- **Three years**, for other complaints

after the date the complaint was received

7.1.8 Complaints reporting

Firms must provide a complete **report to the regulator** on complaints received **twice a year**. There is a standard format for the report, which must show, for the reporting period:

- Complaints broken down into categories and generic product types

- Numbers of complaints closed by the firm: within four weeks of receipt; within four to eight weeks; and more than eight weeks from receipt

- Numbers of complaints: upheld; known to have been referred to and accepted by the FOS; outstanding at the beginning of reporting period; outstanding at the end of the reporting period

- Total amount of redress paid in respect of complaints

7.2 The Financial Ombudsman Service

7.2.1 Function of the Ombudsman

Learning objective	3.6.3 **Explain** the role of the Financial Ombudsman Service (DISP Introduction & DISP 2)

A **complainant** must first go to the authorised firm against which the complaint is being made. If the authorised firm does not resolve the complaint to his satisfaction, the complainant may refer it to the **Financial Ombudsman Service (FOS)**.

The FOS offers an informal method of independent adjudication of disputes between a firm and its customer, which is relatively cheap compared with the alternative of taking action through the Courts.

7.2.2 Powers of the FOS

Learning objective	3.6.5 **Distinguish** between compulsory and voluntary jurisdiction (DISP Introduction)

The FOS is a body set up by statute and, while its Board is appointed by the FCA, it is **independent** from the regulator and authorised firms. The FOS is, however, accountable to the regulator and is required to make an annual report to the regulator on its activities. The Board is all non-executive – and so, they have no involvement with individual complaints.

The FOS can consider a complaint against an authorised firm for an act or omission in carrying out any of the firm's regulated activities together with any ancillary activities that firm does. This is known as the **Compulsory Jurisdiction** of the FOS.

In addition to the Compulsory Jurisdiction, the FOS can consider a complaint under its **'Voluntary Jurisdiction'**. Firms or businesses can choose to submit to the voluntary jurisdiction of the FOS by entering into a contract with the FOS. This is available, for example, to unauthorised firms, and can cover activities such as credit and debit card transactions and ancillary activities carried on by that voluntary participant where they are not regulated activities.

A further **Consumer Credit Jurisdiction** applies under the Consumer Credit Act 2006, which gives to the FOS powers to resolve certain disputes regarding loans against holders of licences issued by the Office of Fair Trading under the Consumer Credit Act 1974.

7.2.3 Eligible complainants

Only **eligible complainants** (as defined earlier) who have been customers of authorised firms or of firms which have voluntarily agreed to abide by the FOS rules may use the FOS.

Where an eligible complainant refers a matter to the Ombudsman, a firm has no definitive right to block the matter being referred, but may dispute the eligibility of the complaint or the complainant. In such circumstances, the Ombudsman will seek representations from the parties. The Ombudsman may investigate the merits of the case and may also convene a hearing if necessary.

7.2.4 FOS time limits

The following **time limits** apply to taking a complaint to the FOS.

- When **six months** have passed since the firm sent the consumer a final response (which has to mention the six-month time limit)

- When more than **six years** have passed **since the event** complained about, or

- More than **three years** since the person became aware of or could reasonably be expected to have become **aware** of the problem

After these time limits have expired, the firm complained about can choose to object to the Ombudsman looking at the complaint on the grounds that it is 'time-barred'.

7.2.5 Outcome of FOS findings

Learning objective | **3.6.4 Apply** the rules relating to determination by the Financial Ombudsman Service (DISP 3)

The FOS may dismiss a complaint where, in its view:

- The complainant has not suffered financial loss, material inconvenience or material distress
- The complaint is frivolous or vexatious
- The firm has already made a reasonable offer of compensation

Where a complaint is determined in favour of the complainant, the Ombudsman's determination may include one or more of the following.

- A **money award** against the respondent
- An **interest award** against the respondent
- A **costs award** against the respondent
- A **direction** to the respondent

The Ombudsman may give a **direction** to the firm to take just and appropriate steps to remedy the position including to pay a money award of up to a **maximum of £150,000**, plus reasonable costs (although awards of costs are not common). This figure will normally represent the financial loss the eligible complainant has suffered but can also cover any pain and suffering, damage to their reputation and any distress or inconvenience caused. If the Ombudsman considers that a sum greater than the specified maximum would be fair, he can recommend that the firm pays the balance, although he cannot force the firm to pay this excess.

An **interest award** may provide for interest from a specified date to be added to the money award.

Once the Ombudsman has given a decision, the complainant may decide whether to accept or reject that decision.

- If the complainant **accepts** the Ombudsman's decision, **the authorised firm is bound** by it
- If the complainant **rejects** the decision, they can pursue the matter further through the **Courts**

7.3 Compensation

7.3.1 Purpose of FSCS

Learning objective | **3.6.8 Explain** the purpose of the Financial Services Compensation Scheme (FSCS) (COMP 1.1.7)

The **Financial Services Compensation Scheme (FSCS)** is set up under FSMA 2000 to compensate **eligible claimants** where a relevant firm is unable or likely to be unable to meet claims against it. The scheme will apply where the firm becomes **insolvent** or has ceased trading. The FSCS is seen as part of the 'toolkit' the FCA will use to meet its statutory objectives.

The compensation scheme is independent of, but accountable to, the FCA and HM Treasury for its operations, and it works in partnership with the regulator in delivering the FCA's objectives, particularly that of consumer protection. The FSCS is funded by **levies on authorised firms**.

7.3.2 Entitlement to compensation

Learning objective | **3.6.9 Identify** the circumstances under which the FSCS will pay compensation (COMP 1.3.3, 3.2.1, 4.2.1 & 4.2.2)

To be entitled to compensation from the scheme, a person must:

1. Be an **eligible claimant**. This covers most individuals and small businesses. Broadly, an eligible claimant is defined as a claimant who is **not**:

    –   An individual with a connection to the insolvent firm (except for, following a 2009 rule change [COMP 4.3.1], directors of the failed entity and their close relatives, in respect of **deposits**)

    –   A large company or large partnership/mutual association. What is meant by a large company and partnership depends on rules established under the Companies Act, which are amended from time to time

    –   An authorised firm, unless they are a sole trader/small business and the claim arises out of a regulated activity of which they have no experience, ie do not have permission to carry out

    –   An overseas financial services institution, supranational body, government and local authority

2. Have a '**protected claim**'. This means certain types of claims in respect of deposits and investment business. **Protected investment business** means designated investment business carried on with the claimant or as agent on his behalf, or – where the claim is made by a unit holder – the activities of the manager/trustee of an authorised unit trust or of authorised corporate director/depository of an OEIC/ICVC. These activities must be carried on either from an establishment in the UK or in an EEA State by a UK firm which is passporting their services there.

3. Be claiming against a '**relevant person**' who is **in default**. A relevant person means:

    –   An authorised firm, except an EEA firm passporting into the UK (Customers who lose money as a result of default by an EEA firm must normally seek compensation from the firm's Home State system, unless the firm has **top-up cover** provided by the FSCS in addition to, or in the absence of, compensation provided by the Home State.)

    –   An appointed representative of the above

4. Make the claim within the relevant **time limits** (normally six years from when the event giving rise to the claim occurred)

The scheme will normally award financial compensation in cash. The FSCS may require the eligible claimant to assign any legal rights to them in order to receive compensation as they see fit.

Consumer awareness of the FSCS is promoted by a rule requiring firms to **provide information** on the existence of the **FSCS** and level of **protection** it offers to depositors, as well as proactively informing customers of any **additional trading names** under which the firm operates.

7.3.3 Compensation limits

Learning objective 3.6.10 **Identify** the limits on the compensation payable by the FSCS (COMP 10.2.1, 10.2.2 & 10.2.3)

The maximum compensation levels are as follows.

	Compensation limits
Protected investments and home finance	£50,000 (ie 100% of the first £50,000)
Protected retail deposits	£85,000 (ie 100% of the first £85,000)
Long-term insurance policies	90% of the claim
General insurance	100% for compulsory insurance; in other cases, 90% of the claim

The limits are per person and per claim, and not per account or contract held.

The **Deposit Guarantee Schemes Directive (DGSD)** requires payout of compensation within twenty days. The FCA expects that payout will be faster, with a target of seven days.

8 FINANCIAL CRIME

8.1 Money laundering and counter-terrorism

Learning objective 3.7.1 **Explain** the various sources of money laundering and counter-terrorism regulation and legislation (FCA rules, Money Laundering Regulations, Proceeds of Crime Act 2002)

8.1.1 Money laundering: introduction

Money laundering is the process by which money that is illegally obtained is made to appear to have been legally obtained. By a variety of methods, the nature, source and ownership of these criminal proceeds are concealed.

- Criminal conduct is any crime that constitutes an offence in the UK, or any act abroad that would constitute an offence if it had occurred in the UK.

- Property is criminal property if it constitutes a person's benefit from criminal conduct and the alleged offender knows or suspects that it constitutes this benefit.

This means that UK anti-money laundering legislation applies to the proceeds of all crimes no matter how small.

8.1.2 Terms and definitions

Learning objective 3.7.4 **Explain** the three stages involved in the money laundering process

There are three typical phases in the laundering of money: **placement**, **layering** and **integration**.

- If the money launderer is able to deposit illicit proceeds within an institution or a state (**placement**), which requires little or no disclosure concerning the ownership of those funds, it may be difficult, if not impossible, to trace the property back to its criminal source.

- In the second instance, if property is passed through a complicated series of transactions (**layering**), involving legitimate as well as illegitimate enterprises, it may again be impossible to identify the owner or origin of that property.

- If the ownership or origin of the funds cannot be ascertained, it is virtually impossible to establish that they are the product of criminal activity. The funds can then be reused in legitimate activity (**integration**).

8.1.3 Money Laundering Regulations 2007

The latest **Money Laundering Regulations 2007 (MLR 2007)** repeal earlier regulations and implement the EU's **Third Money Laundering Directive**, which came into force on **15 December 2007**.

The main changes brought about by the Third Directive are as follows.

- The term '**occasional transaction**' (with a monetary limit of transactions of a value below €15,000) is now used, instead of 'one-off' transaction as in earlier Regulations.

- A **risk-based approach** is mandatory, in respect of risk management generally, and in applying customer due diligence.

- There is detailed coverage of **customer due diligence** in the 2007 Regulations, with substantial guidance on how firms should meet their obligation of identifying customers, and mandatory monitoring of customer relationships.

- There is **enhanced** due diligence on a **risk-sensitive basis**, including for 'politically exposed persons' ('PEPs') from outside the UK.

- There is additional scope for **relying on other appropriately qualified regulated firms**, although the 'relying firm' retains ultimate responsibility for meeting the obligations under the Regulations.

The **Money Laundering Regulations 2007 (MLR 2007)** relate to institutional liability generally. They require internal systems and procedures to be implemented to deter criminals from using certain institutions to launder money. They also aim to enable money laundering to be more easily detected and prosecuted by the law enforcement agencies.

The following 'risk-sensitive' policies and procedures must be established.

- Customer due diligence measures and ongoing monitoring
- Internal reporting
- Record-keeping procedures (for five-year period)
- Internal control
- Risk assessment and management
- Compliance monitoring, management and communication of the policies and procedures
- Recognition of suspicious transactions
- Reporting procedures, including appointing a Money Laundering Reporting Officer (MLRO)
- Staff training programmes

Failure to implement these measures is a **criminal offence**. The **FCA** may institute proceedings (other than in Scotland) for money laundering regulation breaches. This power is not limited to firms or persons regulated by the FCA. Whether a breach of the Money Laundering Regulations has occurred is not dependent on whether money laundering has taken place: firms may be sanctioned for not having adequate **anti-money laundering (AML)** /**counter-terrorism financing (CTF)** systems.

Penalty. Failure to comply with any of the requirements of the ML Regulations constitutes an offence punishable by a maximum of two years' imprisonment and an unlimited fine.

8.1.4 The Proceeds of Crime Act 2002

3.7.5 Explain the four offence categories under UK money laundering legislation

The four main offences are:

- **Assistance**
- **Failure to report**
- **Tipping off**
- **Failure to comply – covered above**

8.1.5 Assistance (POCA S327, S328, S329)

If any person knowingly helps another person to launder the proceeds of criminal conduct, he or she will be committing an offence. This covers obtaining, concealing, disguising, transferring, acquiring, possessing, investing or using the proceeds of crime. The legislation historically covered the laundering of the proceeds of **serious crime**, however as a result of the POCA it now covers the proceeds of **all crimes**, no matter how small. This could include evasion of tax.

The maximum penalties for assisting a money launderer are **14 years' imprisonment** and/or an **unlimited fine**.

8.1.6 Failure to report

If a person discovers information during the course of his employment that makes him **believe or suspect** money laundering is occurring, he must inform the police or the appropriate officer (usually the **Money Laundering Reporting Officer (MLRO)**) of the firm as soon as possible. If he fails to make the report as soon as is reasonably practicable, he commits a criminal offence.

For those working in the **regulated sector** (for an authorised firm), this offence covers not only where the person had actual suspicion of laundering (ie subjective suspicions) but also where there were **reasonable grounds for being suspicious**. The grounds are when a hypothetical **reasonable person** would in the circumstances have been suspicious (ie **objective suspicions**).

This offence is punishable with a maximum of **five years' imprisonment** and/or an **unlimited fine**.

8.1.7 Tipping off (POCA s333A)

Even where suspicions are reported, the parties must generally be careful not to alert the suspicions of the alleged launderer since, within the regulated sector, this can itself amount to an offence.

Under s333A, a person within the regulated sector commits an **offence** if, based on information they acquire in the course of business that is likely to prejudice any investigation, they disclose:

- That information has been passed to the police, HMRC, a Nominated Officer (generally, the firm's MLRO) or the National Crime Agency (NCA) (which replaced the former Serious Organised Crime Agency from 7 October 2013), or

- That an investigation into money laundering allegations is being contemplated or carried out

Tipping off under Section 333A is punishable with a maximum of **two years' imprisonment** and/or an **unlimited fine**.

(Under the earlier Section 333 which was replaced by Section 333A, the penalty was five years and not two years – but note the offence of prejudicing an investigation under Section 462 – described in what follows.)

8.1.8 Prejudicing an investigation (s342 POCA, as amended)

For a person **outside the regulated sector**, the offence of **prejudicing an investigation** is related to tipping off. It involves the offence, for those who know or suspect that a money laundering investigation is being carried out, of either:

- In the **non-regulated sector** (s342 (2)(a)), making a disclosure which is likely to prejudice the investigation, or

- For **all persons** (s342 (2)(b)), falsifying, concealing or destroying documents relevant to the investigation

Section 342 carries a maximum custodial penalty of **five years** and/or an **unlimited fine**.

8.1.9 Senior management arrangements, systems and controls (SYSC)

Rather than providing detailed rules on money laundering, the FCA has high level provisions together with guidance that are to be found in **Senior management arrangements, systems and controls (SYSC)** within the FCA Handbook.

SYSC provides that a firm must take reasonable care to establish and maintain effective systems and controls for compliance with applicable regulations and for countering the risk that the firm might be used to further financial crime.

The systems and controls laid down should enable the firm to identify, assess, monitor and manage **money laundering risk**, which is, the risk that a firm may be used to further money laundering. In addition, the systems and controls should be **comprehensive** and **proportionate** to the **nature**, **scale** and **complexity** of its activities and be regularly assessed to ensure they remain adequate. Failure by a firm to manage money laundering risk will effectively increase the risk to society of crime and terrorism.

The SYSC rules require firms to ensure that their systems and controls include:

- Allocation to a director or senior manager (who may also be the MLRO) overall responsibility within the firm for the **establishment** and **maintenance** of effective anti-money laundering systems and controls

- Appropriate provision of information to its governing body and senior management, including a report at least annually by that firm's **MLRO** on the operation and effectiveness of those systems and controls

- **Appropriate training** for its employees in relation to money laundering

- Appropriate **documentation** of its risk management policies and risk profile in relation to money laundering, including documentation of its application of those policies

- Appropriate measures to ensure that **money laundering risk** is taken into account in its day-to-day operation eg in the development of new products, the taking on of new customers and changes in its business profile

- Appropriate measures to ensure that **identification procedures** for customers do not unreasonably deny access to its services

8.1.10 The Money Laundering Reporting Officer (MLRO)

The MLRO which each authorised firm must appoint has responsibility for oversight of its compliance with the FCA's SYSC rules on money laundering.

The MLRO:

- Must act as the focal point for all activity within the firm relating to anti-money laundering
- Must have a level of authority and independence within the firm
- Must have access to sufficient resources and information to enable them to carry out that responsibility
- Should be based in the UK

8.1.11 Joint Money Laundering Steering Group Guidance 2007

Learning objectives

3.7.2 Explain the role of the Joint Money Laundering Steering Group (JMLSG)

3.7.3 Explain the main features of the guidance provided by the JMLSG

The Joint Money Laundering Steering Group (JMLSG) is made up of representatives of trade bodies such as the British Bankers Association. The purpose of the guidance notes is to outline the requirements of the UK money laundering legislation, provide a practical interpretation of the MLR 2007 and provide a base from which management can develop tailored policies and procedures that are appropriate to their business.

The latest **2007 version** of the JMLSG Guidance Notes enables the UK financial services industry to take the required **risk-based approach** to the international fight against crime.

The courts must take account of industry guidance, such as the JMLSG Guidance Notes, which have been approved by a Treasury Minister, when deciding whether:

- A person has committed the offence of failing to report money laundering under POCA 2002
- A person has failed to report terrorist financing under the Terrorism Act 2000, or
- A person or institution has failed to comply with any of the requirements of MLR 2007

When considering whether to take disciplinary action against an FCA-authorised firm for a breach of SYSC, the FCA will have regard to whether a firm has followed relevant provisions in the JMLSG Guidance Notes. The guidance will therefore be significant for individuals or companies subject to regulatory action.

The Guidance Notes provide a sound basis for firms to meet their legislative and regulatory obligations when tailored by firms to their particular business risk profile. Departures from good industry practice, and the rationale for so doing, should be documented and may have to be justified to the regulator.

8.1.12 Directors' and senior managers' responsibility for money laundering precautions

Senior management of regulated firms must provide direction to, and oversight of, the firm's **anti-money laundering (AML)** and **combating the financing of terrorism (CFT)** systems and controls.

Senior management in FCA-authorised firms have a responsibility to ensure that the firm's control processes and procedures are appropriately designed, implemented and effectively operated to manage the firm's risks. This includes the risk of the firm being used to further financial crime.

Senior management of FCA-authorised firms must also meet the following specific requirements.

- Allocate to a director or senior manager (who may or may not be the MLRO) overall responsibility for the establishment and maintenance of the firm's AML/CTF systems and controls;

- Appoint an appropriately qualified senior member of the firm's staff as the MLRO

8.1.13 High level policy statement and risk-based approach

The FCA requires authorised firms to produce adequate documentation of its risk management policies and risk profile in relation to money laundering, including documentation of the application of those policies.

A statement of the firm's AML/CFT policy and the procedures to implement it will clarify how the firm's senior management intend to discharge their legal responsibility. This will provide a framework of direction to the firm and its staff, and will identify named individuals and functions responsible for implementing particular aspects of the policy. The policy will also set out how senior management makes its assessment of the money laundering and terrorist financing risks the firm faces, and how these risks are to be managed.

The **policy statement** should be tailored to the circumstances of the firm as the use of a generic document might reflect adversely on the level of consideration given by senior management to the firm's particular risk profile.

8.1.14 The risk-based approach

A **risk-based approach** is mandatory under MLR 2007. The approach requires the full commitment and support of senior management, and the active co-operation of business units. The risk-based approach needs to be part of the firm's philosophy, and as such reflected in its procedures and controls. There needs to be a clear communication of policies and procedures across the firm, together with robust mechanisms to ensure that they are carried out effectively, any weaknesses are identified and improvements are made wherever necessary.

There are the following **steps** in adopting the required risk-based approach to money laundering.

- Identify the money laundering and terrorist financing risks that are relevant to the firm

- Assess the risks presented by the firm's particular customers, products, delivery channels and geographical areas of operation

- Design and implement controls to manage and mitigate these assessed risks

- Monitor and improve the effective operation of these controls, and

- Record appropriately what has been done, and why

What is the **rationale** of the risk-based approach? To assist the overall objective to prevent money laundering and terrorist financing, a risk-based approach:

- Recognises that the money laundering/terrorist financing threat to firms varies across customers, jurisdictions, products and delivery channels

- Allows management to differentiate between their customers in a way that matches the risk in their particular business

- Allows senior management to apply its own approach to the firm's procedures, systems and controls, and arrangements in particular circumstances, and

- Helps to produce a more cost-effective system

8.1.15 Risk assessment and 'Know Your Customer'

Firms are expected to 'know their customers'. The **Know Your Customer (KYC)** requirements:

- Help the firm, at the time customer due diligence is carried out, to be reasonably satisfied that customers are who they say they are, to know whether they are acting on behalf of others, whether there are any government sanctions against serving the customer, and

- Assist law enforcement with information on customers or activities under investigation.

Based on an **assessment of the money laundering / terrorist financing risk** that each customer presents, the firm will need to:

- **Verify the customer's identity (ID)** – determining exactly who the customer is

- **Collect additional 'KYC' information**, and keep such information **current and valid** – to understand the customer's circumstances and business, and (where appropriate) the sources of funds or wealth, or the purpose of specific transactions

Many customers, by their nature or through what is already known about them by the firm, carry a **lower** money laundering or terrorist financing **risk**. These might include:

- Customers who are employment-based or with a regular source of income from a known source which supports the activity being undertaken; (this applies equally to pensioners or benefit recipients, or to those whose income originates from their partners' employment)

- Customers with a long-term and active business relationship with the firm

- Customers represented by those whose appointment is subject to court approval or ratification (such as executors)

8.1.16 Due diligence

One of the most important ways in which money laundering can be prevented is by establishing the identity of clients, thus making it difficult for those trading under assumed names or through bogus companies to gain access to the financial markets. This emphasises, again, the obligation to '**know your customer**'.

In the context of **conduct of business rules**, the firm may generally accept at face value information which customers provide. The **money laundering regulations**, however, require that the firm takes positive steps to verify the information that they receive. The **JMLSG** Guidance Notes lay down some basic, but not exhaustive, procedures that can be followed.

8.1.17 CDD, EDD and SDD

MLR 2007 regulations require detailed **customer due diligence (CDD)** procedures and these are explained in the **JMLSG** guidance.

CDD involves:

- Identifying the customer and verifying his identity

- Identifying the beneficial owner (taking measures to understand the ownership and control structure, in the case of a company or trust) and verifying his identity

- Obtaining information on the purpose and intended nature of the business relationship

A firm must apply CDD when it:

- Establishes a business relationship
- Carries out an occasional transaction, of €15,000 or more
- Suspects money laundering or terrorist financing
- Doubts the veracity of identification or verification documents

As well as standard CDD there is:

- **Enhanced due diligence (EDD)** – for higher risk situations, customers not physically present when identities are verified, correspondent banking and **politically exposed persons (PEPs)**

- **Simplified due diligence (SDD)** – which may be applied to certain financial sector firms, companies listed on a regulated market, UK public authorities, child trust funds and certain pension funds and low risk products

Firms' information demands from customers need to be '**proportionate, appropriate and discriminating**', and to be able to be **justified to customers**.

8.1.18 Enhanced due diligence

EDD measures when a customer is not present include obtaining additional documents, data or information to those specified below, requiring certification by a financial services firm, and ensuring that an initial payment is from a bank account in the customer's name.

The category '**politically exposed persons**' (**PEPs**) comprises higher-ranking **non-UK** public officials, members of parliaments other than the UK Parliament, and such persons' immediate families and close associates. Prominent PEPs can pose a higher risk because their position may make them vulnerable to corruption. Senior management approval (from an immediate superior) should be sought for establishing a business relationship with such a customer and adequate measures should be taken to establish sources of wealth and of funds.

8.1.19 Simplified due diligence

SDD means not having to apply CDD measures. In practice, this means not having to identify the customer, or to verify the customer's identity, or, where relevant, that of a beneficial owner, nor having to obtain information on the purpose or intended nature of the business relationship.

8.1.20 Evidence of identity

How much identity information to ask for in the course of CDD, and what to verify, are matters **for the judgement of the firm**, based on its **assessment of risk**.

For **private individuals**, the firm should obtain full name, residential address and date of birth of the personal customer. Verification of the information obtained should be based either on a document or documents provided by the customer, or electronically by the firm, or by a combination of both. Where business is conducted face-to-face, firms should request the original documents. Customers should be discouraged from sending original valuable documents by post.

Firms should therefore obtain the following in relation to **corporate clients**: full name, registered number, registered office in country of incorporation, and business address.

The following should also be obtained for private companies:

- Names of all directors (or equivalent)
- Names of beneficial owners holding over 25%

The firm should verify the identity of the corporate entity from:

- A search of the relevant company registry, or
- Confirmation of the company's listing on a regulated market, or
- A copy of the company's Certificate of Incorporation

8.1.21 Ongoing monitoring

As an obligation separate from CDD, firms must conduct ongoing **monitoring of the business relationship**, even where SDD applies. Ongoing monitoring of a business relationship includes scrutiny of transactions undertaken including, where necessary, sources of funds.

CDD and **monitoring** is intended to make it more difficult for the financial services industry to be used for money laundering or terrorist financing, but also helps firms guard against fraud, including impersonation fraud.

8.1.22 Reporting of suspicious transactions

All institutions must appoint an 'appropriate person' as the **Money Laundering Reporting Officer (MLRO)**, who has the following functions.

- To receive reports of transactions giving rise to knowledge or suspicion of money laundering activities from employees of the institution

- To determine whether the report of a suspicious transaction from the employee, considered together with all other relevant information, does actually give rise to knowledge or suspicion of money laundering

- If, after consideration, he knows or suspects that money laundering is taking place, to report those suspicions to the appropriate law enforcement agency, the National Crime Agency (NCA)

For the purpose of each individual employee, making a report made to the MLRO concerning a transaction means that the employee has fulfilled his statutory obligations and will have **no criminal liability** in relation to any money laundering offence in respect of the reported transaction.

8.2 Terrorism

8.2.1 Terrorist activities

Acts of terrorism committed since 2001 have led to an increase in international efforts to locate and cut off funding for terrorists and their organisations.

There is a considerable overlap between the movement of terrorist funds and the laundering of criminal assets. Terrorist groups are also known to have well-established links with organised criminal activity. However, there are two major differences between terrorist and criminal funds.

- Often only small amounts are required to commit a terrorist atrocity, therefore increasing the difficulty of tracking the funds.

- Whereas money laundering relates to the proceeds of crime, terrorists can be funded from legitimately obtained income.

The **Terrorism Act 2000** defines **terrorism** in the UK as the use or threat of action wherever it occurs, designed to influence a government or to intimidate the public for the purpose of advancing a political, religious or ideological cause where the action:

- Involves serious violence against a person, or
- Involves serious damage to property, or
- Endangers a person's life, or
- Creates a serious risk to the health or safety of the public, or
- Is designed to interfere with, or seriously disrupt an electronic system, eg a computer virus

Although **MLR 2007** focuses on firms' obligations in relation to the prevention of money laundering, **POCA 2000** updated and reformed the obligation to report to cover involvement with any criminal property, and the **Terrorism Act 2000** extended this to cover terrorist property.

The JMLSG Guidance states that the risk of terrorist funding entering the financial system can be reduced if firms apply satisfactory money laundering strategies and, in particular, **know your customer** procedures. Firms should assess which **countries** carry the highest risks and should conduct careful scrutiny of transactions from countries known to be a source of terrorist financing.

For some countries, public information about known or suspected terrorists is available. For example, terrorist names are listed on the US Treasury website.

A **duty to report** occurs where a person believes or suspects that another person has committed a terrorist offence and where the belief or suspicion has arisen in the course of a trade, profession, business or employment.

In addition to the offences in POCA 2002, there is specific UK legislation relating to terrorism. The main legislation is the **Terrorism Act 2000** which is supplemented by the **Anti-Terrorism Crime and Security Act 2001** and the **Terrorism Act 2000 and Proceeds of Crime Act 2000 (Amendment Regulations) 2007**.

Under s21A Terrorism Act 2000 (as amended), it is an offence for those working in the **regulated sector** to fail to report (as soon as practicable) knowledge, suspicion or reasonable grounds for suspicion of offences or attempted offences relating to the following.

- Terrorist fund raising
- Use and possession of funds for terrorism
- Arrangements facilitating the retention or control of terrorist property

Thus, as with POCA 2002, there is an objective test for reporting. Reports should be made to the police or MLRO as soon as practicable.

8.3 Insider dealing

Learning objective 3.7.6 **Explain** the meaning of 'inside information' covered by Criminal Justice Act (CJA) 1993

8.3.1 Overview

Insider dealing is the offence of acting with information that is not freely and openly available to all other participants in the market place. This became an offence in 1980 but the current legislation making it a criminal offence is found in **Part V** of the **Criminal Justice Act 1993**. HM Treasury is responsible for insider dealing legislation.

The Act makes it a **criminal offence** for connected persons who receive inside information to act on that information, in respect of the following instruments.

- Shares
- Debt securities issued by the private or public sector
- Warrants
- Depository receipts
- Options, futures or contracts for a difference on any of the above

The offence covers dealings on any investment exchange, off-market dealings arranged by professional intermediaries, including underwriting arrangements and placings of securities.

An **insider** is defined under CJA 1993 as an individual who has **information** in his possession that he **knows** is **inside information** and **knows** is from an **inside source**.

Inside information in this context refers to **unpublished price-sensitive information** that is **specific or precise** and **relates to a security or its issuer**.

What is **published** information? The following information is deemed to be 'published'.

- Information published via a regulated market, eg an RIE
- Information contained in public records
- Information which can otherwise be readily acquired by market users, eg in the financial press
- Information derived from public information
- Information which can only be acquired by expertise or by payment of a fee
- Information which is published only to a section of the public, rather than the public in general, or published outside the UK
- Information which can be acquired by observation, eg a factory burning down

An inside source is **an individual** and would include a **director, employee** or **shareholder** of an issuer of securities or a person having access to the information by virtue of their employment, office or profession.

A person will also be an inside source if he receives the information directly or indirectly from one of the above and satisfies the general definition above.

8.3.2 Offences

Learning objective	**3.7.7 Explain** the offence of insider dealing covered by the CJA

If a person satisfies the definition of an insider, it is an offence for that person to:

- **Deal** in the affected securities either on a regulated market or through a professional intermediary
- **Encourage another** person to deal with reasonable cause to believe that dealing would take place on a regulated market or through a professional intermediary
- **Disclose the information** to another person other than in the proper performance of their duties

8.3.3 Defences

Learning objective	**3.7.8 Identify** the penalties for being found guilty of insider dealing

General defences

An individual is not guilty of insider **dealing** if he can show that:

- He did not, at the time, expect the dealing to result in a profit attributable to the fact that the information was price sensitive
- At the time, he believed on reasonable grounds that the information had been disclosed widely enough to ensure that none of those taking part in the dealing would be prejudiced by not having the information
- He would have done what he did even if he had not had the information

A similar series of defences are available to the charge of **encouraging** another to deal in price-affected securities.

An individual is not guilty of insider dealing by virtue of a **disclosure** of information if he shows that:

- He did not, at the time, expect any person, because of the disclosure, to deal in securities either through a regulated market or via a professional intermediary
- Although he had such an expectation at the time, he did not expect the dealing to result in a profit attributable to the fact that the information was price sensitive in relation to the securities

Market makers

A market maker is a person who holds himself out at all normal times in compliance with the rules of a RIE as willing to acquire or dispose of securities and is required to do so under those rules. An individual is not guilty of insider dealing by virtue of dealing in securities or encouraging another to deal if he can show that he acted in **good faith** in the course of market making.

Market information

An individual is not guilty of an offence under the Act if he can show that the information which he had as an insider was **market information** (information concerning transactions in securities that either have been or are about to be undertaken) and that it was reasonable for an individual in his position to have acted in that manner when in possession of inside information. Consideration will be taken as to the content of the information, the circumstances of receiving the information and the capacity in which the recipient acts, to determine whether it is reasonable.

This defence will also cover the **facilitation of takeover bids**.

Price stabilisation

An individual is not guilty of insider dealing where a new issue is stabilised under the regulator's **price stabilisation rules**.

8.3.4 Enforcement by the FCA

Learning objective	3.7.9 **Explain** the FCA's powers to prosecute insider dealing

The FCA has powers under s401 & s402 FSMA 2000 to prosecute a range of criminal offences, including **insider dealing**, in England, Wales and Northern Ireland.

Under s168 FSMA 2000, inspectors from the FCA have the power to require persons who they believe may have information to:

- Produce any relevant documents
- Attend before them
- Give all assistance possible

In addition to prosecuting for insider dealing, the FCA may revoke the authorisation of an authorised firm where individuals have been allowed to insider deal. They could also remove a person's approval.

Amendments made in 2009 to the Serious Organised Crime and Police Act 2005 give the FCA additional statutory powers, including the **power to grant 'immunity notices'**, when investigating criminal cases such as insider dealing.

While the Department for Business, Innovation and Skills has the power to prosecute, the **FCA** will now normally prosecute insider dealing cases. Accordingly, the London Stock Exchange (as the person who often initiates an investigation) will pass information directly to the FCA.

Insider dealing is a **criminal offence** carrying a maximum penalty of seven years' imprisonment and an unlimited fine in a Crown Court, or six months' imprisonment a maximum £5,000 fine in a Magistrates' Court.

There are no automatic civil sanctions contained in CJA 1993. In addition, no contract is automatically void or unenforceable by reason only that it is the result of insider dealing.

8.4 Market abuse

Learning objective	3.7.10 **Describe** the behaviours defined as market abuse (MAR 1.3, 1.4, 1.5, 1.6, 1.7, 1.8 & 1.9)

8.4.1 Overview

Market abuse is a **civil offence** under **S118 FSMA 2000,** which provides an alternative civil regime for enforcing the criminal prohibitions that apply to insider dealing and (under Part 7 of the Financial Services Act 2012) to misleading statements or impressions.

The UK market abuse rules conform with the **EU Market Abuse Directive**.

The **territorial scope** of market abuse is very wide. It covers everyone, not just authorised firms and approved persons. Firms or persons outside the UK are also covered by the offence.

As market abuse is a **civil offence**, the FCA must prove, on the balance of probabilities, that a person:

- Engaged in market abuse, or
- By taking or refraining from action, required or encouraged another person to engage in market abuse

As shown in the following diagram, there are seven types of behaviour that can amount to market abuse.

In relation to qualifying investments trading or to be traded on a prescribed market

Which falls into one or more of the types of behaviour
- Insider Dealing
- Improper Disclosure
- Misuse of Information
- Manipulating Transactions
- Manipulating Devices
- Dissemination
- Misleading Behaviour and Distortion

8.4.2 Requiring and encouraging

Section 123(1)(b) FSMA 2000 allows the FCA to impose penalties on a person who, by taking or refraining from taking any action, has required or encouraged another person or persons to engage in behaviour, which if engaged in by A, would amount to market abuse.

The following are **examples** of behaviour that might fall within the scope of Section 123(1)(b).

- A director of a company, while in possession of inside information, instructs an employee of that company to deal in qualifying investments or related investments in respect of which the information is inside information. (This could amount to **requiring**.)

- A person recommends or advises a friend to engage in behaviour which, if he himself engaged in it, would amount to market abuse. (This could be **encouraging** market abuse.)

8.4.3 Qualifying investments and prescribed markets

Behaviour will only constitute market abuse if it occurs **in the UK or in relation to qualifying investments traded on a prescribed market**. The term 'behaviour' is specifically mentioned as the offence of market abuse can cover both action and inaction.

A **prescribed market** means any UK RIE, and any regulated market. **Qualifying investment** thus means any investment traded on a UK RIE or a regulated market. **Regulated markets** comprise the main EEA exchanges.

The definition of prescribed market and qualifying investment are amended slightly with reference to the offences of '**Misuse of Information**', '**Misleading Behaviour**' and '**Distortion**'. Here, a prescribed market means any UK RIE. Qualifying investment thus means any investment traded on a UK RIE. Therefore, these offences are only relevant to the UK markets.

In addition, the rules confirm that a prescribed market accessible electronically in the UK would be treated as operating in the UK.

As behaviour must be **in relation to** qualifying investments, the regime is not limited to on-market dealings. A transaction in an OTC (Over The Counter) derivative contract on a traded security or commodity would be covered by the regime. In addition, abusive trades on foreign exchanges could constitute market abuse if the underlying instrument also trades on a prescribed market. This makes the regime much wider than the criminal law offences.

8.4.4 The definition of market abuse

Market abuse is behaviour, whether by one person alone or by two or more persons jointly or in concert, which occurs in relation to:

- Qualifying investments admitted to trading on a prescribed market, or

- Qualifying investments in respect of which a request for admission to trading on a prescribed market has been made, or

- Related investments of a qualifying investment (strictly, this is only relevant to the offences of 'Insider Dealing' and 'Improper Disclosure' – see below)

and falls within one or more of the offences below.

8.4.5 The seven types of market abuse offence

The seven types of behaviour that can constitute market abuse are as follows:

1. **Insider Dealing**. This is where an insider deals, or attempts to deal, in a qualifying investment or related investment on the basis of **inside information**.

2. **Improper Disclosure**. This is where an insider discloses **inside information** to another person otherwise than in the proper course of the exercise of his employment, profession or duties.

3. **Misuse of Information**. This fills gaps in '1' or '2' above and is where the behaviour is

    – Based on information which is not generally available to those using the market but which, if available to a regular user of the market, would be regarded by him as relevant when deciding the terms on which transactions in qualifying investments should be effected, and

    – Likely to be regarded by a regular user of the market as a failure on the part of the person concerned to observe the standard of behaviour reasonably expected of a person in his position.

4. **Manipulating Transactions**. This consists of effecting transactions or orders to trade (otherwise than for legitimate reasons and in conformity with accepted market practices) which

    – Give, or are likely to give a false or misleading impression as to the supply, demand or price of one or more qualifying investments, or

    – Secure the price of one or more such investments at an abnormal or artificial level.

5. **Manipulating Devices**. This consists of effecting transactions or orders to trade which employ fictitious devices or any other form of deception.

6. **Dissemination**. This consists of the dissemination of information by any means which gives, or is likely to give, a false or misleading impression as to a qualifying investment by a person who knew or could reasonably be expected to have known that the information was false or misleading.

7. **Misleading Behaviour** and **Distortion**. This fills any gaps in '4', '5' and '6' above and is where the behaviour

   – Is likely to give a regular user of the market a false or misleading impression as to the supply of, demand for, or price or value of, qualifying investments, or

   – Would be regarded by a regular user of the market as behaviour that would distort the market in such an investment and is likely to be regarded by a regular user of the market as a failure on the part of the person concerned to observe the standard of behaviour reasonably expected of a person in his position.

8.4.6 Intention

The market abuse regime is **effects based** rather than 'intent based'. Thus, whether the perpetrator intended to abuse the market is largely irrelevant – the key question is whether the action **did** abuse the market.

8.4.7 Code of Market Conduct

While the law is set out in FSMA 2000, the FCA also has a duty to draft a **Code of Market Conduct (MAR)**.

The main provisions of the Code of Market Conduct are that it sets out:

- Descriptions of behaviour that, in the opinion of the regulator, do or do not amount to market abuse. Descriptions of behaviour which do not amount to market abuse are called '**safe harbours**'

- Descriptions of behaviour that are or are not **accepted market practices** in relation to one or more identified markets

- Factors that, in the opinion of the regulator, are to be taken into account in determining whether or not behaviour amounts to market abuse

The Code does not exhaustively describe all types of behaviour that may or may not amount to market abuse.

8.4.8 Enforcement and penalties

Learning objective	3.7.11 **Explain** the enforcement powers of the FCA relating to market abuse (MAR 1.1.4, 1.1.5 & 1.1.6)

The FCA may impose one or more of the following **penalties** on those found to have committed market abuse.

- An unlimited **fine**

- Issue a **public statement**

- Apply to the court to seek an **injunction** or **restitution order**

- Where an authorised firm or approved person is guilty of market abuse, they will also be guilty of a breach of the FCA's Principles and they could, in addition to the above penalties, have disciplinary proceedings brought against them, which may result in withdrawal of authorisation/approval.

In addition to being able to impose penalties for market abuse, the FCA is given criminal prosecution powers to enforce insider dealing. The regulator has indicated that it will not pursue both the civil and criminal regime.

8.5 Part 7 Financial Services Act 2012

Under **Part 7 (ss89-95) Financial Services Act 2012 (FSA 2012)**, the FCA has the power to enforce the following offences (in the UK). (These offences replace the repealed older section 397 FSMA 2000.) What counts as a 'relevant' agreement, investment or benchmark in the summary below is determined by Treasury order.

- **Misleading statements**. A person commits this offence if they make a false or misleading statement knowingly or recklessly, or conceal material facts, with the intention of inducing another person to enter (or refrain from entering) into a relevant agreement, or exercising (or refraining from exercising) rights conferred by a relevant investment.

- **Misleading impressions**. This offence is committed when a person intends to create a false or misleading impression of the market in or the price or value of any relevant investments, in order to induce another person to take actions of buying, selling, subscribing or underwriting (or refrain from taking such actions) regarding the investments. It is also committed if a person knowingly or recklessly creates such a false or misleading impression in order to make gains for the person or for another person, or to create losses or the risk of loss for another person.

- **Misleading statements or impressions relating to benchmarks**. An offence is committed if a person knowingly or recklessly makes a false or misleading statement to another person in the course of arrangements for setting a relevant benchmark. An offence is also committed if a person intentionally and knowingly or recklessly acts so as to create a false a misleading impression of the price or value of an investment or of an interest rate, if the impression affects the setting of a benchmark.

Misleading statements or impressions relating to benchmarks would include misleading other parties in relation to the setting of **LIBOR**, for example. Making this an offence is in line with the recommendation of the **Wheatley Commission** on the manipulation by traders of the LIBOR benchmark, which is used to set various interest rates, for example on mortgages.

The **maximum penalty** for these offences is a prison term of seven years and a fine.

8.6 Law on bribery

Learning objective 3.7.12 **Explain** the main features of the Bribery Act 2010

8.6.1 Overview

The **Bribery Act 2010 (BA 2010)** has replaced previous anti-corruption legislation, introducing a new offence for commercial organisations of negligently failing to prevent bribery.

A commercial organisation will commit an offence if a person acting for it, or on its behalf, makes corrupt payments. Organisations and individuals will face heavy penalties if prosecuted and convicted under BAS 2010.

It will be a defence for a firm if it can demonstrate that it has '**adequate procedures**' to prevent such conduct by persons associated with it.

Only firms with a '**demonstrable business presence**' in the UK will be subject to BA 2010, and a 'common sense approach' will be adopted in interpreting this. Having a UK subsidiary will not necessarily mean that the parent company is subject to BA 2010. The **Serious Fraud Office (SFO)** has expressed the opinion that a UK listing would mean that a company would fall under BA 2010.

The **FCA** does not have responsibility for enforcing the criminal offences in BA 2010 for authorised firms. Where the FCA finds evidence of criminal matters, it will refer them to the SFO, which is the UK lead agency for criminal prosecutions for corruption. However, authorised firms who fail to address corruption and bribery risks adequately remain liable to regulatory action by the FCA.

8.6.2 Bribery offences

There are four **main offences** under BA 2010:

- **Section 1: Active bribery** – Offering, promising or giving a bribe

- **Section 2: Passive bribery** – Requesting, agreeing to receive or accepting a bribe (passive bribery)

- **Section 6: Bribing a foreign public official** – A breach of this section may also breach s1 BA 2010, and prosecutors will need to decide which is the more appropriate offence for the case

- **Section 7: Failure of firms to prevent bribery** – Failure by a commercial organisation to prevent persons associated with it from bribing another person on its behalf

8.6.3 Adequate procedures as a defence

An organisation has a defence against the s7 offence (failure to prevent bribery) if it can prove that, despite a particular instance of bribery having occurred, the organisation had **adequate procedures** in place to prevent persons associated with the organisation from committing bribery.

Associated persons include anyone performing services for the commercial organisation, but suppliers of goods are not necessarily 'associated persons'. The legal relationship between a joint venture entity and its members does not automatically mean that they are associated: this would depend on the degree of control the joint venture has over a bribe paid by its employee or agent.

Under s9 BA 2010, the **Minister of Justice** is required to publish **Adequate Procedures Guidance** on the defence. After much discussion, the final Guidance was published on 30 March 2011, and is supplemented by a Quick Start Guide aimed at smaller businesses, which does not form part of the statutory guidance.

- The guidance seeks to reassure senior management of properly organised businesses that BA 2010 is not intended to bring the force of the criminal law to bear in relation to single instances isolated incident. The guidance seeks instead to assert the importance of the matter of bribery and to encourage effective procedures to be established.

- The guidance also seeks to define the circumstances in which bribery may or may not have been committed. For example, it makes clear that genuine client entertainment, for example at sporting events, would not be caught by the legislation.

8.6.4 Ministry of Justice Guidance: principles

The **Ministry of Justice's Guidance** sets out **six principles** to help firms, which can be summarised as follows.

- **1: Proportionate procedures.** Procedures should be proportionate to the risks faced by the organisation, with tailored procedures based on a **risk assessment**.

- **2: Top-level commitment.** Senior management in the organisation need to help create a **culture of integrity** with a **commitment to zero tolerance to bribery**.

- **3: Risk assessment**. The organisation's assessment of the risks it faces should be periodic, informed and documented.

- **4: Due diligence**. In alignment with the requirement for a **proportionate** and **risk-based** approach, the extent of due diligence for different relationships will vary greatly depending on the particular relationship and the associated risks.

- **5: Communication (including training)**. Internal communications should include a clear **statement of the policies and procedures** of the organisation, and of how concerns about instances of bribery can be raised.

- **6: Monitoring and review**. An organisation must be able to demonstrate that it regularly monitors and reviews the adequacy and suitability of policies and procedures and adapts them to reflect organisational changes.

8.6.5 Penalties

Under BA 2010, the maximum jail term for bribery by an individual is 10 years. A company that is convicted of failing to prevent bribery is subject to an unlimited fine.

CHAPTER ROUNDUP

- European Union legislation has an increasing importance, and takes precedence over UK law. 2011 changes created the European Systematic Risk Board and three new pan-European Supervisory Authorities covering banking, insurance and securities markets and replacing the former Level 3 committees.

- The Markets in Financial Instruments Directive (MiFID) opened up European markets by making it easier for firms to passport their activities across the European Economic Area (EEA). MiFID applies to a range of 'core' investment services and activities.

- The European Market Infrastructure Regulation (EMIR) comprises a set of standards for regulation of OTC derivatives markets. EMIR should increase transparency and reduce the risk of counterparty default in OTC derivatives trading, and may thus help to reduce systemic risks.

- The Office of Fair Trading seeks to promote good practice in business, and has a role in ascertaining whether proposed takeovers will lessen competition. The OFT is empowered to refer bids to the Competition Commission, which may block a takeover.

- The Panel on Takeovers and Mergers, funded by a levy on larger share transactions, regulates takeovers through the City Code on Takeovers and Mergers, with statutory force under the Companies Act 2006.

- The Financial Services and Markets Act (FSMA) 2000 provides for a system of statutory regulation of the financial services industry. The 2013 re-structuring the regulation of the UK financial services industry have resulted in the replacement of the previous regulator (the FSA) with the Prudential Regulation Authority (PRA) and the Financial Conduct Authority (FCA).

- FSMA 2000 establishes the regime of authorisation of firms to carry out regulated activities relating to specified investments. The general prohibition (S19 FSMA 2000) states that no person may carry on a regulated activity in or into the UK by way of business or purport to do so, unless they are authorised or exempt. The relevant regulator must be satisfied that the firm meets the 'threshold conditions' for the activity concerned and must pass a 'fit and proper' test.

- The SYSC section of the FCA Handbook seeks to encourage directors and senior managers of authorised firms to take appropriate responsibility for their firm's arrangements and to ensure they know their obligations.

- The Trustee Act 2000 gives wide investment powers and powers of delegation for trusts where the trust deed does not already specify otherwise.

- The Pensions Regulator is the regulatory body for work-based pension schemes in the UK. The Pensions Act 2004 introduced a Pension Protection Fund to protect employees in the event their company scheme is not able to meet its obligations.

- The FCA's overall single strategic objective is, in summary, to make markets work well. The FCA's three operational objectives cover ensuring consumer protection, integrity of the financial system, and promoting effective competition in the interests of consumers. The Authority also has a duty to address financial crime.

- The FCA Handbook is divided into seven blocks. Within each block there are various sourcebooks. The High Level Standards known as the Principles for Businesses apply to every authorised firm carrying out a regulated activity. Approved persons are subject to a separate set of principles, known as Statements of Principle.

- Controlled functions include exerting significant influence on the firm, and dealing with customers or their property. There are different FCA and PRA controlled functions, to minimise duplication of approvals in dual-regulated firms.

- A firm is responsible for ensuring that there is appropriate training for employees and that employees remain competent. There are appropriate examination requirements for those carrying out specified regulated activities with retail clients.

- Retail investment advisers (RIAs) must hold a Statement of Professional Standing, backed by the ethical code of their professional body.

- The UK derivatives exchanges, which include Liffe and the London Metals Exchange, are Recognised Investment Exchanges. Accordingly, the exchange mainly regulates the market, with the FCA being responsible for the financial soundness and conduct of business of exchange members.

- The level of protection given to clients by the regulatory system depends on their classification, with retail clients being protected the most. Professional clients and eligible counterparties may both be either *per se* or elective. Both professional clients and eligible counterparties can re-categorise to get more protection.

- Firms doing designated investment business, except advising, must set out a basic client agreement. Firms must provide to clients appropriate information about the firm and its services, designated investments and their risks, execution venues and costs. Firms managing investments must establish a performance benchmark and must provide information about valuations and management objectives.

- A financial promotion – inviting someone to engage in investment activity – must be issued by or approved by an authorised firm. Communications must be fair, clear and not misleading. Prospectus advertisements must clearly indicate that they are not a prospectus. Communications with retail clients must balance information about benefits of investments with information about risks. Unwritten financial promotions rules cover cold calling – limited to an 'appropriate time of day'.

- The FCA is given a power of product intervention power by FSA 2012. The Authority has the power to intervene quickly – making temporary rules without the normal consultation requirement, if it is expedient to do so – where it considers that a product or product feature is likely to result in significant consumer detriment.

- Rules on assessing suitability of a recommendation apply when a firm makes a personal recommendation in relation to a designated investment. For personal recommendations of certain products – eg, collective investments and life policies – a suitability report is required, specifying the client's demands and needs and explaining the firm's recommendation.

- There are obligations to assess 'appropriateness' – based on information about the client's experience and knowledge – for MiFID business other than making a personal recommendation and managing investments.

- A firm must in general take all reasonable steps to obtain, when executing orders, the best possible result for its clients: this is the requirement of best execution. There must be arrangements for prompt, fair and expeditious client order handling, and a fair order allocation policy. Unexecuted client limit orders must normally be made public, to facilitate early execution.

- Firms must establish arrangements designed to prevent employees entering into personal transactions which are prohibited forms of market abuse. Staff must be made aware of the personal dealing restrictions.

- The Retail Distribution Review brought to an end the current commission-based system of adviser remuneration. Retail investment advisers must disclose whether they are providing independent advice – based on the full range of retail investment products available – or restricted advice on a limited range of products or providers. In the case of both independent advice and restricted advice, advisers will no longer receive commission from product providers, and clients will pay adviser charges.

- Retail clients must be given the opportunity to change their mind (cancel) after agreeing to the purchase of a retail investment product.

- Inducements must not be given if they conflict with acting in the best interests of clients, and there are controls on the use of dealing commission.

- Minimum periods are set down for retaining records (five years for MiFID business) and there are requirements on reporting executions of trades and on periodic reporting.

- Firms must make adequate arrangements to safeguard clients' money, and to prevent the use of client money for the firm's own account.

- In its supervision process, the FCA allocates firms to one of four conduct supervision categories. The larger and more significant C1 and C2 firms will experience the most intensive focus and shorter, two-year regulatory cycles. C3 and C4 firms will too have their business models evaluated, but this will be done on a four-year cycle and through a combination of risk profiling, which will determine which firms will be interviewed.

- The FCA has wide powers, for example to visit firms' premises without notice and to require documents to be produced. Regulatory enforcement measures include public censure, unlimited fines, restitution orders and cancellation of authorisation or approval.

- Firms must have transparent and effective complaints procedures, and must make customers aware of them. Firms must investigate complaints competently, diligently and impartially.

- Time limits apply to complaints processing, and the firm must report data on complaints to the regulator twice-yearly.

- If the firm does not resolve a customer's complaint to the customer's satisfaction, the Financial Ombudsman Service is available to adjudicate the dispute. The FOS has a Compulsory Jurisdiction (covering authorised firms' regulated activities) and a Voluntary Jurisdiction (for unregulated activities where a firm opts for it). The Ombudsman can order a firm to pay up to £150,000 plus costs, in respect of a complaint.

- The Financial Services Compensation Scheme – set up under FSMA 2000 – will pay out within the claim limits to eligible depositors and investors if a firm becomes insolvent.

- Money laundering has three typical stages: placement, layering, integration. Those in the financial services industry must keep alert to, and report, possible offences relating to the proceeds of any crime.

- Joint Money Laundering Steering Group guidance requires firms to assess risks when implementing money laundering precautions. The 'Know Your Customer' principle implies that firms should, where appropriate, take steps to find out about the customer's circumstances and business.

- It is a criminal offence to assist laundering the proceeds of crime, to fail to report it satisfactorily or, in the regulated sector, to tip off someone who is involved in laundering the proceeds of crime.

- The Money Laundering Regulations 2007 apply to all authorised firms and individuals. Each firm must have a Nominated Officer, who will decide whether to report suspicions to the National Crime Agency.

- Fund raising, use and possession, funding arrangements and money laundering are offences under the Terrorism Act 2000. There is a duty to report suspected terrorism to the police.

- To act on information not freely available to the market is to commit the criminal offence of insider dealing. Various types of behaviour, including insider dealing and manipulation of transactions, can constitute market abuse.

- The Bribery Act 2010 makes it an offence to give a bribe or to accept a bribe. It is also an offence for a firm to fail to prevent bribery, and firms should have adequate procedures in place, which will constitute a defence against this offence.

TEST YOUR KNOWLEDGE

1.   What is the main purpose of the European Market Infrastructure Regulation?

2.   What are the two core purposes of the Bank of England?

3.   How is the Panel on Takeovers and Mergers financed?

4.   Outline the main purposes of the Takeover Code.

5.   Which of the following is not a specified investment – Share warrant; NS&I Savings Certificate; Contract for Differences?

6.   List six of the regulators' Principles for Businesses.

7.   Which Statements of Principle apply to all approved persons?

8.   Give two examples of behaviour that would breach Statement of Principle 1.

9.   All trustees must follow the rules on investment powers in the Trustee Act 2000, as these take precedence over anything to the contrary in the trust deed. True or False?

10.   What is the purpose of the Pension Protection Fund?

11.   What is the normal medium for providing periodically to members of work-based pension schemes information regarding the investment of money held within the pension scheme and the investment returns received?

12.   Outline the FCA's statutory objectives.

13.   List the seven blocks of the FCA Handbook.

14.   Outline what is meant by 'passporting'.

15.   Outline the threshold condition that relates to effective supervision.

16.   What are the important considerations a person must show to the regulator in order to become approved?

17.   Name the regulator of recognised clearing houses.

18.   What is the main requirement of IAS 39?

19.   Name the three main categories of client.

20.   Name three types of per se eligible counterparty.

21.   A firm's communications and financial promotions must be '...................... , ... and not ....'. *Fill in the blanks.*

22.   What information will the firm need to obtain from the client to enable it to assess the appropriateness of a product or service to the client?

23. What does the rule on best execution require?

24. Mrs Willard consults an adviser who offers restricted advice. None of the restricted range of products offered by the adviser meets suitability requirements for Mrs Willard's needs and circumstances. Mrs Willard is offered an investment product from the adviser's restricted range which most closely matches her needs. Comment on the adviser's action in offering this product.

25. What are the different types of retail investment product?

26. 'The FCA must consult the public before making product intervention rules.' Is this statement True, or False?

27. How much notice must the FCA give if it wants to seek entry to a firm's premises?

28. What is the FCA's 'Firm Systematic Framework'?

29. Within what time period after receiving a customer complaint does the regulator require the firm to send a final response or alternatively a holding response?

30. What is the maximum award the Financial Ombudsman may make?

31. What are the three typical stages of money laundering?

32. What is the definition of an insider under criminal law?

33. Outline the main offences under the Bribery Act 2010.

TEST YOUR KNOWLEDGE: ANSWERS

1. To enhance stability in EU over-the-counter (OTC) derivatives markets of the EU, implementing a G20 commitment to have all EU standardised OTC derivatives cleared through central counterparties.

    (See Section 1.6)

2. To ensure monetary stability and to contribute to financial stability.

    (See Section 1.6)

3. A flat £1 levy on all transactions dealt on the LSE above £10,000, plus document charges and exemption charges.

    (See Section 2.11.6)

4. To ensure that shareholders are treated fairly and are not denied an opportunity to decide on the merits of a takeover, and that shareholders of the same class are afforded equivalent treatment by the offeror.

    (See Section 2.11.6)

5. Warrants and CfDs are specified investments, but the products of National Savings & Investments (a Government agency) are not.

    (See Section 2.12.7)

6. You could have listed any six of the following: Integrity, Skill, Care & Diligence, Management and Control, Financial Prudence, Market Conduct, Customers' Interests, Communications with Clients, Conflicts of Interest, Customers: Relationships of Trust, Clients' Assets, Relations with Regulators.

    (See Section 3.4.1)

7. The first four Statements of Principle apply to all approved persons. These are the Statements covering: Integrity; Skill, care and diligence; Proper standards of market conduct; Deal with the regulators in an open way.

    (See Section 3.5.2)

8. The first Statement of Principle is: 'An approved person must act with integrity in carrying out his accountable functions.' This would be breached if someone, for example:

    ■   Deliberately misleads clients, his firm or the regulator, or

    ■   Deliberately fails to inform a customer, his firm, or the regulator, that their understanding of a material issue is incorrect

    (See Section 3.5.2)

9. False. Trustees and their advisers need to follow the Act only if the trust deed does not overrule the Act.

    (See Section 2.14)

10. To protect employees in the event that their work-based pension scheme is not able to meet its obligations.

    (See Section 2.15.3)

11. The Statement of Investment Principles (SIP).

    (See Section 2.15.4)

12. Strategic objective of FCA: ensuring that the relevant markets function well. Operational objectives: securing an appropriate degree of protection for consumers; protecting and enhancing the integrity of the UK financial system; promoting effective competition in the interests of consumers in the market for regulated financial services and for services provided by a recognised investment exchange.

    (See Section 3.2)

13. ■ High level standards
    ■ Prudential standards
    ■ Business standards
    ■ Regulatory processes
    ■ Redress
    ■ Specialist sourcebooks
    ■ Listing, prospectus and disclosure

    (See Section 3.3)

14. The idea of a 'passport' enables firms to use their domestic authorisation to operate not only in their home state, but also in other host states within the EEA.

    (See Section 3.6.1)

15. No impediment to the firm's effective supervision should arise from: the nature and complexity of regulated activities undertaken, products offered, and the business organisation. This condition also covers the effect of close links of the applicant with other entities, eg other members of the same group, and whether these have an effect on effective supervision by the regulator.

    (See Section 3.7.2)

16. Honesty, integrity and reputation; competence and capability; financial soundness.

    (See Section 3.8.2)

17. The Bank of England.

    (See Section 4.3)

18. The key requirement of IAS39 is that all derivatives held by an institution, except those designated as a hedge, must be stated in accounts at their fair value.

    (See Section 4.5.4)

19. Eligible counterparties, professional clients and retail clients.

    (See Section 5.2.1)

20. Investment firms, national governments and central banks are all examples.

    (See Section 5.2.5)

21. Fair, clear and not misleading.

    (See Section 5.4.2)

22. The firm will need to ask the client for information about his knowledge and experience in the relevant investment field, so that it can assess whether the client understands the risks involved.

    (See Section 5.6)

23. The best execution rule requires a firm to take all reasonable steps to obtain, when executing orders, the best possible result for its clients, taking into account the execution factors.

    (See Section 5.8)

24. The adviser would be in breach of regulatory requirements. The adviser should not offer an unsuitable product to a client.

    (See Section 5.16.3)

25. RIPs comprise: life policies; unit trust or OEIC units; stakeholder and personal pension schemes; shares in investment trusts and IT savings schemes; other designated investments offering exposure to underlying financial assets, in a packaged form which modifies that exposure when compared with a direct holding; Structured capital-at-risk products (SCARPs).

   (See Section 5.16.4)

26. S138M makes a specific exemption for making temporary product intervention rules (TPIRs) where the FCA considers it necessary or expedient in order to advance its objectives. Such TPIRs, made without consultation (under s138M FSMA 2000), are limited to a maximum duration of 12 months.

   (See Section 5.17)

27. None. The regulator may seek access to an authorised firm's premises on demand. Where this is refused, a court warrant may be obtained.

   (See Section 6.3)

28. The FSF is preventative work, based on analysing firms' business models and strategies so that the FCA can form a view of the sustainability of the business from a conduct perspective and where future risks might lie; and assessment of how the fair treatment of customers and ensuring market integrity is embedded in the way in which the firm runs its business.

   (See Section 6.7)

29. Eight weeks.

   (See Section 7.1.5)

30. £150,000 plus costs.

   (See Section 7.2.5)

31. Placement, layering and integration.

   (See Section 8.1.2)

32. Under CJA 1993, an insider is an individual who knowingly has inside information and knows it is from an inside source.

   (See Section 8.3.1)

33. Offering, promising or giving a bribe (active bribery); requesting, agreeing to receive or receiving a bribe (passive bribery); bribing a foreign public official; for a commercial organisation, failing to prevent bribery.

   (See Section 8.6.2)

4

Legal concepts

INTRODUCTION

In this Chapter, we cover some key legal concepts, whose meanings are quite precise. An important concept in law and business is that a company is a 'legal person' separate from its owners (its shareholders).

From time to time, a client of a financial adviser might run into financial difficulties, and face bankruptcy or a corporate client might face insolvency proceedings. It is important for the adviser to have a broad understanding of the legal and financial implications for the client in these circumstances.

We also gain an understanding of powers of attorney, the law on which was changed by the Mental Capacity Act 2005, and of trusts and trusteeship.

CHAPTER CONTENTS

1 LEGAL PERSONS AND POWER OF ATTORNEY

1.1 Legal personality

A **legal person** possesses legal rights and is subject to legal obligations. In law, the term **person** is used to denote two categories of **legal person**.

- An individual human being is a **natural person**

- The law also recognises **artificial persons** in the form of corporations, co-operatives, and sovereign states

A corporation, such as a limited company, is distinguished from an unincorporated association. An **unincorporated association** (for example, a partnership) is not a separate legal entity; it does not have a legal identity separate from that of its members.

1.2 Companies and limited liability

The most important consequence of registration of an enterprise as a company is that a company becomes a **legal person distinct from its owners**. The owners of a company are its members, or shareholders.

A significant consequence of the fact that the company is distinct from its members is that its members therefore have **limited liability**.

The **company** itself is **liable without limit for its own debts**. If the company buys plastic from another company, for example, it owes the other company money.

Limited liability provides that the creditors of the company cannot demand the company's debts from members of the company, for example if the company fails.

A company, as a separate legal entity, may also have liabilities in tort (eg, to pay damages for negligent acts) and crime. To prosecute a company on criminal charges, as it is necessary to show a *'mens rea'*, or controlling mind. Unless a company is very small it is difficult to show that the mind controlling the company was connected with the criminal act.

A company may be identified with those who control it, for instance to determine its residence for tax purposes. The courts may also ignore the distinction between a company and its members and managers if the latter use that distinction to **evade** their **legal obligations**.

1.3 Power of attorney

A **power of attorney** is a legal document made by a person ('the donor') which appoints another person ('the attorney' or 'the donee') or persons, to act for the donor in legal matters. An example of the use of a power of attorney is where the donee is given power to sign documents on behalf of the donor.

The power of attorney may be a **general** power, to allow the donee to act for the donor in all matters, or restricted to a **specific** act, for example to execute a specific document. In either case, the donor can still act himself. The donor is liable for the acts of the donee, for example, the donor would be bound by a document signed by the donee, provided that the donee has acted within the terms of the power of attorney.

1.4 Making a power of attorney

A general power of attorney may be set out in the form set out in s10 of the Powers of Attorney Act 1971. This shows the names of the donor and donee and states that the donee is appointed as attorney for the donor. The document must be executed as a deed.

1.5 Length of a power of attorney

An ordinary power of attorney (whether given as an individual or as a trustee) is only valid while the donor is capable of giving instructions. It can be revoked by the donor and is automatically revoked if the donor or attorney become bankrupt or die.

The power will also cease at the end of a time specified in it or when a specific act has been carried out, or if the donee dies or becomes incapacitated. Therefore it will cease to have effect if the donor becomes mentally incapacitated. For this reason, a **lasting power of attorney (LPA)** – explained below – may be advisable for many people, and it is probably a good idea to consider this at the same time as executing a **will**.

1.6 Mental Capacity Act 2005

The **Mental Capacity Act 2005** sets out a single **'decision-specific' test** for assessing whether a person lacks capacity to take a particular decision at a particular time. A lack of capacity cannot be established merely by reference to a person's age, appearance, or any aspect of a person's behaviour. Carers and family members have a right to be consulted.

The Act deals with two situations where a designated decision-maker can act on behalf of someone who lacks capacity.

- **Lasting powers of attorney (LPAs).**This is similar to the previous Enduring Power of Attorney (EPA), except that the Act also allows people to let an attorney make health and welfare decisions.

- **Court appointed deputies.** The Act provides for a system of court appointed deputies to replace the previous system of receivership in the Court of Protection.

1.7 Lasting power of attorney (LPA)

A **lasting power of attorney** – as established under the **Mental Capacity Act 2005** –is a legal document that the Donor makes using a special form available from the **Office of the Public Guardian (OPG)**. It allows the Donor to choose someone now (the Attorney) that he or she trust to make decisions on the Donor's behalf about things such as the Donor's property and affairs or personal welfare at a time in the future when the Donor no longer wishes to make those decisions or may lack the mental capacity to make those decisions for himself or herself.

An LPA **can only be used** after it is registered with the **Office of the Public Guardian (OPG)**.

Anyone aged 18 or over, with the capacity to do so, can make an LPA appointing one or more Attorneys to make decisions on their behalf. Someone cannot make an LPA jointly with another person; each person must make his or her own LPA.

If no lasting power of attorney is made before a person becomes incapable, it may be necessary to apply to the **Court of Protection** – a more cumbersome and possibly expensive procedure. The Court of Protection is intended to protect the finances of people who are no longer able to manage their own affairs.

There are two different types of LPA:

- **Personal Welfare LPA** – enabling decisions to be made about care and medical treatment, including decisions to give or to refuse consent for treatment, and about where the person is to reside

- **Property and Affairs LPA** – providing for choices to be made about a person's financial affairs

1.8 Personal Welfare LPA

A **Personal Welfare Lasting Power of Attorney (LPA)** allows a person to plan ahead by choosing one or more people to make decisions on their behalf regarding personal healthcare and welfare.

These personal welfare decisions can only be taken by somebody else when the person lacks the capacity to make them for himself or herself – for example, if the person is unconscious or because of the onset of a condition such as dementia.

The **Personal Welfare Attorney(s)** will only be able to use their power once the LPA has been registered and provided that the person cannot make the required decision for himself or herself.

A person can decide to give the Attorney the power to make decisions about any or all of their personal welfare matters, including healthcare matters. This could involve some significant decisions, such as:

- Giving or refusing consent to particular types of health care, including medical treatment decisions, or

- Whether the person continues to live in their own home, perhaps with help and support from social services, or whether residential care would be more appropriate

There is provision on the LPA form to give the Attorney(s) the power to make decisions about 'life-sustaining treatment', but this power must expressly be given.

1.9 Property and Affairs LPA

A **Property and Affairs Lasting Power of Attorney (LPA)** allows someone to plan ahead by choosing one or more people to make decisions on their behalf regarding their property and financial affairs.

Someone can appoint a **Property and Affairs Attorney** to manage their finances and property while they still have capacity as well as when they lack capacity. For example, it may be easier to give someone the power to carry out tasks such as paying bills or collecting benefits or other income.

This might be easier for lots of reasons: someone might find it difficult to get about or to talk on the telephone, or they might be out of the country for long periods of time.

1.10 Pre-existing Enduring Power of Attorney (EPA)

The Mental Capacity Act 2005 replaced the former Enduring Powers of Attorney (EPA). It is not possible to make any changes to an **existing EPA** or make a new one. However, an unregistered EPA set up before 1 October 2007 can still be used and the Attorney will still need to register it with the OPG if they have reason to believe the person is, or is becoming, mentally incapable in the future.

Someone can also make an LPA to run alongside an EPA if they wish. For example, someone may have an existing EPA that makes provision for decisions about their property and affairs, and decide to make a Personal Welfare LPA to run alongside that, to provide for decisions concerning their healthcare and welfare.

2 CONTRACT AND AGENCY

2.1 Elements of a valid contract

A contract is a legally binding agreement between mutually consenting two parties who intend to enter into a legal relationship.

There are **three essential elements** to look for in the formation of a valid contract: **agreement, consideration** and **intention**.

The first essential element of a binding contract is **agreement**. To determine whether or not an agreement has been reached, the courts will consider whether one party has made a firm **offer** which the other party has **accepted**.

In most contracts, offer and acceptance may be made **orally** or in **writing**, or they may be implied by the conduct of the parties. Contracts for the sale of land, and tenancy agreements, must be in writing. The person making an offer is the offeror and the person to whom an offer is made is the offeree.

In life assurance, the **proposal form** makes up the offer which the life assurance company can either accept at standard rates or on special terms, or reject. If the assurance company accepts on special terms, it is effectively rejecting the proposal and making a counteroffer, which the proposer then either accepts or rejects.

The second of the three essential elements of a contract is **consideration**. The promise which a claimant seeks to enforce must be shown to be part of a bargain to which the claimant has himself contributed.

Third, an agreement is not a binding contract unless the parties **intend to create legal relations**. What matters is not what the parties have in their minds, but the inferences that reasonable people would draw from their words or conduct.

The requirements of standardisation in business have led to the **standard form contract**. The **standard form contract** is a document prepared by many large organisations setting out the terms on which they contract with their customers. The individual must usually take it or leave it.

2.2 Legality of object

If you enter into an agreement with an accomplice to steal property, such a contract would be **illegal** and the contract would **not be valid**.

2.3 Form of a contract

As a general rule, **a contract may be made in any form**. It may be written, or oral, or inferred from the conduct of the parties. For example, a customer in a self-service shop may take his selected goods to the cash desk, pay for them and walk out without saying a word.

However, certain contracts must be in **writing**, such as for the purchase of land and property. Also bear in mind that specific consumer legislation or regulations may require certain agreements to be in a specified form, such as in writing or transmitted through a website.

2.4 Capacity to contract

Capacity to contract is the legal ability to enter into a contract.

- Someone who is **insane** may have their capacity to contract limited by law.
- **Minors** – that is, those under 18 – do not have unrestricted capacity to enter into contracts.

2.5 Breach of contract

A contract may be breached when one party does not fulfil one or more of the specified terms of the contract – for example, if a contractor makes the other party aware that it will not be performing some of the agreed tasks, or if work carried out is defective. A contract dispute may ensue, and a court may award damages to the other party. Financial damages will only be due if the party to the contract can prove that they have suffered financial loss.

2.6 Contract discharge

A contract may be discharged – come to an end – through **breach, performance, agreement, or frustration**. If all the terms of the contract have been met, the contract is discharged by performance. Both parties may agree to end the contract, or one party may release the other party from all their obligations under the contract. If events have occurred that make it impossible to complete the contract, then it is said to be discharged through 'frustration'.

2.7 Utmost good faith

If you buy a used car from a private seller and find that it falls apart soon after you bought it, that usually is your problem. Provided that the seller answered honestly any questions that you asked, they were not obliged to volunteer information that you did not seek. The general principle here is: *caveat emptor* – 'let the buyer beware'.

However, if you make a proposal for insurance, including life insurance, you are expected to give to the insurance company **all relevant information** which will enable the company to assess the risk, eg if you are seriously ill or in a dangerous occupation or have a risky lifestyle, or whether you are a normal risk for which the company would issue a contract on standard terms.

This requirement to **disclose all relevant information** is fundamental to an insurance contract. If the rule is not observed the policy can be treated by the insurer as **voidable**. The requirement is termed **'utmost good faith'** or *uberrimae fidei*.

2.8 The agency relationship

'Agents' are engaged by **'principals'** generally in order to perform tasks which the principals cannot or do not wish to perform themselves, because the principal does not have the time or expertise to carry out the task. In normal circumstances, the agent discloses to the other party that he (the agent) is acting for a principal whose identity is also disclosed.

Agency is a relationship which exists between two legal persons (the **principal** and the **agent**) in which the function of the agent is to form a contract between his principal and a third party.

The relationship of principal and agent is usually created by mutual consent. The consent need not generally be formal nor expressed in a written document. **It is usually an 'express' agreement**, even if it is created in an informal manner.

When an agent agrees to perform services for his principal for reward there is a contract between them.

2.9 Examples of agency relationships

There are many examples of agency relationships which you are probably accustomed to, although you may not be aware that they are examples of the laws of agency. Some examples are as follows.

- **Partnerships.** A feature of partnerships is that the partners are agents of each other.

- **Brokers.** Any broker is essentially a middleman or intermediary who arranges contracts in return for commission or brokerage. For example, an **insurance broker** is an agent of an insurer who arranges contracts of insurance with the other party who wishes to be insured. However, in some contexts (for example, when the broker assists a car owner to complete a proposal form) he is also treated as the agent of the insured.

- **Appointed representatives of product providers.** A financial adviser who works as an appointed representative (tied adviser) for a product provider firm (such as a life office) is an **agent of the product provider firm**, while the firm is principal. The firm, as principal, is responsible for the acts and omissions of its appointed representatives (its agents) and must ensure that its agents comply with the regulator's rules.

- An **retail investment adviser (RIA)**, who offers advice on products from a full range of providers, is the **agent of his client** in respect of the advice or recommendations offered to the client. This is the case whether or not the RIA is a member or appointed representative of a **network**. The RIA owes a duty of care to his or her client.

2.10 Obligations of an agent

Even if the agent undertakes his duties without reward, the agent has obligations to his principal.

- **Performance and obedience.** The agent must **perform** his obligations, following his principal's instructions with **obedience**, unless to do so would involve an illegal act.

- **Skill and accountability.** The agent must act with the standard of **skill and care** to be expected of a person in his profession and to be **accountable** to his principal to provide full information on the agency transactions and to account for all moneys arising from them.

- **No conflict of interest.** The agent owes to his principal a duty not to put himself in a in a situation where his own interests conflict with those of the principal; for example, he must not sell his own property to the principal (even if the sale is at a fair price).

- **Confidence.** The agent must keep in **confidence** what he knows of his principal's affairs even after the agency relationship has ceased.

- **Any benefit** must be handed over to the principal unless he agrees that the agent may retain it. Although an agent is entitled to his agreed remuneration, he must account to the principal for any other benefits. If he accepts from the other party any commission or reward as an inducement to make the contract with him, it is considered to be a bribe and the contract is fraudulent.

2.11 Authority of the agent

The **contract** made by the agent is **binding** on the principal and the other party **only if** the **agent was acting within the limits of his authority** from his principal.

3 OWNERSHIP OF PROPERTY

3.1 Legal ownership and beneficial or equitable ownership

Legal ownership and equitable or beneficial ownership are distinct in English law.

Client money may be held in an account in the name of the firm, who are thus its **legal owners**. But the money is held in trust for the clients, who are its **beneficial owners**. **Shares** may be registered in the name of a **nominee company** who is not the beneficial owner. Beneficial ownership is the valuable part of ownership.

Most people who own their own home will do so as legal and beneficial owners.

3.2 Forms of co-ownership of land

It is possible for more than one person to own **land**. If land (and the property built on it) is purchased or transferred to two or more persons, these persons become either **joint tenants** or **tenants in common**. (Note that this applies to owning freehold land outright, even though the word 'tenant' is used.)

- **Joint tenancy** is where two or more people acquire land but no words of 'severance' are used. This means that the transfer does not state what share in the land each person has. The land is merely 'held by X and Y'. It is both legal and equitable co-ownership. **Joint tenancy** is a convenient and commonly used way for a husband and wife to own the matrimonial home. If one of the couple dies, the other will have title to the whole property.

- **Tenants in common** have shares in the land. For instance, a conveyance may state that the land should go to 'P, Q and R equally' – each then owns one-third part of the interest. It is equitable ownership. If P subsequently dies, his or her one-third share goes into P's estate: Q and R still own a one-third share each.

3.3 Significance of the type of ownership

The importance of the distinction is that if a **joint tenant** dies his interest lapses and the land is owned wholly by the survivor(s). He may not pass his interest on by **will**. The advantage is that only a limited number of interests can exist. The disadvantage is the fact that survival decides ownership. With tenants in common, each tenant can bequeath his interest which means that a house owned by tenants in common (A, B and C equally) will, if C dies and leaves his interest to D, E, F and G, be owned by A, B, (one-third part each) D, E, F and G (one-twelfth part each). While perhaps being fairer, this can be cumbersome!

The Law of Property Act 1925 achieved a compromise by providing that, where land is owned by two or more persons, no more than four of those persons hold the **legal estate** as joint tenants and trustees, for the **beneficial** or **equitable interest** of themselves and other co-owners. Thus transfers can be effected by four signatures but the sale proceeds are subject to trusts so that all the owners get fair shares.

4 INSOLVENCY AND BANKRUPTCY

4.1 Insolvency

A **company** that can no longer meet its obligations on time is in a state of insolvency. The company will need to take action to generate cash and/or re-negotiate terms with its creditors. If the company cannot recover and achieve solvency, it may face bankruptcy proceedings, possibly leading to the appointment of court '**administrators**', debtholders' **receivers**, or **liquidators** who will wind up the company.

The purpose of insolvency law is to govern what should happen to the property of a company that is insolvent. There are three types of corporate insolvency 'officials', depending on whether a company goes into **administration, receivership** or **liquidation**.

The basic aims of company insolvency law are to:

- **Protect** the creditors of the company
- **Balance** the interests of competing groups
- **Control or punish** directors responsible for the company's financial collapse
- **Encourage** 'rescue' operations

While **insolvency** may be described as a **state** in which liabilities exceed assets, **bankruptcy** is a **legal** matter.

4.2 Bankruptcy

4.2.1 Overview

Bankruptcy occurs when an individual's financial affairs are taken over by a court. The individual's assets are transferred into a **trust** which is used to repay as much debt as possible.

A sole trader or partner who owes money (a debtor) and is unable to pay the debt could be faced with bankruptcy proceedings.

Inability to pay a debt will occur when the individual cannot find the money. Inadequate cash flow, rather than a loss-making business, may be the problem. Typically, the business will have insufficient cash coming in to meet its various payment obligations, and will be unable to borrow more money. In this situation, the individual's business will have more current liabilities than liquid assets.

The current legislation dealing with bankruptcy is the **Insolvency Act 1986**, as amended by the **Insolvency Act 2000** and the **Enterprise Act 2002**.

4.2.2 Bankruptcy proceedings

Bankruptcy proceedings against an individual begin with the presentation of a petition for a **bankruptcy order** to the court. (This could be the High Court or a County Court with power to deal with such proceedings.)

The petitioner may be a creditor, or several creditors acting jointly. (However, a debtor may petition to have himself/herself declared bankrupt.) The court will not entertain a petition from a creditor unless the creditor is owed at least **£750** on an unsecured debt.

A creditor's petition must allege that the debtor is unable to pay the debt or has very little prospect of being able to pay it.

When a bankruptcy order has been made, the **Official Receiver** takes control of the debtor's assets, as **receiver and manager**. The Official Receiver is an official of the Department of Business, Innovation and Skills and an officer of the court.

The duty of the receiver and manager is to protect the bankrupt's property until a **trustee in bankruptcy** has been appointed.

Every bankruptcy is under the general control of the court, which has wide powers to control the trustee. All property owned by the debtor on the date of the bankruptcy order, and any property acquired subsequently, passes to the trustee.

5 WILLS AND INTESTACY

Learning objective	4.1.5 **Explain** wills and intestacy

5.1 Wills and administration of an estate

A **will** is a legal document which gives effect to the wishes of an individual (the **testator**, if male, the **testatrix** if female) as to how their estate should be distributed after their death. It appoints the persons who will have the responsibility for dealing with the estate (the **executors**, also called **personal representatives**) and gives instructions as to how the estate should be distributed.

The person making the will must be aged at least 18 years, and must have the mental capacity to understand the effect of making a will. The will must not have been made as a result of pressure from another person.

A will must be signed in the presence of two witnesses. A **witness** or the **spouse of a witness** cannot benefit from a will. If a witness or the spouse of a witness is named as a beneficiary, the will is not made invalid, but that person will not be able to inherit under the will.

The executors need to obtain a **Grant of Probate** from the Probate Registry to show they are entitled to **administer the estate**. Then they can collect the assets of the estate. The executors are responsible for settling all liabilities of the estate before paying out the money to the beneficiaries.

The assets comprising the estate are held by the executors on trust for the beneficiaries until they are distributed to them. Usually this will only last as long as it takes to administer the estate. However, longer term **trusts** are frequently created by wills. The trustees of these can be separate individuals to the executors and the trust terms can be the same as those of lifetime (*inter vivos*) trusts. Trusts are typically created to cater for minors. Another common use is the creation of a **discretionary trust** to use the inheritance tax nil rate band of the first of a married couple to die.

A will is made **invalid** if the testator **marries**, unless the testator expressly stated that the will was made in contemplation of marriage. If the testator **divorces**, bequests in favour of the **ex-spouse** no longer have effect.

5.2 Reasons for making a will

There are the following reasons for making a will.

BPP
LEARNING MEDIA

- To arrange for beneficiaries other than those appointed under the intestacy rules to benefit. Unmarried partners and stepchildren cannot benefit other than by a will. Children of a previous marriage might also lose out if the testator remarries.
- To use tax reliefs and allowances
- To create trusts to cater for the long-term needs of the beneficiaries or to enable capital to skip generations
- To choose executors and trustees and to extend their statutory powers
- To specify funeral arrangements

5.3 Intestacy

An individual who dies without a will is referred to as **intestate**. The estate of an intestate individual is dealt with under the laws of intestacy which direct that the estate be distributed to next of kin according to specific rules.

6 TRUSTS AND THEIR USES

Learning objective | 4.1.6 **Identify** the main types of trusts and their uses

6.1 What is a trust?

A **trust** is an equitable obligation (see below for an explanation of 'equitable') in which certain persons (the **trustees**) are bound to deal with property over which they have control (the **trust property**) for the benefit of certain individuals (the **beneficiaries**).

The trustees may also be beneficiaries of the trust. An individual who transfers assets into a trust during his lifetime is known as a **settlor** and such trusts are known as **settlements**. A settlor may also be a trustee and/or a beneficiary. A trust may also be set up in a **will** and is then usually called a **will trust**. Where the trust is set down in writing, this document is called the '**trust instrument**'.

6.2 Trustees and beneficiaries: equitable interest

The word **'equity'** derives from the Latin word meaning justice or fairness. Trusts are an invention of the law of equity. Originally the law of England was made up primarily of ancient customs which varied from one region to another. This was eventually compiled into a law which was uniform throughout England and known as the **common law**.

Over time, common law attained a definite shape but it did not tend to evolve sufficiently fast to cater for the changing needs of society. In particular, it tended to look at the form of a transaction (eg in a land purchase whose name appeared on the title deeds) rather than the substance (eg who provided the purchase money). Eventually definite principles evolved and these were compiled into a system of rules that became known as **equity**. For example, equity would recognise the interest of the provider of purchase monies whether or not that person's name appeared on the title deeds.

The Judicature Act 1873 provided that equity should override common law. The Act also provided that all courts could administer both types of law. The two types of law, however still remain distinct. Legal rights (those derived under common law) and equitable rights (those derived under equity) therefore need to be distinguished from each other.

Trusts encompass both types of interest. The **legal title** (ie legal ownership) to the property in a trust will be held by the **trustees** whereas the **equitable (or beneficial) interest** will belong to the **beneficiaries**. For example, land could be transferred to the trustees and the legal title would be in their names. Equity would recognise that the land was not transferred to the trustees for their own benefit but to be held for the benefit of the beneficiaries in accordance with the terms of the trust. If the trustees do not act in accordance with the terms of the trust, the beneficiaries may apply to the Court to enforce the trust.

6.3 Types of trust

A trust may be a **bare trust**, also known as a **simple trust**, where there is a sole beneficiary. In such a trust, the trustee has no discretion over payment of income or capital to the beneficiary, who has an immediate and absolute right to both capital and income. The beneficiary of the trust can instruct the trustee how to manage the trust property, and has the right to take actual possession of the trust property at any time.

An **interest in possession trust** arises where a beneficiary, known as an 'income beneficiary' or a 'life interest', has a legal right to the income or other benefit derived from the trust property as it arises. For example, the **life interest** may have the right to occupy a house during his or her lifetime, or an **income beneficiary** the right to receive income from the trust property for a specified period or until death. On the death of the life interest/income beneficiary, the assets of the trust will be held for the benefit of the second class of beneficiary, known as the **remainderman** or the reversionary interest. A trustee of an interest in possession trust has the duty to safeguard the interests of both classes of beneficiary.

A trust may be a **discretionary trust** where the trustees exercise their discretion as to which beneficiaries will be entitled to receive income or capital from the trust. The exact rights of each beneficiary are not determined in advance. This can be of use in family situations. First of all, it may enable the settlor to control the conduct of the beneficiaries by the trustee's use of discretionary powers. Second, it keeps the trust flexible. For example, the settlor can constitute a discretionary trust for the benefit of a class of people, such as his grandchildren. If a new grandchild is born after the trust is set up, the grandchild will automatically rank as a beneficiary.

For **inheritance tax (IHT)** purposes, there is a **chargeable lifetime transfer (CLT)** when a discretionary trust or an interest in possession trust is set up. The trust suffers an IHT **principal charge** once every ten years and an **exit charge** when property leaves the trust.

A **charitable trust** is a trust – that is, a relationship between the donor of assets, trustees, and beneficiaries – that has charitable purposes, as set out by the **Charities Act 2006**. The 2006 Act gave new emphasis to the requirement for all charities' aims to be, demonstrably, **for the public benefit**. Charitable trusts enable the settlor to give some degree of individuality to a gift, specifying how it may be used and, as **charities**, are basically free from tax.

6.4 Uses of trusts

6.4.1 Overview

Trusts are useful vehicles for non-tax reasons such as to preserve family wealth, to provide for those who are deemed to be incapable (minors, and the disabled) or unsuitable (due to youth or poor business sense) to hold assets directly.

6.4.2 Will trusts

A discretionary trust may be set up by will. The rate of inheritance tax on principal charges and exit charges within the trust will then depend on the settlor's cumulative transfers in the seven years before his death and the value of the trust property. The discretionary trust allows the transferee flexibility about who

BPP
LEARNING MEDIA

is to benefit from the trust and to what extent. This can be useful if there are beneficiaries of differing ages and whose financial circumstances may differ.

6.4.3 Lifetime trusts

Although gifts to trusts during lifetime can lead to an IHT charge (a CLT), there can be tax benefits from setting up trusts during the settlor's lifetime. As long as the cumulative total of CLTs in any seven-year period does not exceed the nil rate band, there will be no lifetime IHT to pay on creation of the trust. The trust will be subject to IHT at 0% on the ten-year anniversary and later advances, unless the value of the trust property grows faster than the nil rate band.

If a discretionary trust is used, the settlor can preserve the maximum flexibility in the class of beneficiaries and how income and capital should be dealt with.

If the settlor is included as a beneficiary of the trust the gift will be treated as a gift with reservation.

6.4.4 Family settlements

As mentioned above, the purpose of many trusts is to enable the wealthy to retain their wealth. Trusts will tie up wealth within the family and will often be constructed to minimise tax liabilities. They may be created through a will but will often be set up when the settlor is alive, to make tax planning easier.

Key benefits to the family

- Controlling who owns and receives benefit from the property
- Potential reduction of tax liabilities
- Giving someone the benefit of property while preventing them from wasting it through careless actions

For example, a house may be left on trust so that one member of the family can use it during their lifetime (ie have a **life interest in possession**), while another member can receive the house when the person with the life interest dies (ie the **remainderman**).

6.4.5 Those who cannot hold property on their own behalf

Unincorporated associations (for example, some charities, trade unions or clubs) are unable to own property, since they are not legally recognised as persons. In such a case, the property can be held on behalf of the association by a trustee.

Children under the age of 18 are not allowed to have legal ownership of land. In order to give land to a child, a trust will need to be set up for the benefit of the child, who can receive legal ownership of the land on reaching his or her majority.

6.4.6 Marriage

Whereas most of the trusts mentioned above will be expressly made, a trust in the context of marriage or cohabitation will often be a **resulting trust**. An example would be a situation where a house is held in the name of one of the two partners (X) but the other partner (Y) has contributed money to purchase the house. Since the house is intended to be occupied jointly, X may have legal ownership of the house but is holding part of the interest on trust for Y, even if this were not stated explicitly.

6.4.7 Confidentiality

Leaving property through a trust can protect the identity of the beneficial owner, who will only be known to the trustee. Such a trust will be referred to as a '**secret trust**'.

CHAPTER ROUNDUP

- In law, an individual human being is a natural person, while a corporation, such as a limited company, is also a legal person: a legal entity separate from the natural persons connected with it, for example its members or shareholders.

- A power of attorney is a document made by a person ('the donor') which appoints another person ('the attorney' or 'the donee') or persons, to act for the donor in legal matters. With Lasting Powers of Attorney, established under the Mental Capacity Act 2005, an attorney can make health and welfare decisions, or the attorney may be limited to making decisions about property and affairs of the person.

- A contract is a legally binding agreement between mutually consenting two parties who intend to enter into a legal relationship. Elements to look for in the formation of a valid contract are: agreement, consideration and intention. As a general rule, a contract may be made in any form.

- An insurance contract requires the proposer of the contract to disclose all relevant information, as it is an 'utmost good faith' (*uberrimae fidei*) contract.

- Agency is a relationship which exists between two legal persons (the principal and the agent) in which the function of the agent is to form a contract between his principal and a third party.

- It is possible for more than one person to own land. If land and the property built on it is purchased or transferred to two or more persons, these persons become either joint tenants or tenants in common.

- The basic aims of the law on corporate insolvency are to: protect the creditors of the company; balance the interests of competing groups; control or punish directors responsible for the company's financial collapse; and encourage 'rescue' operations.

- When an individual is declared bankrupt, his or her financial affairs are taken over by a court and the individual's assets are transferred into a trust used to repay debt.

- A will is a legal document giving effect to the wishes of the testator (male), or the testatrix (female) on how their estate should be distributed after their death. It also appoints the executors (or 'personal representatives'), who have responsibility for dealing with the estate.

- The process of establishing ownership of the estate before the assets of a deceased person are distributed is known as 'probate'.

- The estate of an intestate individual who dies intestate (leaving no will) is dealt with under rules laid down in law.

- A trust is an equitable obligation in which the trustees are bound to deal with the trust property for the benefit of the beneficiaries of the trust. Typical ways in which trusts are applied include: will trusts; lifetime trusts; family settlements; unincorporated associations; land gifted for children; protecting the identity of a beneficial owner.

TEST YOUR KNOWLEDGE

1. What types of legal person does the law recognise?

2. What types of power of attorney may be set up under the Mental Capacity Act 2005?

3. What are the three essential elements of a valid contract?

4. Give two cases or persons who do not have the legal capacity to enter into a contract.

5. A contract may be discharged through any of the following, except

   A   Breach
   B   Consideration
   C   Frustration
   D   Performance

6. Outline what is meant by an agency relationship.

7. Chris and Martin are in a civil partnership and own their house in such a way that, if one of them dies, the other will own it in full. What form of joint ownership is this?

8. Outline what a will is, and what it does.

9. Outline what a trust is.

TEST YOUR KNOWLEDGE: ANSWERS

1. An individual human being is a natural legal person. The law also recognises artificial legal persons in the form of corporations.

    (See Section 1.1)

2. Two types of Lasting Power of Attorney (LPA) are possible:

    - Personal Welfare LPA
    - Property and Affairs LPA

    (See Section 1.7)

3. The three essential elements to look for in the formation of a valid contract are: agreement, consideration and intention.

    (See Section 2.1)

4. Someone who is insane; someone who is under 18 years of age.

    (See Section 2.4)

5. The correct answer is B. A contract may be discharged through breach, performance, agreement, or frustration. Consideration (B) is one of the essentials of a valid contract.

    (See Section 2.6)

6. Agency is a relationship which exists between two legal persons (the principal and the agent) in which the function of the agent is to form a contract between his principal and a third party.

    (See Section 2.8)

7. A joint tenancy.

    (See Section 3.2)

8. A will is a legal document giving effect to the wishes of an individual (the testator, if male, the testatrix if female) as to how their estate should be distributed after their death. It appoints the persons who will have the responsibility for dealing with the estate (the executors, also called personal representatives) and gives instructions as to how the estate should be distributed.

    (See Section 5.1)

9. A trust is an equitable obligation (see below for an explanation of 'equitable') in which certain persons (the trustees) are bound to deal with property over which they have control (the trust property) for the benefit of certain individuals (the beneficiaries).

    (See Section 6.1)

5

Client advice

INTRODUCTION

The investment adviser needs to identify a client's objectives and make recommendations or construct portfolios to meet these objectives. The adviser must operate within the confines of the risk tolerance of the client whilst facing the general economic financial circumstances.

Investment management may be conducted at an institutional level for companies or at an individual level. There are different approaches and philosophies behind managing money, ranging from hands-on active approaches, to more passive approaches.

When dealing with retail clients, or consumers who are not yet clients, the adviser needs to adapt his or her communication to suit the capabilities of the individual involved. In practice, there is a wide range of investment solutions to suit different circumstances.

1 OBLIGATIONS TO INDIVIDUAL CLIENTS

Learning objectives	5.1.1 **Describe** and **compare** the different types of investors
	5.1.2 **Explain** the obligations of a firm towards retail clients
	5.1.3 **Explain** the main needs of retail clients and how they are prioritised
	5.6.2 **Identify** and apply suitable investment solutions to suit different needs of retail clients

1.1 Individual and institutional investors

Investors can broadly be categorised into **two types**:

- Individuals or retail investors
- Institutional investors

Although some **individuals** are full-time investors or may spend much of their time on their investment activities, individuals are generally limited in the time and resources they have for investing compared with **institutional** investors. Institutional investors, such as pension funds and mutual funds (a term used in the US for collective investment funds), employ professional fund managers who manage funds on a large scale. Given the size of many financial institutions and professionally managed funds, such managers can put a lot of resources into collecting and analysing information. Other examples of institutional investors include hedge funds, charitable and philanthropic trusts (eg, the Bill & Melinda Gates Foundation), and sovereign wealth funds, such as the Abu Dhabi Investment Authority, and Norway's sovereign wealth fund, said to be the world's largest in October 2013 with funds of $800 billion.

As we saw in Chapter 1 of this Study Text, **institutional investors** specialise in providing capital and act as intermediaries between those firms and individuals who supply funds and those who require finance.

We will be looking at the features and objectives of institutional investors in Section 3 of this Chapter.

Individual investors are generally classified by firms according to their wealth, with typical categories being, for example:

- Retail
- High net worth
- Very high net worth

As we saw in Chapter 3, the Financial Promotions Order allows regulatory exemptions for individual investors with certain levels of wealth and experience ('certified high net worth individuals' – with a net income of £100,000 or more, or net assets excluding principal property of £250,000 or more – and sophisticated investors – who are certified as being knowledgeable enough to understand the risk of a specified investment.

1.2 Regulation of retail financial services

Authorised **firms** have an obligation to abide by the regulators' Principles for Businesses and detailed rules, as set out in the relevant regulatory Handbook (FCA or PRA), in their dealings with consumers. Over-arching principles include the requirement to treat customers fairly, while detailed rules cover many areas, including disclosures to be made to customers.

Beyond these requirements, firms will clearly serve themselves best if they work hard to maintain and enhance the **reputation** of the firm and of the financial services industry among consumers.

The **Retail Distribution Review (RDR)** set up new arrangements – from 31 December 2012 – that are intended to enhance **consumers' confidence** in using retail financial services.

1.3 Consumers' ethical perceptions

In DP 18 *An Ethical Framework for Financial Services* (2002), the regulator recognised that consumers are increasingly understanding an ethical stance.

- Professional conduct and ethical behaviour could **strengthen the level of confidence** enjoyed by the industry.

- On the other hand, if consumers have **diminishing trust** in the sector and in individual firms, they will hesitate to use the products and services available.

Furthermore, there is increasing pressure from consumers and Government to 'put something back'. An example of this is the growing interest in policies to combat **social exclusion**, particularly from a financial standpoint.

Higher business and individual standards of behaviour promoting the integrity and the general probity of all working in financial services will, the FCA believes, enhance public perceptions and trust in the firms and individuals concerned.

1.4 Customer trust and confidentiality

The consumer must have every reason to **trust** a financial adviser. Trust is gained through respect, and an adviser will be able to project the attitudes needed by professional presentation at all times, and through the way the adviser deals with customers.

Acting as a professional means that it should be clear in the way business is conducted that all relevant regulations are being adhered to. Regulations exist to **protect the consumer**, and a client will be reassured if there is no suggestion that regulatory rules might be breached.

If the adviser is trusted, the client will be more open about his or her circumstances, and a more satisfactory basis for giving financial advice will be created. The adviser must always treat personal information with the utmost **confidentiality**.

Regarding confidentiality, all professional people need to be aware of the provisions of the **Proceeds of Crime Act 2002**. This Act requires a professional to disclose to the relevant authorities any information regarding possible crimes having been committed. These provisions mean that, by law, there are some circumstances – for example, if an adviser became aware of tax evasion having been committed – in which the professional requirement of confidentiality is overridden by the statutory requirement to breach that confidentiality by informing the authorities.

1.5 The adviser's fiduciary duty

The regulatory system codifies many obligations and many of the expectations that apply to professional investment advisers. Even where obligations have not been codified through written regulations and regulator's principles, the adviser may still owe a fiduciary duty to his or her client.

A decision in the Federal Court of Australia – *Australian Securities and Investment Commission v Citigroup Global Markets (2007)* – is likely to be persuasive in UK courts. In that decision, the court held that the parties' rights and liabilities could be excluded or modified by the terms of the contract between the parties (although **unfair terms regulations** discussed below would affect exclusions in consumer contracts). Citigroup's letter of engagement with a company it was advising had excluded any fiduciary relationship, and that exclusion was found to be effective by the court. The court stressed that, where there were **no explicit contractual exclusion or alteration**, a court would be likely to find that **a financial adviser has a fiduciary duty** towards its client.

An **adviser's fiduciary responsibility** implies that the adviser ought not to take advantage of a client's trust in him or her. The adviser (or firm) agrees to act in the sole interests of the client, to the exclusion of his or her own interests.

- The adviser's fiduciary duty implies that the adviser should act so as to avoid an influence being exerted by any conflict of interest the adviser may have.

- In fulfilling his or her fiduciary duty, the adviser must always act in the client's best interests. This is codified in the **client's best interests rule**.

- The adviser must make a full and fair disclosure of material facts, particularly where there may be a conflict of interest.

The adviser's fiduciary duty runs through all of his or her work and his or her relationships with clients. The adviser must do more than merely stick to the letter of the regulations. Under its **principles-based regulation** approach, the FCA expects the industry to pay due attention to the **higher level Principles for Businesses**, rather than only to slavishly tick checklists of detailed regulations and codes.

1.6 Fair treatment of customers

The FCA aims to maintain efficient, orderly and clean markets and to help retail customers achieve a fair deal. As previous regulator, since 2000 the FSA had examined what a fair deal for retail customers actually means and this has led to much discussion of the concept of **TCF** – 'treating customers fairly'.

The regulator does not define **treating customers fairly (TCF)** in a way that applies in all circumstances. **Principle for Businesses 6** states that a firm must pay due regard to its customers and treat them fairly. By adopting a 'principles-based approach' to TCF through Principle 6, the regulator puts the onus on firms to determine what is fair in each particular set of circumstances. Firms therefore need to make their own assessment of what TCF means for them, taking into account the nature of their business.

The emphasis of the Authority's philosophy is not so much on the principles themselves. It is on the actual consequences of what firms do. Increasingly, the term used for the regulators' recent approach has been **outcomes-focused regulation**.

TCF is treated as a part of the **FCA's core supervisory work**. Firms – meaning senior management, including the Board – are expected to be able to demonstrate to themselves and to the regulator that they deliver **fair outcomes to their customers**.

With regard to TCF, the FCA specifically expects firms to focus on delivering the following six **consumer outcomes**.

- **Corporate culture**: consumers can be confident that they are dealing with firms where the fair treatment of customers is central to the corporate culture.

- **Marketing**: products and services marketed and sold in the retail market are designed to meet the needs of identified consumer groups and are targeted accordingly.

- **Clear information**: consumers are provided with clear information and are kept appropriately informed before, during and after the point of sale.

- **Suitability of advice**: where consumers receive advice, the advice is suitable and takes account of their circumstances.

- **Fair product expectations**: consumers are provided with products that perform as firms have led them to expect, and the associated service is both of an acceptable standard and also as they have been led to expect.

- **Absence of post-sale barriers**: consumers do not face unreasonable post-sale barriers imposed by firms to change product, switch provider, submit a claim or make a complaint.

1.7 Requirements for fair agreements

In communications relating to designated investment business, a firm must not seek to **exclude or restrict any duty or liability** it may have under the **regulatory system**. If the client is a retail client, any other exclusion or restriction of duties or liabilities must meet the 'clients' best interests rule' test.

The general law, in particular the **Unfair Terms in Consumer Contracts Regulations 1999**, also limits a firm's scope for excluding or restricting duties or liabilities to a consumer. As a qualifying body, the FCA has an agreement with the Office of Fair Trading – the lead enforcer of these Regulations – that the Authority will apply the Regulations to financial services contracts issued by regulated firms and appointed representatives for carrying out regulated activities.

- As well as its principles and rules which require firms to treat their customers fairly, the FCA has powers under the Regulations to challenge firms that use unfair terms in their standard consumer contracts.

- The Authority may consider the fairness of consumer contracts, make recommendations to firms, and apply for injunctions against them to prevent the use of such terms.

- The FCA also has a statutory duty to consider all complaints made to it about unfair contract terms.

The regulator has made clear that it considers fairness in consumer contracts to be an important visible factor in firms treating their customers fairly.

The Regulations state that an unfair term is not binding on the consumer but that the contract will continue to bind the parties if it is capable of continuing in existence without the unfair term. Therefore, if the court finds that the term in question is unfair, the firm would have to stop relying on the unfair term in existing contracts governed by the Regulations.

The FCA may consider the fairness of a contract following a complaint from a consumer or another person.

Under the Regulations, the regulator has the power to request, for certain purposes:

- A copy of any document which that person has used or recommended for use as a pre-formulated standard contract in dealings with consumers

- Information about the use, or recommendation for use, by that person of that document or any other such document in dealings with consumers

Terms are regarded as **unfair** if, contrary to the requirement of good faith, they cause a significant imbalance in the parties' rights and obligations **to the detriment of the consumer**.

Unless the case is urgent, the regulator will generally first write to a firm to express our concern about the potential unfairness of a term or terms (within the meaning of the Regulations) and will invite the firm to comment on those concerns. If we still believe that the term is unfair, we will normally ask the firm to stop including the term in new contracts and to stop relying on it in any concluded contracts. If the firm either declines to give an undertaking, or gives an undertaking but fails to follow it, the regulator will consider the need to apply to the courts for an injunction.

2 GIVING INVESTMENT ADVICE

2.1 The financial planning process

The **financial planning** process can be summarised as comprising the following six stages.

1. **Obtaining relevant information** – sometimes termed fact finding
2. **Establishing and agreeing** the client's financial objectives
3. **Processing and analysing the data** obtained
4. **Formulating recommendations** in a comprehensive plan with objectives
5. **Implementing the recommendations** as agreed with the client
6. **Reviewing and regularly updating** the plan

It is helpful to consider **client objectives** below (stage **2** in the process) before we go on to discuss the **fact-find** (stage **1** in the process).

2.2 Client objectives

2.2.1 Overview

Broadly speaking, the requirements of clients fall into one of two categories:

- To **maximise returns**, eg for positive net worth individuals looking for a portfolio to match their risk/return preferences

- To **match liabilities**, eg in the case of pension funds, where the aim is to match assets and liabilities or minimise any mismatch

2.2.2 Return maximisation

Given the choice, most investors seeking a collective fund investment would elect to have a high performance fund with minimal risk. However, this is not achievable and some trade-off between the two will have to take place. Understanding the **risk/reward trade-off** is crucial to understanding the overall objectives of a return-maximising fund and then to establishing the policy of a fund.

Lower risk aversion or greater risk tolerance will tend to result in greater allowable portfolio risk, along with greater potential gains (and potential losses).

The primary concern in this type of fund is, therefore, to fully understand the client's risk tolerance, whether the clients are private or institutional clients.

2.2.3 Liability matching

The only way to guarantee the matching of any liability is through investment in government bonds where the income and capital inflows exactly match those liabilities.

If the return from bonds is insufficient to achieve this required return, then we must use other assets. The result of the use of other assets is that we may achieve the higher return required. However, the risk associated with the use of these other assets means that the liabilities may not be exactly met – there may be a mismatch.

Again, a key requirement here will be to establish the client's attitude to risk, though here we have more specific financial objectives to meet, ie a future liability to satisfy.

2.2.4 Mixed requirements

For most institutional clients, the primary requirement will be quite clear-cut – collective investments are generally return-maximising funds whereas pension funds are liability-driven.

For many individual clients, however, the requirements may be more mixed. A wealthy individual client may have certain liabilities to meet such as paying for children's/grandchildren's school and college fees, repaying loans/mortgages or providing financial protection for relatives/dependents, but may wish that any 'spare' resources be managed to maximise returns.

There are a number of stages that need to be undertaken when considering client objectives.

2.3 Quantifying and prioritising clients' objectives

Learning objective | 5.2.1 **Explain** the importance of establishing and quantifying a client's objectives

The first stage is to determine all of the objectives that the client is looking to meet and to prioritise and quantify those objectives, especially quantifying any liability targets since they will invariably be the top priorities.

From a priority viewpoint, this will clearly be specific to and determined by the client.

From a quantification viewpoint, the fund liabilities may include such factors as school/college fees, loans, dependent pensions, and a primary consideration here will be whether those liabilities are nominal or real.

- A **nominal liability** is one that is fixed in monetary terms irrespective of future inflation. An example of a nominal liability would be a bank loan or mortgage where the monetary sum borrowed must be paid off at the end of the term and does not alter with inflation over that time.

- In contrast, a **real liability** is one which changes in monetary terms as we experience inflation. For example, in order to maintain a standard of living a pension needs to pay out the same amount each year in real terms, ie a rising monetary amount to cover the impacts of inflation, and this sum needs to be paid for the remaining life from the retirement – an indeterminate term.

Whatever the liability, assessment will involve a **present value analysis** of the anticipated future liabilities that the fund is aiming to meet. For example, to pay a pension of £20,000 pa for a period of 20 years when real returns (asset returns in excess of inflation) are 3% will require a fund value at retirement of almost £300,000 and so we would be looking to achieve this fund value at the retirement date.

2.4 Affordability of client's objectives

Learning objective | 5.2.2 **Explain** the need to prioritise objectives to accommodate a client's affordability

Based on the quantification, the investment adviser will be able to determine any lump sum or annual contributions that need to be made in order to establish the required pool and at this stage the issue of affordability needs to be considered. **Affordability** is the primary issue since if a client cannot afford a proposal then it is not suitable.

If the current assets and/or disposable income of the client are more than sufficient to meet the liability needs then the surplus funds are available for (return-maximising) savings. If, on the other hand, there is a deficit or shortfall then the client's targets and, potentially, priorities will need to be reconsidered.

2.5 The fact find process

Learning objectives

5.3.1 Explain the importance of the fact find process in establishing a client's current financial circumstances and requirements

5.3.2 Identify the factors shaping a clients' circumstances

Key to the assessment of the affordability, therefore, is the client's current personal and financial circumstances which may be determined through the fact find. There are no specific regulatory requirements regarding the nature and content of the fact find.

The fact find will seek to establish both personal and financial information. **Personal information** detailed in the fact find would, for a retail client, include family names and addresses, dates of birth, marital status, employment status, tax status. **Financial information** would include current income and expenditure levels, levels of savings and investments, the scale of any financial liabilities (usually mortgages, loans and credit cards), the existence of any life assurance policies and pensions etc.

The client will have much of this information readily to hand, however certain information may need to be obtained from third parties. For example, the current performance and value of any pension schemes or life policies such as endowments will probably need to be obtained from the relevant pension fund manager or life assurance fund manager. The overall financial plan will need to take account of any payments that are committed to such funds, any receipts that may be expected from them and whether it is worth considering changing providers.

Other areas that may be considered at this stage are current mortgage terms and the terms of other loans as it may again be appropriate to refinance at better rates.

In order to obtain this information from a third party, the adviser will require a **letter of authority** from the client that authorises the release of the information. Such enquiries typically take several weeks to get resolved and so this may cause a significant delay.

The objective information regarding the client's personal and financial situation may be referred to as **hard facts**. One final aim of the fact find will be to seek to understand the more subjective information that may be relevant, such as client requirements or aspirations, risk tolerances and any other subjective factors such as their attitude towards issues such as socially responsible investment. This type of information, which cannot be verified using documentary evidence, may be referred to as **soft facts**.

Understanding such soft facts requires face-to-face meeting with the client to discuss and consider the issues alongside them. Establishing a client's risk tolerance, for example, is far from straightforward as standard risk measures are far from familiar to most retail clients and approaches are covered below.

2.6 Risks affecting investors

Learning objectives

5.4.1 Analyse the main types of investment risk as they affect investors

5.4.2 Explain the role of diversification in mitigating risk

5.4.3 Analyse the impact of timescales on a client's attitude to risk

5.4.4 Explain the key methods of determining a client's attitude to risk

2.6.1 Overview

The main risks that a **client** faces and that they need to understand are as follows.

- **Capital risk** – the potential variability in the principal (capital) value of an investment

BPP
LEARNING MEDIA

- **Inflation risk** – the potential variability in inflation rates, which will impact significantly on return requirements for funds looking to finance real liabilities

- **Interest rate risk** – the risk of changes in bank base rates and the knock-on effect that this may have on asset returns

- **Shortfall risk** – the risk of the return on an investment falling short of the amount needed for a client to achieve their objectives. This might be reduced by minimising targets, increasing sums invested or extending investment terms

2.6.2 Diversification

One of the key benefits of utilising collective funds, such as unit trusts, exchange traded funds (ETFs) or OEICs, is that the investor's funds are being pooled with those of other investors. This pooling allows the investor's money to be spread over a range of assets.

Consider an **investment** in shares (equities). Two sorts of risk can be distinguished:

- The general **market risk** (or **'systematic' risk**) of investing in shares or bonds
- The **specific risk** (or **'non-systematic' risk**) of any individual investment

For example, if an investor were to put all their money into the shares of a company, there would firstly be the risk that the market in all shares would fall, causing the value of the investment to fall, and secondly the risk that the specific company itself may suffer from a specific incident causing the share price to fall.

If an investor is able to buy more investments, he will be taking on board specific risks of different companies. Eventually, there will be a situation where, because of specific risks, some of the investments will fall but others will rise. Overall, through this process of **diversification**, investors are able to rid themselves of the specific risk of a stock. It is, however, impossible to remove the market risk.

Having established the general principle of diversification, we can see that there are the following different types of diversification:

- **Diversification by asset class.** This is achieved by holding a combination of different kinds of asset within a portfolio, possibly spread across: cash, fixed interest securities, equity investments, property-based investments, and other assets.

- **Diversification within asset classes.** An investor can diversify a portfolio by holding a variety of investments within the particular asset types that he holds. This may be achieved by holding various fixed interest securities, by holding equities in a number of different companies, by spreading investments across different industry sectors and geographical markets, and by holding a number of different properties or property-based investments.

- **Diversification by manager.** Diversifying risk across different funds with different managers reduces the risks from a manager performing poorly. This is one of the attractions of '**manager of manager**' and '**fund of fund**' structures.

The **principle of diversification** should be clearly explained to the client as it will have a significant impact on the potential asset allocations. As part of the fact find, the investment adviser will probably illustrate various possible asset allocations and discuss in detail the potential returns and risks of each.

2.6.3 Timescales

A client's attitude to risk may be influenced by **investment timescales**.

If, for example, we are managing a pension fund or portfolio, our attitude to risk will be highly dependent on timescales. If the fund is a young scheme with 30 or 40 years to client retirement, then it can afford to take a reasonably aggressive attitude to capital risk and invest in what may be regarded as the riskier assets. By taking a high risk, we may experience some poor years but we are also likely to experience some very good years. The effect is that risk averages out over time, giving rise to a good overall long-term return, thus minimising shortfall risk.

If, on the other hand, the scheme is very mature and retirement is imminent, then there is insufficient time for this averaging effect to take place. As a result, any poor performance this year may have a significantly adverse effect on the portfolio, ie a high capital risk in this circumstance increases the shortfall risk.

The investment adviser's approach will, therefore, be very much affected by investment timescales.

2.6.4 Client's risk tolerance

There are two approaches that an investment adviser will utilise in order to get an understanding of the client's risk tolerance, specifically the fact find soft facts discussion, and a review of any current investments.

The process will probably start with **a review of the client's current investments and risks**, which will clearly illustrate the client's historical attitude to risk. As we noted above, however, risk tolerance changes over time, so this historical information, whilst a very useful insight, is not of itself sufficient for a full understanding of the client's risk tolerance.

To augment this, the investment adviser will also undertake the **fact-find soft facts review**. The standard fact-find approach is to ask the client to select a mix of, say, equities and bonds, to give an idea of the normal mix (and hence risk) that the client wishes to face. We noted above that as part of the fact find process the investment adviser will illustrate various possible asset allocations and discuss in detail the potential returns and risks of each. Such targeted discussions should enable the manager to get an understanding of the clients general risk tolerance. The investment adviser will also be looking to establish limits for each asset class, maximum and minimum holdings of the different assets available, representing investment risk limits.

The client's mental approach and desire for security may imply a lower tolerance of risk.

2.6.5 Investment risks and rewards

We have already mentioned the trade-off between risk and potential reward. This is fundamental to an understanding of investment management.

- **Low risk** investments offer low returns, but low probability of loss
- **High risk** investments offer the possibility of high returns, and a high probability of loss

The following table gives a broad indication of where various investments can be placed in a 'spectrum' of overall investment risk.

Negligible risk	NS&I deposit products Gilts (income) Gilts (redemption)
Low risk	Bank deposits Building society deposits Cash ISAs Annuities
Low / medium risk	Gilts (pre-redemption capital) With-profits funds
Medium risk	Unit-linked managed funds Unit trusts and OEICs/ICVCs (UK funds) Investment trusts (UK) Residential and commercial property
Medium / high risk	Unit-linked overseas funds Unit trusts and OEICs/ICVCs (overseas funds) UK single equities Commodities
High risk	Venture Capital Trusts Unlisted shares Warrants Futures and Options when used to speculate Enterprise Investment Scheme Enterprise Zone Property

Before offering any investment advice, it is vital to ensure that the risk and prospective returns match the customer's criteria.

2.7 The investment management process

The objectives and constraints of a fund or portfolio lead the fund or portfolio manager to consider a variety of strategies or possible asset allocations, and within these to select specific stocks that meet the fund or portfolio objectives.

The approach to portfolio management

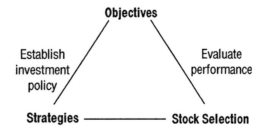

Once the objectives and constraints of the particular portfolio have been established, the next stage is to develop the investment policy/strategies that will be used in order to achieve these objectives. All these considerations will be detailed as recommended investment policy/strategy options.

These recommendations must then be submitted to the client for approval. In simple situations there may be one obvious approach for the manager to adopt, in more complex situations, several alternatives may be presented to the client forming the basis of a discussion leading to the finally agreed investment policy/strategy statement.

2.8 Asset allocation

The resultant investment policy/strategy statement forms the basis of the management approach. This strategy will detail the long term **strategic asset allocation** options selected to achieve the client's objectives. Asset allocations should not, however, be set in stone. Different asset categories perform better in different economic situations and the investment adviser must be ready to respond to such circumstances.

Along with the long-term strategic **asset allocation**, the strategy may also detail **market timing/tactical asset allocation** options that may be adopted in those differing circumstances. The strategy details asset allocations and limits but will not detail **stock or product recommendations**.

Finally, the investment strategy will probably detail any performance **benchmarks** against which the portfolio performance is to be assessed.

2.9 Investment and product selection

2.9.1 Introduction

When the overall strategy and policy of the portfolio have been determined, the final stage is to select the stock that will make up the portfolio.

The precise approach adopted depends on the investment management style adopted, ie **active** or **passive**.

2.9.2 Active versus passive management

There are broadly two styles that the investment manager can adopt. On the one hand, an **active** investment manager is one who intervenes with the portfolio on a regular basis, attempting to use individual expertise in order to enhance the overall return of the fund. **Passive** investment management, on the other hand, establishes a strategy which, once established, should guarantee the appropriate level of return for the fund. These are, perhaps, two extreme versions of investment management. There are alternatives that represent hybrids between the two extremes.

2.9.3 Active management

As mentioned above, active investment management means that the investment adviser constantly takes decisions and appraises the value of investments within the portfolio. Whilst, to many, this may seem the only thing an investment adviser could do, it has to be appreciated that in practice there are costs involved with all transactions, and hence limits on the number of active interventions taking place are likely to be to the advantage of the fund holder.

Moreover, from a more theoretical point of view, there are a number of theories (such as efficient market hypothesis) that indicate that the market itself is efficient and therefore the prices currently quoted in the market contain within them all available information. If this is so, then the only reason that a price will move is because of information which is not already known to the market and, as such, investment

advisers buying and selling (switching between stocks) will only make money if they are 'lucky' and switch to the right stock at the right time.

Active fund managers do not believe that the securities markets are continuously efficient. Instead, they believe that securities can be mis-valued and that at times **winners** can be found. They also attempt to correctly **time** their purchase or sale on the basis of specific stock information, market information, economic factors and so on.

Active fund managers may obtain research from external sources such as investment banks. In this instance analysts are referred to as 'sell-side' analysts. Alternatively they may establish an in-house research department, made up of 'buy-side' analysts. The benefit of generating unbiased internal research needs to be weighed against the costs of setting up the department.

2.9.4 Passive management

Passive management involves the establishing of a strategy with the intention of achieving the overall objectives of the fund. Once established, this strategy should not require active intervention, but should be self-maintaining. The simplest strategy is to 'buy and hold'. However, perhaps the most common form of passive management is indexation.

2.9.5 Indexation

With **indexation**, the fund manager selects an appropriate index quoted in the market place. Having established the index, the fund manager builds a portfolio which mimics the index, the belief being that this portfolio will then perform in line with the index numbers. Such funds are known as **index** or **tracker** funds.

Overall, the likelihood is that the fund will underperform the index for a number of reasons. Firstly, there is the initial cost of creating the portfolio. Secondly, and perhaps more importantly, all index funds tend to be based on a sampling approach and consequently exhibit a degree of **tracking error**.

It should be noted that indexation itself is not a totally passive form of investment management since the constitution of each index will, over time, change and the portfolio will also be required to change. Tracker funds will, however, incur lower transaction costs as a result of the lower levels of turnover, an advantage over actively managed funds.

2.9.6 Hybrids

Seeking to out-perform indexes, rather than merely track them, inevitably requires a less than fully passive, and more interventionist, approach – possibly with an **indexed core fund**, and a **peripheral** or **satellite fund** which is more actively managed and could involve the use of derivatives in order to establish larger trading positions than the fund itself can obtain.

Alternatively, the fund manager may combine both active and passive fund management methods by **tilting** the fund. Tilting involves holding all (or a representative sample) of the constituents of an index (like a passive tracker fund), but with larger proportions in areas that the manager favours. This asset allocation decision constitutes the active management component.

Research suggests that many 'active' funds can be viewed partially as '**closet trackers**' – committing much of their funds to stocks within an index without declaring that policy, perhaps in order to avoid having performance move too far from the performance of benchmark indices.

2.10 Review

The review process will evaluate whether a portfolio is achieving its objectives through a consideration of its performance. Portfolio performance should be **reviewed** no less than once a year, or more regularly for short term funds, and will look to achieve a number of objectives.

- **Client circumstances** – we should firstly look to determine whether any client circumstances have altered as this may result in an alteration of the client's objectives. Any significant changes may require a modification to the investment strategy.

- **Performance review** – we need to monitor the performance of the portfolio against the selected benchmark to ensure that it is achieving its objectives.

- **Portfolio rebalancing** – following on from the performance review we should consider whether there is any need to update the agreed asset allocations. Care needs to be taken here in respect of the tax liabilities that may arise from the effects of any rebalancing.

The fund or portfolio management process cannot, however, be thought of as a step-by-step process that finishes at this stage, rather it is an ongoing process. This review will establish the strategy for the next period and the process will continue.

2.11 Benchmarks

2.11.1 Overview

An investor who has been paying someone to actively manage their portfolio will wish to monitor how well the investment manager is doing his job. Such information can then be used to:

- Alter or update the portfolio investment constraints in order to achieve a particular objective

- Communicate investment objectives to the manager to ensure that the portfolio is managed efficiently

- Identify strengths and weaknesses of particular managers

When measuring performance of a portfolio, it is important to establish whether the performance was relatively good, or bad, and so a performance measure is required.

There are three main forms of comparable analysis of performance.

- Comparison to relevant stock/index, eg a published market index

- Comparison to similar funds, ie performance of other managers with similar objectives and constraints. PPM consultants maintain extensive databases on statistical performance, eg CAPS Ltd and WM Company, Micropal. These companies measure:

    – Short and long-term investment return
    – Asset distribution of funds
    – Review specific client portfolio performance against peer groups and/or market indices
    – Portfolio performance relative to benchmarks and market medians

- Comparison with a customised benchmark for funds that have a unique objective or constraint, eg ethical funds that cannot invest in arms/tobacco (although the standardised FTSE4Good indices meeting ethical criteria are available)

2.11.2 Using indices

Movements of an **index** over a period of time can be used by analysts to give an indication of general trends, and also indicate whether the market appears overpriced or underpriced relative to previous years. To be useful in this context, however, the index must be comparable over the period being considered, and great efforts must be made to ensure that any index is both **relevant** and **comparable**. If an index is to be used as a performance yardstick against which the performance of a portfolio is to be assessed, it must provide a reasonable comparison.

This is particularly important when a client wants to compare the performance of a collective fund in which they are investing. There are various performance indices available for individual investors, including for example the WM Performance Indices, in addition to FTSE Indices. The WM Performance Indices include a series of benchmarks based upon **income**, **growth** as well as a **balanced fund** index.

An investor will need to understand how the index deals with the payment of income by a security (dividends for shares and interest for bonds). The normally quoted **FTSE Indices** do **not** include dividend income in their evaluation. In contrast, bond indices, such as the **Citigroup World Government Bond Indices**, most frequently **do** include the value of coupon payments and hence represent **total return indices**.

2.11.3 Benchmark indices

Indices may be used for a variety of reasons. Historically, their main purpose was to give an indication of the mood of the market. More frequently now, they are used as a benchmark for performance assessment.

To be appropriate for benchmarking purposes, an index must be indicative of the performance that could realistically have been achieved.

The characteristics that are required to render an index suitable as a benchmark are therefore that it is:

- Specified and unambiguous

- Appropriate to the nature of the fund (eg, a UK blue chip fund may utilise the FTSE 100 Index)

- Appropriate to the currency of the fund

- Investable, ie composed of investments that could conceivably be held in the fund

- Measurable, ie the return can be calculated on a frequent basis as required

- Representative of achievable performance, ie it has an arithmetic weighted composition (remember that the return of a portfolio is an arithmetic weighted average of the individual stock returns)

- Measures the relevant component of performance, ie total return indices for total return performance and capital value indices for capital growth

2.12 Recommending funds

2.12.1 Introduction

Where a portfolio is too small to be efficiently managed or the client's objectives are too specialised to be handled in-house, the fund management may be **outsourced**. The decision to outsource will be determined when the overall strategy and policy are developed, towards the end of the initial investment management process.

The range of funds that a manager can use may be restricted if the manager is 'tied', however if they are independent then they will have the whole market to choose from. Irrespective of the range available to them there are certain factors to consider, including the following.

2.12.2 Past performance

Although appropriate warnings must be given on how the past is not a guide to future performance, consistently positive past performance – for example, as measured relative to against benchmarks or relative to the peer group of funds – is accepted as an indication of the manager's skill.

2.12.3 Charges

The best fund manager in the world will not be worth using if his charges eat up all of the fund's returns so it is essential that these are considered. Fund charges tend to come in one of two forms

- Entry and exit charges – charges made when funds are invested or when funds are withdrawn

- Annual charges – generally charged as a percentage of the value of funds under management, though they may include a performance related element

The higher the overall fee burden, the greater the fund performance needs to be in order to outperform its peer group.

2.12.4 Financial stability of the provider

For many funds this is of little relevance, however it is key to 'with profits' funds run by life assurance companies whose performance accumulates over many years. 'With profits' funds aim to smooth the fund returns across the years through the application of bonuses. In very good years part of the fund return will be retained rather than being allocated as an annual bonus. In poorer years these retained funds can be called on to continue to provide the annual bonus. For this process to function requires a good degree of financial stability within the provider.

2.12.5 Stability, independence and standing of trustee, fund custodians and auditors

Financial regulation came into being as a result of certain financial scandals and despite these regulations scandals still arise, though they are now much rarer in the UK. In many respects, fund management is an industry ripe for fraud. One individual, the fund manager, has control of potentially quite substantial funds owned by others, the investors. As a result, there needs to be controls and checks in place to ensure that neither the fund manager nor anyone else involved in the process is either tempted or able to abuse their position.

Typically, within a fund where a trustee is involved:

- The fund manager controls how and where the assets are invested but never personally has access to them

- Any trades are transacted by a broker

- The funds are held in the name of the trustee who is charged with the task of ensuring that the fund manager operates in accordance with his remit

- Periodically, the fund accounts are checked by the fund auditor

Any action taken by any one of these parties is immediately transparent to the others, so this segregation of duties should ensure the safety and security of the investor's funds (except in the case of collusion between all of the parties involved).

The trustee and auditor are the primary controlling influences in this system, hence their independence from the fund manager and each other as well as their reputation and standing in those roles are of great importance to the investor.

3 INSTITUTIONAL INVESTORS

5.7.1 Explain the features and objectives of the following funds in the UK: pension funds (defined benefit (DC) and defined contribution (DC)), life assurance, general insurance

5.7.2 Distinguish among the typical asset allocations for DB and DC pension funds, life assurance and general insurance funds

5.7.3 Explain the return objectives of the major fund types

5.7.4 Classify funds by their income/capital growth requirements

5.7.8 Identify the other types of legal requirements that affect pension funds, insurance funds and private retail clients

3.1 Overview

Institutional investors are major participants in modern financial markets. Much of individuals' wealth is tied up in retirement and other savings that are held within institutional investment vehicles. Occupational pension funds, insurance companies, pooled investment vehicles such as OEICs, unit and investment trusts, and other financial institutions such as charities, endowments and educational institutions, hold more than half the equity capital of UK-listed companies.

Each type of institutional fund has its own particular risk/reward profile stemming from:

- Its objectives, return maximising/liability matching
- The value and time horizons of the liabilities it has to meet (if any)
- The assets it can invest in
- The liquidity they require within the fund
- The risk they can tolerate in the fund
- Its tax status
- Legislation governing its powers

Here, we consider the features and objectives of:

- Pension funds
- Life assurance funds
- General insurance funds

3.2 Pension funds

3.2.1 Assets and liabilities

A pension fund is an example of a liability matching fund or a return maximising fund. It represents a pool of money to be invested now, to achieve either:

- A specific return based on the employee's salary and number of years' service with the company – a **defined benefit (DB)/final salary scheme**, or

- A general increase in value of the contributions paid on behalf of the employee – a **defined contribution (DC)/money purchase scheme**

Occupational pension schemes, where the scheme is set up by the employer for the benefit of the employees, tend to be DB schemes, though defined contribution schemes are becoming increasingly popular.

A DB pension fund has an obligation to ensure that the present value of liabilities equals the present value of assets. The stream of future pension liabilities is reasonably predictable by actuaries. This suggests that it is desirable to ensure the future cash flows from assets required to meet those pension payments are also reasonably predictable. This, in turn, suggests that bonds should play a significant role in the portfolios of pension funds.

Personal pension plans, set up by an individual who is, perhaps, self-employed or is not a member of an occupational scheme, are DC pensions.

Generally speaking, pension funds have fairly **long-term horizons** and, therefore, are prepared to take on board a higher degree of risk, since any shortfall in the fund can be made up in future investment performance. This **investment policy** depends on the **maturity** of the fund. If the fund beneficiaries are close to retirement, then it would be more appropriate to select relatively short-term safe investments. However, in general the above comment is applicable.

Pension funds also have to keep control over the real rate of return that they earn since their liabilities, the potential pension payments calculated by the fund actuaries, will be expanding in line with inflation. As a consequence, pension funds tend to invest in slightly more speculative assets often referred to as **real assets**, such as **equities** and **property**, since these offer a degree of protection against the impact of inflation.

In addition, they tend to keep only a small proportion of the fund in fixed interest instruments. In particular, they will tend to be substantial holders of index-linked stocks, partly because these guarantee real returns over a period of time, but also because the bonds themselves tend to have fairly high durations and are therefore sensitive to movement in real interest rates.

Equally, the pension fund will need to keep some assets in a liquid form and government bond markets represent a highly liquid market place in which to invest money gaining a moderate but **risk-free** return.

DB pension funds need to consider **longevity risk** – the risk that liabilities to pay pensions will increase as pensioners live longer. It could be difficult to meet this risk through investment in bonds. The Pensions Regulator has estimated that the addition of two years to life expectancies can increase scheme liabilities by 5%.

3.2.2 Tax status

Within certain limits, **contributions** paid to registered pension schemes are **tax-free**, ie no income tax burden is suffered by individuals on contributions paid on their behalf, and tax relief can be claimed on contributions that they pay themselves.

In addition, pension funds approved by HMRC pay no UK tax on either fund income or capital gains.

However, pension funds are not able to reclaim the notional 10% income tax that is deemed to have been paid on UK dividends received. In addition, there may be withholding tax on overseas investments that may not be recoverable.

The only occurrence of tax in relation to pension funds is the deferred **income tax payable on pensions in retirement**.

3.2.3 Trends in the pensions sector

During the last fifteen years, there has been a general **decline in defined benefit (DB) schemes** and a **rise in defined contribution (DC) schemes**.

There are the following reasons for this.

- Increased liabilities of DB schemes, due to increased longevity

- Falling returns on scheme assets resulting in higher contributions being needed to maintain DB schemes

- Increasing pension deficits resulting from the poor financial position of many DB schemes

- Requirements for disclosure of the schemes' funding position in the company's financial statements

A less certain financial outlook has led many DB schemes to change asset allocations to reduce equity holdings and to increase fixed interest (bond) holdings. **Liability-driven investment (LDI)** strategies have been developed that use derivatives such as swaps to match more closely assets and liabilities.

3.3 Life assurance companies

3.3.1 Assets and liabilities

Life assurance is a form of insurance against an eventuality that is **assured** (hence the name) to arise, ie that people will die. As such, it is another form of liability matching fund. Life assurance policies take a number of forms.

- **Term assurance policies** – where an individual's life is insured for a specific period or term (usually ten years or more) in a similar way to normal car or household insurance.

- **Whole of life policies** – where a capital sum will be paid upon the death of the policyholder, whenever that may be.

- **Endowment policies** – which combine life insurance and savings. These policies are generally associated with mortgages where the savings element is designed to pay off the capital borrowed at the end of the term of the policy, and the life insurance will repay the mortgage should the policyholder die before the end of that term.

In common with pension funds, life assurance companies tend to have reasonably **long-term** liabilities and, as such, are able to take on board a higher degree of risk. Once again, this tends to involve a high proportion of their assets being invested into equities and property with only a smaller proportion being invested into the fixed interest markets.

As holders of long-term funds, life assurance companies are able to take reasonably higher degrees of risk and again may be tempted towards the higher duration stocks in the bond markets.

Within the industry there are a variety of policies available ranging from with profits policies, which share in the profits of the fund but attract higher premiums, to without profits policies, where the premiums are lower but the profits go to the insurance company.

3.3.2 Tax status

There is **no tax relief on the payment of life assurance premiums** on new policies (although there is on certain older policies).

All fund income and capital gains are taxable, which will result in the investment manager selecting investment vehicles that are more tax-efficient.

Proceeds paid from life policies are taxable unless the policy is a **qualifying** policy, in which case the proceeds are **tax-free**.

3.3.3 Regulation

In terms of regulation, there is a considerably stronger regime imposed upon the insurance industry than that operating in the pensions market. The regulator of insurance companies is the PRA which, under FSMA 2000, is given a range of interventionist powers.

Both life assurance funds and general insurance funds are closely monitored to ensure that the solvency of the company is in no way called into question. Overall, this tends to make both of them more risk adverse than pension funds, but there is a marked difference between life assurance companies and general insurance companies in the risk/reward profile they adopt.

The basic measure of solvency is that the assets of the fund must exceed the liabilities of the fund, both derived using prudent measures. Where there are concerns about the solvency of a fund, then they may intervene in order to guarantee the policyholders' rights.

3.4 General insurance companies

3.4.1 Assets and liabilities

General insurance companies aim to be able to match their liabilities. They have a much shorter liability profile than life funds.

The insured person pays the company the premium. The insurance company makes money if they are able to take in this premium and earn investment income on it that, together with the premium *less* administrative costs, exceeds the amounts of any claims arising on the policy.

Since claims are likely to arise in the immediate future, for example in the next year, then they are unable to take substantial risks with part of their funds, leading them to invest a greater proportion of their fund into **short-term** 'risk-free' government securities. Returns will be fairly low, but the fund must limit its risk.

3.4.2 Tax status

General insurance business profits are subject to normal corporation tax rates.

3.4.3 Regulation

General insurance business is governed by similar rules and regulations as life insurance business, which was discussed above.

3.5 Constraints on funds

Learning objective	5.7.5 **Explain** the effect of each of the following on a fund's asset allocation: time horizons; liability structure, liquidity requirements

Given the client's objectives, the key to understanding the investment strategy is to appreciate the various constraints that operate on the fund itself. We commented above on the risk/reward trade-off, which impacts on the ways in which the fund's requirements can be achieved.

3.6 Time horizons and liability structure

The **time horizon** for the attainment of the return, or the matching of the liabilities, will clearly influence the types of investments that will be worthwhile for the fund.

A fund whose purpose is to meet some liabilities in, say, two years' time, may find that the investment vehicle is low coupon gilts. This will especially be the case if the client is a high rate taxpayer as he will be able to benefit from a tax-free capital gain on these gilts at redemption.

For a fund that has liabilities to meet in 20 years' time, such investments would be inappropriate.

The time horizon will also influence the level of risk that can be taken in order to achieve the objectives. A fund with a long-term time horizon can probably stand a higher risk, as any poor returns in one year will be cancelled by high returns in subsequent years before the fund expires. Clearly, this sort of risk cannot be taken in a very short-term fund which may only span a couple of years and, therefore, may not have counterbalancing good and bad years.

As mentioned earlier, certain funds have liabilities that they are obliged to meet and the investment manager's objective must take these into consideration. For example, pension funds and life assurance companies will have statistical projections of their liabilities into the future and the fund must attempt to achieve these.

A further consideration is the exposure to currency risk. A pension fund may have all its liabilities denominated in sterling. If the fund were to invest heavily in overseas assets this would expose it to an additional risk, other than the risk inherent in the assets themselves. However, if the pension fund has liabilities in, say, dollars, then buying US investments matches their currency exposure and, therefore, minimises risk as well as taking on board an acceptable investment.

3.7 Liquidity needs

Within any fund, there must be the ability to respond to changing circumstances and, consequently, there needs to be a degree of liquidity. Government fixed interest instruments can guarantee a tranche of the investment portfolio which will give easy access to cash should the fund need it. In general, exchange traded investments (equities and bonds) tend to be highly liquid whilst investments that are not exchange traded, such as property, have low liquidity.

3.8 Asset allocation

Asset allocation is the allocation of the funds available between the various instruments or financial markets.

All fund managers require a knowledge of asset allocation according to more fundamental principles. This is perhaps the most subjective area of fund management, and one where there will never be a single correct answer. Given the same fund and client, it is unlikely that any two fund managers would produce exactly the same asset allocation and make exactly the same investment decisions. However, it would be reasonable to assume that any allocations would have a broadly similar effect. The justification for this last statement is that the fund or portfolio manager has a legal and professional duty to **base the asset allocation on the client's wishes** with particular regard to the criteria discussed above when identifying the client's objectives, specifically the following.

- Matching liabilities
- Meeting any ethical considerations
- Remaining within risk tolerances
- Maximising fund performance

Asset allocation must, therefore, be the first step in the investment management process.

There are three basic rules the fund manager should bear in mind when trying to satisfy the client's investment objectives.

- The fund manager should take every step to diversify risk, a process requiring an understanding of the different risk factors affecting all the investments in which he may be investing as well as the impact of foreign exchange.

- The fund manager should be aware that the best way to match the client's liabilities if they are fixed in money terms is by investing in bonds, since this will generate cash flows from interest and redemption proceeds which will allow the liabilities to be met as they arise.

- Asset allocation is effectively a compromise between matching investments to client liabilities and investing assets in more attractive markets in order to maximise fund performance.

The optimal asset allocation should be based on the objectives and constraints of the fund and the fund manager's estimate of the risks and returns offered by the various securities.

The idea is that the objectives and constraints of a fund direct the investment manager towards certain asset classes and away from others, leading towards the asset allocation decision. For example, if real liabilities are to be met, these must be matched by real assets (equities/property/index-linked bonds), or if high liquidity is needed, then property is inappropriate.

As an illustration of this, we consider in the table below the various constraints for common liability matching funds and some possible resultant asset allocations.

Constraint	Young pension fund	Mature pension fund	Life assurance fund	General insurance fund
Time	Long-term	Short-term	Long-term	Short-term
Liability	Real	Real	Nominal	Nominal
Liquidity	Very low	High	Low	Very high
Risk tolerance	High	Low	Medium/High	Very low
Tax status	No tax on income or gains*	No tax on income or gains	Tax on income and gains	Tax on income and gains
Asset allocation				
Equities	60% - 80%	20% - 30%	55% - 65%	0%
Property	5% - 10%	0% (illiquid)	0% - 5%	0%
Bonds	15% - 25%	55% - 65%	15% - 30%	100%
Cash	0% - 5%	15% - 25%	5% - 15%	

3.9 Tax status

Learning objectives   5.7.6 **Explain** the taxation of the various types of funds in the UK
5.7.7 **Explain** the effect that tax legislation may have on the stock selection and asset allocation of a fund

Taxation is a consideration for all investment managers. The investment portfolio and the strategy adopted must be consistent with the fund's tax position. In some cases, such as pension funds, the fund does not suffer taxation. For these **gross funds**, the manager should, normally, avoid those stocks which involve the deduction of tax at source. For, even though it may be possible to reclaim any tax suffered, the fund will have incurred the opportunity cost of the lost interest on the tax deducted.

4   ADVISING INDIVIDUALS

Learning objectives

5.6.1   Describe the need for advisers to communicate clearly, assessing and adapting to the differing levels of knowledge and understanding of their clients

5.6.2   Identify and apply suitable investment solutions to suit different needs of retail clients

4.1 Client questionnaire

Information collected about the client should be **recorded carefully and meticulously**. The standard method of doing this is the use of a **questionnaire** designed to ensure that all relevant information is sought.

Comprehensive information gathering can serve the function of helping to generate business for the adviser but it is also important from the compliance point of view. It ensures that a proper record is kept, that information was sought from a client, that it was either given or refused and, combined with documents recording recommendations made to a client, can confirm that the advice given to the client was sound and suitable.

4.2 Client's attitudes

The following questions concern attitudes of the client.

- What is the client's attitude to existing savings/investment/protection?
- Are existing arrangements **sufficient**?
- Are they **suitable**?
- Have they been **reviewed recently**?
- Is the level of **investment risk acceptable** to a client?
- Is the client prepared to accept **more or less risk**?
- Are there any **constraints** on investment, eg ethical investments?
- Does the client consider that the **existing investments meet current needs**?
- **Do you consider that they meet current and existing needs**?

4.3 Client's objectives

The **client's objectives** and **expected liabilities** should be considered under headings such as the following.

- Dos the client face **major purchases or expenses**?
- What is the client's **timespan** for investments, ie short-term or long-term or both?
- How **accessible** must the client's funds be?
- What is the client's **current and future tax position**?
- Are the client's needs for **income or growth** or both?
- Does the client want any **personal involvement** in the direction of investment?
- Does the client have **ethical views or preferences** which could influence their investment choices?

4.4 Present client circumstances

The analysis of a client's current circumstances begins with an analysis of the financial figures for the client's current circumstances. For a typical retail client, this would show a list of the client's **assets and liabilities**, and reveal whether there is a surplus or a deficit. A **cash flow statement** can also be prepared to reveal whether there is **surplus** or a **shortfall**: this is effectively a **budget**.

- If there is a **surplus**, it will enable the client to put into effect at least some of any recommendations which involve an additional outlay.

- If there is a **shortfall**, this reveals the need for the client to take action not to increase liabilities and perhaps to reduce existing liabilities.

Current income needs should be measured and this will enable you to check whether or not the **protection** against death and disability is adequate to meet those needs.

4.5 Future client circumstances

The adviser must also analyse the client's possible **changing circumstances** and **lifestyle**.

- What are the consequences, for example, of moving to another house or a prospective job change or children approaching fee paying school age? There may be additional housing or education costs, for example.

- If the client is employed and is planning to become self-employed, are any arrangements in hand for replacing company group life and disability cover with personal life and disability cover?

- Are arrangements in hand to ensure that finance is available to enable the move to take place?

4.6 Analysing client needs

In order to formulate a **recommendation** for a client, an adviser must always **identify** and **analyse** the **client's needs**.

By now, you have all the information necessary regarding the client and you can quantify a client's protection needs against the existing provision and compare future income needs against expectations.

You can also assess the client's current and future **tax position** and evaluate the tax efficiency of existing investments.

After all this has been done, the chances are that **most clients will not be able to achieve all of their objectives**. This will mean prioritising their objectives according to their resources.

An adviser must take into account all the **regulatory compliance requirements** that apply before dealing with the client (such as giving to the client a **business card**, a **services and costs disclosure document (SCDD) or combined initial disclosure document (CIDD)**, and **terms of business letter**) through the process to the stage where recommendations are given, when the reasons for those recommendations are required.

4.7 Discretionary and non-discretionary portfolio management

If the client is to own a portfolio, we should be clear about the nature of the advice being given.

- With **discretionary portfolio management**, the investment manager makes and implements decisions to buy and sell investments in the portfolio without asking the client each time.

- The **non-discretionary portfolio manager** provides advice to the client to assist the client in making their own investment decisions.

4.8 Execution-only customers

Execution-only customers are those who are not given any advice by the firm when they make investment decisions. The only responsibility of the firm to such customers is one of 'best execution': to implement the customer's investment decisions at the best price available.

4.9 Client needs and circumstances

It is possible to characterise individual investors by their situation, which may cover:

- Source of wealth
- Amount of wealth
- Stage of the life cycle

4.10 Wealth and investment exposure

When considering investment, the **wealth** of the investor is clearly an important consideration. If there is free capital to invest, then clearly it is sensible for the individual to take steps to make the best use of that capital.

It is possible, although not generally advisable, for someone with little wealth to gain exposure to investment markets, for example by **borrowing money to invest**, or by using investments such as derivatives or spread betting to gain a greater exposure than the individual's free resources. When investing in **risky assets** such as **equities**, a good principle is the often-stated one that **someone should only invest what they can afford to lose**. Someone who borrows to invest without having other capital to back it up if things go wrong, has the problem that they may end up with liabilities in excess of their assets.

An investor who uses instruments such as derivatives to increase their exposure should maintain other accessible resources (for example, cash on deposit) that can be used to meet losses that may arise. Clearly, it is also important that they understand the risks they are undertaking.

Major investments, including housing, should be appropriately **safeguarded**. For investments, the soundness of institutions holding funds, and any compensation arrangements where applicable, should be considered. Good title to housing should be ensured, and appropriate insurance taken out against risks such as fire.

4.11 Source of wealth

The way in which people received their wealth may affect their characteristics as investors. Investors may have acquired their wealth **actively** or **passively**.

Passive wealth

- People who have acquired their wealth passively, for example, through inheritance, or those who have acquired savings gradually from their salaries.

- These people are frequently less experienced with risk and do not believe that they could rebuild their wealth were they to lose it.

- They have a greater need for security and a lower tolerance for risk.

Active wealth

- People who have earned their own wealth, often by risking their own capital in the process.
- These types of people are assumed to be more confident and familiar with risk.

- They have a higher tolerance for risk.
- They dislike losing control over anything, including their investments.

4.12 Amount of wealth

The amount or **measure** of someone's wealth will affect his views on risk, since it will affect a person's sense of financial health. However, this sense of financial health is highly subjective. This makes it difficult to use this approach as a means of categorising investors.

Generally, if people perceive their wealth to be small, they are less inclined to take risks with their portfolios.

A portfolio that is only just sufficient to cover lifestyle needs could be viewed as small. A portfolio that is well in excess of that needed for the person's lifestyle could be considered large.

4.13 Taxation

4.13.1 Tax planning points

In giving financial advice in other aspects, there are of course tax considerations to be borne in mind:

- Is the client a non-taxpayer, savings income starting rate (10%), basic rate (20%), higher rate (40%) or additional rate (45%) taxpayer? (**2013/14** rates)

- Are all personal allowances for income tax purposes being used?

- What is the likely capital gains tax position, and is there a way for the client to make use of annual CGT exemptions, or any brought forward capital losses that can be set against capital gains?

- What is the tax position of financial products being considered? Are proceeds exempt from tax? Are there planning steps that can ensure that tax effects are mitigated?

- At the **end of a tax year**, key issues are whether an individual wishes to top up **pension plans** or **ISAs,** for which there are limits on contributions within a tax year.

4.13.2 Tax planning in context

It is important to consider tax planning in the light of all the client's circumstances and needs, and in the context of all of their plans and wishes.

Any **tax advantages** should not be sought at all costs, without considering other aspects. For example, there will be no benefit to a client if a particular financial product carries a tax advantage which is cancelled out by the effect of higher charges on that particular product, or by exposure to **investment risks** that the client would not otherwise wish to be exposed to.

We consider **tax planning** issues in Chapter 6 of this Study Text.

4.14 Factors shaping individual circumstances

There are various **life stages**, and people have differing financial needs. Every case is different, and there may be many variations in individual circumstances that cannot easily be fitted into easily formulated categories.

As an individual gets older, different priorities and needs take effect. Each person will clearly be different and therefore it is difficult to generalise to any degree. However, analysing by reference to where someone is in their life cycle will give some insight into investor characteristics.

Typically, but not always, **risk tolerance** declines as someone passes through his life cycle. Younger people have a long time horizon and a lower net worth. They may be more willing and able to take risk as a result.

As a person gets older, his net worth may increase and long-term spending goals will start to appear. The investor is still investing for the long term, but risk tolerance has declined, reflecting a fear of capital losses. These will be harder to recover over the shorter time available.

Later in a person's life, when they have paid off all their liabilities (eg mortgage), they will find that their personal net worth increases more quickly. The person who is close to retirement age has the prospect that earnings will no longer be able to counterbalance falls in the portfolio value. As a result, risk tolerance will fall even more.

4.15 Life cycle, age and commitments

The **age** of an investor, the stage of **life cycle** that he is at, and his **commitments**, all affect the investor's **risk profile**.

Adventurous risk-taking may be unwise for someone with heavy financial **commitments**, for example to children and other dependants. Another aspect of an investor's commitments is that of how much time he has available: if he works full-time and has a family, there may be little time left for him to manage his own investments even if he has an interest and knowledge to do so, and his commitments may mean that he is more likely to wish to seek professional financial advice.

4.16 An individual's risk profile

The financial adviser must recognise that each client has their own views, aspirations and attitudes. **Attitudes to risk** vary widely, and accordingly investment choices vary widely too. Some individuals will be reluctant to take on any significant risk of loss of their capital while others are prepared to 'gamble' with their savings.

People are likely to take notice of the growth potential of an investment while some could be less willing to appreciate the risk involved. The adviser needs to take especial care to make such a client aware of risks.

Attitudes to risk vary according to the different objectives of the investor. An investor may have a core holding of deposits that he wishes to keep as an emergency fund, while he may be prepared to take greater risks with other funds he holds. If a client has a specific target for a particular investment – for example, to pay for children's education, or to pay for a vacation – then he may choose lower risk investments for the funds intended to reach that target than for other his other investments.

One way of classifying investors is to look at an investor's views on risk and the way that investor makes decisions. This will give a classification system based on how **cautious**, **methodical**, **spontaneous** or **individualistic** the investor is.

	Decision making is rational/based on thought	Decision making is emotional/based on feeling
High risk aversity	Methodical	Cautious
Low risk aversity	Individualist	Spontaneous

Source: Bronson, Scanlan, Squires

The following is a general guide to typical characteristics.

Cautious investors

- Highly loss averse
- Need for security
- Want low-risk investments with safe capital
- Do not like making decisions but do not listen to others
- Tend not to use advisers
- Portfolios are low risk and with low turnover

Methodical investors

- Analytical and factual
- Make decisions slowly
- Little emotional attachment to investments and decisions
- Tend to be conservative in investment approach

Spontaneous investors

- High portfolio turnover

- Do not trust the advice of others

- Some are successful investors, but most do less well, particularly because of high transaction costs due to high turnover

- Make decisions quickly and are fearful of missing out on opportunities

Individualist investors

- Self-confident
- Prepared to do analysis and will expect to achieve their long-term goals

4.17 Customer understanding

It is a basic regulatory requirement that a firm should not recommend a transaction or act as an investment manager for a customer unless it has taken reasonable steps to help the customer **understand the nature of the risks** involved. In the case of **warrants** and **derivatives**, the firm should provide to the customer any appropriate **warrants and derivatives risk warnings**.

If recommending to a retail customer transactions in investments that are not readily realisable, the adviser should explain the difficulties in establishing a market price.

Following the recording of recommendations in a **report**, the adviser can check whether the client has read and understood the contents of the report, and can be asked whether he has any **questions** to ask about it.

4.18 Affordability and accessibility

The **affordability** of any investments and protection policies to be recommended for the client must be considered. The client's prospective disposable income should be ascertained in order to assess the affordability of regular contributions to policies and investment plans. Existing assets and policies, such as life assurance contracts and other savings need to be taken into account in quantifying the sizes of investments needed to meet client needs.

4.19 Client reviews

The adviser is concerned with identifying and satisfying client needs. This is not just a 'one-off' process. Clients will have a continuing need for financial advice. Their circumstances will change, and there may need to be a review of whether products initially recommended continue to be suitable.

Regular **reviews** of client circumstances will enable the adviser to make best use of future business opportunities with that client. For the client, there are the benefits of the advice arising from the review.

4.20 Review dates

Many financial advisers conduct client reviews **annually**. This may fit well with the client's needs, if pay or bonuses are reviewed annually for example, or to fit in with the accounting cycle of a business. A review at the time of a client's birthday is another possibility: some life assurance risks are assessed in annual steps linked to the birth date.

Client reviews should not be restricted to **pre-determined review dates**. Clients' circumstances may change in unpredictable ways. An individual may be made redundant, or may start a new job. There could be a change in family health circumstances, or a new baby may be expected. These are examples of changes that could have a significant impact on financial planning, and so the client should be encouraged to seek advice and appropriate review of their circumstances, when such events occur.

Events in the financial world may produce an opportunity for the adviser to contact the client to review their effect on his or her circumstances.

- For example, **new tax rules** may be announced, or investment conditions may change, for example if there are significant movements in share prices.

- A **new tax year** can present possible **tax planning** opportunities, for example relating to ISA investments and pension contributions.

It may be most appropriate for an adviser to agree with the client that there will be an annual review date, but with the proviso that either client or adviser may make contact if an additional review is appropriate.

5   CLIENT INTERACTION

Learning objective	5 **Demonstrate** an understanding of the range of skills required when advising clients

5.1 The financial adviser

The adviser must work within the scope of the activities for which their firm is **authorised** or for which they are individually **approved**. The adviser needs to be aware of the extent of their own **professional competence** and not attempt to work outside this, or beyond the **job description** laid out by their firm.

5.2 Communication techniques

Good **communication skills** are important for the financial adviser and wealth manager. Much of the information the adviser acquires is likely to be by interviewing – asking questions of – the client.

You should appreciate the difference between objective **factual information** and evaluative statements which express opinions or feelings. The latter type of statement may be expressed in terms of someone's hopes, wants or plans.

Examples of factual information

- Disregarding dividends, the Clearfield Unit Trust has grown in value by more than the FTSE 100 benchmark index over the three-year period to 31 December 2010.

- Brenda has fallen into two months' arrears on her mortgage payments.

Examples of non-factual statements

- Graham thinks that he should invest more money in foreign stocks, in order to diversify risk.
- Matilda was disappointed by the service provided by her previous financial adviser.

Closed questions ask for a **specific** piece of **information**, for example a National Insurance number or a figure for the value of a property. Examples could be:

- Could you please tell me your address?
- Do you have any ISAs?

The answer to a closed question is typically a single word, or a short phrase, or 'Yes' or 'No'. The client may tire of having too much of this form of questioning quickly, and the questioner will not find out much about the client's views or feelings in the process.

Open questions give the client more opportunity to **express his views** or **feelings** in a **longer response**. Examples of open questions are:

- How do you feel about taking risks with your investments?
- What do you think are the most immediate financial needs to be addressed?

5.3 'Know your customer'

You will be well aware of the need to possess a lot of **information** about your client before you can give them advice. This need is reflected in the tenet: **'know your customer'** (KYC). This is one of the basic requirements of the regulatory regime as well as being part of the **fiduciary duty** of the adviser.

This includes obtaining sufficient information about a customer's personal and financial situation, before giving advice or (if applicable) before constructing a portfolio for the customer. The process of obtaining this information is not only essential in ensuring that you give suitable advice on a current issue. It can also reveal further areas where you might help your clients in the future.

A further aspect of knowing one's customer is to know the **customer's capabilities**, so that one can **adapt** one's communication to suit the customer. Such adaptation should cover the extent of use of technical terminology and the extent of quantitative analysis presented to the customer. The adaptation should cover both **spoken and written communication**.

Earlier, we mentioned initiatives such as **Money Guidance**, which targets consumers generally, many of whom may have had limited if any contact with financial services firms. Firms themselves can help to widen their customer base and be more inclusive through initiatives to write **printed and website content** in plain English, and to train advisers in communicating with a range of consumers.

In **presentations** to clients, the adviser who is an effective communicator will be checking for indications that the client understands what is being said as the presentation develops, so that the adviser can explain a point again if necessary, perhaps simplifying aspects of the explanation. Checks on understanding can be made by asking open questions. Just to ask 'Do you follow what I am saying?' will not be sufficient: the less assertive client may say 'Yes' even if they do not fully understand.

5.4 Written reports to clients

Providing a **written report** to clients is an important part of the process of giving financial advice.

The **parts of a financial planning report** to a client are typically as follows.

- A statement of the client's objectives

- A summary of the client's income and assets and other relevant circumstances or problems

- Recommendations, including any proposals for immediate action as well as longer-term suggestions for the client to consider in the future

- Appendices, including any data that is best presented separately, if appropriate

Product quotations, illustrations and brochures should be presented in an orderly way, possibly with an index listing the various items being sent to the client.

The **language** in the report should be phrased as concisely as possible and, again, with explanations to suit the capabilities of the particular client while also meeting all regulatory requirements. Jargon should be avoided except where necessary to explain points being made.

When a client has agreed a set of recommendations, there will be a considerable amount of work involved in arranging investments, along with any pension arrangements and protection policies also being taken out.

5.5 Formulating a plan

The prime objective of the **comprehensive plan** is to make **recommendations** regarding the action needed to meet the client's stated and agreed objectives. As well as **regulatory considerations,** the plan must **take account of economic conditions** which could affect the client, such as the possibility of redundancy, the prospects for a self-employed person's business and the effect of inflation.

The plan should take account of a client's **current financial position**. Is there a surplus of assets over liabilities? If so, is the surplus in a form where it can be better used?

If liabilities exceed assets then can **liabilities be rearranged**? For example, if part of the reason is an expensive loan, can the loan be repaid (provided any repayment charges are acceptable) and replaced by a more effective loan such as borrowing on the security of a with profits policy where interest rates tend to be below average?

How liquid are the client's assets? How much of the client's assets is in a form which can be turned into cash quickly, if necessary? The client's current **tax position** is of prime importance.

The client's protection requirements will be affected not only by current needs but also by **changing economic conditions**.

Full account must be taken of the **client's attitude and understanding of risk** when it comes to arranging investments. Widows with small capital sum and whose only income is the state pension should not be advised to invest in futures and options! Equally, high net worth individuals with substantial excess of income over expenditure could spread their investments in a way which provides a balanced mix of caution, medium risk and high risk.

5.6 Ethical preferences

In taking account of any **ethical preferences** affecting investment choice that a client may have, the adviser needs to bear in mind the differences between funds. As we have seen, there are many **'ethical' funds**, but these cover a range of criteria, for example between 'dark green' funds that use **negative criteria** to exclude companies to other 'lighter green' funds that use **positive criteria** to include companies that pursue positive policies on the environment or social factors. The adviser should ensure that funds chosen match the expressed concerns of the client.

CHAPTER ROUNDUP

- Investors can be categorised broadly into two types: individual investors, who range from retail investor who may have relatively small savings to invest, to high net worth and very high net worth individuals, and institutional investors, a category that includes fund managers, pension funds, hedge funds, charitable trusts and sovereign (country) wealth funds.

- Given consumers' experience and perception of financial services, firms will do well to treat customers fairly, as the regulator requires, and to ensure that ethical practices prevail in their business.

- The financial planning process involves six stages: 1: Obtaining relevant information – fact finding. 2: Establishing and agreeing the client's financial objectives. 3: Processing and analysing the data obtained. 4: Formulating recommendations in a comprehensive plan with objectives. 5: Implementing the recommendations as agreed with the client. 6: Reviewing and regularly updating the plan.

- Clients' objectives may need to be prioritised and quantified, resulting in a present value analysis of anticipated future liabilities. Affordability should be assessed.

- Information on the client's current personal and financial circumstances is collected through the fact find process.

- Higher risk investments are needed to produce the potential of high returns, but also bring the chance of loss. Specific risks of investments can be diversified away, but general market risk will remain. A client's attitude to risk may be influenced by investment timescales.

- The objective of a fund may either be to match future liabilities or to maximise returns within given risk parameters.

- There are two main types of pension scheme: defined benefits schemes, which pay a proportion of final salary at retirement; and defined contribution schemes, which pay a pension based on the amount of contributions and investment performance up to retirement.

- Life assurance and general insurance companies also invest the premiums they receive to generate returns.

- Discretionary, advisory and execution-only are different service levels offered to clients.

- The investment management process involves asset allocation, market timing and stock selection, asset allocation being the primary step since it is based on the client's objectives and fixed constraints.

- Investment managers may follow an active process of trying to outperform the market, or a passive approach of merely aiming to track the market.

- Differences in individuals' circumstances include variability in sources of wealth (whether passively or actively acquired), amount of wealth and the current life cycle stage of the individual. The level of an individual's tolerance to risk needs to be considered by an adviser.

- Advisers should aim to employ good communication skills. The desirability of avoiding social exclusion underlines the idea that communications with consumers be adapted suit the capabilities of the consumer to which the communication is directed.

TEST YOUR KNOWLEDGE

Check your knowledge of the chapter here, without referring back to the text.

1. What does it mean to say that the adviser owes a fiduciary duty to the client?

2. Outline the six stages of the financial planning process.

3. What different types of diversification might an investor or adviser consider?

4. What term describes the risk that index tracking funds will not follow the index?

5. What are the two main different types of pension schemes?

6. Name three different types of life assurance product.

7. Distinguish discretionary and non-discretionary portfolio management, and execution only business.

8. In the context of communicating verbally with a client, give examples of closed questions and open questions.

TEST YOUR KNOWLEDGE: ANSWERS

1. An adviser's fiduciary responsibility implies that the adviser ought not to take advantage of a client's trust in him or her. The adviser (or firm) agrees to act in the sole interests of the client, to the exclusion of his or her own interests.

    (See Section 1.5)

2. Stages of the financial planning process: (1) Obtaining relevant information – fact finding, (2) Establishing and agreeing the client's financial objectives, (3) Processing and analysing the data collected, (4) Formulating recommendations in a comprehensive plan, (5) Implementing the agreed recommendations, (6) Reviewing and regularly updating the plan.

    (See Section 2.1)

3. Diversification may be:

    - By asset class
    - Within asset classes
    - Across different fund managers

    (See Section 2.6.2)

4. Tracking error.

    (See Section 2.9.5)

5. Defined contribution and defined benefit schemes.

    (See Section 3.2)

6. Term assurance policies, whole of life policies and endowment policies.

    (See Section 3.3.1)

7. With discretionary portfolio management, the investment manager makes and implements decisions to buy and sell investments in the portfolio without asking the client each time. The non-discretionary portfolio manager provides advice to assist the client in making their own investment decisions.

    Execution-only customers are not given any advice by the firm when they make investment decisions. The only responsibility of the firm to such customers is to implement the customer's investment decisions at the best price available ('best execution').

    (See Section 4.7-4.8)

8. Closed questions:

    - Could you please tell me your address?
    - Do you have any ISAs?

    Open questions:

    - How do you feel about taking risks with your investments?
    - What do you think are the most immediate financial needs to be addressed?

    (See Section 5.2)

6

Taxation in the UK

INTRODUCTION

Individuals are liable to pay income tax on any salary, interest and dividends earned. Gains made from assets are also potentially liable to capital gains tax if they rise above the annual exemption.

Companies are liable to pay corporation tax on their profits. The amount varies dependent on the size of a company's profits.

There are tax implications of direct investments such as cash and cash equivalents, fixed interest securities, equities and property, and of indirect investment such as ISAs, REITs, collective investment schemes, VCTs and the Enterprise Investment Scheme.

Tax planning refers to the process of organising one's affairs so as to take best advantage of tax rules. With some of the more complex ways of taking advantage of tax rules, HMRC will review them to ensure that the main aim is not to avoid tax.

CHAPTER CONTENTS

1 INCOME TAX FOR INDIVIDUALS

1.1 Introduction

1.1.1 Who pays income tax?

Income tax is payable by all individuals and trusts (see later) **resident in the UK** on their **worldwide income**. Non-residents are only liable to income tax if they have a source of income derived in the UK (see later).

1.1.2 Tax years

Income tax is calculated by reference to the tax year. It runs from 6 April one year to 5 April the next year. The 2013/14 tax year is the year ending 5 April 2014.

1.2 Taxable income

1.2.1 What is taxable income?

Taxable income is virtually any income that an individual receives from whatever source.

1.2.2 Tax-free income

Some income is specifically **tax-free** (free of both income tax and capital gains tax (CGT)), such as the income and/or gains from:

- **National Savings & Investments (NS&I) Savings Certificates**
- **NS&I Children's Bonus Bonds**
- **Individual Savings Accounts (ISAs)**
- Existing **Child Trust Funds (CTFs)**
- **Qualifying life assurance policies** in the hands of the original owner
- Save As You Earn (SAYE) schemes (interest and gains)
- **NS&I Premium Bond** prizes
- Gambling wins, such as from the National Lottery
- Compensation payments of up to £30,000 when employment ends (redundancy payments)
- **Life assurance bond withdrawals** of up to 5% pa (cumulative) of the original premium (withdrawals above this level are taxable)

1.3 Income tax liability

1.3.1 Tax rates

Different tax rates apply to different types of income, so it is important to determine what income an individual has received.

The main types of income you will see in your exam are:

- Income from employment or self-employment ('earnings')
- Savings income, including interest (eg bank interest and interest from securities – see later) and dividends
- Investment income, including property income

If a taxpayer receives income from a number of different sources, it is taxed in the following order:

(1) Earnings and property income ('non-savings' income)
(2) Interest
(3) Dividends

1.3.2 Calculating tax

Before applying the appropriate tax rate(s), an individual can deduct the **personal allowance** from his income to arrive at his taxable income. In 2013/14, the personal allowance is **£9,440**. If an individual's net income exceeds £100,000, the personal allowance is reduced: this is explained later.

The personal allowance is deducted from non-savings income first, then from savings income and lastly from dividend income (see later).

1.3.3 Income tax rates for non-savings income

There are three different rates of income tax that apply to non-savings income:

Tax rates for earnings	2013/14
20% – Basic rate	The basic rate is charged on the **first £32,010** of taxable income
40% – Higher rate	The higher rate is charged on any taxable income above **£32,010**.
45% – Additional rate	The additional rate is charged on taxable income above **£150,000**.

Employment earnings are received after income tax has been deducted by the employer under the **Pay As You Earn (PAYE)** system (see later).

Self-employment earnings and property income are only taxed at the end of the tax year under the self-assessment system (see later).

Example

Mr Anderson is an employed electrician. In the tax year 2013/14, his total earnings were £66,000 (PAYE tax deducted £16,100).

Requirement

Calculate Mr Anderson's tax due for the year.

Solution

	£
Total earnings	66,000
Less: personal allowance	(9,440)
Taxable income	56,560
Tax on first £32,010 @ 20%	6,402
Tax on next £24,550 @ 40%	9,820
Total tax liability	16,222
Less: tax deducted at source via PAYE	(16,100)
Tax due	122

1.3.4 Income tax rates for interest income

There is a starting rate of 10% for the **first £2,790 of interest** income (2013/14). This **only applies** where **savings income falls below the starting rate limit**.

Remember that non-savings income is taxed first. In most cases, an individual's non-savings income will exceed the starting rate limit and the savings income starting rate will not be available on savings income. Where an individual's non-savings income exceeds the starting rate limit, the individual's savings income will be charged to tax at 20% up to the basic rate limit of £32,010, 40% up to the higher rate limit of £150,000, and 45% thereafter.

Example

Sandra is a self-employed hairdresser. In the tax year 2013/14, she has earnings of £51,000 and interest of £8,000. Calculate Sandra's tax due for the year.

Solution

	Earnings £	Interest £
Total earnings	51,000	
Interest £8,000 × 100/80*		10,000
Less: personal allowance	(9,440)	
Taxable income	41,560	10,000
Tax on first £32,010 @ 20%	6,402	
Tax on next £9,550 @ 40%	3,820	
Tax on £10,000 @ 40%	4,000	
Total tax liability	14,222	
Less: tax deducted at source Interest: £10,000 × 20%	(2,000)	
Total tax due	12,222	

*£8,000 is the net amount received, representing 80% of the gross amount, due to the 20% tax that is automatically deducted. Therefore the gross amount is £10,000.

1.3.5 Income tax rates for dividend income

UK dividends are treated as if received net of a deemed (or 'notional') 10% tax credit so are grossed up by 100/90.

Dividends falling in the basic rate tax band are taxed at 10%. As they come with a 10% deemed or 'notional' tax credit, no further tax is payable on dividends for basic rate taxpayers. Dividends falling into the higher rate tax band are taxed at 32.5%, and for additional rate taxpayers at 37.5%.

The 10% tax credit on dividends is deductible from the tax liability. However, since it is not a real tax credit, it cannot be repaid to the taxpayer.

Example

In the tax year 2013/14, Nikki receives earnings from employment of £50,000, interest of £8,000 and dividends of £27,000.

Requirement

Calculate Nikki's tax due for the year.

Solution

	Earnings £	Interest £	Dividends £
Total earnings	50,000		
Interest £8,000 × 100/80		10,000	
Dividends £27,000 × 100/90*			30,000
Less: personal allowance	(9,440)		
Taxable income	40,560	10,000	30,000

	£
Tax on first £32,010 @ 20%	6,402
Tax on next £8,550 @ 40%	3,420
Tax on £10,000 @40%	4,000
Tax on £30,000 @ 32.5%	9,750
Total tax liability	23,572
Less: tax deducted at source	
On dividends: £30,000 × 10%	(3,000)
On interest: £10,000 × 20%	(2,000)
Total tax due	18,572

*£27,000 is the net amount received, representing 90% of the gross amount, due to the 10% notional tax credit that is deemed to have been deducted. Therefore the gross amount is £27,000 x 100/90 = £30,000.

1.4 Allowances

1.4.1 Introduction

There are various allowances and reliefs available through the UK tax system. These either reduce the amount of income that is taxable, or reduce the tax liability. It is essential to distinguish between the different types. First, we consider allowances.

1.4.2 Personal allowance

An individual (including a child) is allocated the **personal allowance of £9,440** in the tax year 2013/14.

The allowance is deducted from the individual's net income before arriving at his taxable income. It is deducted from **non-savings income** first, then from **savings income** and lastly from **dividend income**.

If an individual's net income for 2013/14 exceeds £100,000, the personal allowance is reduced by £1 for every £2 excess income. So, an individual with net income of £118,880 receives no personal allowance in 2013/14.

Those born before 6 April 1948 may have a higher age-rated personal allowance.

1.5 Interest payments

Certain loan interest payments can be deducted from total income. An individual who pays interest in a tax year is entitled to relief in that year if the loan is for one of the following purposes, subject to certain conditions:

- Loan to buy plant or machinery for partnership use (interest allowed for three years)
- Loan to buy plant or machinery for employment use (interest allowed for three years)
- Loan to buy interest in unquoted employee-controlled company
- Loan to invest in a partnership
- Loan to invest in a co-operative

Tax relief is given by deducting the interest from total income for the tax year in which the interest is paid. It is deducted from non-savings income first, then from savings income and lastly from dividend income.

1.6 Relief for gifts to charity

1.6.1 Payroll giving

Under the **payroll giving scheme**, employees can authorise their employer to deduct charitable donations from their gross salary before calculating tax via the PAYE system (see later), giving the employee automatic tax relief at his or her marginal (ie highest) rate of tax.

1.6.2 Gifts of shares and securities

If an individual makes a gift of certain shares and securities to a charity, he can deduct the market value of the shares or securities at the date of the charitable gift, again giving the employee automatic tax relief at his marginal rate of tax.

The shares must be listed on a recognised stock exchange in the UK or overseas. A gift of AIM shares can qualify.

1.6.3 Gift Aid

The tax calculation may be affected by cash donations to charity made under the **Gift Aid** scheme.

All cash donations are treated as being paid net, ie after deduction of income tax at the basic rate (20%). So, a net donation of £800 is worth £1,000 (£800 × 100/80) as the charity can claim £200 (20% × £1,000) from Her Majesty's Revenue & Customs (HMRC).

If the donor is a higher or additional rate taxpayer, their basic rate band is increased by an amount equal to the gross amount of the gift (£1,000, in our example). This has the effect that an additional £1,000 of income is taxed at the basic rate instead of the higher or additional tax rate providing additional relief.

1.7 Pension contributions

1.7.1 Contributions to occupational pension schemes

Within certain limits (see later), an individual's contributions to his employer's pension scheme can be deducted from his earnings from that employment. This provides tax relief at the individual's highest rate.

1.7.2 Personal pension contributions

Within the same limits as for occupational schemes, an individual's contributions to a personal pension scheme may affect his tax rate if he is a higher or additional rate taxpayer. Relief is given in broadly the same way as for cash gift aid donations (see later).

1.8 Tax reductions

Tax reductions do not affect income: they reduce the amount of tax calculated on income.

The tax reductions, which are both covered in more detail later in this Chapter, are:

(a)   Investments in **venture capital trusts (VCTs)**, and
(b)   Investments under the **enterprise investment scheme (EIS)**

VCT and EIS investments may qualify for a tax reduction of up to the lower of:

(a)   A percentage of the amount subscribed for qualifying investments, and
(b)   The individual's tax liability

For investments in VCTs and under the EIS, the percentage is 30% (2013/14).

A tax reduction can only reduce an individual's tax liability to zero. It cannot create a repayment.

If an individual is entitled to both tax reductions, the VCT reducer is deducted first.

1.9 Overseas aspects of income tax

1.9.1 Introduction

A taxpayer's **residence** and **domicile** have important consequences in establishing the treatment of his UK and overseas income.

The UK Government has introduced a new **statutory residence test** that applies from **6 April 2013**. As part of the changes, the concept of 'ordinary' residence has been abolished for tax purposes.

The test is summarised in the following diagram.

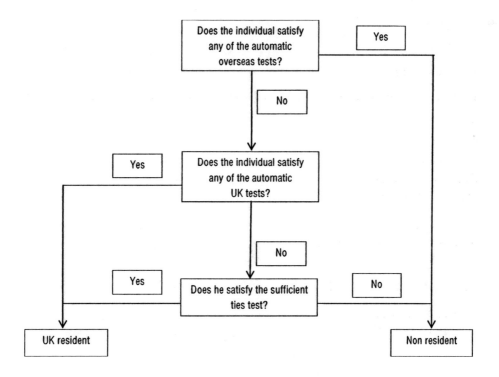

1.9.2 Automatically non-resident test

The **automatic overseas test** treats an individual as **not resident** in the UK if he:

(a) Was resident in the UK for one or more of the three previous tax years and spends fewer than 16 days in the UK in the current tax year

(b) Was not resident in the UK for any of the previous three tax years and spends fewer than 46 days in the UK in the current tax year

(c) Leaves the UK to carry out full-time work overseas, or

(d) Dies in the current tax year, subject to conditions which include spending fewer than 46 days in the UK

As implied by the earlier diagram, if he does not meet any of the **automatic overseas tests**, the individual will be automatically UK-resident if he meets any of the **automatic UK tests**.

1.9.3 Automatic UK-resident test

The **automatic UK test** treats an individual as **UK-resident** if:

(a) He spends 183 days or more (ie more than six months) in the UK during the tax year

(b) There is a period of more than 90 days, part of which falls within the tax year, when he has a home in the UK and no home overseas (disregarding any home at which he is present for fewer than 30 days in the tax year)

(c) He dies in the current year, subject to conditions which include having been UK-resident in the previous three tax years, or

(d) He meets the **full-time UK work test**

The **full-time UK work test** is satisfied if **all** of the following conditions are met:

■ There is a 365 day period, all or part of which falls within the tax year, when the taxpayer works an average of 35 hours a week in the UK. This is calculated excluding annual leave, sick leave, gaps of up to 15 days between employments and days when he works overseas.

■ Within that 365 day period, there are no significant breaks of more than 30 days when he does not work in the UK (excluding annual leave and sick leave).

■ Within that 365 day period, the taxpayer works in the UK on at least 75% of his working days.

■ There is at least one day in the tax year when he does at least three hours work in the UK.

1.9.4 Sufficient ties test

If the individual meets none of the automatic overseas tests and none of the automatic UK tests, he must look at the **'sufficient ties' test**. This test compares the number of days spent in the UK against a small number of connection factors.

An individual who was not UK-resident in any of the previous three tax years (ie someone arriving in or returning to the UK) must determine whether they have any of the following ties:

(a) UK-resident family
(b) Substantive UK work (employment or self-employment)
(c) Available accommodation in the UK
(d) More than 90 days spent in the UK in either or both of the previous two tax years

The application of this test is quite complex, and is beyond the requirement of the syllabus. Broadly, the number of ties that must apply in order for the individual to be treated as UK-resident in the current tax year depends on the number of days spent in the UK.

1.9.5 Days spent in the UK

A day spent in the UK is normally one where the individual is in the UK at the end of that day, unless he is in transit through the UK, leaves the UK the day after arrival, and does not engage in any activities substantially unrelated to his transit.

1.9.6 Domicile

A person is **domiciled** in the country in which he has his **permanent home**. Domicile is distinct from nationality or residence. A person may be resident in more than one country, but he can be domiciled in only one country at a time.

A person acquires a domicile of origin at birth; this is normally the domicile of his father (or that of his mother if his father died before he was born or his parents were unmarried at his birth) and therefore not necessarily the country where he was born.

A person retains this domicile until he acquires a different domicile of dependency (if, while he is under 16, his father's domicile changes) or domicile of choice. A domicile of choice can be acquired only by individuals aged 16 or over.

To acquire a domicile of choice a person must sever his ties with the country of his former domicile and settle in another country with the clear intention of making his permanent home there. Long residence in another country is not in itself enough to prove that a person has acquired a domicile of choice: there has to be evidence that he firmly intends to live there permanently.

1.9.7 Application of the rules

Generally, a UK resident is liable to UK income tax on his UK and overseas income.

A resident and domiciled individual is taxed on his general earnings on a receipts basis.

A non-resident is taxed on his general earnings in respect of UK duties on the receipts basis but there is no UK income tax on foreign earnings (those in respect of non-UK duties). A non-UK resident is liable to UK income tax only on income arising in the UK.

EEA citizens, residents of the Isle of Man and the Channels Islands, those enabled to do so by a double taxation treaty, and current or former Crown employees, can claim the UK personal allowance to reduce the amount of UK income tax due.

An individual who is UK-resident but not UK domiciled ('**non-dom**') may **claim** for a particular tax year to be taxed on overseas income on the remittance basis (unless it applies automatically – where the individual's unremitted income is less than £2,000 in the tax year). This means that the person is only liable to UK income tax on overseas income only to the extent that it is brought in (remitted) to the UK. However, the **remittance basis charge** may apply – see below.

1.9.8 Remittance basis

Where the remittance basis applies, the income is taxed in the same way as earnings, ie at 20% in the basic rate band, 40% in the higher rate band and 45% for additional rate taxpayers, even if it is dividends.

An individual aged 18 or over is liable to a **remittance basis charge** if he **claims the remittance basis** for a tax year, subject to the following residence rule.

- If the individual has been UK-resident for at least 7 of the 9 tax years preceding that tax year, the remittance basis charge payable is **£30,000** annually

■ If the individual has been UK-resident for at least 12 of the 14 tax years preceding that tax year, the remittance basis charge payable is **£50,000** annually

Resident 'non-doms' who have been resident in the UK for less than 7 years can still elect for the remittance basis of tax, but there is no annual charge.

The remittance basis charge is a charge on non-UK income and gains not paid to the UK. The individual remains liable to UK tax on his UK source income and non-UK income remitted to the UK in the usual way.

2 NATIONAL INSURANCE CONTRIBUTIONS

2.1 Introduction

Learning objectives	6.1.4 **Explain** the system of national insurance contributions (NICs) 6.2.4 **Calculate** the most common elements of NICs

2.1.1 Who pays National Insurance Contributions?

National insurance contributions (NICs) are payable by employees and their employers and also by self-employed individuals. Certain benefits are only paid if sufficient NICs have been paid.

2.2 Classes of NIC

Both employees and employers pay Class 1 NICs, in amounts that are related to the **employee's earnings. Primary Class 1 NICs** are paid by employees under the State Pension Age, on part of their earnings, through a deduction from their pay. The employer adds their own contribution (**secondary Class 1 NICs**) and remits the total to HMRC.

Class 1A NICs are payable on most benefits in kind, and and are paid by the employer not the employee. Class 1A NICs do not count towards any state benefits.

Class 1B NICs are paid by an employer if they have entered into a PAYE Settlement Agreement (PSA) with HMRC.

Class 2 contributions are payable at a flat rate by self-employed persons, unless annual profits are below the small earnings exception limit.

Class 3 NICs are mainly **voluntary contributions** paid by those who do not have to pay compulsory NICs.

Class 4 NICs are paid by self-employed persons, based on the level of their taxable business profits.

3 CAPITAL GAINS TAX

3.1 Introduction

Learning objectives	6.1.5 **Explain** the principles of capital gains tax (CGT) in the UK 6.1.8 **Explain** the implications of residence and domicile in relation to liability to capital gains tax 6.2.5 **Calculate** the most common elements of CGT

Capital gains tax (CGT) is payable by **UK-domiciled residents** on the **chargeable disposal** of a **chargeable asset**.

The rules for a person who is UK-resident but **not domiciled** in the UK are explained later below (*Overseas aspects of CGT*).

Chargeable persons for CGT purposes include:

- Individuals
- Partnerships
- Companies
- Trusts

Virtually all assets are chargeable assets, wherever in the world they are situated, except for certain exempt assets.

Be aware of the following **exempt assets**.

- **National Savings & Investments (NS&I) certificates** and **Premium Bonds**
- **Betting and lottery winnings**
- **Foreign currency** for private use
- **Decorations** awarded for bravery (unless purchased)
- **Damages** for personal or professional injury
- **Gilt-edged securities** (eg, Treasury Stock)
- **Qualifying corporate bonds (QCBs)**
- Single **chattels** (ie, tangible movable property) up to £6,000 gross proceeds per item
- **Wasting chattels** (ie, with a predictable life of 50 years or less)
- **Private cars**
- **Debts** (except debts on a security)
- Investments held in **individual savings accounts (ISAs)** and **child trust funds (CTFs)**
- The **principal private residence (PPR)** of an individual or a married couple or civil partnership

There are also exemptions (covered later) for **enterprise investment scheme (EIS)**, **seed enterprise investment scheme (SEIS)** shares, and **venture capital trust (VCT)** shares.

Chargeable assets include shares and other investments, and foreign currency bought and sold for gain.

If an asset is an exempt asset, any gain is not chargeable and any loss is not allowable.

A **chargeable disposal** occurs when an asset is sold (in whole or in part), is given away or is received as a result of a liquidation of a company. When an individual dies, the assets disposed of as a result, through inheritance etc, are not subject to CGT, but inheritance tax is charged instead.

The disposal can occur either in the UK or overseas, but is only treated as subject to CGT when made by a UK resident.

Disposals to spouses or civil partners are tax-neutral for CGT purposes (ie there is no gain and no loss).

3.2 Overseas aspects of CGT

3.2.1 General principles

Individuals with UK domicile are liable to CGT on the disposal of assets situated anywhere in the world if, for any part of the tax year in which the disposal occurs, they are resident in the UK.

By concession, new arrivals who have not lived in the UK for any of the previous five tax years are not normally charged to CGT on gains arising before their arrival.

If a person is UK-resident but **not domiciled** in the UK (a 'non-dom'), gains on the disposal of assets situated overseas are taxable only to the extent that the sale proceeds are **remitted** to the UK **if** the individual has made a claim for the **remittance basis, or** if it applies automatically because his unremitted income and gains are less than £2,000 in the tax year. As with non-UK income, there is no charge on remitted money from gains that is brought into the UK in order to pay the Remittance Basis Charge, or to acquire shares in or make a loan to a trading company. An individual who claims the remittance basis is not entitled to an annual exempt amount against chargeable gains.

3.2.2 Domicile

If a person is UK-resident but is not UK-domiciled, they may be able to use the remittance basis of taxation usually by making a claim. If the remittance basis applies, the individual's gains on the disposal of assets located overseas are only chargeable to CGT when the gains are remitted to the UK.

If a non-UK domiciled individual over the age of 18 makes a claim to use the remittance basis (ie, it does not apply automatically) then, subject to the past residence record, he or she may be liable to pay the **remittance basis charge**, as described earlier in this Chapter.

3.3 Calculation of capital gains and losses

3.3.1 The basic computation

The calculation of a capital gain on the disposal of an asset in a tax year can be illustrated as follows.

	£
Disposal value (say)	10,000
Less: assumed allowable deductions	(3,000)
Capital gain	7,000

If allowable deductions exceed the disposal value, a capital loss will arise.

The disposal value will typically be the **sale proceeds**. The allowable deductions will be the purchase price and other relevant costs of acquisition and disposal such as stamp duty land tax (SDLT) paid on purchase (see later), legal fees and estate agency commission.

3.3.2 The annual exempt amount

An individual pays CGT on his net chargeable gains (his gains minus his losses) for a tax year, less unrelieved losses brought forward from previous years and the annual exempt amount.

There is an **annual exempt amount** for each tax year. In 2013/14 it is £10,900.

This is the last deduction to be made in the calculation of taxable gain.

Trustees (see below) are entitled to half of the individual's annual exempt amount, ie £5,450 for 2013/14.

3.3.3 Capital losses

Allowable losses of the same year

- Capital losses in a tax year are deducted from capital gains arising in the same tax year to come to a net overall position for the year. Only then is the annual exempt amount deducted.

- Any loss which cannot be set off is carried forward to set against future gains. Losses must be used as soon as possible (but see below).

Allowable losses brought forward

- Allowable losses brought forward are only set off to reduce current year gains less current year allowable losses to the annual exempt amount. No set-off is made if net chargeable gains for the current year do not exceed the annual exempt amount.

Example

George has gains for 2013/14 of £11,000 and allowable losses of £6,000. What is his net CGT position for the year?

Solution

As the losses are current year losses, they must be fully relieved against the £11,000 of gains to produce net gains of £5,000, despite the fact that net gains are below the annual exempt amount.

Example

Bob has gains of £14,000 for 2013/14 and allowable losses brought forward of £6,000. What is his net CGT position for the year?

Solution

Bob restricts his loss relief to £3,100 so as to leave net gains of £(14,000 − 3,100) = £10,900, which will be exactly covered by his annual exempt amount for 2013/14. The remaining £2,900 of losses will be carried forward to 2014/15.

Example

Tom has gains of £10,000 for 2013/14 and losses brought forward of £4,000. What is his net CGT position for the year?

Solution

Tom will leapfrog 2013/14 and carry forward all of his losses to 2014/15. His gains of £10,000 are covered by his annual exemption for 2013/14.

3.4 Calculating CGT payable

For 2013/14, the following rates apply, where taxable gains less the annual exemption are added to the individual's income to determine in which tax band the gains fall:

- **18%** – for taxable gains falling within the individual's basic rate tax band
- **28%** – for taxable gains above the individual's basic rate band

The CGT rate for **trusts** is 28% (2013/14).

Example

Lucinda has a taxable income of £10,000 and has sold the following assets in 2013/14.

	Proceeds £	Cost £
Plot of land	100,000	80,000
Painting	40,000	15,000
Shares in XYZ plc	50,000	68,000

Requirement

Calculate the CGT payable by Lucinda.

Solution

	£	£
Land		
Proceeds	100,000	
Less: cost	80,000	
Gain		20,000
Painting		
Proceeds	40,000	
Less: cost	(15,000)	
Gain		25,000
Shares		
Proceeds	50,000	
Less: cost	(68,000)	
Loss		(18,000)
Net gains		27,000
Less: annual exemption		(10,900)
Taxable gains		16,100
CGT @ 18% on £16,400		2,898

Lucinda's taxable income of £10,000 plus capital gains of £16,100 total £26,100 – within the basic rate band of £32,010.

Example

Joshua has a taxable income of £24,000 in 2013/14 and has sold shares worth £40,000 on 12 October 2013. The original cost of the shares was £15,000.

Requirement

Calculate the CGT payable by Joshua.

Solution

	£
Shares	
Proceeds	40,000
Less: cost	(15,000)
Net gains	25,000
Less: annual exemption	(10,900)
Taxable gains	14,100
CGT @ 18% on £8,010	1,441
CGT @ 28% on £6,090	1,705
Total CGT payable	3,146

Joshua's taxable income of £24,000 plus £8,010 of the capital gain lies within the basic rate band of £32,010.

3.5 Entrepreneurs' relief

Entrepreneurs' relief is available to reduce the gains on a material disposal of business assets.

There is a **lifetime limit** of **£10 million** of gains on which entrepreneurs' relief can be claimed.

Gains qualifying for entrepreneur's relief up to the lifetime limit are subject to a reduced rate of CGT of **10%**.

The relief results in an effective 'lifetime' saving of £1,800,000.

Losses on assets not qualifying for entrepreneurs' relief and the annual exemption are deducted after the application of entrepreneurs' relief.

In determining the individual's **CGT rate on any other gains**, the gains qualifying for entrepreneurs' relief are set against any unused basic rate band before non-qualifying gains. Therefore, any gains in excess of the lifetime limit will normally be subject to the CGT rate of **28%**.

The relief applies to gains arising on the disposal of:

- The whole or part of a trading business
- Assets used in a business that has ceased
- Shares in a trading company where the individual held 5% or more of the voting shares
- Assets used in a partnership
- Certain disposals by trustees

Where a material disposal of business assets results in both gains and losses, losses are netted off against gains before entrepreneurs' relief is applied.

An individual must claim entrepreneurs' relief: it is not automatic. The **claim deadline** is the **first anniversary of the 31st January following the end of the tax year of disposal**. So, for a 2013/14 disposal, the taxpayer must claim by 31 January 2016.

4 INHERITANCE TAX AND TRUSTS

6.1.6 **Explain** the principles of inheritance tax (IHT)

6.1.8 **Explain** the implications of residence and domicile in relation to liability to inheritance tax

6.1.3 **Explain** the taxation of the income of trusts and beneficiaries

6.2.4 **To carry out computations** on the most common elements of IHT, including the impact of lifetime transfers and transfers at death

4.1 Basic principles of inheritance tax

IHT is a tax on gifts, or **'transfers of value'**, made by **chargeable persons**. This generally involves a transaction as a result of which wealth is transferred by one person to another, either directly or via a trust.

IHT is primarily a tax on **wealth left on death**. It also applies to **gifts within seven years of death** and to certain **lifetime transfers of wealth to trusts**.

For income tax and CGT we asked the basic question: how much money has the taxpayer made?

For IHT, we generally need to ask: how much has he given away?

We tax the amount which the taxpayer has transferred (the 'transfer of value') – the amount by which he is worse off.

IHT applies to:

- **Lifetime gifts to trusts** (see below)
- **Gifts on death (usually in someone's will)**, and
- **Lifetime gifts if the person making the gift (the 'donor') dies within seven years of making that gift**

UK-domiciled individuals are liable to inheritance tax (IHT) on their **worldwide assets**. For individuals who are **not domiciled in the UK, only transfers of UK assets** are liable to IHT. UK assets are broadly assets located in the UK.

4.2 IHT on death

The **chargeable estate** on death is calculated as the value of all assets owned by the individual at the time of death, valued at that date (**probate value**), minus all liabilities of the individual, minus any exempt legacies, transfers and other allowances.

IHT is generally charged at the rate of **40%** on the total value of the chargeable estate that exceeds **£325,000** (2013/14). The first £325,000 does not suffer any IHT at all.

A **reduced rate** of 36% applies where **10% or more** of the net estate on death is **left to charity**.

Example

Ms S died on 3 July 2013. The value of her assets at the date of death was £550,000 and she had liabilities totalling £100,000.

Requirement

Calculate the liability to IHT on the chargeable estate.

Solution

	£
Total assets	550,000
Liabilities	(100,000)
Chargeable estate	450,000
Inheritance tax due = (£450,000 – £325,000) × 40%	50,000

4.3 Transfer of nil rate band between spouses/civil partners

Where a spouse or civil partner dies, any **unused proportion** of the **nil rate band** of his deceased spouse or civil partner can be claimed on the death of the surviving spouse or civil partner.

Where a claim to transfer unused nil-rate band is made, the nil-rate band that is available when the surviving spouse or civil partner dies will be increased by the proportion of the nil-rate band unused on the first death.

The maximum nil rate band available on the surviving spouse or civil partner's death is twice the nil rate band applicable on the survivor's death, so the maximum nil rate band in 2013/14 is 2 × £325,000 = £650,000.

Example

Derek died in January 2008 leaving an estate of £500,000. In his will, he left £210,000 to his son and the remainder of his estate to his wife, Felicity. The nil rate band applicable at Derek's death was £300,000 (2007/08). Derek's unused nil rate band is therefore £300,000 – £210,000 = £90,000. The unused proportion in percentage terms is therefore:

$$\frac{90,000}{300,000} \times 100 = 30\%$$

Felicity dies in December 2013 leaving an estate of £450,000 to her son. The nil rate band applicable at her death (in 2013/14) is £325,000. What is Felicity's chargeable estate?

Solution

Felicity's chargeable estate will be as follows.

	£
Estate passing to son	450,000
Less: Felicity's nil-rate band	(325,000)
Derek's unused nil-rate band: 30% x £325,000	(97,500)
Chargeable estate	27,500

4.4 Lifetime gifts

A **potentially exempt transfer (PET)** is a **lifetime gift made by an individual to another individual**.

A PET is exempt from IHT when made, and will remain so if the donor survives for at least **seven years** from making the gift. If he dies within seven years of making the gift, it will become chargeable to IHT.

Any other lifetime transfer by an individual (eg gift to a trust) not covered by an exemption (see below) is a **chargeable lifetime transfer (CLT)**.

4.5 Exemptions

4.5.1 Introduction

Various exemptions are available to eliminate or reduce the chargeable amount of a lifetime transfer or property passing on an individual's death.

- Some exemptions apply *only* to lifetime transfers
- Other exemptions apply to both lifetime gifts and property passing on death, including those for gifts between spouses and civil partners

4.5.2 Exemptions applying to lifetime transfers only (including PETs)

Small gifts exemption. Outright gifts to individuals totalling £250 or less per donee in any one tax year are exempt. If gifts are more than £250 the whole amount is chargeable. A donor can give up to £250 each year to each of as many donees as he wishes. The small gifts exemption cannot apply to gifts into **trusts**.

Annual exemption. The first £3,000 of value transferred in a tax year is exempt from IHT. The annual exemption is used only after all other exemptions (such as for transfers to spouses/civil partners – see below). If several gifts are made in a year, the £3,000 exemption is applied to earlier gifts before later gifts. The annual exemption is used up by PETs as well as CLTs, even though the PETs might never become chargeable.

Any **unused portion of the annual exemption** is **carried forward for one year** only. Only use it in the following year after that year's annual exemption has been used.

Normal expenditure out of income. IHT is a tax on **transfers of capital**, not on **gifts of income.** So the gift is exempt if it is:

(a) Made as part of the donor's normal expenditure
(b) Out of income, and
(c) Leaves the transferor with sufficient income to maintain his usual standard of living

This exemption mainly covers such gifts as paying grandchildren's school fees.

Wedding gifts, and gifts made on the occasion of a **civil partnership** ceremony, are exempt up to:

(a) £5,000, if from a parent of a party to the marriage or civil partnership
(b) £2,500, if from a grandparent of one of the parties to the marriage or civil partnership
(c) £1,000, if from any other person

The limits apply to gifts from any one donor per marriage or civil partnership.

4.5.3 Exemptions applying to both lifetime transfers and transfers on death

Gifts to UK charities are exempt from IHT.

Gifts between spouses/civil partners are exempt if the donee is domiciled in the UK. The exemption covers lifetime gifts between them and property passing on death.

If the donor is UK-domiciled but the donee is not UK-domiciled, the exemption is limited to the level of the nil rate band: £325,000 in total (2013/14). Any lifetime gift over £325,000 will be a PET.

If neither spouse/civil partner is domiciled in the UK, there is no limit on the exemption.

A claim can also be made to transfer any unused nil rate band from one spouse/civil partner to the surviving spouse/civil partner.

4.6 Lifetime IHT

After all available exemptions have been applied, the first £325,000 of a CLT is taxed at 0% (the **nil rate band** for 2013/14), and is therefore effectively tax-free.

To stop people from avoiding IHT by, for example, giving away £1,625,000 in five lots of £325,000, the IHT rules look back seven years every time a transfer is made to decide how much of the nil rate band is available to set against the current transfer.

Any excess over the available nil rate band is taxable at 20%.

4.7 Death tax on lifetime transfers

Although PETs are exempt from IHT when they are made, if the donor dies within seven years of making the gift, it will become chargeable to IHT.

In addition, if a donor dies within seven years of making a CLT, additional IHT may become due on the gross gift amount. In this case, any lifetime tax already paid can be deducted.

Gross gifts in the seven years before the original gift use up the nil rate band. On death, therefore, you need to look back for up to 14 years to work out how much nil rate band is left.

The rate of IHT on death is 40%. However, the longer the transferor survives after making the gift, the lower the rate applied. This is because a taper relief applies to lower the amount of death tax payable as follows:

Years between transfer and death	% reduction in death tax	Effective IHT rate
3 years or less	0	40%
More than 3 but less than 4	20	32%
More than 4 but less than 5	40	24%
More than 5 but less than 6	60	16%
More than 6 but less than 7	80	8%

IHT on a lifetime transfer on death is payable by the **transferee**.

4.8 Trusts and taxation

4.8.1 Types of trust

A trust may be either:

- An **interest in possession (IIP) trust**, where the beneficiaries are automatically entitled to receive all of the income of the trust as it arises, or

- A **discretionary trust**, where the trustees can determine which beneficiaries to make payments to and how much they will receive.

Although both trusts are treated the same for IHT purposes, it is essential to recognise the type of trust, as the income tax treatment is very different for each.

You are likely only to have to deal with the taxation of savings and investment income of a trust.

4.8.2 Income tax for IIP trusts

IIP trustees' tax position (2013/14)

- Interest income is taxed at **20%**
- **Dividends** are taxed at **10%**

Interest is usually received net of a 20% tax credit by the trust (as it is by an individual). Dividends are received with a 10% notional tax credit. As both of these tax credits satisfy the trustees' liability for these types of income, no further tax is due from the trustees.

IIP beneficiary's tax position. The IIP beneficiary (sometimes called the 'life tenant') is entitled to receive the trust income once the trustees have paid the tax due.

The beneficiary will receive a statement of income from the trust showing the amounts they are entitled to receive along with the associated tax credit (ie the tax paid by the trustees). They will then include these amounts in their own tax calculation.

The income paid to the beneficiary retains its nature so, if it is interest income in the trustees' hands it will be taxed as interest income on the beneficiary, and so on.

4.8.3 Income tax for discretionary trusts

Discretionary trustees' tax position. Discretionary trusts have a **standard, or basic rate, band of £1,000**. The first £1,000 of income is taxed at basic rates, ie at 10% (dividends) – the **'dividend ordinary rate'** – and at 20% (interest and other income) – the **'basic rate'** (2013/14). As for individuals, the basic rate band is applied first to non-savings income, then savings income and finally dividends. Many smaller trusts will have no further tax to pay.

Any **remaining income** is taxed at the rates that apply to additional rate taxpaying individuals:

- Interest and other income is taxed at **45%** (the **'trust rate'**)
- **Dividends** are taxed at **37.5%** (the **'dividend trust rate'**)

Beneficiaries of discretionary trusts are only taxed if they receive income payments from the trust.

Any payments of income to beneficiaries are made **net of tax at 45%** and are taxed on them at the rates that apply to earnings income. The trustees will again provide a statement of income to the beneficiaries showing the relevant figures.

If the trustees have not paid sufficient tax to cover this tax credit, they must make an additional payment. Beneficiaries who are basic or higher rate taxpayers may obtain repayments. Additional rate taxpaying beneficiaries will have no further tax liability.

5 UK TAX COMPLIANCE

Learning objective	6.1.9 **Describe** the system of UK tax compliance including self-assessment, Pay As You Earn (PAYE), tax returns, tax payments, tax evasion and avoidance issues

5.1 Introduction

In earlier sections of this Chapter, we have explored the principles of income tax, capital gains tax and national insurance.

In this section, we see how individuals and trusts must 'self-assess' their tax liability. We outline the PAYE system for individuals in employment, and we also consider the difference between tax avoidance and tax evasion.

In subsequent sections of the Chapter, we will consider other taxes within the syllabus: stamp taxes, corporation tax and Value Added Tax.

5.2 Self-assessment

5.2.1 General principles

The self-assessment system relies upon the taxpayer completing and filing a tax return and paying the tax due on time.

Many taxpayers have very simple affairs: an individual receiving a salary under deduction of tax through PAYE or an IIP trustee receiving only interest. These individuals and trustees will not normally have to complete a tax return. Self-employed taxpayers and trustees with more complicated affairs will have to complete a self-assessment tax return.

5.2.2 Tax returns

Individuals who are chargeable to income tax or CGT for any tax year and who have not received a notice to file a return must notify HMRC that they are chargeable within six months from the end of the year, ie by 5 October 2014 for 2013/14. HMRC will then send them a multi-page tax return to complete.

The **latest filing date** for a self-assessment tax return for a tax year (Year 1) is:

- 31 October in the next tax year (Year 2), for a non-electronic return (ie a paper return)
- 31 January in Year 2, for an electronic return (ie completed online at the HMRC website)

If the taxpayer is filing a paper return, he may make the tax calculation on his return, or he may ask HMRC to do so on his behalf.

If the taxpayer wishes HMRC to make the calculation for Year 1, a paper return must be filed on or before 31 October in Year 2.

If the taxpayer is filing an electronic return, the calculation of tax liability is made automatically when the return is made online.

There are penalties for late returns.

5.2.3 Payment of tax

The self-assessment system may result in the taxpayer making three payments of income tax and Class 4 NICs.

Date	Payment
31 January in the tax year	1st payment on account
31 July after the end of the tax year	2nd payment on account
31 January after the end of the tax year	Final payment to settle the remaining liability

Payments on account are usually required where the income tax and Class 4 NICs due in the previous year exceeded the amount of income tax deducted at source; this excess is known as **the relevant amount**. Income tax deducted at source includes tax suffered (eg, 20% on interest income), PAYE deductions and tax credits on dividends.

The payments on account are each equal to 50% of the relevant amount for the previous year.

Payments on account of CGT are never required.

Payments on account are not required if the relevant amount falls below a *de minimis* limit of £1,000. Also, payments on account are not required from taxpayers who paid 80% or more of their tax liability for the previous year through PAYE or other deduction at source arrangements.

The balance of any income tax and Class 4 NICs together with all CGT due for a year, is normally payable on or before the 31 January following the year.

5.2.4 Late payment of tax

If tax is paid late, interest is chargeable from the due date until the day before the actual date of payment.

If the tax is still unpaid at 30 days, six months and twelve months, there are **penalties** of 5% of the unpaid tax at these dates.

5.3 Pay As You Earn (PAYE)

5.3.1 General principles

PAYE is the method by which income tax and national insurance contributions are **deducted from the earnings of employees.**

5.3.2 Payment of PAYE

Employers are **required to pay PAYE and NIC deductions** made on paydays falling between 5th of a calendar month and the 6th of the next calendar month to HMRC **within 14 days of the end of the tax month**. For example, PAYE deducted on 26 September 2013 payday must be paid by 19 October 2013.

If **payments are made electronically** the payment **date is extended by three days,** ie to 22 October 2013 in this example.

5.3.3 PAYE end of year reporting

After the end of each tax year, the employer must provide each employee with a **form P60.** This shows total taxable earnings for the year, tax deducted, tax code, NI number and the employer's name and address. The P60 must be provided by **31 May** following the tax year so that the employee can complete his self-assessment tax return on time.

5.4 Tax avoidance and evasion

Tax avoidance is a valid way for a taxpayer to use existing tax rules to his advantage so that he does not pay more than is legally due.

Tax evasion, on the other hand, is illegal and includes, for example, a taxpayer not reporting all of his income on his tax return to reduce his tax liability.

6   STAMP TAXES

<table>
<tr><td>Learning objectives</td><td>6.1.10 Explain the principles of stamp duty land tax (SDLT) as applied to property transactions – buying, selling and leasing
6.1.11 Explain the principles of stamp duty reserve tax (SDRT)</td></tr>
</table>

6.1 Stamp Duty Land Tax (SDLT)

6.1.1 Basic principles

Stamp duty land tax (SDLT) applies to land transactions. A land transaction is a transfer of land or an interest in, or right over, land.

SDLT is generally payable as a **percentage of the consideration paid** for the land and on the **premium paid for a new lease** or the **assignment of an existing lease**. It is **payable by the purchaser**.

6.1.2 SDLT rates

The amount of the charge to SDLT depends on whether the land is residential or non-residential.

Stamp duty land tax rates (2013/14)

Rate	Residential land	Non-residential land
0%	£0 – £125,000	£0 – £150,000[1]
1%	£125,001 – £250,000	£150,001 – £250,000
3%	£250,001 – £500,000	£250,001 – £500,000
4%	£500,001 – £1,000,000	Over £500,000
5%	£1,000,001 – £2,000,000	N/a
7%[2]	Over £2,000,000	N/a

Notes
(1) The rate is 1% for non-residential land up to £150,000 if the annual rent is £1,000 or more.

(2) Where residential property over £2 million is purchased by a company or similar entity, an anti-avoidance rate of 15% applies.

The following land transactions are **exempt** from SDLT:

- A transfer for no chargeable consideration (except a gift to a connected company)
- A transfer on divorce, annulment of marriage or judicial separation
- Variations of a will or intestacy made within two years of death for no consideration
- Transfers to charities if the land is to be used for charitable purposes

Example

What is the difference in the stamp duty land tax (SDLT) payable on a house which sells for £249,000 and the SDLT on a house which is sold for £251,000?

Solution

Sale at £249,000: £249,000 × 1% = £2,490

Sale at £251,000: £251,000 × 3% = £7,530

Difference: £7,530 – £2,490 = £5,040

This calculation shows the significant effect of the SDLT threshold levels arising from the SDLT charge being levied on the total price paid. A purchase at a little above £250,000 will cost the buyer approximately £5,000 more in SDLT than a purchase slightly below £250,000.

New leases – SDLT on lease rentals (2013/14)

Rate	Net present value (NPV) of rent	
	Residential	**Non-residential**
Zero	£0 – £125,000	£0 - £150,000
1%*	Over £125,000	Over £150,000

When a new residential lease has a substantial rent, SDLT is payable on the net present value (NPV) of the rent in addition to SDLT on any lease premium.

* ie 1% of the value that exceeds £125,000/£150,000.

6.2 Stamp Duty Reserve Tax (SDRT)

Stamp Duty Reserve Tax (SDRT) is a tax on electronic (ie paperless) share transactions. It is also payable on electronic purchases of units in unit trusts or shares in open-ended investment companies (OEICs) (see later).

SDRT is payable by the purchaser at a flat rate of 0.5% based on the amount paid for the shares.

For example, if an individual buys shares for £1,000, they must pay SDRT of £5.

7 CORPORATION TAX

Learning objective	6.1.12 **Explain** how companies are taxed in the UK

7.1 Who pays, and when

A UK-resident company is liable to corporation tax on its worldwide profits (subject to an opt-out for non-UK branches) and on capital gains in the accounting period. Other companies are liable to corporation tax on profits earned in the UK. Tax treaties between countries cover instances of potential double taxation.

An **accounting period** is the period for which corporation tax is charged and cannot exceed 12 months.

An accounting period is based on the company's **period of account**, which is the period for which it prepares its financial accounts. Usually this will be 12 months in length but it may be longer or shorter than this. If it is longer, the period of account must be split into two accounting periods. The first accounting period is always twelve months in length.

Most companies pay their corporation tax nine months and one day after the end of their accounting period. Large companies, however, must pay their corporation tax in four quarterly instalments. The instalments are based on the company's estimate of its current year tax liability.

7.2 Taxable profits

7.2.1 General principles

Corporation tax is self-assessed by the company and is calculated as a percentage of the taxable profits of the company.

The taxable profits are based on the profit before tax figure in the company's annual financial accounts. There is scope for a company to manipulate this profit, for example by using particular depreciation rates (see below) for assets. For this reason, tax legislation requires that a number of adjustments be made to this profit figure.

7.2.2 Trading profit

Disallowed expenses. Certain expenses that are deducted from profits in the financial accounts cannot be deducted for tax purposes. Examples include **client or supplier entertainment expenditure** and provisions for **uncertain debts** (although **bad debts** are allowed).

Depreciation charged by a company in its financial accounts is not allowable expenditure for tax purposes, since the company determines the depreciation rates. However, the company can deduct **capital allowances** instead. This is essentially a form of tax depreciation, calculated by reference to special rules in the tax legislation.

7.2.3 Interest

Companies receive interest gross, ie without deduction of 20% tax at source. As interest is investment income and not trading income, it **must be deducted from the profit before tax** shown in the accounts when calculating taxable profits. It is then added to the rest of the company's income and gains to arrive at total profits.

Interest paid by a company, for example on debentures (see later), **is deductible for tax purposes** and does not usually have to be adjusted for.

7.2.4 Dividends

Dividends received by a company from another company are tax-free and do not form part of the company's taxable profits.

Although dividend income is exempt from corporation tax, the gross dividend (ie the dividend received plus the 10% notional tax credit) is added to the company's total profits to arrive at the augmented profits, which determine the rate of corporation tax that it must pay.

However, it is only the total profits are actually taxed.

7.2.5 Capital gains

Capital gains made by a company on the disposal of its fixed assets are **chargeable to corporation tax** and not to capital gains tax. Only individuals pay capital gains tax.

A company's chargeable gains are calculated in a similar way as an individual's gains are calculated, but with an additional deduction to strip out the effect of inflation on the value of the asset.

7.3 Corporation tax rates

The **rates of corporation tax** are set for **financial years. A financial year** runs from 1 April to the following 31 March and is **identified by the calendar year in which it begins**.

For example, the year from 1 April 2013 to 31 March 2014 is the Financial Year 2013 (FY 2013). This should not be confused with a tax year which, as we saw earlier, runs from 6 April to the following 5 April.

UK Corporation Tax Rates (FY 2013)
The **main rate** is 23%.
The **small profits rate** is 20%.

The **main rate** of corporation tax of 23% is payable by companies with 'augmented' profits (ie total profits plus gross dividends) of **£1,500,000 or more** in their chargeable accounting period.

The **small profits rate** of 20% is payable by companies with profits of **less than £300,000** in their chargeable accounting period.

Companies whose profits lie between £300,000 and £1,500,000 receive marginal relief so that they pay a rate that effectively lies between 20% and 23%.

7.4 Corporation tax losses

If a company suffers a trading loss, it can set this off against any other income and gains in the year (say from investments).

If it is still showing a loss for the year, then clearly there will be no tax charge for that year. In this case the company can make a claim to carry these losses back against the income and gains of the prior year (but usually just the prior year) in order to obtain tax relief and thus generate a tax repayment.

If the company does not make a claim to carry the losses back, it can carry them forward indefinitely and offset them against future profits **from the same trade**.

8 VALUE ADDED TAX

Learning objective	6.1.13 **Describe**, in outline, the principles of Value Added Tax (VAT)

8.1 The scope of VAT

VAT is a **tax on turnover**, not on profits.

The basic principle is that VAT should be borne by the final consumer. VAT-registered traders may deduct the tax which they suffer on supplies to them (input tax) from the tax which they charge to their customers (output tax) at the time this is paid to HMRC.

So, at each stage of the manufacturing or service process, the net VAT paid is on the value added at that stage. The burden is borne by the final consumer.

8.2 Rates of VAT

VAT is charged on taxable supplies. A taxable supply is a supply of goods or services other than an exempt supply.

A taxable supply can either be **standard-rated** or **zero-rated**. The current standard rate is 20%.

Energy products and services are charged at a **reduced rate of 5%**.

Zero-rated supplies are taxable at 0%. An example is the supply of books. A taxable supplier whose outputs are zero-rated but whose inputs are standard-rated will obtain repayments of the VAT paid on purchases.

An exempt supply is not chargeable to VAT. An example is the supply of financial services or insurance. A person making **exempt supplies** is **unable to recover VAT on inputs**. The exempt supplier thus has to shoulder the burden of VAT. Of course, he may increase his prices to pass on the charge, but he cannot issue a VAT invoice which would enable a taxable customer to obtain a credit for VAT, since no VAT is chargeable on his supplies.

The following table summarises the impact of VAT on investment services.

Service provided/Fee charged	VAT status
Commissions	Exempt
Advisory services	Standard rated if invoiced separately, otherwise exempt
Nominee services	Exempt
Portfolio management fees	Standard rated

9 TAXATION OF INVESTMENTS

9.1 Direct investments

Learning objectives

6.1.14 Analyse the taxation of direct investments including cash and cash equivalents, fixed interest securities, equities and property

6.2.4 Calculate the most common elements of income tax and NICs, CGT, and IHT, including the impact of lifetime transfers and transfers at death

We now look at direct investments, which involve the investor spending their money, either personally or through a broker, on a particular investment, for example shares or property.

9.2 Cash and cash equivalents

9.2.1 General principles

Cash investments, or deposits, are used by individuals looking for secure, low risk, liquid investments.

9.2.2 Cash investments

The principal UK deposit takers are **banks and building societies**.

National Savings & Investments (NS&I) is a government agency that also takes cash deposits. NS&I investments are guaranteed by the government so are completely secure. NS&I currently offers two savings accounts, the Direct Saver and the Investment Account. NS&I also offers other products including, for example, the Direct ISA and Children's Bonds.

Other types of cash investment include:

- Time deposits (or term accounts)
- Money market accounts, which allow deposits for periods ranging from overnight to five years
- Foreign currency accounts

9.2.3 Income from cash investments

The **income receivable** from cash investments is **interest.**

9.2.4 Tax treatment of cash investments

Income tax

We have already seen that UK-resident individuals are taxable on bank and building society interest in the **tax year the interest is paid**.

The rates, which we saw earlier are:

- 10% starting rate (where there is non-savings income below £2,790 for 2013/14)
- 20% basic rate
- 40% higher rate
- 45% additional rate

Bank and building society interest is generally paid **net of 20% income tax**.

The investor's tax position will be as follows:

- Non-taxpayers can reclaim the full 20% tax deducted

- Starting rate taxpayers can reclaim a 10% refund
- Basic rate taxpayers have no further tax liability
- Higher rate (40%) taxpayers pay a further 20% through their self-assessment tax return
- Additional rate (45%) taxpayers pay a further 25%, also via self-assessment

Interest on **NS&I Direct Saver** and **Investment Account** is taxable but **paid gross**. This means that no tax is deducted by NS&I, and the taxpayer cannot claim a 20% tax credit. The tax liability will usually have to be paid through the self-assessment system.

Interest from **NS&I Savings Certificates** (no issues currently on sale) and **Children's Bonds** is tax-free (exempt).

Cash on a deposit investment does not grow in value: it simply produces income, so there is no charge to **capital gains tax.**

9.3 Fixed interest securities

9.3.1 Overview

Fixed interest or 'fixed income' securities are securities that pay a pre-specified return, in the form of capital and income. Such securities are also generally called **bonds. Gilts, corporate bonds, loan stock, debentures** and **loan notes** are names given to types of bond.

Bonds are **loans**, with the investor as the lender. The holder of the bond – that is, the investor – will receive any interest payment (the coupon), and normally repayment of capital on maturity of the bond.

As you will be aware, the issuers of bonds include:

- Government ('gilts' is the name for UK Government stock), and
- Companies (corporate bonds)

9.3.2 Features of fixed interest securities

Fixed interest securities generally have:

- A **fixed redemption value** which the issuer will repay to the bondholder on maturity

- A **fixed rate of interest** (the coupon) expressed as a percentage of face value, usually paid every six months

- A **pre-specified redemption date** (or maturity date)

For example, a holding of £10,000 Provident Financial PLC 7% 2017 corporate bond (trading on the LSE's Order Book for Retail Bonds as PF17) will pay £350.00 interest every six months until its maturity date of 4 October 2017, when the holder will be repaid the £10,000.

9.3.3 Tax treatment of fixed interest securities

Income tax. Interest received from fixed interest securities is taxed at the same rates as other (eg bank) interest.

Interest from government stocks (gilts) is paid gross unless:

- The investor elects to have 20% tax deducted from it, or
- The gilt was purchased before 6 April 1998 and the investor has not elected for gross payments

Interest on corporate bonds (or 'debentures') is generally paid **net of 20% income tax.**

The investor's tax position is as shown above for other interest.

Capital gains tax. Individuals pay **no CGT** on disposals of their holdings of:

- **Gilts**
- **Qualifying corporate bonds** (most company loan stock and debentures)

Gains on such disposals are exempt and losses are not allowable (ie, cannot be set off against other gains).

9.4 Equities

9.4.1 Income tax

Shareholders who receive **dividends** from **equities (ordinary shares)** are **paid with a notional 10% tax credit**. The tax credit equals: 1/9 × Dividend received. As the tax credit is only 'notional', it cannot be repaid to the taxpayer, although it can **reduce the taxpayer's liability**.

The position for a dividend received of £90 for different types of taxpayer can be summarised as follows.

	Non-taxpayer £	Basic rate taxpayer (10%) £	Higher rate taxpayer (32.5%) £	Additional rate taxpayer (37.5%) £
Net dividend	90.00	90.00	90.00	90.00
Tax credit (net × 1/9)	10.00	10.00	10.00	10.00
Gross dividend (net × 100/90)	100.00	100.00	100.00	100.00
Additional tax due	Nil	Nil	22.50	27.50
Net income	90.00	90.00	67.50	62.50

You can see that the **effective rate of tax on the net dividend** for a higher rate taxpayer is (22.5/90 × 100) 25%, and for an additional rate taxpayer is (27.5/90 × 100) around 30.5%.

9.4.2 Capital gains tax

If the investor makes a **capital gain** on the disposal of shares, it may be subject to capital gains tax at 18% (if within the basic rate tax band) or at 28% (above the basic rate band), after deduction of the annual exempt amount (£10,900 for 2013/14).

The basic calculation is:

Profit = Proceeds (less expenses of sale) *less* costs of investing in the shares.

Expenses of sale include broker's commission.

The main costs of originally investing in shares that can be deducted are:

- Purchase cost
- Broker's commission
- Stamp duty reserve tax (SDRT) (0.5% on electronic purchases of UK equities)

If the investor holds at least 5% of the shares in a company that he also works for and has owned the shares for at least one year, he can get **entrepreneurs' relief** up to a lifetime limit. This reduces the effective tax rate to 10% (as explained earlier).

9.5 Property

9.5.1 Income tax

Profits from renting out **property** are taxed in the same way as earnings, ie they are taxed as **non-savings income at 20%, 40% or 45%**.

Mortgage interest on the let property is a deductible expense when calculating the letting profit.

Other costs normally also deductible include:

- Maintenance costs

- 10% (× the rental income) 'wear and tear' allowance or, alternatively, the cost of replacing (but not the original purchase price of) furniture, fixtures and fittings

- Estate agent's commission

- Management expenses

Improvement expenditure (eg adding an extension to the property) is **not** normally **deductible.**

If a landlord is **non-UK resident**, the tenant or letting agent must deduct basic rate tax from the property income before paying the rent to the non-resident landlord. The landlord may apply to HMRC to be allowed to receive gross payments of rent if he completes a self-assessment tax return and keeps his tax affairs up to date.

9.5.2 Capital gains tax

If a property being let has ever been the investor's **principal private residence (PPR)** (main home) that he has lived in at any time, the gain on the sale of the property may be fully or partly exempt from capital gains tax, depending on how long he has owned the property and how long he actually lived in it before renting it out. A married couple or civil partnership can only have one PPR at one time.

If the property has never been the investor's PPR, the gain will be taxable in full.

Expenses of sale that can be deducted include **legal fees**.

The main **costs of originally investing in property** that can be deducted when calculating the gain:

- Purchase cost
- Legal fees
- **Stamp duty land tax (SDLT)** (percentage based on original value of the property)

The property will not usually qualify for **entrepreneurs' relief.**

9.6 Indirect investments

In the remainder of this Section of the Chapter, we look at the tax treatment of various forms of **indirect investment**.

9.7 Pension arrangements

9.7.1 Introduction

Tax relief on pension provision includes relief for qualifying contributions to a pension and an exemption from tax on income and gains arising in a pension fund.

For the tax advantages to apply to a pension scheme, the scheme must be registered with HMRC.

An individual may make pension provision in different ways:

- **Personal pension schemes**, set up by an individual who could be self-employed or not a member of an occupational scheme, are **defined contribution** pensions. This means that the level of pension that the member can draw from such schemes will depend on the investment performance of the money invested.

- **Occupational pension schemes**, where the scheme is set up by the employer for the benefit of the employees, historically tended to be **defined benefit** (final salary) schemes, where the pension depends on the period for which the individual has been a member of the scheme and his salary at the time of retirement. Modern occupational schemes are more likely to be defined contribution schemes.

9.7.2 Tax treatment of pension funds

Income from investments within the pension is tax-free, as is any growth in value when the pension fund disposes of the investments.

A pension arrangement acts as a **tax-free wrapper** around the investments within it.

9.7.3 Tax treatment of pension contributions

Subject also to the **annual allowance** limit (see below), an individual who has not yet reached the age of 75 can make tax-relievable contributions to his pension arrangements up to the **higher of**:

- His **earnings** (employment and self-employment income) in the tax year, and
- **£3,600**

The **annual allowance** is an overriding limit on the total contributions (including from the employer) that can receive tax relief for each tax year. The amount of the annual allowance for **2013/14** is **£50,000**. A member of a registered pension scheme can **carry forward** unused annual allowances from the **three previous tax years**. For the purpose of this carry forward, the annual allowances for the tax years **2008/09, 2009/10 and 2010/11** are deemed to be **£50,000**.

If the amount put into the pension exceeds this annual allowance, there is an income tax charge, determined by adding the amount subject to the charge to the individual's net income.

Contributions to personal pensions are paid net of basic rate tax, which gives immediate relief to all taxpayers. Further tax relief is given if the individual is a higher or additional rate taxpayer. The relief is given by increasing the basic rate limit for the year by the gross amount of contributions for which the taxpayer is entitled to relief.

No tax relief is available on **contributions made after age 75**.

Example

Joe is aged 47 and has earnings of £61,000 in 2013/14. He pays a personal pension contribution of £7,200 (net). He has no other taxable income.

Requirement

Show Joe's tax liability for the year.

Solution

	£
Total earnings	61,000
Less: personal allowance	(9,440)
Taxable income	51,560
Tax on first £32,010 @ 20%	6,402
Tax on next £9,000 @ 20% (£7,200 × 100/80)*	1,800
Tax on next £10,550 @ 40%	4,220
Tax liability	12,422

* Note that pension contributions are paid net. The provider reclaims 20% tax from HMRC. Joe is a higher rate taxpayer and here gets 40% − 20% = 20% additional tax relief by the extension of his basic rate tax band.

Employers normally operate a **'net pay' arrangement** in respect of employees' contributions to their **occupational schemes**. In this case, as we saw earlier, the employer will deduct gross pension contributions from the individual's earnings before operating PAYE. The individual therefore obtains tax relief at his marginal rate of tax through PAYE without having to make any claim.

9.8 Tax treatment of pension benefits

No pension payment can be made before the member reaches **normal minimum pension age (55)**, unless the member is incapacitated by ill health. At this age the member may take:

- An income pension, and/ or
- A lump sum

from the pension scheme.

Up to **25% of the pension fund** can be taken as a **tax-free pension commencement lump sum**, subject to the lifetime allowance limit (see below). The **remainder** must be used to provide a **pension income**.

Pension income is **taxable as non-savings income.**

An individual is not allowed to build up an indefinitely large pension fund. There is a maximum value for a pension fund (for money purchase arrangements) or for the value of benefits (for defined benefits arrangements). This is called the **lifetime allowance** – a limit on the total value of the benefit accumulated.

The lifetime allowance is tested as benefits crystallise (for example, on retirement), and is set at £1,500,000 for the year 2013/14, subject to certain ways of protecting the limit that were available in the past (up to 5 April 2012).

If the pension fund exceeds the lifetime allowance, this will give rise to an **income tax charge** on the **excess value of the fund**.

The rate of the charge depends on the type of benefit that will be taken from the excess funds:

- **Lump sum**: charge at **55%** on the value of the lump sum
- **Pension income**: charge at **25%** on the value of the vested funds

9.9 Individual savings accounts (ISAs)

9.9.1 What is an ISA?

An ISA is a tax-free savings account. There are two types of ISA:

- **Cash**, including all the kinds of bank and building society accounts as well as NS&I products and similar, and

- **Stocks and shares**

9.9.2 Who can invest in an ISA?

Individuals over 18, who are **resident in the UK**, can invest in **two ISA accounts each year**, one for cash deposits, and one for stocks and shares, so long as they keep within the investment limits (see below).

Trustees cannot invest in ISAs.

9.9.3 Main features of ISAs

The main features of ISAs are as follows.

- There is an **annual subscription limit (2013/14)** of **£11,520**, of which no more than **£5,760** may be in the cash component

- There is no statutory lock-in period or minimum subscription

- There is **no lifetime limit**

Individuals under 18 but over 16 are allowed to subscribe up to the £5,760 pa limit into a cash only ISA account.

Once the maximum amount has been subscribed for in any type of ISA for a year, it is not possible to make further investments even after a withdrawal is subsequently made.

9.9.4 Tax treatment of ISAs

All income (eg interest, dividends) and gains in respect of investments within an ISA are **exempt from tax**. You can think of an ISA as a **tax-free wrapper** around the investments within it.

A full or partial withdrawal may be made from an ISA at any time without loss of tax exemption.

Where an investor ceases to qualify by becoming **non-resident**, the benefits, including tax reliefs, of any ISAs held up to that time may be retained but **no further subscriptions** may be made (unless UK residence status is regained).

9.10 Junior ISA (JISA)

Junior ISAs (JISAs) are long-term tax-free savings accounts for children.

The JISA has replaced the Child Trust Fund (CTF) and is open to UK-resident children who are under 18 and are not eligible to have a CTF (ie, born after 2 January 2011).

There are cash JISAs, and stocks & shares JISAs, with a single overall limit for each child of £3,720 per tax year (2013/14).

All income and gains within the Junior ISA is tax-free.

Anybody can put money into a JISA. The JISA is in the child's name, but the person who opens the account is the '**registered contact**' who is responsible for managing it. The child can choose to become the registered contact from age 16 and can withdraw money from age 18, when the JISA converts to an ISA.

9.11 Collective investment schemes

9.11.1 Types of collective investment scheme

Collective investment schemes include:

- **Unit trusts**
- **Investment trusts**
- **Open-Ended Investment Companies**

9.11.2 Taxation of the fund

If the **unit trust or OEIC is an equity fund it receives dividends** from its underlying investments net of a 10% tax credit and **has no further tax to pay**.

If the **unit trust or OEIC is a non-equity fund** it receives income from its underlying investments (eg, interest or rental income) gross and has to pay **corporation tax at 20%** (equivalent to the basic rate of income tax).

This income is then passed on to investors at the distribution dates.

HMRC- approved **investment trusts** are exempt from tax on capital gains. Their non-dividend income is subject to corporation tax.

Unit trusts and OEICs are exempt from tax on their gains when they dispose of their investments. This allows the fund managers to trade in and out of shares without having to worry about the tax implications.

9.11.3 Taxation of the investor

Income tax

The tax regime for investors in **unit trusts** and **OEICs** is as follows.

- **Dividend distributions** to investors are taxed in the same way as dividends on holdings of individual shares.

- **Interest distributions** – for a 'bond fund', ie one that holds more than 60% of its investments in interest-bearing securities – are deemed to be interest income and are subject to a 20% tax deduction at source for UK residents unless the funds are held within an ISA.

An **investment trust shareholder** will only ever receive dividends, which are taxed in the same way as other dividends.

Capital gains tax

Investors in a unit trust are liable for CGT on gains they make when they sell their units, or shares in collective funds or investment trusts, regardless of whether the fund is investing in exempt assets such as gilts or not.

The chargeable gain is the difference between what the investor paid for the units or shares and what they sell them for.

9.11.4 Offshore funds

An offshore fund will generally not itself pay tax, although a small local tax may be payable in some jurisdictions. The taxation of the individual investor in an offshore fund will depend upon whether the fund is granted **reporting** or **non-reporting** status by HMRC.

These rules replaced the previous distributor / non-distributor status rules when the **Offshore Funds (Tax) Regulations 2009** came into force in December 2009.

The intention of the offshore fund rules generally is to prevent the **roll-up of income** in pooled investment arrangements, with a subsequent realisation at (or nearly at) net asset value, or (by reference to an indexed value) in capital form.

An offshore entity that meets the definition of an offshore fund (under section 40A(2) Finance Act 2008) can, on meeting certain conditions, apply to be a 'reporting fund'.

- The relevance of **reporting fund status** for UK investors is that **gains realised on disposals of investments in reporting funds will in most circumstances be subject to tax on chargeable gains**, whereas

- Gains realised on disposals of investments in **non-reporting funds** ('offshore income gains' or OIGs) will be subject to less favourable treatment as they will generally be **charged to tax on income** on gains arising

Thus:

- **Gains** realised in reporting funds attract tax at CGT rates (18%/28%), while

- **Gains** on a non-reporting fund are subject to income tax at the investor's marginal rate of income tax (20%/40%/45%), and losses cannot be set against other gains

The charge to income tax for non-reporting funds (previously termed 'roll-up' funds) is designed to penalise investors who by investing in such funds (which report little by way of dividends) in order to turn income (taxed at income tax rates) into capital growth (taxed at lower CGT rates).

Distributions of income received by UK investors in offshore funds (reporting or non-reporting) will be charged to UK income tax in accordance with usual rules depending on the type of the income in question – eg, dividend income or interest. Investors in reporting funds must declare as income their share of the fund's reportable income, as well as their distributed income, which is paid gross.

To maintain **reporting status**, a fund must:

- Prepare accounts in accordance with an acceptable accounting policy

- Provide reports of their 'reportable income', which is the accounts figure for the total return of the fund adjusted in accordance with certain rules set out in the Offshore Funds (Tax) Regulations 2009. (They must provide reports both to HMRC, to include a computation showing their reportable income, and to participants (investors) that show their proportionate share of that income.)

- Make certain information available to HMRC when requested to do so

9.12 Life assurance policies

9.12.1 Overview

There are two types of life assurance policy:

- Contracts for **protection (insurance) purposes** only, and
- Contracts with **both protection and investment elements**, which are the focus of this section

Unlike a pension fund, a **life assurance fund** is not a tax-free vehicle: it suffers corporation tax on its income and gains at a rate of 20%.

As the fund itself suffers tax, payouts from policies are often completely free of income tax and capital gains tax. This is the case if it is a qualifying policy.

A **qualifying policy** is one where premiums have been paid for a minimum of one of the following:

- Life of the life assured
- 10 years
- Three quarters of the term

If it is a **non-qualifying policy**, there may be an income tax charge on encashment of the policy. A non-qualifying policy is a **single premium bond** where a lump sum is invested in a life fund a small part of which buys cover in the event of death with the balance being invested. These are also known as **investment bonds** or **property bonds.**

The encashment or partial encashment (withdrawal) of such a policy, is a **chargeable event** for **income tax** purposes. Depending on the circumstances, this event may produce an additional income tax charge in the year in which the event occurs.

A chargeable event may arise in certain circumstances where any withdrawal/encashment is **received by a higher rate or additional rate taxpayer**.

For such a bond, up to 5% of the original premium for each year of the bond's life **(including the year of the chargeable event)** may be withdrawn from the bond with no **immediate** tax implications until 100% is reached. For withdrawals above this 5% level the excess will be taxable.

Example: Chargeable event gain & top slicing relief

If an investor purchases a single premium bond for £10,000 and after 3 years withdraws a sum less than or equal to £1,500 (3 years at £500 pa), then no chargeable event arises.

If this sum exceeds £1,500, the excess represents a chargeable event. So, if the investor withdraws £1,800 then £300 excess is potentially taxable.

This £300, however, is the total withdrawal for 3 years, representing £100 pa, the income has been 'sliced' or annualised. This £100 slice will be added as the 'top slice' of the investor's income and if the investor is a higher or additional rate taxpayer then tax must be paid at either 20% (the difference between the higher and basic rate for savings income) which would be £20 here on each £100 slice (£60 in total on the three slices), or 30% (the difference between the additional and basic rate for savings income) which would be £90 in total).

On the final encashment of such bonds, any gains realised will be considered in a similar manner and will be subject to income tax in the hands of a higher rate taxpayer.

The gain will be 'sliced' as above to establish the annual gain, this annual gain will be added to the investors income to determine his tax status (basic/higher rate) with any higher rate part/region being taxed at 20%.

The total tax payable will be the tax on one slice × the number of slices.

9.12.2 Offshore life policies

An offshore life policy, often called an **offshore bond**, is broadly the same as a UK non-qualifying policy.

The advantage of an offshore bond is that the **underlying life funds suffer little or no tax (gross roll up)** compared with UK life funds which are taxed at 20%.

Withdrawals of up to 5% of the original investment may be taken for 20 years with no immediate tax liability. If the 5% allowance is not used in one year, then it can be carried forward to the next.

The taxation of offshore policies on encashment is more stringent than for onshore products. The chargeable gain on the bond is subject to basic, higher and additional rate tax.

When dividing to find the slice of gain, we use the **number of years since the beginning of the bond** not the years since the last chargeable event as with an onshore bond.

If the investor had been non-UK resident for part of the time he held the bond, then he receives **relief for the time that he was non-resident**. For example if he was non-UK resident for five of the ten years that he held the bond then the chargeable gain on encashment would be reduced by 50%.

If the investor is **non-UK resident** when the bond is encashed there are no UK tax consequences.

9.13 Real Estate Investment Trusts (REITs)

A REIT is a listed company (AIM does not count for this purpose) owning, managing and earning rental income from commercial or residential property.

The investor can use a REIT to spread his risk over a number of different properties.

REITs can elect for their property income (and gains) to be exempt from corporation tax and must withhold basic rate (20%) tax from distributions paid to shareholders (who cannot own more than 10% of a REIT's shares) out of these profits.

These distributions are taxed as property income on the investor, not as dividends.

Distributions by REITs out of other income (ie not property income or gains) are taxed as dividends in the normal way.

It is possible to hold REITs within **ISAs** and **existing Child Trust Funds.**

If the investor makes a capital gain on the disposal of REIT shares it may be **subject to capital gains tax** in the same way as shares in any other company.

9.14 EIS and SEIS

9.14.1 The schemes

The **Enterprise Investment Scheme (EIS)** is a scheme designed to promote enterprise and investment by helping high-risk, unlisted trading companies raise finance by the issue of ordinary shares to individual investors who are unconnected with that company.

Individuals can invest directly in the EIS company itself or via an EIS fund to diversify their exposure to risk. Only shares in certain companies qualify for the EIS.

The company must be an **unquoted trading company** that carries on a qualifying business activity for at least three years. Shares in AIM companies can qualify.

Non-qualifying business activities include:

- Banking
- Dealing in commodities
- Property development

The company must not be a subsidiary of, or be controlled by, any other company. Any subsidiary it has must be at least 90% owned and the group taken as a whole must qualify in respect of its business activities.

Qualifying companies must have **250 or fewer employees** and may **raise no more than £5 million through EIS, VCTs and similar schemes in a 12-month period**.

The **assets of the company** (including assets of group companies) must **not exceed £15 million** immediately before the share issue and must **not exceed £16 million** immediately afterwards.

The **Seed Enterprise Investment Scheme (SEIS)** is a tax-advantaged venture capital scheme similar to the EIS, available since 6 April 2012. The SEIS is focused on smaller, early stage companies carrying on, or preparing to carry on, a new business in a qualifying trade. The scheme makes available up to 50% tax relief to investors who subscribe up to £100,000 for shares and have a stake of less than 30% in the company.

9.14.2 EIS: income tax

When an individual subscribes for eligible shares in a qualifying company, the **amount subscribed** is a **tax reduction**, saving income tax at **30%**.

The **maximum total investment** that can qualify for this income tax relief in a tax year is **£1,000,000**, resulting in a maximum tax saving at 30% of £300,000.

A 2013/14 investment will attract relief against the tax liability for that tax year. However, a taxpayer can claim to **carry back** all or part of the investment to the previous year, using any unused part of that year's limit (£1,000,000 in 2013/14).

The **relief may be withdrawn** if certain events, such as the sale of the shares, occur within three years.

Dividends from EIS shares are **taxable** under the normal rules.

Trustees cannot obtain any income tax relief.

9.14.3 EIS: capital gains tax

Where EIS income tax relief is available, there are also **capital gains tax reliefs** when the investor sells his EIS shares:

- Where an individual disposes of EIS shares after the three year period any **gain is exempt** from CGT. If the shares are disposed of within three years any gain is computed in the normal way.

- If the EIS shares are disposed of at a loss at any time, the **loss is allowable** but the acquisition cost of the shares is reduced by the amount of EIS relief attributable to the shares. The loss can be **set against capital gains**, as normal, and can also be **set against the investor's income**.

EIS CGT reinvestment or 'deferral' relief allows the taxpayer to defer chargeable gains arising on the disposal of any asset if he invests in EIS shares in the period starting **one year before and ending three years after the disposal of the asset**. Note that this relief does not depend on income tax relief being available and is also available to trustees.

9.14.4 EIS: inheritance tax

Under **business property relief** rules, EIS investments that have been held for at least two years are normally **exempt from inheritance tax**.

9.15 Venture Capital Trusts (VCTs)

9.15.1 Overview

Venture capital trusts (VCTs) are **listed companies that invest in unquoted trading companies** and meet certain conditions. The VCT scheme differs from EIS in that the individual investor may spread his risk over a number of individually higher-risk, unquoted companies.

Similarly to the EIS rules:

- Each company in a VCT must have **250 or fewer employees**

- Each qualifying company may **raise no more than £5 million through EIS and VCTs in the 12 months ending on the date of the relevant investment**

- The assets of the company (including assets of group companies) must not exceed **£15 million immediately before** the share issue and must not exceed **£16 million immediately afterwards**

9.15.2 Income tax

An individual investing in a VCT obtains the following **income tax benefits** on a **maximum qualifying investment of £200,000** in the tax year:

- A tax reduction of 30% of the amount invested. There is a withdrawal of relief if the shares are disposed of within five years or if the VCT ceases to qualify

- Dividends received are tax-free income

No relief is available for **trustees.**

9.15.3 Capital gains tax

Capital gains on the sale of shares in the VCT are exempt from CGT (and losses are not allowable).

In addition, capital gains which the VCT itself makes on its investments are exempt, so are not subject to corporation tax.

There is no minimum holding period requirement for the benefits of tax-free dividends and CGT exemption.

10 TAX PLANNING

Learning objectives	**6.2.1 Evaluate** the tax considerations shaping clients' needs and circumstances
	6.2.2 Analyse the key principles of income tax planning
	6.2.4 Calculate the most common elements of income tax and NICs, CGT, and IHT, including the impact of lifetime transfers and transfers at death
	6.2.5 Select elementary tax planning recommendations in the context of investments and pensions advice

10.1 Introduction

Strategies for reducing the amount of income tax make use of the fact that not all income is subject to income tax and that all individuals are entitled to personal allowances. Investing in assets and products that produce exempt income, such as ISAs, is a simple and important way of reducing taxable income.

10.2 Spouses and civil partners

10.2.1 General principles

Spouses and civil partners are taxed as **two separate people.** Each spouse/civil partner is entitled to a personal allowance (or an age-related personal allowance, depending on income).

If one spouse's or civil partner's marginal rate of tax is higher than the other's marginal rate, it would be tax-efficient to transfer the income-yielding asset (or part of it) to the individual with the lower rate to utilise their personal allowance and lower marginal tax rate.

10.2.2 Joint property

When spouses/civil partners **jointly own income-generating property**, it is assumed that they are entitled to equal shares of the income.

If the spouses/civil partners are not actually entitled to equal shares in the income-generating property, they may make a joint declaration to HMRC specifying the proportion to which each is entitled. These proportions are used to tax each of them separately, in respect of income arising on or after the date of the declaration.

Example

Mr Buckle is a higher rate taxpayer who owns a rental property producing £20,000 of property income on which he pays tax at 40%, giving him a tax liability of £8,000. His spouse has no income.

What tax planning advice would you give Mr Buckle to reduce the couple's overall income tax liability?

Solution

If Mr Buckle transfers a small interest in the property, say 5%, to his wife, they will be treated, for income tax purposes, as jointly owning the property and will each be taxed on 50% of the income.

Mr Buckle's tax liability will be reduced to £10,000 x 40% = £4,000. His wife's liability is only £112 (= (£10,000 – £9,440) x 20%), giving an overall tax saving of £3,888.

10.3 Children

A **child** is a **separate taxable person** for tax purposes and so is entitled to a personal allowance in his or her own right.

There are rules to prevent the parent of a minor child (under the age of 18) from transferring income to the child to use his personal allowance and starting and basic rate tax bands. These rules treat income received by the child that is directly transferred by the parent, or is derived from capital transferred by the parent (eg by setting up a bank account in the child's name), as income of the parent, rather than the child's, for income tax purposes.

The child's income is not, however, treated as his parent's if it does not exceed £100 (gross) a year.

The rules only apply to gifts from parents, so a tax saving is possible if other relatives (eg grandparents) make the gifts. It is also possible to use the child's personal allowance and starting and basic rate bands if the child is employed in the parent's trade, because in this case there is no element of gift.

These rules do not apply to income from a **Child Trust Fund (CTF)** or **Junior ISA (JISA)**, so a parent can make contributions to their child's CTF or JISA, depending on which they have qualified for, and the income will not be taxed on them (nor on the child, as the income is tax-free).

10.4 Tax-efficient investments

The following strategies involving tax-efficient investments may help to reduce someone's income tax liability.

- **Investing in a pension.** All taxpayers receive tax relief as contributions are paid **net of basic rate tax**. **Additional relief** is given to higher rate and additional rate taxpayers by increasing the basic rate limit for the year by the gross amount of contributions. However, income drawn as a pension is taxable (at whatever rate the individual pays tax when benefits are taken), and so there is an effect of tax deferral – except with regard to the 25% tax-free lump sum that can be taken when benefits are crystallised.

- **Employer contributions to a pension.** If an individual's **employer makes contributions** to his pension (within the annual allowance), there is no tax or NICs on the amount paid. It is therefore tax-efficient for an individual to receive part of his earnings as a pension contribution rather than salary.

- **Open a cash and/ or share ISA account.** Income and gains are exempt within the ISA. Higher and additional rate taxpayers benefit from the fact that they have no further tax to pay on dividends in a stocks and shares ISA. Before making any other investments, an individual should be encouraged to open an ISA account.

- **Contribute to an existing Child Trust Fund account.** Income and gains are exempt within the account. Even parents can make contributions to a CTF with no adverse tax consequences. (CTFs are not available for children born after 2 January 2011, who are eligible for the **Junior ISA**.)

- **Invest in EIS company** shares to obtain an **income tax reduction** of 30% (2013/14). If the individual's tax rate was higher in the year before the investment, they should claim to deduct the tax reduction from the tax liability of the **previous year**. There are also CGT reliefs available for investments in EIS shares. The Seed Enterprise Investment Scheme (**SEIS**) is another tax-advantaged scheme.

  EIS shares are **high risk investments** due to the size and nature of EIS qualifying companies. Only investors who are willing to accept this high level of risk, and possible losses on the eventual sale of the shares, should be advised to invest in EIS companies directly, although an EIS fund may be appropriate for a more risk-averse investor.

- **Invest in VCT company shares** to obtain a 30% **income tax reduction. Dividends received from VCTs are exempt** from income tax. **Less risky than EIS shares** as the investor is able to spread his risk across a number of higher-risk unquoted companies while investing in a listed company.

- **Invest in a single premium bond** (non-qualifying life policy). Can make **regular withdrawals up to 5%** of the original premium each year, with no tax until the bond is encashed. Withdrawals come with **20% tax credit so no further liability** if investor is a basic rate taxpayer by that time. May be tax-efficient for **investors nearing retirement age expecting a lower level of income**, although the high charges typical for this type of product tend to erode tax advantages.

- **Invest in National Savings & Investments (NS&I) Certificates** (when available) and NS&I Children's Bonds. Income is tax-free.

10.5 Capital gains tax planning

6.2.3 Analyse how the use of annual CGT exemptions, the realisation of losses, the timing of disposals, and sale and repurchase of similar assets, can mitigate CGT

6.2.4 Calculate the most common elements of income tax and NICs; CGT; IHT including the impact of lifetime transfers and transfers at death

6.2.5 Select elementary tax planning recommendations in the context of investments and pensions advice

10.5.1 Introduction

Strategies for reducing the amount of capital gains tax make use of the fact that not all assets are subject to capital gains tax and that all individuals are entitled to an annual exempt amount as well as relief for their capital losses.

10.5.2 Planning points

As we have seen, each individual can make gains every year up to the level of the annual CGT-exempt amount.

Only gains, net of losses for the year, in excess of the annual exempt amount are subject to CGT. Any unused annual exempt amount cannot be carried forward to future years.

Strategies to reduce CGT liability

- **Transfer the ownership of assets to a spouse or civil partner.** The transfer will be tax-neutral for CGT purposes and will allow the gifting spouse/ civil partner to use their annual exempt amount.

- **Phase asset disposals over more than one tax year** if possible, to use more than one annual exempt amount. For example, make two separate disposals in March 2014 and later in April 2014, which uses two annual exempt amounts, ie those for the tax year 2013/14 and 2014/15.

- **Realise gains within the annual exempt amount**, so that there is no actual taxable gain, and repurchase a similar asset. This has the effect of increasing the base cost of the asset, reducing the risk of future gains exceeding future annual exempt amounts.

- **Realise gains within the basic rate band**, if anticipating being a higher or additional rate taxpayer in the following year. Gains within the basic rate band will be taxed at 18%, but at 28% above this band.

- **Dispose of EIS shares** (after three years of ownership) **or VCT shares** as any gain will be exempt. However, the investor should not sell an investment that he would prefer to keep just for the tax benefits. Do not let the 'tax tail' wag the dog!

- **Dispose of other exempt assets**, such as cars, treasury stock (gilts) or Qualifying Corporate Bonds (corporate stock).

- **Dispose of assets standing at a loss.** Remember that capital losses must be set against gains of the same year. If there are any losses remaining, they can be carried forward and must be set against gains in future years, but only if those gains are not already covered by the annual exempt amount. Losses arising on the disposal of EIS-type shares can be set against income as well as gains.

10.6 Inheritance tax planning

10.6.1 Introduction

Inheritance tax (IHT) arises as a result of the transfer of wealth in excess of the settlor's nil rate band. IHT is primarily a tax on wealth left on death and therefore most IHT planning focuses on reducing an individual's estate through lifetime gifts. It is, however, necessary to balance the desire to reduce the potential IHT liability through the gifting of assets versus the need to maintain sufficient assets to support the required standard of living.

10.6.2 Spouses and civil partners

Spouses and **civil partners** are **taxed separately** for IHT purposes. On the death of one spouse or civil partner, it is necessary to value his or her estate. That estate includes only the property (or share of property) actually belonging to the deceased. Each spouse or civil partner has their own **nil rate band**, exemptions and reliefs independently of the other spouse or civil partner.

Transfers between spouses or civil partners (whether or not living together) are **exempt**.

A simple planning point follows from this exemption. Spouses/civil partners may avoid IHT, at least in the short term, if each makes a will leaving his property to the other.

Transferable nil rate band. As we saw earlier, when one spouse or civil partner dies, the unused portion of their nil rate band is **transferred** to the surviving spouse or civil partner. So, the second person's nil rate band on death will be their own remaining nil rate band plus the unused portion of the first person's (based on the nil rate band available on the second death).

10.6.3 Gifts with reservation of benefit (GWR)

One aspect of IHT planning is to make lifetime gifts rather than to keep property and gift it on death as, if the donor survives seven years from the date of a lifetime gift, there is no further IHT to pay if it was a chargeable lifetime transfer or becomes completely exempt if the gift was a PET.

Many individuals would like to make lifetime gifts, but are unwilling to do so because they want to continue using the asset (for example, a house or a work of art). One way around this would be for the individual to give the asset away and for the donee to allow the donor to continue to use the asset. However, this type of arrangement does not work because of the **gift with reservation of benefit (GWR)** rules.

A GWR occurs when an individual gifts property and continues to enjoy the benefit of the asset, either rent free or at reduced cost, or the person getting the gift does so with conditions attached.

The following are the most common examples of a GWR:

- **Giving away a house but continuing to live in it rent-free** (or at a rent lower than a market rent)
- Giving away a holiday cottage but continuing to spend long holidays there without paying a market rent

- **Giving away a painting but the donor continuing to keep it hanging on his wall** without paying a market rent for its use

- Creating a trust from which the settlor can benefit

Where a GWR is made, it is treated in the same way as any other gift at the time it is made, ie as either a PET or a CLT.

However if the reservation still exists at the date of the donor's death, the asset is included in the donor's estate at its market value at the date of death (probate value) and not its value at the date the gift was made.

If the donor has died within seven years of making the original GWR then, under basic principles, that gift will have death tax consequences (become chargeable if a PET, additional tax due if a CLT). There will therefore be two IHT charges on the same asset. To avoid this double taxation HMRC will choose the higher total tax.

Note that if the donor pays a full market rent for use of the property gifted, he will not be treated as having reserved a benefit and there will be no GWR implications.

Example

George gives his house to his son Owen on 1 April 2010 when it is worth £400,000. However, he continues to live in the house rent-free. George died on 2 January 2014. The house was then worth £460,000. George has made no previous transfers, other than to use his annual exemption each year. What are the inheritance tax consequences of these events?

Solution

George makes a PET in April 2010 of £400,000. As he dies within seven years of the transfer (in January 2014), the PET becomes chargeable. However, he is also treated as still owning the house and this will be included in his death estate at the value at the date of death (£460,000).

This results in a double charge to IHT on the same property, so the 'double charges' rules ensure that only the IHT calculation that produces the higher tax applies. In this case, the charge on the house in the death estate will apply (higher value and no taper relief available for the death estate). The effect is the same as if George had never made the gift.

10.6.4 Other IHT planning

Other IHT planning steps

- **Make full use of all available exemptions** (eg annual gifts, marriage / civil partnership gifts, and small gifts).

- **Use the normal expenditure out of income exemption**, for example to pay grandchildren's school fees.

- **Make lifetime gifts.** IHT will only be due on the asset gifted if the donor dies within seven years. The IHT charge will usually be based on a lower value (as the asset will often have increased by the date of death), and will take into account the lifetime annual and other exemptions as well as taper relief if the donor survives at least three years.

- **Make CLTs before making PETs in a tax year**. Annual exemptions are allocated chronologically during the tax year. CLTs are immediately chargeable to IHT so make these first, otherwise PETs will use up the annual exemption(s) if they are made earlier in the tax year. Remember, PETs only become chargeable if the donor dies within seven years of making PETs first will waste the annual exemption(s) if the donor survives for at least seven years.

- **Write life assurance benefits into trust** (ie, make someone else – eg, a family member – the beneficiary of the life policy) so that the policy proceeds are paid to another person and do not become part of the deceased's death estate.

- **Use life assurance policies (written into trust) to cover future IHT liabilities**, eg a seven -year policy to cover the potential liability on a PET or additional liability on a CLT.

- **Leave assets to spouse/ civil partner.**

CHAPTER ROUNDUP

- Income tax is payable on earnings, savings and investments. These are taxed at different rates.

- A number of reliefs and allowances are available to either reduce income (eg the personal allowance) or the tax liability (eg investments in the EIS).

- UK-resident and domiciled individuals are taxed on their worldwide income. UK-resident non-UK domiciled individuals may be taxed on their foreign income on the remittance basis, but a remittance basis charge may apply. Non-UK residents are only taxable in the UK on their UK income.

- Capital gains tax is payable by individuals and trustees on the disposal of chargeable assets (ie assets that are not exempt, such as cars).

- Inheritance tax is payable on death, and on lifetime gifts to trusts (CLTs). It is also due if an individual dies within seven years of making any gift (ie to a trust (CLT) or to an individual (PET)).

- Individuals and trusts may need to complete a self-assessment tax return and make three payments of tax (two payments on account and a balancing payment). PAYE is the system used for deducting income tax and Class 1 NIC from employees' earnings.

- Companies calculate their tax liability based on their taxable profits in a chargeable accounting period.

- Bank and building society interest is usually paid net of 20% basic rate tax, while interest from NS&I accounts is paid gross (income from NS&I Certificates is exempt). Income tax is payable on interest income at 10%, 20%, 40 and 45%.

- Interest from government stocks (gilts) is paid gross while interest on corporate bonds (debentures) is generally paid net of 20% income tax. The accrued income scheme applies when an investor buys or sells securities, so they are treated as receiving interest for the time they have owned the stock. Gilts and qualifying corporate bonds are exempt from CGT.

- Dividends from equities (ie shares) are paid with a 10% non-refundable tax credit. The gross dividend is taxed at 10%, 32.5% (higher rate) or 37.5% (additional rate).

- Property income (ie rent) is taxed as non-savings income at 20%, 40% or 45%. The gain on disposal of property is chargeable to CGT unless it has been the investor's main residence (PPR) at any point, in which case the gain may be fully or partly exempt.

- Income and gains within a pension fund are exempt from income tax and CGT. Individuals obtain tax relief when making contributions to their pension within the annual allowance. When an individual starts taking their pension they can take up to 25% of the fund (up to the lifetime allowance) as a tax-free lump sum. The rest is taken as an income pension and is taxed at the non-savings rates.

- Income from unit trusts and OEICs may be either interest or dividends and are taxed as such on the investor. Investment trusts are listed companies so distributions are always taxed as dividends. Capital gains tax is due on any growth in value when an investor disposes of their units or shares in any collective investment scheme.

- Payouts from qualifying life assurance policies are free of tax. Up to 5% of the original premium paid into a non-qualifying single premium life policy (bond) can be withdrawn tax free each year. Any excess is chargeable to income tax, but comes with a 20% tax credit. There may be further income tax (but not CGT) when a non-qualifying policy is encashed. Top slicing relief may apply for higher and additional rate taxpayers.

- Distributions from the tax-exempt income of a REIT are taxed as property income on the investor, not as dividends. CGT will apply when the investor sells shares in a REIT.

- Income tax relief (a 30% tax reduction) is available for investments in EIS companies and VCTs. Dividends from EIS companies are taxable as normal. There is no CGT if the investor sells the EIS shares after three years. Dividends from VCTs are exempt from income tax. There is no CGT when the investor sells his VCT shares.

- Successful income tax planning can involve simple steps such as ensuring both spouses / civil partners are using their personal allowances and lower rate bands.

- Parents' gifts of assets or income to their children can lead to any income being taxed on them rather than the child, unless the income arises from a CTF or Junior ISA, or is less than £100 a year.

- Pensions can be a tax-efficient way for individuals to make provision for retirement but they should be aware that they cannot use the pension fund until they reach retirement age.

- Capital gains tax planning includes making use of the annual exempt amount (of both the investor and their spouse/ civil partner) and losses. Phasing asset disposals over more than one tax year allows for more than one annual exempt amount to be used. Disposing of assets standing at a loss will allow offset of that loss against other gains in the same or later years.

- Transfers between spouses, both during lifetime and on death, are exempt for IHT purposes. The unused proportion of nil rate band on the death of one spouse/ civil partner can be transferred to the other on the second death. Lifetime gifts are effective for making use of available IHT lifetime exemptions.

TEST YOUR KNOWLEDGE

1. Who must pay Class 1 National Insurance Contributions?

2. Briony is an additional rate taxpayer and has made capital gains of £8,400 in 2013/14. She has no allowable losses brought forward. How much capital gains tax is she due to pay?

3. How long must someone survive from the date of making a PET for it to be completely exempt?

4. What rate of tax is generally withheld from interest payments to individuals and trustees?

5. Is interest from gilts generally paid net or gross?

6. David is a higher rate taxpayer who is aged 52. He pays £10,000 into his registered pension scheme. By what amount will his basic rate band be extended?

7. What is the maximum amount that can be withdrawn from a single premium bond each year?

8. Warren, who is an additional rate taxpayer, receives a distribution of £2,500 from a REIT. What rate of tax must he pay on the income?

9. What is the income tax reduction available for individual investors in an EIS company?

10. Wayne sells his shareholding in Baronsmere plc, a venture capital trust, making a gain of £10,000. How much CGT must he pay?

11. Mr and Mrs Smith own a holiday cottage jointly. The rental income during the year is £12,000. Mr Smith owns 15% of the property and Mrs Smith owns the remaining 85%. How much income is taxable on Mr Smith?

12. Celia Jones sets up a bank account, which is not an ISA, for her daughter, Camilla, who is 12 years old. The interest received during the tax year was £240 (net). What is the income tax position in respect of the interest received on the account?

13. Madeleine gifts the family home to her daughter, Cynthia, but continues to live in the property, rent free. Explain whether Madeleine has successfully reduced the value of her estate for IHT purposes.

14. Keith wishes to make a gift to his son, Sam, and a gift to a trust. Advise Keith which of the gifts he should make first and why.

TEST YOUR KNOWLEDGE: ANSWERS

1. Both employers (secondary Class 1) and employees (primary Class 1).

   (See Section 2.2)

2. Nil, as Briony's gains are covered by her annual exemption of £10,900.

   (See Section 3.3.2)

3. 7 years.

   (See Section 4.4)

4. 20%.

   (See Section 4.8.2)

5. Gross.

   (See Section 9.3.3)

6. £12,500 (= £10,000 × 100/80).

   (See Section 9.7.3)

7. 5% of the original premium.

   (See Section 9.12.1)

8. 45% (taxed as property income not a dividend).

   (See Section 9.13)

9. 30%.

   (See Section 9.14.2)

10. Nil. There is no CGT liability on a profit on sale of VCT shares.

    (See Section 9.15.3)

11. Mr Smith is taxable on half of the income as the couple is treated as owning the property jointly. Mr Smith is therefore taxable on £6,000.

    (See Section 10.2.2)

12. The interest is treated as taxable on Celia because Camilla is her minor child and the interest is more than £100 gross. Celia is therefore taxable on £300 (£240 × 100/80).

    (See Section 10.3)

13. Madeleine has made a gift with reservation of benefit as although she has made a PET of the house to her daughter, she continues to benefit from the asset so it is treated as still belonging to her. The gift is ineffective for IHT purposes.

    (See Section 10.6.3)

14. Keith should make the gift to the trust before the gift to Sam. This is because the gift to the trust is a CLT and is immediately chargeable to IHT, whereas the gift to Sam is a PET. If he were to make the PET first, it would needlessly use up the annual exemption(s), and the tax due on the CLT, if any, would be higher.

    (See Section 10.6.4)

INDEX